LUMPENCITY

Discourses of Marginality

Marginalizing Discourses

edited by:
Alan Bourke
Tia Dafnos and
Markus Kip

© Red Quill Books Ltd. 2011
Ottawa

www.redquillbooks.com

ISBN 978-1-926958-16-3

Printed on acid-free paper. The paper used in this book incorporates post-consumer waste and has not been sourced from endangered old growth forests, forests of exceptional conservation value or the Amazon Basin. Red Quill Books subscribes to a one-book-at-a-time manufacturing process that substantially lessens supply chain waste, reduces greenhouse emissions, and conserves valuable natural resources.

"LUMPEN-CITY"

Run by an editorial collective, Red Quill Books is dedicated to the following three principles:

1. Consciousness Raising: We are committed to disseminating critical academic works to a mass readership in formats that are accessible and that raise awareness and promote political engagement.

2. Ecology: We aim to build a sustainable and Green publishing house. Our processes are digital with minimal supply-chain waste. We are an on-demand producer of books, which also ensures our books are never out of print.

3. Community: We offer academic prizes and graduate research grants to support the next generation of critical scholars. We seek to actively promote future critical scholarship.

[RQB is a radical publishing house.
Part of the proceeds from the sale of this book will support student scholarships.]

ACKNOWLEDGEMENTS

Before seeing the light of day, an anthology such as this is necessarily the product of much collaboration and combined effort. There were many people who were generous in their advice, support, and encouragement at various stages of its completion.

First and foremost, we would like to thank members of the organizing committee of *Lumpencity: Discourses of Marginality|Marginalizing Discourses* held at York University on March 12 and 13 in 2009. It is largely due to the success of this conference, and the degree of interest it generated, that you now hold before you this volume. As prospective conference papers began flooding in, it rapidly became clear to us the extent to which the themes we wished to interrogate resonated both within and beyond the academy. In particular, we are indebted to the invaluable support and dedication of Burak Köse, Heather McLean, Michael Romandel, and Philip A. Steiner in helping organize the conference. We would like to extend our deepest gratitude as well to all those who took part as participants and volunteers for their assistance in making the conference such a memorable event. We would also like to thank Ashanti Alston, Viviane Saleh-Hanna, Rinaldo Walcott, and David Wilson, distinguished activists and scholars who honoured us with their participation as keynote speakers.

If bringing the conference to a close saw the completion of one journey, the nurturing and development of this volume witnessed the beginning of another. We are grateful to the following people for the assistance and guidance they were able to provide in helping us put this anthology together: Nouk Bassomb, Irena Bourke, Ian Hussey, Miriam Kip, Mike Larsen, Radhika Mongia, AK Thompson, Debra Wong, the City Institute of York University, the Graduate Program in Sociology at York University, York University Office of the Vice-President for Research and Innovation, and the Youth Action Network (YAN) in Toronto.

We are also very thankful for the immense patience and encouragement of George Rigakos and the editorial collective of Red Quill Books through all stages of the publication process, as well as for the constructive criticism provided by two anonymous reviewers. We are excited to be part of the project being initiated by Red Quill Books in publishing critical work and supporting young scholars.

And last, but not least, we would like to thank the contributors to this volume. It was a pleasure to work with and to learn from them. Their patience and perseverance was truly tested by the number of requests and demands we made of them.

Any royalties resulting from the publication will be donated to the G20 Legal Defense Fund to support detainees' legal costs. The 2010 G20 summit in Toronto was a clear reminder of the necessity to fight against the criminalization of dissent and the shackling of social protest.

TABLE OF CONTENTS

Acknowledgements 5
1. **Lumpen-City:** Discourses of Marginality|
   Marginalizing Discourses
   Alan Bourke, Tia Dafnos, and Markus Kip 9

Part I | Contesting Discourses of Marginality
2. **Understanding Obama's Discourse on
   Urban Poverty**
   David Wilson and Matthew Anderson 43
3. **Legitimizing Violence and Segregation:** Neoliberal
   Discourses on Crime and the Criminalization of Urban
   Poor Populations in Turkey
   Zeynep Gönen and Deniz Yonucu. 75
4. **Homelessness as Neoliberal Discourse:**
   Reflections on Research and the Narrowing
   of Poverty Policy
   Mark Willson. 105
5. **Samuel Delany's Lumpen Worlds and
   the Problem of Representing Marginality**
   Lisa Estreich 131

Part II | Contested Representations
6. **Indigeneity and the City:** Representations,
   Resistance, and the Right to the City
   Julie Tomiak 163

7. **Palestinian Refugees and Citizens:** Trajectories of Group Solidarity and Politics
   Silvia Pasquetti 193
8. **Sexual Violence and the Creation of a Postcolonial Ordinary:** Engagements Between Street-Based Sex Workers and the Police in Machala, Ecuador
   Karen O'Connor 227
9. **Making Sense of Failure:** Why German Trade Unions Did Not Mobilize Against the Hartz-IV Reforms—Partisan Research in Frankfurt, Germany
   Markus Kip 257

Part III | Methodological Reflexivities
10. **Participatory Practices:** Contesting Accountability in Academic-Community Research Collaborations
    Alan Bourke 291
11. **Lost in Translation:** The Social Relations of an Institutional Ethnography of Activism
    Kate M. Murray 323
12. **Shifting the Gaze "Upwards":** Researching the Police as an Institution of Power
    Tia Dafnos 355
13. **Our Streets!** Practice and Theory of the Ottawa Panhandlers' Union
    Matthew R. McLennan 389
14. **Afterword:** A Call to Activist Scholarship . . . 409
(End)Notes. 417
Contributors 442

Lumpen-City
Discourses of Marginality | Marginalizing Discourses

Alan Bourke, Tia Dafnos, and Markus Kip

> I still feel the same contempt for and still reject so-called objective decisions made without passion and anger. Objectivity, like the claim that one is nonpartisan or reasonable, is usually a defensive posture used by those who fear involvement in the passions, partisanships, conflicts, and changes that make up life; they fear life. An "objective" decision is generally lifeless. It is academic and the word "academic" is a synonym for irrelevant. (Saul Alinsky, *community activist,* 1909-1972)

In 1971, Saul Alinsky proclaimed the word "academic" to be a synonym for irrelevant. While much has since been done to challenge the methods and mythologies of scholarly "objectivity", the charge of irrelevance is arguably one which has continued to haunt the vicissitudes of scholarly practice, and yet it is an accusation we refuse to accept as definitive. Having embarked upon an academic path in the hope of instantiating a socially responsive and relevant form of scholarly practice, many of us remain troubled by the extent to which our institutional affiliations and disciplinary identities pre-empt the practice of an inclusive and emancipatory activist-scholarship. By activist-scholarship, we are referring to a range of political practices. These include practices that challenge oppressive hegemonic discourses and those modes of scholarly knowledge production that sustain them, as well as practices of analysis contributing to the clarification of goals, strategy, and tactics for collective action. Radha D'Souza (2009:28) has queried, "is activist scholarship about activists *and* scholars or about activism *in* scholarship, or scholarship *about* activism?" The first conceptualization refers to a relationship among people with shared values working in different institutional settings towards a common purpose. In the second and third conceptions, universities and formal research centres are the points of departure. The term "activist scholar" as it is used throughout the volume encompasses all three conceptions, reflecting the ways in which contributors embrace the passions, partisanships, conflicts, and challenges of their work.

Although our research is driven by the desire to locate the experiences of oppression within their social and political contexts, and to render them intelligible for a collective activist praxis, disciplinary norms and institutional orthodoxies often relegate such work to that of a lesser status. In light of this, Hale (2006:108) attests to the difficulties encountered when making the case for activist research, as it entails being held accountable to both an academic and an activist audience. While the dictates of academic protocol call for compliance with convention, we are compelled, nevertheless, to critically interrogate our relation to such traditions. If our experience as scholars is enabled by the institutional foundations of academia, then surely the conditions for the possibility of activist-scholarship reside among the cracks. Moreover, in subjecting the conceptual and methodological repertoires of our respective disciplinary heritages to critical scrutiny, we strive to sustain a scholarly praxis of emancipatory intent.

A focus on urban marginality points to a further set of contradictions with which we seek to engage. Augmented by neoliberal ideology and structures, social inequalities are inextricably linked to the de-politicizing and de-radicalizing forces of capital that manifest in the city, as Alinsky would have well understood (Feagin and Vera 2001:144). To this end, a critique of neoliberalism initially requires sensitizing our gaze to the complex web of institutional practices and policies that serve to perpetuate and multiply various forms of interlocking oppression. As Day (2005:6) notes, state domination, class antagonisms, and capitalist exploitation are possible because of the division of neoliberal societies along multiple lines of inequality. Too often has scholarship remained impervious to its collusion with and in such politics.

Locating marginality in the city is also an apparent contradiction to the inherent claim of the urban that "any point can become central" (Lefebvre 2003:116). It is from this notion of centrality that Lefebvre develops the "right to the city" which has become a battle cry for activists involved in urban social movements (Mayer 2009). In this view, social movements generate new knowledge, challenge the efficacy of theory, and pose new questions. As Kelley (2002:8) states "the most radical ideas often grow out of a concrete intellectual engagement with the problems of aggrieved populations confronting systems of oppression." As the sphere of the collective every-day, the urban remains a promising field within which to re-articulate relationships between "activists" and "academics"—and between "researchers" and "researched". The confluence between these relationships is suggested by Foucault (1980:126-127):

> I believe intellectuals have actually been drawn closer to the proletariat and the masses, for two reasons. Firstly, because it has been a question of real, material, everyday struggles, and secondly because they have often been confronted, albeit

in a different form, by the very same adversary as the proletariat, namely the multinational corporations, the judicial and police apparatuses, the property speculators, etc. ...This new configuration has a further political significance. It makes it possible; if not to integrate, at least to rearticulate categories which were previously kept separate.

As urban activist-scholars, we cannot reduce our relationship to marginality to the detached or "objective" conceptualization of social problems as if viewed from a separate realm. Such would be the "consolidating glance" as Lefebvre describes the "urbanist" activity of organizing and administrating the ruling order (2003:116). For us, the crucial issue becomes that of connecting the representation of marginal space to a radical practice. Following Lefebvre (1996), a dialectical analysis of urban space and its inherent contradictions has increasingly become a pivotal element for the articulation of social movements centred on the "right to the city." Contrary to a liberal conception of rights, "the right to the city" expresses a counter-hegemonic demand and is a right "that exists only as people appropriate it (and the city)" (Mayer 2009:367). It is not only about rights for a marginalized group, but implies a different sociality. In liberating urban space from the dominance of exchange value, the city emerges as an *oeuvre*—a work shaped by the participation of its inhabitants. Thus, rather than seeking and being granted recognition by the state, such appropriation of the city amounts to what Day (2005) describes as the "politics of the act" in which the city is produced by its inhabitants and users according to their needs and criteria. As the appropriation of the city implies a "right to centrality" for all, it also entails a "right to difference"—that is, freedom from externally imposed classifications (Lefebvre 1996:174).

While it has been fashionable to think of academic research as benefiting marginalized groups, scholars such as Robin D.G. Kelley (1997), Herbert Gans (1995), and

Alice O'Connor (2001) have problematized this idea in demonstrating how methodological choices in academic research have often legitimized marginalizing practices. As such work makes clear, scholarship does not remain immune from the neoliberal and state-sanctioned processes which exert a delineating effect on methodological orientations and determine who is to qualify as the "researched." To this end, Feagin and Vera (2001:11) claim that mainstream sociology throughout the twentieth century has been reticent to engage with issues of power in regard to class, race, and gender oppression—typically choosing instead to explore social strata below that of the ruling class. This has raised the ethical and practical issue of rethinking academic undertaking as part of a praxis by which to overcome marginalization. The contributors to this volume share a commitment to the unsettling of these regulatory frameworks of analysis while seeking to explore how, often quite inadvertently, those same commitments collude in strengthening the very patterns of systemic exclusion they seek to expose. Instead of assuming that a "critical stance" towards the object of research feeds directly into a praxis resisting marginalization, we seek to explore the extent to which activist-scholarship becomes less about activism and more about maintaining the hierarchies and privileges of academia.

Conceived as an act of collaboration that strives to instantiate a reflexive activist-scholarship practice, this volume is an attempt to revitalize the vocabulary of activism that scholars may utilize in combating the exigencies of urban marginalization. The contributions reveal how authors have sought to engage with and transform their scholarly repertoires into the tools of analysis useful for political action. Although we remain troubled by Alinsky's accusation of irrelevance, we contend that the perennial contradictions surrounding the relationship between theory and practice, and the tensions which emerge in the practice of activist-scholarship, open up spaces of resistance and create the possibility of change.

The contributions collected in the volume emerge from a context in which access to academia is considered both a privilege and a mechanism of social exclusion. Indeed, to speak from the privileged and conservative spaces of academia to a radical cause is a contradiction we seek to productively exploit. The challenge that this volume takes up is to consider through what methodological practices we can remain accountable and politically committed to social justice and equality, even as we work from within the compromised spaces of the university. In embracing an oppositional perspective (Feagin and Vera 2001; Hale 2008), we make no pretence to encompass a full spectrum of approaches. Rather, we aim to encourage activists and scholars alike to recognize and question the limitations of their respective institutional and disciplinary settings, as understanding the barriers impeding knowledge production and its application is a necessary condition for an emancipatory and activist-oriented epistemology and practice (Day 2005; D'Souza 2009). As we outline in the afterword of this volume, such engagement requires maintaining a critical consciousness in regard to partisanship, praxis, and solidarity.

Our intention with this volume is simultaneously critical, reflexive, and interrogative. Firstly, the volume offers a critical inquiry of the epistemic practices enveloping representations of urban marginality. In such terms, discourses of marginalization are ideological due to the role they play in perpetuating systems of domination. Following Hale (2008), we hold that activist scholars may inform both activism and scholarship by pursuing critical knowledge of the mechanisms of systemic oppression. It is an orientation that combines the effort to understand how things are with the imperative of imagining how they could be otherwise. Secondly, the volume builds upon a growing tradition of reflexive activist-scholarship (Gitlin 1994; Day 2005; Frampton et al. 2006; Shukaitis, Graeber, and Biddle 2007; Sanford and Angel-Ajani 2006; Hale 2008; Sudbury and Okazawa-Rey 2009) which calls into question the role of the "researcher" and their relation to the "researched". In claiming that research and other forms of political engagement can be mutually enriching, the volume draws upon a broad range of epistemological and methodological approaches in critically interrogating how such dualisms can be challenged and undermined. Thirdly, and crucially, we call into question the institutional conventions that distinguish between "critical scholarship" and "activism" which serve to valorize the former whilst denigrating the latter. In eschewing Alinsky's claim of the academic as irrelevant, we refute the common accusation that activist scholars seek reductive, politically motivated truths at the expense of social complexity. In acknowledging the differences in how contributors to this volume have interpreted the practice of activist-scholarship, there thus emerges a common critical and reflexive awareness of contradiction—and a commitment to work with such contradiction rather than expect its resolution.

Urban Marginality and the "Right" to the Lumpencity

In thinking through these contradictions, we feel that these tensions and contestations, and the imperative of addressing them, are well captured with reference to Marx and Engels' problematic conceptualization of the lumpenproletariat. For Marx and Engels ([1848]1978), the politics and passion of whom have arguably been one of the pre-eminent points of inspiration for activist-scholars, the truly revolutionary class is the urban working class—the proletariat—the exploitation and subjugation of whom continues to increase amidst the ever-multiplying contradictions of class antagonism and capitalist accumulation (see also Engels [1892]1952). While Marx and Engels (1968) foresaw the possibility of the proletariat developing a militant class-consciousness, as inspired by the exigencies of shared circumstances in the close quarters of life and work in the industrial city, their condemnation of the lumpenproletariat rejects the idea that the condition of material destitution alone is a sufficient premise for revolutionary action. It is their representation of the lumpenproletariat that is particularly salient in three respects. First, the moralistic tone of such representation, or discourse, appears to resonate with that of a bourgeois morality distinguishing between the "deserving" and the "undeserving" poor which continues to be evident in contemporary neoliberal thinking. The second aspect of interest is that such representation of the marginalized "other" is made from positions of relative privilege and power. Third, the representation of the lumpenproletariat made by Marx and Engels *as activist-scholars* reflects an elitist or vanguardist model of activism.

In *The Eighteenth Brumaire of Louis Napoleon* ([1852]1963:75), Marx refers to the lumpenproletariat as a politically distinct category encompassing the "scum, offal, the refuse of all classes." Engels ([1874]1962:646) characterizes the lumpenproletariat in similar terms: "the depraved elements of all classes, which establishes its headquarters in the big cities, is the worst of all possible allies. This rabble is absolutely venal and absolutely brazen... Every leader of the workers who uses these scoundrels as guards or relies on them for support proves himself by this action a traitor to the movement." In this view, the lumpenized will not be participants in the radical changes to come as they occupy a space of abject and moral depravity beyond that of the "formal" labour market. In *The Communist Manifesto* ([1848]1978:482), furthermore, Marx and Engels claim that although "[t]he 'dangerous class', the social scum, the passively rotting mass thrown off by the lowest layers of the old society, may, here and there, be swept into the movement by a proletarian revolution, its conditions of life, however, prepare it far more for the part of a bribed tool of reactionary intrigue." As such, Marx and Engels caution that conservative forces may easily seduce the most destitute parts of society with the lure of power and wealth. Lacking class-based political vision, the lumpenproletariat is represented as a raggedy population living parasitically outside the realms of both proletarian and bourgeois consciousness, with a particular susceptibility to the conservatism of counter-revolutionary sentiment. They were, therefore, to be treated with suspicion, if not contempt, and excluded from participation in revolutionary movements.

Disconcertingly, the distinctions that Marx and Engels make between the proletariat and lumpenproletariat echoes dominant perceptions reflected in philanthropic reformist discourses. According to Rimke (2003:254), the diagnosed degenerative physical and moral conditions of the labouring classes as "filthy", "unruly", and "disorderly" became a chief concern for medical and philanthropic ends in the nineteenth century. In consequence, liberal reformists intervened in their living quarters and implemented paternalistically conceived ideas of well-ordered spaces (Rimke and Hunt 2002; Hunt 1999). Whereas the proletariat could be reformed and were, therefore, "redeemable," the lumpenproletariat were held to be beyond redemption and thusly required containment by the coercive security apparatus of the state (Neocleous 2008). This distinction not only moralizes but also provides the justification for the differential treatment of those perceived to be a threat to the social order (see Wilson and Anderson, this volume). Beyond that, reformist interventions were a defence against what was categorized as a veritable "regression in human evolution" (Rimke and Hunt 2002:74). Such discourses fed into emerging ideas of "race" as a biologically defined conception of a "healthy people". In this view, the diagnosed pathologies of the "undeserving poor" were considered a threat to the health of the species and thus required segregation practices (Foucault 1997). As Goldberg (1993:54-55) argues, the racialization of discourses of cleanliness, hygiene, purity, pollution, and disease provided the justification for exclusion.

While the prefix "lumpen" should not necessarily be held as synonymous with poverty and marginality, its inherent definitional imprecision has been both its danger and appeal. In contrast to the perceived unified class identity of the proletariat, Marx (1973:52) depicts the lumpenproletariat as without stable collective determination—as "a people without a definite trace." Influenced by later psychoanalytic and poststructuralist frameworks, such ambiguity has led to a re-conceptualization of the lumpenproletariat, not as a distinct social group, but rather as signalling a heterogeneity problematic for Marx's conceptual schema. Given that a growing population of unwaged, marginalized, excluded, and counter-cultural groups were seen to be unrepresented in the conventional figure of the proletariat, Guattari (1995:61) argues that the category of the lumpenproletariat has since been deployed to excise and condemn the part of the "masses" that do not fall behind the revolutionary party line:

> One always finds the old schema: the detachment of a pseudo-avant-garde capable of bringing about synthesis, of forming a party as an embryo of state apparatus, of drawing out a well brought up, well-educated working class; and the rest is a residue, a lumpen-proletariat one should always mistrust.

While under-theorized by Marx and Engels, similar categorizations of the lumpenproletariat have been adopted in subsequent Marxian writing. In describing Mussolini's rise to power in fascist Italy, Trotsky (2002) elaborated upon Marx's view of the lumpenproletariat as being especially vulnerable to reactionary thought, evoking the "declassed and demoralized, all the countless human beings whom finance capital itself has brought to desperation and frenzy." Paul Hirst (1972) suggests that such condemnation of the lumpenproletariat should not be dismissed as the replication of Victorian bourgeois moralism on the part of Marx and Engels—but rather that such views are directly consistent with a nuanced materialist understanding of the perceived reactionary nature of the marginal and criminalized classes under existing conditions. Such representation of the lumpenproletariat has served to perpetuate ideas of marginalized groups in morally vacuous and criminalizing terms, while refusing to adequately acknowledge how the "declassed and demoralized" can be interpreted as victims of, or resisters to, capitalist development. As Shantz (1999:25) notes, the legacy of Marxism from the beginning established a distaste for the "lumpen flavour" of revolutionary action. In essence, Marxian views of the lumpenproletariat have continued to this day in terms defined by its tangential relationship to capitalist processes of production and exchange and, by extension, the necessities of class consciousness.

However, if the Marxian conceptualization of the lumpenproletariat stands as indicative of the contradictions of class-based activism, it also, paradoxically, promises its redemption. Indeed, with the influence of Black liberation movements and anti-colonial struggles in the 1960s, some radical Marxists came to view the proletariat as being too close to the bourgeoisie and turned to the lumpenproletariat as the decisive agent of historical transformation. To this end, the racialized character of lumpenproletariat became a cornerstone for a class-based Black politics. In the late 1960s, Huey Newton, founding member of the Black Panther Party, came to believe that the lumpenproletariat could, in fact, play a progressive role in revolutionary politics: "as the ruling circle continue to build their technocracy, more and more of the proletariat will become unemployable, become lumpen, until they have become the popular class, the revolutionary class" (quoted in Epps 1970). Similarly, Frantz Fanon argues that revolutionary movements in colonized countries must, by necessity, include the lumpenproletariat in revolutionary action as they constitute both a counterrevolutionary and a revolutionary potential. In *The Wretched of the Earth*, Fanon ([1961]1963:129) described the lumpenproletariat as "one of the most spontaneous and the most radically revolutionary forces of a colonized people.... It is within this mass of humanity, this people of the shanty towns... that the revolution will find its urban spearhead." In such terms, Fanon claims that the inclusion and education of the dispossessed masses should be made central to revolutionary strategy, lest they become co-opted by reactionary forces. Such a view, typical of the vanguardism present in both Marxist and non-Marxist thought, exhibits both distrust and faith in the capacity of the lumpenproletariat in effecting progressive change.

Even as the above authors alternately accuse or defend Marx of a moralizing depiction of the lumpenproletariat, it has continued to remain a curiously undertheorized representational trope. Whilst the suspicion and contempt of the lumpenproletariat (as arguably evident in Marx's writings) is no longer explicitly present in contemporary urban research on the poor, the urban outcast, the socially excluded, or the marginalized, we contend that the representation of such populations as lacking in social and political agency, and as exhibiting socially dysfunctional, pathological behaviours—as irredeemably *lumpen*—is implicitly affirmed. According to Loïc Wacquant's (2002) provocative appraisal of Chicago-style ethnography, much contemporary urban scholarship perpetuates a moralizing "culture of poverty" conceptualization in which marginalized populations are depicted as being agents in their own misfortune. For example, the ethically neutral "unemployed," who were the subject matter of economic and social policy for most of the twentieth century, have been reconstructed as "welfare scroungers" in a way that is reminiscent of the "paupers" and "undeserving poor" inhabiting earlier periods (Hunt 1999). Moreover, Robin D.G. Kelley (1997) charges that the fascination with the "ghetto" has served to produce and reproduce a racialized and moralizing bourgeois discourse that has rarely captured the social agency and political efficacy of its "captive" population. Whilst it is not our intention to present an exhaustive account of such marginalizing discourses, or indeed of the many nuanced evocations of the "lumpen", we argue, following Gans (1995), that the periodic emergence or re-invention of new labels for "the poor"—as the disadvantaged, the outcast, the underclass, and so on—has often played as a disquieting soundtrack accompanying the dismantling of welfare provisions and support for those populations most vulnerable to the vicissitudes of capitalist accumulation. The challenge facing the activist-scholar lies in remaining cognizant of how the objectivist processes of state-sanctioned policies, in the guise of benevolence and recognition, create new subjugated positionalities which serve merely to reproduce, if not exacerbate, existent social inequalities. At the same time, we have to remain reflexive in our own practices in terms of how they might contribute to such processes (Day 2005). Indeed, it is our contention that perhaps nowhere are these contradictions more apparent than in contemporary research on urban marginality.

Researching the Urban Margins

As the human casualties of capitalism and global conflict struggle to be heard amidst the clamour for property and profit in contemporary processes of urbanization, the unique character and context of such configurations of exclusion calls upon urban activist-scholars to reflexively interrogate their commitment to social justice in the city (Harvey 2009). The significance of the interplay between urbanization, intensifying processes of class polarization, increasing social and political stratification, state oppression, and the growing precariousness of labour bears witness to the need to fundamentally rethink the categorization and representation of those at the urban margins. According to the "global city" thesis (Sassen 2001), changes in the composition and circulation of capital have contributed to the formation of new strategic sites in the world economy. Privileging an economic rationality and dominative capitalist logic that is buttressed by security ideology, the restructuring of the global economy has produced a highly differentiated labour force. In such terms, the accelerated growth of a small, modernized, highly waged sector is coupled with a large sector of informal and often precarious survival strategies. Under these conditions, the numbers of those relegated to the marginal spaces of the lumpen is growing exponentially.

Conversely, the rise of "gated communities" and "fortified urban enclaves" (Caldeira 2000) has served to exacerbate this discrepancy in class-based and psychological urban division through the production of mere simulacra of belonging. To this end, segregating processes along racial, ethnic, and class-based divisions, and physical barriers such as gates and walled fortifications, act as markers of material and symbolic exclusion instantiating a veritable "ecology of fear" in the city (Davis 1999). The power of these patterns of segregation, discrimination, and criminalization, augmented by declining community capacity, exclusionary labour market practice, the withdrawal of social services, the erosion of welfare provision, and pervasive stigmatization have thus combined to complicate attempts at structural change. Such transformations call for a revitalized practice of activist-scholarship that problematizes the ruptures and continuities found in the history of representing the subaltern.

Contemporary social research on urban exclusion has arguably remained content with mapping the contours of marginalization through a range of representational and discursive choices—variously evoking ghettos, hyper-ghettos, ethnic enclaves, hyper-segregation, the underclass, slums, and so on. While there is considerable value in deconstructing these phenomena in order to reveal their inherently socially constructivist character, the search for ever-more refined theories of such processes nevertheless appears a limited strategy—a form of "luxury production" among academics that is potentially productive of that which they seek to contest (Gilmore 1993; Hale 2006). Analyses which conclude with policy recommendations typically directed to state agencies, or which reveal "both the common and distinctive elements of humanity" (Duneier 2011), can certainly provide material for political strategies. Yet, they operate within the discursive parameters of prevailing hegemonies of control, aimed at changing the *content* of structures of domination rather than at dismantling their *form* (Day 2005:88). Such dilemmas, furthermore, gesture toward Bauman's notion of "asymmetric surveillance" and the separation of watchers from the watched in which techniques of moralization are ever-present (Hunt 1999:8). At best, such accounts help to create significant and much needed awareness and identification of neglected social issues. At worst, they indulge a deeply problematic cultural predilection in bearing witness to what has become journalistically known as "poverty porn". This fuels, as Day (2005:12) notes, the distrust among activists of university-based researchers seeking to "satisfy a voyeuristic urge to participate in the 'real world'." Consequently, raising awareness can lead to the reification or even aestheticization of conditions of marginality. From the perspective of activist-scholarship, the critical litmus test of such accounts is whether they are useful for action and mobilization of, for, among, or with, the marginalized rather than encouraging mere spectacularization in the act of representation.

The questions such contestations raise for activist-scholars are complex: to what extent does the invocation of the poor, the outcast, the underclass, the ghettoized, the disadvantaged, the homeless, and more, prove complicit with hegemonic representational tropes? To what extent do such conceptualizations perpetuate the representation of marginalized populations as lacking in social and political efficacy? In what ways can our conceptual and methodological tools become useful for urban social movements in a transformative rather than merely reformist manner? Is attempting to span the disparity between the conventions of academia and the commitment to activism a bridge too far? For some, such contradictions lead to a precariously balanced, albeit reflexively constituted, bifurcation of activist-scholar identity. For others, recognizing such contradiction assists in collaborating with and giving voice to those historically othered by hegemonic evocations of urban space.

If the urban sphere remains a contradictory site of capitalist accumulation, we thus contend that it is also an arena that provides the conditions for the possibility of a coordinated resistance to such exclusionary regimes of power and capital. Historically, a broad range of urban social movements has emerged to politicize the exclusionary exigencies of capitalist logic and render them visible in the search for social change. Indeed, urban spaces, as opposed to the university, have traditionally been the battlegrounds for activists fighting against oppression. During the turbulence of the 1960s, for instance, the locale of knowledge production was based not within the institutional confines of the university but in grassroots political organizations with agendas of emancipation (D'Souza 2009:21). In this regard, too often has academic scholarship remained on the periphery of, if it has not simply ignored, such movements. In parallel fashion, it is surely of great significance to note that the transformative social movements of modernity—abolitionism, labour movements, suffragette movements, anti-colonial liberation struggles, civil rights movements, black power and red power movements, and queer activism—have received little support from the academic establishment, which has remained largely oblivious to radical social and political thought.

Yet, in contradiction to this, the university has also, at times, remained one of the few sites of intellectual resistance to reactionary discourse, and has often assumed the mantle of nurturing what Alvin Gouldner (1979:45) has referred to as "the production of dissent, deviance, and the cultivation of an authority-subverting culture of critical discourse." Drawing upon the history of activist and critical scholarship, the contributors to this volume seek to build upon and advance such contested discourses of marginalization. In so doing, it is imperative that present contestations remain cognizant of the successes and failures of past practices. What is required, claims Day (2005:205) is both a "practical theory" and a "theoretical practice," the symbiotic alignment of which avoids the quiescence brought on by excessive abstraction and the frustrations inherent in setting out to "do something" without adequately acknowledging what others have done before. To this, we add the imperative of nurturing what Paulson (2010:35) calls the "radical imagination"—maintaining a range of creative and activist engagements with present circumstance whilst remaining cognizant of the historical conditions of social struggles.

One of our intentions with this volume is to encourage activists, scholars, and activist-scholars alike to question the limitations of their respective disciplinary orthodoxies and institutional settings, as understanding the nature of such impediments remains the first, and crucial, step to take in their contestation. Indeed, the borders we seek to contest are not only those of disciplinary identity or geographical focus. More substantively, the authors have utilized the tools of analysis at their disposal in targeting the politics and practice of conducting research at a time when the divide between being a "scholar" and an "activist" is perhaps being more regularly and systematically policed than ever before. The individual and collective acts of critique and resistance documented throughout this volume emphasize the importance of paying attention to local, embodied strategies as the sites from which change occurs. This applies to individual researchers and the disciplinary effects of an academic habitus which simultaneously facilitates while constraining research activity. To this end, recognition of the power of discourse, praxis engagements, experiential learning, and tales from the field are all means of challenging the regimes and conventions of academic practice which serve to reproduce and legitimize the status quo. Our focus on urban space is intended to encourage an analysis of the interconnectedness of locales through which flows of labour, capital, discourses, images and power converge—connecting Istanbul to Frankfurt, Frankfurt to Machala, Machala to New York, New York to Jalazon, Jalazon to Ottawa, and so on. Analyzing the linkages, continuities, and ruptures that shape discourses of marginality/ marginalizing discourses is an important condition in fostering dialogic engagement between differing enactments of scholarly-activism. Such analyses re-centre the urban margins as the centrifugal spaces in which the contradictions of capitalism and neoliberal hegemonies are exposed. It is when noting this promise of activist-scholarship that, to paraphrase Italian Marxist Antonio Gramsci, our pessimism of the intellect is tempered by an optimism of the will.

Contesting Practices

The prospects for such reinvigoration encounter a range of forces which threaten to render activism and academia as ever more antagonistic collaborators. In Gramscian terms, scholars are experiencing more pressure than ever before to become the organic intellectuals of the status quo. In practice, this has been evident in the incremental blunting of the radical force of inclusive, collaborative, and activist methodologies (see Bourke, this volume). To this end, the entrenchment of capitalism and neoliberal governance characterizing the contemporary "knowledge economy" is nothing if not resourceful in seeking to counter the expressions of discontent which seek to challenge its dominance. As argued by Jordan (2003), one general effect has been to assimilate and reconstitute participatory methodologies within existing forms of social organisation which conserves rather than contests existing relations of ruling. The work of Piven and Cloward (1997), for instance, suggests that as long as poor people's movements rely on themselves and their most effective instrument—militant action—the more they are able to gain. It is only when they start conforming to mainstream constraints, especially by seeking to become a "respectable" organization with legitimate institutional affiliations, that they lose their autonomy in the struggle for social justice.

The fostering of alliances between universities and communities can thus be seen as indicative of an intensifying neoliberal mandate for research practices in higher education, one eager to capitalize upon the social agency of community capacity and local knowledge (Cancian 1993). Shragge and colleagues (2006) situate such movement within the wider context of the neoliberal "re-discovery" of community by government, one which pushes community organizations into de-politicized roles wherein they act as veritable subcontractors for the state in delivering community-level services. Miraftab (2004) argues that neoliberal discourse operates as an "authorizing narrative" linking thematics of community empowerment, social capital, and democratic participation in order to further the effects of its governance. Once the weapons of critique wielded by community activists, such concepts as "empowerment" and "inclusion" have now become the de-radicalized tools of the neoliberal trade. Feagin and Vera (2001:177), furthermore, cite the emergence of a new dynamic between North and South in terms of how participatory and sustainable development, human rights, feminist, antiracist, and other critical actions against the societal status quo "have been relentlessly subjected to efforts at co-optation and domestication." In this view, such discourses of symbolic inclusion as "partnership", "participation", "collaboration", and so on, operate as a subterfuge disguising the perpetuation of practices of material exclusion. Such concerns, however, are by no means novel—Thorstein Veblen (1957) claimed in 1918 that business principles were transforming higher education into a "merchantable commodity."

Making the case for activist research in university settings remains difficult, as even in cases where universities champion their ties to the community, the internal rewards system of academia invariably moves to discourage it. The inclination to adhere to disciplinary standards of methodological rigour, even when adopting radical methodologies, is ingrained through disciplinary training and institutional policing which valorizes forms of knowledge produced according to established practice—and by implication denigrates knowledge generated outside of its sphere. The manner in which research is produced and distributed; the ways in which funding practices influence or impede the research question; the bureaucratization of ethical protocols; the manner in which the ubiquitous peer-review process and various gate-keeping mechanisms of academe serve to maintain and conserve disciplinary "standards"—all coalesce and congeal to produce an adversarial climate for activist work which aspires towards social change. On this, bell hooks (1994:5) notes that non-conformance to the dictates of academia is often viewed as "defiance aimed at masking inferiority and substandard work." Clearly, academic norms accord relative privilege—material, social, and symbolic—to those recognized as legitimate "researchers". In such terms, the oppressive binaries of researcher and researched, and activist and scholar, are implicitly reaffirmed.

A key site of struggle confronting the methodological practice of activist-scholars thus continues to be the dichotomizing of the social relations of research into the dualisms of researcher and researched, basic and applied research, and between theory and practice. Feminist and post-colonial scholars have long been critical of the structural universalism implicitly present in traditional research design. In such terms, its emphasis upon delivering a realist, objectivist, and rationalist research narrative has been problematized as reinforcing gendered and racialized class relationships (e.g. Smith 1990; Harding 1991; Collins 1991). Such critiques have led to the opening of representational spaces in which the local, experiential, and indigenous can be voiced. With regard to ethnographic scholarship, the ongoing critique of representation and realism is one which has been rigorously sustained ever since the publication of Clifford and Marcus' *Writing Culture: The Poetics and Politics of Ethnography* (1986). The primary consequence for much subsequent political and comparative ethnography has been the encouragement and awareness of constructivist perspectives within the research process itself, thereby undermining (if not overthrowing) the rationale and dominance of a hegemonic realism. These perspectives have effectively sought to expose the implicit methodological scaffolding and rhetorical complicities of the ethnographer with ethnocentric and supremacist ideologies.

Besides this, researchers often face the dilemma of engendering either vanguardism or valorization in their research—of subjugating or romanticizing "problematic identities" (Day 2005:86). If, on the one hand, one assumes the role of vanguard in issuing prescriptions or guidelines in struggles for social justice, one risks ascribing a lack of political agency to marginalized populations. On the other hand, an overly sanitized representation of marginalized populations as inhabiting the only true standpoint from which to strive for emancipation risks abdicating both political and ethical responsibility by virtue of deference to the leadership of such populations while evading interrogation of one's own privileged subject position. This appears scarcely progressive, if not counter-productive, when challenging the reproduction of internal contradictions of communities as based upon positivistic conceptualizations of class, race, ethnicity, gender, and sexuality (Thompson 2010). Indeed, encountering such positivism is especially problematic given that the majority of critically-minded scholars typically place a post-positivistic worldview at the centre of their praxis.

Clearly, issues pertaining to the role and responsibility of the researcher in representing struggles for social change have been and will continue to be ongoing sources of debate, reflection, and transformation. Rather than becoming immobilized by this challenge of optimal practice orientation, by which we mean navigating the contradictory position of the researcher and their role and responsibility in the (re)production of discourses of marginalization, we contend that researchers engage with(in) social justice struggles in order to distance themselves from succumbing to disciplinary orthodoxy. Building upon, whilst not being subservient to, previous traditions of critical scholarship and activist praxis, we hold that activist-research can only be sustained through the maintenance of an ongoing dialectic of praxis, critique, and reflexivity. Although a commitment to social justice implores us to "take sides" (Becker 1967), doing so does not release researchers from engaging in reflexive practice (Day 2005). This requires a practitioner-level act of methodological decolonization (Smith 1999) in breaking with the disciplinary socialization many of us have received, coupled with the maintenance of an ongoing critical reflexivity regarding the interlocking aspects of subjectivities with(in) research practice.

What we have gathered with this volume is a range of perspectives on the experiential facets of a scholarly practice that seek to bring into critical relation their academic and activist dimensions. Too often are each of these aspects caricatured in terms of mutual exclusivity—as when the shoring up of scholarly credentials is seemingly premised upon its distancing from an activist practice. In counter-point, activist practice is often couched in terms of denigrating scholarly work as irrelevant, content with privileging theory over practice. Rather, with this volume we seek to advance the blending which can be achieved when scholarship and activism are brought into a dialogic relation of mutual confrontation. Perhaps more importantly, and as we discuss in the afterword to the collection, activist-scholarship both prefigures and is prescient to alternative relationships based on praxis, partisanship, and solidarity. In other words—discourses of marginalization are best repelled when their contestation is collectively orchestrated. If such categorizations have been bolstered by the legitimacy accrued through their association with academic discourse, so too should such academic discourse be implicated in their dismantling.

Organization of the Volume

The collection is organized to address and bring into discussion a variety of ways in which scholars have aligned their research with activist goals. Part I *Contesting Discourses of Marginality* consists of four chapters which open a theoretical space for thinking critically about the representation of marginality in a range of settings. Applying different approaches to discourse analysis, the contributing authors reveal a range of conceptual inconsistencies embedded in such evocations of poverty, homelessness, and the criminalization of the urban poor. Although these opening chapters are ostensibly "on" marginalized populations, we contend that exposing the constructivist nature of such dominant discourses is an initial, and crucial, step to take in their contestation, and sets the foundation for the articulation of alternative research practices for and with marginalized populations.

In our opening chapter, David Wilson and Matthew Anderson confront the contemporary reality of urban poverty in the United States, explicating how political discourse serves to both absorb and placate mainstream America's fear regarding the potentially incendiary political voice of the urban poor and, more recently, the country's dramatic economic and political slippage. In demonstrating how the voice of the poor is neutralized in Obama's poverty discourse, Wilson and Anderson bring into discussion the structural logics in American society that foster and sanction poverty. To this end, their usage of the tools of critical discourse analysis develops a critical consciousness of language as the basis for a mode of ideological struggle.

In the following chapter, Zeynep Gönen and Deniz Yonucu examine how the association of crime with the urban poor legitimizes segregation practices and the remaking of urban space in accordance with neoliberal urbanism. In contemporary Turkey, the urban poor are increasingly seen as a "race apart" and their particular culture as productive of "degeneracy" and "criminality" concentrated in the neighbourhoods in which they reside. Augmented by the representational violence prevalent in mainstream media and as produced through academic criminology, the authors argue that these characterizations legitimize both civilian and state violence against urban poor populations.

In chapter 4, Mark Willson explores how approaches to, and representations of, homelessness tells us more about contemporary social anxieties, ethical ambiguities and economic imperatives than it does about the "homeless" that are often taken as the object of study or concern. In this reading, Willson aims to highlight how homelessness, construed as a distinct object of popular and professional knowledge and practice, has come to be understood in terms antithetical to social justice claims for safe and secure housing and adequate social benefits for all. Reflecting on these contradictions raises questions about possible engagements between activism and scholarship, contends Willson, as this relationship is shaped both by the particularities of political struggles and by the shifting conditions for research within the university.

Lisa Estreich's chapter on the writings of Samuel R. Delany addresses the often neglected connection between literature, representation, and marginalization. Widely known as a prolific writer of science fiction, Delany's suturing of vignette, prose portrait, autobiographical account and social analysis in the mode of "'ethnographic' memoir" provides a unique vantage point from which to portray the experiential complexities of the interlocking of race, class, gender and sexuality in marginalized urban subjectivities. Estreich examines how Delany, in *The Mad Man* and *Dark Reflections*, sketches fragments of socially and economically liminal existences that the underclass discourse erases from view.

In Part II *Contested Representations*, four contributions focus on the marginalizing effects of representational practice as they are encountered in a variety of fieldwork contexts. In embedding themselves as researchers in the life-worlds of oppressed groups, these contributions deconstruct prevailing ideas about power relationships through a view from the "bottom up". Cities are shown to be uneven terrains of struggle and resistance over access to resources, representation, and urban space itself. In engaging contestations that have been silenced in hegemonic representations of the city, the authors thus propose counter-hegemonic ways to conceive of the agency of the othered.

Unmapping the socio-spatial containment and colonialist imaginaries which have marginalized and erased Indigenous peoples from city life, Julie Tomiak explores how indigeneity and the city are constructed as two mutually exclusive categories. Addressing this through the overlapping discourses of erasure, ghettoization, and assimilation, Tomiak looks at how practices of Indigenous place-making, re-territorialization, and alternative urban geographies and histories in Ottawa and Winnipeg, have been mounting crucial resistance in asserting an indigenous "right to the city." In this view, popular and academic discourses are positioned among a range of technologies of power, including law, private property, state policies and population control, through which the settler city is produced and reproduced.

Silvia Pasquetti presents a comparative political ethnography of local politics and communal life in a Palestinian refugee camp in the West Bank, and a Palestinian urban minority neighbourhood inside Israel. Through these two contexts, her fieldwork compares issues of collective organization and self-identification and their relation to class and nationalist politics. Pasquetti demonstrates that close ethnographic engagement is a necessary tool for an analytical perspective that explains and ties together the institutional policies from above with the practices of subject populations below.

Karen O'Connor's ethnography reveals the casual manner in which postcolonial state violence is materialized through multiple engagements between sex workers and the police in Machala, Ecuador. Drawing upon fieldwork which chronicles street sweeps encouraged by urban regeneration schemes, O'Connor deconstructs how representations of race, class, gender, sexuality, and mestizo nationalisms are interwoven in the urban politics of the street. She explores the ways that "flirtatious threats" and "flippant taunts" in street encounters are connected to the desire for sadistic postcolonial violence.

The contribution by Markus Kip concludes part II by advancing the idea of "partisan scholarship." Engaging with this approach, Kip presents a case study in Frankfurt, Germany which inquires into the lack of mobilization of trade unions to resist the Hartz IV welfare reforms. Based on interviews with trade union representatives and unemployment activists, Kip's analysis highlights the issue of motivation for further activist and scholarly reflection. In contributing to the debate on social movement unionism, this chapter calls attention to the challenge of rendering experiences of failure productive. Taking a step back from his experiences as an activist, Kip seeks to rethink the conditions of possibility for activists to mobilize when resources are few and chances of short-term success slim.

The contributions included in Part III *Methodological Reflexivities* contest the dominant methodological practices of knowledge production and the marginalizing implications of research practice. The section begins with Alan Bourke's critique of participatory methods as they are practiced in contemporary paradigms of community-based participatory research. Arguing that such approaches risk being co-opted by neoliberal mandates and disinvested of their emancipatory potential, Bourke cautions that the social sciences are increasingly positioned as *reactive* in their practice in terms of how they are forced to twist and turn within the circumscribed political spaces they are accorded.

Reflecting on her experience of conducting an institutional ethnography (IE) with anti-poverty activists in Ottawa, Kate Murray's chapter attends to the theory-practice disjuncture prevalent in the approach's own "social relations of research." In calling into question whether IE's focus on the explication of *ruling* brings potential for problematic objectification and the misrepresentation of research participants, Murray explores how the approach may be further developed as a means of strengthening and advancing a transformative research praxis.

Tia Dafnos shifts the gaze of the researcher and its problematizing effects away from those conventionally identified as "problematic" and towards the dominant institution of the police in order to render visible and challenge its discursive and material practices of exclusion and marginalization. Blending narrative and essay, Dafnos details the reflexive and ethical tensions permeating the methodological base of "studying-up" as a form of activist research in the context of radical criminology.

In the final contribution, Matthew McLennan, a participant/activist of the Ottawa-Outaouais General Membership Branch of the Industrial Workers of the World, chronicles union strategies and tactics in organizing the poorest segment of the population against "aggressive panhandling" legislation in Canada's capital, which is marked by a visibly increasing disparity between rich and poor. In noting both its successes and difficulties in combating such discursive violence, and assessing his own role as activist, McLennan details how the Ottawa Panhandlers' Union has provided a democratic union structure for homeless and street-affected people.

We conclude the collection with an afterword—*A Call to Activist Scholarship*—which reflects upon the contributions featured throughout the volume. We believe that much inspiration can be drawn from discussing the tensions and contradictions which exist between the complimentary approaches as exemplified by the contributions in this volume. To some degree, the diversity of activist-scholarship assembled here assists in combating the tendencies of specialization and narcissism systematically encouraged in academic culture. Only by speaking through and across disciplinary protocols can a praxis of activist-scholarship be nurtured and sustained. The challenge we face is to link the practice of activist research with key moments of theoretical and critical innovation—the conditions of possibility of which are likely to be collective rather than individual. To this end, we hope to encourage scholars, activists, and scholar-activists to reflect upon the complementarity of their academic and activist praxis, and to remain committed to unsettling both disciplinary norms and institutional boundaries. Acknowledging patterns of exclusion and marginalization which exist within academic spaces, and the differential distribution and impact of the "costs" of engaging in transgressive activist research, we feel that there is immense value to be derived from the sharing of our dilemmas, struggles, success stories, barriers, and limitations among those who identify as activist-scholars. It is an invitation we extend to the readers of this volume.

References

Alinsky, Saul. D. (1971)1989. *Rules for Radicals: A Practical Primer for Realistic Radicals.* New York: Vintage Books.

Becker, Howard. 1967. "Whose side are we on?" *Social Problems* 14(Winter):239-247.

Cancian, Francesca M. 1993. "Conflicts between activist research and academic success: participatory research and alternative strategies." *American Sociologist* 24(1):92-106.

Caldeira, Teresa Pires do Rio. 2000. *City of Walls: Crime, Segregation, and Citizenship in São Paulo.* Berkeley: University of California Press.

Clifford, James, and George Marcus. 1986. *Writing Culture: The Poetics and Politics of Ethnography.* Berkeley: University of California Press.

Collins, Patricia Hill. 1991. *Black Feminist Thought: Knowledge, Consciousness, and the Politics of Empowerment.* New York: Routledge.

Davis, Mike. 1999. *Ecology of Fear: Los Angeles and the Imagination of Disaster.* New York: Metropolitan Books.

Day, Richard J. F. 2005. *Gramsci is Dead: Anarchist Currents in the Newest Social Movements.* Toronto: Between the Lines.

D'Souza, Radha. 2009. "The prison houses of knowledge: Activist scholarship and revolution in the era of 'globalization'." *McGill Journal of Education* 44(1):19-36.

Duneier, Mitchel. 2011. "How do science and politics come together in urban ethnography?" Princeton Sociology Department Faculty Page, Accessed August 24, 2011. http://www.princeton.edu/sociology/faculty/duneier/

Epps, Garrett. 1970. "Huey Newton speaks at Boston College, presents theory of Intercommunalism," *The Harvard Crimson,* November 19.

Engels, Friedrich. (1874)1962. "Preface to the peasant war in Germany." In *Marx and Engels: Selected Works,* Vol. 11. Moscow: Foreign Languages Publishing.

———. (1892)1952. *The Condition of the Working Class in England in 1844,* translated by K. Wischnewetzky, London: George Allen and Unwin.

Fanon, Frantz. (1961)1963. *The Wretched of the Earth,* preface by Jean-Paul Sartre, translated by Constance Farrington. New York: Grove Press.

Feagin, Joe R., and Hernán Vera. 2001. *Liberation Sociology.* Boulder, CO: Westview.

Foucault, Michel. 1980. "Truth and power." In *Power/Knowledge: Selected Interviews and Other Writings, 1972-1977,* edited by Colin Gordon, 109-133. New York: Pantheon Book.

———. 1997. *Society Must Be Defended. Lectures at the College de France 1975-1976,* edited by Mauro Bertani and Alessandro Fontana, translated by David Macey. New York: Picador.

Frampton, Caelie, Gary Kinsman, A.K. Thompson, and Kate Tilleczek, eds. 2006. *Sociology for Changing the World: Social Movements/Social Research.* Halifax: Fernwood.

Gans, Herbert. 1995. *The War Against the Poor: The Underclass and Antipoverty Policy.* New York: Basic Books.

Gilmore, Ruth Wilson. 1993. "Public enemies and private intellectuals: Apartheid USA." *Race and Class* 35(1):69-78.

Gitlin, Andrew, ed.1994. *Power and Method: Political Activism and Educational Research.* New York: Routledge.

Goldberg, David Theo. 1993. *Racist Culture: Philosophy and the Politics of Meaning.* Cambridge, MA: Blackwell.

Gouldner, Alvin. 1979. *The Future of Intellectuals and the Rise of the New Class: A Frame of Reference, Theses, Conjectures, Arguments, and an Historical Perspective on the Role of Intellectuals and Intelligentsia in the International Class Contest of the Modern Era.* New York: Seabury Press.

Guattari, Felix. 1995. *Chaosmosis: An Ethico-aesthetic Paradigm*, translated by P. Bains and J. Pefanis. Sydney: Power Publications.

Hale, Charles. 2006. "Activist research v. cultural critique: Indigenous land rights and the contradictions of politically engaged anthropology." *Cultural Anthropology* 21(1):96-120.

———. 2008. *Engaging Contradictions: Theory, Politics, and Methods of Activist Scholarship.* Berkeley: University of California Press.

Harding, Sandra 1991. *Whose Science? Whose Knowledge? Thinking From Women's Lives.* Ithaca: Cornell University Press.

Harvey, David. 2009. *Social Justice and the City.* Athens: University of Georgia Press.

Hirst, Paul Q. 1972. "Marx and Engels on law, crime and morality." *Economy and Society* 1(1):28-56.

hooks, bell. 1994. *Teaching to Transgress: Education as the Practice of Freedom.* New York: Routledge.

Hunt, Alan. 1999. *Governing Morals: A Social History of Moral Regulation.* Cambridge, MA: Cambridge University Press.

Jordan, Steven. 2003. "Who stole my methodology? Co-opting PAR." *Globalisation, Societies and Education* 1(2):185-200.

Kelley, Robin D. G. 1997. *Yo' Mama's Disfunktional: Fighting the Culture Wars in Urban America.* Boston: Beacon Press.

———. 2002. *Freedom Dreams: The Black Radical Imagination.* Boston: Beacon Press.

Lefebvre, Henri. 1996. *Writings on Cities*, translated and edited by Eleonore Kofman and Elizabeth Lebas. Cambridge: Blackwell Publishers.

———. 2003. *The Urban Revolution*, translated by Robert Bonnono, forward by Neil Smith. Minneapolis: University of Minneapolis Press.

Marx, Karl. (1852)1963. *The Eighteenth Brumaire of Louis Napoleon.* New York: International Publishers.

———. 1973. "The class struggle in France: 1848-1850." In *Surveys From Exile*, translated by P. Jackson and edited by D. Fernbach, 35-142. Harmondsworth: Penguin.

Marx, Karl, and Friedrich Engels. 1968. *The German Ideology.* Moscow: Progress Publishers.

———. (1848)1978. "Manifesto of the Communist Party," in *The Marx-Engels Reader*, 2nd ed., edited by Robert C. Tucker, 473-500. New York: Norton.

Mayer, Margit. 2009. "The 'Right to the City' in the context of shifting mottos of urban social movements." *City* 13(2-3):362-374.

Miraftab, Faranak. 2004. "Public-private partnerships: The Trojan horse of neoliberal development?" *Journal of Planning Education and Research* 24(1):89-101.

Neocleous, Mark. 2008. *Critique of Security*. Montreal: McGill-Queen's University Press.

O'Connor, Alice. 2001. *Poverty Knowledge: Social Science, Social Policy, and the Poor in Twentieth-Century U.S. History.* Princeton, NJ: Princeton University Press.

Paulson, Justin. 2010. "The uneven development of radical imagination." *Affinities: A Journal of Radical Theory, Culture, and Action* 4(2):33-38.

Piven, Frances Fox, and Richard Cloward. 1997. *Poor People's Movements: Why They Succeed, How They Fail*. New York: Pantheon Books.

Rimke, Heidi. 2003. "Constituting transgressive interiorities." In *Violence and the Body: Race, Gender, and the State*, edited by Arturo J. Aldama, foreword by Alfred Arteaga, 247-262. Bloomington: Indiana University Press.

Rimke, Heidi, and Alan Hunt. 2002. "From sinners to degenerates: the medicalization of morality in the 19th century." *History of the Human Sciences* 15(1):59-88.

Sanford, Victoria, and Asale Angel-Ajani, eds. 2006. *The Engaged Observer: Anthropology, Advocacy, and Activism,* New Brunswick, NJ: Rutgers University Press.

Sassen, Saskia 2001. *The Global City: New York, London, Tokyo.* Princeton, NJ: Princeton University Press.

Shantz, Jeff. 1999. "Countering convention: Active resistance and the return of anarchy." In *Interrogating Social Justice: Politics, Culture and Identity*, edited by Marilyn Corsianos and Kelly A. Train, 23-50. Toronto: Canadian Scholar's Press.

Shragge, Eric, Jill Hanley, Steve Jordan, Charlotte Baltodano, Jaggi Singh, Martha Stiegman, and Aziz Choudry. 2006. *Community University Research Partnerships: A Critical Reflection and an Alternative Experience*. Accessed August 14, 2011. http://wall.oise.utoronto.ca/resources/Shragge_Partnerships_2006.pdf

Shukaitis, Stephen, David Graeber, and Erika Biddle, eds. 2007. *Constituent Imagination: Militant Investigations, Collective Theorization*. Oakland, CA: AK Press.

Smith, Dorothy. 1990. The *Conceptual Practices of Power: A Feminist Sociology of Knowledge*. Toronto: University of Toronto Press.

Smith, Linda Tuhiwai. 1999. *Decolonizing Methodologies: Research and Indigenous Peoples*. London: Zed Books.

Sudbury, Julia, and Margo Okazawa-Rey. 2009. *Activist Scholarship: Antiracism, Feminism, and Social Change*. Boulder, CO: Paradigm Publishers.

Thompson, A. K. 2010. *Black Bloc, White Riot: Anti-Globalization and the Genealogy of Dissent*. Edinburgh: AK Press.

Trotsky, Leon. 2002. *Fascism: What it is and How to Fight it*. Australia: Resistance Books.

Veblen, Thorstein. (1918)1957. *The Higher Learning in America: A Memorandum on the Conduct of Universities by Business Men*. Introduction by Louis M. Hacke. New York: Hill and Wang.

Wacquant, Loïc. 2002. "Scrutinizing the street: Poverty, morality, and the pitfalls of urban ethnography." *American Journal of Sociology* 107(6):1468-1532.

PART I
CONTESTING DISCOURSES OF MARGINALITY

Chapter 2
Understanding Obama's Discourse on Urban Poverty

David Wilson and Matthew Anderson

United States President Barack Obama today trumpets a new anti-poverty plan for urban America (MacGillis 2007; Gans 2010). Obama speaks of the need to correct for two key things: failed anti-poverty initiatives and a nation's persistent marginalization of the urban poor. This foray comes at a relevant and timely moment: urban poverty has increased 11 percent (35 million people) in America since 2000 (Cornfield 2009). Moreover, in America's two most impoverished cities, Cleveland and Detroit, more than 47 percent of children live below the poverty level (Walsh 2005; Tsoi-A-Fatt 2009). Obama posits a broad-based agenda: to open up new economic opportunity, re-cast a nation's sensibilities about the poor, and re-shape the poor's values. To make his case, Obama aggressively seeks the turf of progressivism. Recent years are marked as "reactionary times" and "the stuff of feudal intervention" amid calls to "eradicate the ills of poverty" and "move America into a new morning of concern, equality, and dignity" (Obama 2009a). In unabashed posture, his commitment to poverty reduction is served up as beyond doubt. "This kind of poverty is not an issue I just discovered for the purposes of a campaign" Obama noted before a national TV audience, "it is the cause that led me to a life of public service almost 25 years ago" (in MacGillis 2007).

In this opening chapter, we use critical discourse analysis (CDA) to decipher Obama's discourse of poverty. This perspective allows the unearthing of the underpinnings for the production of social policy—its system of meanings, values, and intentions (Fairclough 1992, 2000, 2001; Jones 2004). CDA posits, first, that one should not merely analyze texts, but also examine the relations between texts, their shaping of processes, and existent social conditions. It suggests, second, that policy discourses are always mobilized to colonize existing knowledge and dominate fields of discursivity. Thus, such discourses continuously assimilate society's central sentiments, ideals, and fears into their evolving "archive." Third, this perspective posits that discourses are thickly inter-textual, and never de-root from the settings and society that anchor them. Finally, CDA identifies that discourses are populated by a wealth of grounding, knowledge-building imaginative spaces. Such imaginative spaces, it notes, move in and out of discourses as fleeting but unmistakably key signs and signifiers.

Through CDA, we chronicle that Obama's discourse of poverty is a complex and tension-ridden apparatus. It is seen to be rooted in the contemporary of ambiguous liberal-progressive thinking mediating a legacy of past reactionary attempts to explain poverty, and is ultimately based in attempts to both help the poor materially and to contain and manage their voices and actions. We unveil a turbulent, unstable narrative that both illuminates and occludes the dynamics of contemporary urban poverty (Collins 1996; Marshall 2000). On the one hand, we suggest, this discourse is part of a political project (like some of its predecessor narratives about urban poverty) that attempts to reduce poverty as an identified human affliction. Obama and advisors seek progressive political change coming out of a harsh neoliberal Bush regime deemed punishing of the poor (Talbott 2008; Nation 2009). Obama's call for change is unequivocal. Desirous of burying the now widely unpopular Bushian legacy (see MacGillis 2007; Talbott 2008), Obama, akin to Gower Davies's (1972) notion of the evangelistic bureaucrat, fashions and sees himself as a social progressive. There is commitment and benevolence here, paraphrasing commentator and analyst Daniel Schorr (2009), at a time when calls for change and more fairness in society are in the air.

But there is more to this narrative of contemporary urban poverty. As we chronicle, Obama's discourse is also shaped by the desire to muzzle the poor's voice. It absorbs and plays to mainstream America's fear over two things—the poor's always potentially incendiary political voice and, more recently, the country's dramatic economic and political slippage. Here Obama seamlessly assimilates a kind of "societal habitus" into his discursive formation (see Bourdieu 1977), that is, the evolving, regulative, structures of feeling (anxieties, fears, hopes, and desires) seared into the common consciousness. At work, first, is a pervasive, timeless consternation about allowing the poor to speak their truths about their lives and society (hooks 1993; Wilson 2007). The poor, a potential incendiary demographic category, can be agents of social de-stabilization which need to be controlled. At work, second, is a practical reality of erasure: Obama continues another tradition of choking off grim news and bleak critiques of America in a time of immense national fragility. Many are currently traumatized by America's economic unraveling whose leading edges are the recent Wall Street collapse, national economic hemorrhaging, and national home-foreclosure crisis. Obama and the nation strive to de-fuse any notion of one more problematic reality: a deepening, structurally rooted poverty. Both add up to what we call "a trace of a desire" by Obama to render the poor's voice docile and passive even as there is genuine hope to enact policy that can upgrade their lives and communities.

Why is this deconstruction of Obama's explanation for and rendition of urban poverty important? Because a painful and afflicting reality deepens in urban America today: festering poverty, hunger, unemployment, and underemployment. Since 2000 and the implementation of stepped-up neoliberal programs like Workfare, No Child Left Behind, and Faith Based Resource Provision, the magnitude and intensity of racialized urban poverty has deepened (Davis and Shaylor 2001; Berry and Henderson 2002; Palast 2004; Wilson 2007). This is the same population disproportionately affected by another afflicting process—criminal justice policies—that now includes an unprecedented magnitude of incarceration (Davis 2003; Wacquant 2008, 2009). In this context, we find Obama's explanation for urban poverty seriously flawed with profoundly negative implications for one contemporary population: inner city racialized populations. Obama silences the historically racialized contours of urban poverty in America. Here, Obama works through a paradox of desiring to help the urban poor amid accepting the moorings of existent power relations. This finding, in one sense, is not surprising: Obama is a standard "political liberal" set in late capitalist society. What surprises, however, are the specific assumptions and assertions in this setting he accepts and incorporates into his thought.

The result is a discourse whose assumptions and assertions need to be problematized. We write this chapter following the notion that activist scholarship is a necessary first-step in any project of praxis and needs to confront the realities of post-industrial urban marginalization. Progressively changing the world, it follows, requires an illuminating base of critique as its foundation. Our analytic object of appraisal, Obama's discourse on urban poverty, is identified as a piece of social policy which, following Marx's famous axiom, is not merely producing, but also socially reproducing. It is a powerful discursive formation that, as much as any in our world today, needs to be critically examined.

In this context, we chronicle that this tension-ridden discourse takes a precise mode of portrayal: what we call the psycho-healing ethos. Obama's rendition of this poverty is shown to be offered as a social drama put in a sequence of two stages: a sad human fall into poverty, and full dilemma and malfunction. This sequence offers a population that falls into a paralyzing poverty and deprivation that disables them as normatively functioning beings. The story, never challenging of society's power structure and reassuring in its simplicity and closure, reduces "the poverty question" to a group's social and cultural disablement. Society is implicated in this: as an ostensibly brutish force that is momentarily insensitive to this population's plight. American society, rendered enabling and benevolent, but momentarily beset by insensitivity about the poor, is served-up as an object in need of deeper social sensibilities. This psycho-healing ethos ultimately places grief and bad societal values at the issue's core, silencing the poor as a potentially dissident source of knowledge about poverty's societal roots.

Obama and Background

Obama's discourse on the reasons for urban poverty closely parallels his explanations for urban marginality. Obama spoke little about poverty in his presidential campaign, except in a brief flurry that helped counter the growing popularity of "Mr. Poverty Soothsayer," John Edwards (Schorr 2009). In a series of heated exchanges with Edwards, Obama declared that urban poverty had always pre-occupied him and would be a central policy concern in his administration (MacGillis 2007). But when a badly beaten Edwards left the race shortly thereafter, Obama retreated back into his dominant domestic discourse: middle-class tax relief and financial support. This presentation had three prongs: middle class tax reductions, tax benefits for laid-off workers, and relief for households struggling to pay high school and college tuition fees. With the abrupt collapse of Wall Street and the US economy shortly thereafter, this dominant discourse was supplemented by the offering of another one: the narrative of national economic upgrade. Its central planks were "the 700 billion bailout issue," "bailout II," and "the stimulus package issue."

Obama re-centred his discourse on poverty when his stimulus package was signed into law on February 18, 2009. In this context, Obama issued an acclaimed position paper that summarized his policy recommendations to alleviate urban poverty. Five components (jobs, income, community, housing, Faith Based Neighbourhood Partnerships) dominated the presentation; some had been implemented within Obama's first year in office. On the jobs front, Obama has passed a $210 billion stimulus package, termed a 10-year government job-creation package. Nearly three-fourths of this outlay is for what Obama calls "green-collar" jobs devoted to developing clean energy; the rest is to be used to create jobs in construction and maintenance of public infrastructure. On the community front, Obama borrowed a page from the streets of New York and established 20 "Promise Neighbourhoods" in areas of high poverty, high crime, and low student academic achievement (Thabit 2003). The idea, borrowed from the Harlem Children's Zone (see Stein 2009) uses "free-market" solutions (e.g. active use of charter schools, cultivation of competitive curricula) to upgrade these areas. On the income front, Obama focuses on the category "working-class Americans" and proposes national tax reform to alleviate their tax burden. To facilitate this, he supports raising the minimum wage to $7.25 within two years. On the housing front, Obama calls for an Affordable Housing Trust to finance the construction of approximately 100,000 affordable housing units in "mixed income communities." The program is designed to move "lower-income families" from "poverty-ridden" neighbourhoods.

Finally, Obama proposes a new institutional infrastructure to drive these goals: a revamped White House Office of Faith Based and Neighbourhood Partnerships, passed into law in March, 2009. Obama here borrows from George Bush's template, the Office of Faith Based Initiatives. The goal is to deploy active, committed institutions on the ground which can integrate their "responsible religious convictions" with government and private-sector practices. Like Bush, religious groups are seen as unique compositional entities and potentially effective poverty combatants. They, to Obama, have an immense knowledge of the local, a strong spirituality and therapeutic ethos, and an intense guiding idealism (Kiely and Stinson 2008). Spurred by this vision, Obama directs this organization to facilitate four functions: reduce hunger, inculcate individuals with job skills and the values of successful work, reduce the number of abortions, and promote responsible fatherhood (Gorski 2009). The 25 member Partnership is charged to foster innovative collaborations across America's cities that would advance these functions. Unlike Bush's Faith Based Office, Obama prohibits organizations funded or operating under this umbrella from discriminating in hiring practices and the provision of resources.

Policy Discourses and Managing the Voice of the Poor

Policy discourses in America, like Obama's rendition of urban poverty, have a long history of managing the poor's voice. As discussed in this section, post-war discourses on urban education, urban redevelopment, and city policing vividly reflect this. While a multiplicity of voices have been taken up and mediated by these discourses (Mumby 1993; Potter 1996), the poor have been relentlessly caricatured. In this context, they are often focal points in narratives, the objects around which stories are spun (Mumby 1993; Bauder 2001). For the poor, as delineated below, are rich and resonant symbols in policy affairs and in common thought. On the one hand, the poor have been the centre of concern in many of these typically planning-state spearheaded discourses. On the other hand, as society's most marginalized and materially lacking, their existence invokes powerfully complex, contradictory feelings: bewilderment, concern, fear, loathing, compassion, and denial (Piven and Cloward 1978; Jakle and Wilson 1992).

Policy discourses in America (at diverse scales) have typically silenced, pathologized, or morally degraded the poor's voice. This voice has been, in typical treatments, reduced to an anecdotal status or banished into oblivion. Reflecting this, pre-2000, are studies of the discourse on urban policing and education. Reese (1986) reveals how the prominent post-war discourse on best community policing practices obliterates the poor's voice under a privileging of authoritative, technical expertise. The poor, relegated to knowledge deficient subjects in a supposed democratic planning forum, become "bodies without brains." Their voice, heard openly in a context of "citizen input," is reduced to a nuisanced noise: pre-determined policing plans and strategies rule the day. Similarly, educational discourse across urban America commonly projects something similar: an unqualified-to-be-heard poor population (see McCarthy 1995). Curricula construction and best pedagogical techniques, offered ideally as melded through relations between residents and school officials, codes poverty populations ill-prepared to offer innovative suggestions. Negative signifiers ascribed to the poor—emotionally overwhelmed by an everyday poverty, communicatively imprecise and deficient, and lacking knowledge about the tools and techniques of schooling—quash the relevance of their voice.

Recent work on discourses of community development chronicles a deepened stifling of the racialized poor's voice in contemporary neoliberal times. Barraclough (2009) shows how the black poor's voice in Los Angeles is more pathologized than ever before in state-driven renditions of best and most innovative land-use policy. Such policy posits this voice to be barely heard when set against the supposed rights and base of knowledge of two central players: middle-class white citizens and private-sector operatives (developers, builders, and prominent business people). Renditions of best property rights juxtapose a poverty-stained, bordering-on-the-corrosive voice of the black poor against a practical, technical voice of citizens and private-sector entrepreneurs. Moreover, Wilson and Grammenos (2005) document how a low-income stifling discourse of redevelopment in Chicago today deepens a capital-serving depiction of gentrification. Before 1989, to Wilson and Grammenos, prominent media and planner renditions offered gentrification as a new untested redevelopment reality with residents offered as at least partially viable sources of ideas and information. After 1990 (with the rise of the Daley regime), gentrification has been widely re-cast as a potent technocratic tool to be guided by professional expertise. In presentation, it is conspicuously innovative, attuned to new city and global realities, and best propelled by technical experts. Its counter, "low-income oppositional redevelopment," is reduced to being transparently reactionary, ill-informed about new city realities, and emotively rather than analytically driven. In current neoliberalist times where the poor have been imagined and treated more harshly (Davis and Shaylor 2001; Wacquant 2008), muffling their voices in the policy arena has become more flagrant (see also Willson, this volume).

Fear of the Potentially Incendiary Voice

The foundation of this current voice, these studies suggest, is the recognition of the poor's potentially incendiary voice. Barraclough's (2009) analysis excavates the pervasive fear among L.A. planners and politicians of providing a true policy forum for the black poor. This voice, to Barraclough, is potentially explosive and reverberative. To fully enable and "mike it" is to open up land-use planning to something feared by planners: real democratic practice. Similarly, Wilson and Grammenos (2005) reveal the fear of the poor's voice that helps guide Chicago's discourse of redevelopment. This counter voice, they document, cannot be allowed to legitimately stake a claim about best redevelopment form, forgotten and neglected human need, and the desire for political empowerment. Set within the niceties of "impression management," this voice cannot be allowed to flourish and propagate. Power, here, flows from a production of knowledge that is class-biased and exclusionary.

To hooks (1993), the poor are potentially disruptive, vituperative voices. They are society's most disadvantaged, the perceived dregs of America that can easily position themselves as having little to lose by narrating their plight and pushing for solutions. Managing the poor socially and spatially has been a continuous and creative process rooted in an imperative to prevent any meaningful political turf to be ceded to them. To truly represent their interests in policy, to hooks, is to open up power structures (locally, regionally, or nationally) to serious appraisal and scrutiny. To Piven and Cloward (1978), the poor's political aspirations and existing power formations will always be at loggerheads. Poverty, they note, represents the failings of existing social and economic arrangements; its carriers can seldom be allowed to speak their truths in ways that centre this reality. The poor, in these discussions, are a feared population, situated to shed light on realities that can mobilize people and prove disruptive and subversive. There is, to Piven and Cloward, a double-refusal here. Not only do afflictive realities have to be sanitized, so too do the social relations and institutional mechanisms that give rise to them.

At work, we suggest, has been the persistence of a kind of "management economy" (Amin and Thrift 2004; Leitner, Peck, and Sheppard 2007) in which the poor are objects sculpted and contained in a communicative circuitry that links flows of information with levels of political enablement. In a dominant motif, cultural practices regulate the poor's voice to constitute an expedient identity: the perplexing, ambiguous figure. They are configured to speak their truths about plight and realities but in ways that do not grant political terrain to them. Enabled to speak in a supposed inclusive policy community, they are shown to have little to say or contribute. Policy, cast as inclusive, smooth, and rule-driven, reaches out to improve the poor's lives but fails to get meaningful engagement from them. The poor, measured by one notion of creativity and reflexivity, becomes suspended in Wilson, Beck, and Bailey's (2009) permanent-temporariness of political exclusion. In this context, true policy decision-making gets rightfully shouldered by technical experts. The poor become manipulated objects: under the appearance of inclusion and appropriation, there is exclusion and condemnation.

A caveat at this point is important. We do not suggest a conspiracy to translate fear of the poor's voice into their removal from policy decision-making. Rather, following Potter (1996), we submit a more complex and nuanced reality. It is one of predictable rhetorical and instrumental flow in policy discourses and procedures where shared "vocabularies of motive" are conventionalized. A reflexive, evolving structure of fearing the poor's voice gets institutionalized. This structure becomes a convention as influential stakeholders (local, regional, and national planners, policy analysts, politicians, and policy builders) seek to induce positive outcomes. In this process, reflexively managing the poor's voice embeds in the unbroken, taken-for-granted flow of the expected, the desired, and the spatially and temporally contingent. Beneath offers of "impression management" and democratic inclusion, erasure of the poor's voice emerges out of concerns and anxieties to sculpt communicative dynamics. Voices, seen as resonant and influential instruments, the stuff of human striving and ideals, are managed in evolving, contingent ways on two fronts: their content and their veracity.

America's Slippage and Public Angst

But policy discourses in America have also typically reflected a constellation of other societal fears, concerns, and aspirations. A prominent fear infiltrating this discourse has chilled America in ebbs and flows: the fate of individuals, families, and communities in turbulent economic times. Here, a vacillating capitalist economy—its immense fluctuations and instabilities—have affected purchasing power, job availability, and job security to produce near national panics during severe downturns (Harvey 1989; Heilbroner 1995). For example, dramatic stock market crashes following the dramatic "fourth" and "fifth" Kondratief downturns in 1971 and 1987 seared the public psyche. In abruptness and severity of fall, these crashes rivalled the 1929 one. In the 1987 collapse, Federal Reserve Chairperson Alan Greenspan's fervent efforts to forestall a depression by funnelling massive capital into the banking system proved successful. But through the struggle and subsequent months, America experienced Jan Pieterse's (2008) shocking existential paralysis which, to Pieterse, became rooted in America's "culture of economic fear." An essential task of the policy community and media immediately thereafter, to Pieterse, was to work diligently to lessen this fear and instil confidence in America as a stable and still robust economic and political giant. Similar panics and responses followed the turbulent economic downturns of 1929, 1945, and 1971 (Sobel 1968; Harvey 2005).

This fear now engulfs America following the 2008 economic collapse. In 2008-2009, the United States (and much of the global west) plunged into a deep recession. A financial crisis rooted in reckless lending practices (the sub-prime fiasco) set the process off. It immediately exposed and was exacerbated by a sea of unprofitable speculative loans and over-inflated asset prices made available by an extended period of easily available (and irresponsibly lent) credit and inadequate regulation and oversight. This eroding situation has been further exacerbated by two trends. First, a sharp increase in oil and food prices decimated consumption of homes, goods, and services. Second, the paralleling global recession quickly choked off investor possibilities to find quick spatial fixes of new consumption markets abroad (Pieterse 2008). To make matters worse, as share and housing prices continued to plummet, a host of large, seemingly entrenched investment and commercial banks and houses severely contracted or went bankrupt (e.g. Goldman Sachs, Lehman Brothers, Bear Stearns). Negative multipliers materially and psychically reverberated through the national and local economies. To many observers, a once seemingly robust economy suddenly looked lost, vulnerable, and on the verge of disintegration.

This collapse has shaken America. Unemployment has strikingly spiked up since September 2008 to produce immense suffering in the low-income, working and middle classes. The official and unofficial figures in May 2009 were 9.4 and 15.8 percent, respectively (US Department of Labor 2009). Two years earlier, these figures were 3.5 and 11 percent. In two months (May and June of 2009), the US economy shed more than one million private-sector jobs. A spiral of mortgage foreclosures and homelessness has followed to scar many cities and communities and frighten their populations. Whereas the mortgage industry states that a one percent foreclosure rate is alarming, cities like Detroit, Cleveland, Las Vegas, and Baltimore now have rates of more than seven percent. Some neighbourhoods in these cities have foreclosure rates exceeding 17 percent (Foreclosuredata online 2009): they have emerged in the imaginary as the leading edge of a symbolic dystopia (Pieterse 2008). In this context, crude oil prices have shot up to record levels, straining household budgets and serving as a painful reminder at the pump of bewildering economic times. In 2008, crude oil prices established a record high at $102.08 per barrel (Cara Community 2008).

Fear of economic realities in current tumultuous times now visibly imprints numerous policy discourses. Wilson and Sternberg (forthcoming), for example, suggest that this fear currently circulates widely through narratives of city and metropolitan-wide across America. Growth, commonly reduced to a straight-forward calling to upscale downtowns and gentrify neighbourhoods, is articulated as the antidote to further economic eclipse (i.e. less mortgage foreclosures, less job loss, less tax base erosion) (Logan and Molotch 1987; Jonas and Wilson 1999; Smith 2002).

To Wilson and Sternberg, this notion of economic eclipse, a stress card being played, invokes the central symbols of this latest fiscal fear which provides this "new necessary growth" logic. As discussed, this growth thematic is at least two decades old; it has been aggressively pursued in US cities since the rise of neoliberalism and urban entrepreneurial governance (see Harvey 1989; Brenner and Theodore 2002). But, unlike before, this discourse now poignantly plays to a dramatic economic angst. It is now the central rhetorical trope that in robust, aggressive utterance, rationalizes this growth vision.

Equally illustrative, this fear now circulates within contemporary discourses of urban education (Johnson 2006). For example, to Rizvi (2008), this economic foreboding now gets skilfully and aggressively incorporated into renditions of best curricula content in public school systems. To Rizvi, this economic foreboding embeds in an already pronounced call for science and technical dominated curricula. This economic fear, unlike before, gets wielded like a cudgel to lash critics and dissenters. In utterance, the only way to prepare kids for a sound future, and to ensure community and city prosperity, is to endow them with technical and scientific knowledge. To stray from this path, it is suggested, is to create Morford's (2009) "next generation's... pile of idiots" and risk a re-emergence of what people now profoundly fear: massive unemployment, increased poverty, community collapse, and a tidal wave of human failures. This economic fear gets deployed in a strategy of political containment where only one proper policy course is sanctioned. This fear, so used, becomes a central building block in creating an emotively-laced, emotively manipulating story. The invoking of emotion and logic meshes in a seamless, complementary relation.

The analysis that follows unveils Obama's discourse on urban poverty as a complex, contradictory formation. Conflicting desires to both help extricate the poor from poverty and to manage their voice and actions are shown to embed within a dominant thematic: a psycho-healing ethos.

We reveal this ethos as simultaneously sensitive to, insensitive to, illuminating of, and concealing of the complexities of this poverty. Its emphasis on psychic turmoil, tumultuous social falls, and emotive instability is shown to be a society protecting, mainstream "feel-good" narrative that explains urban marginality in tidy, acceptable ways while ultimately failing to confront the foundations of this poverty.

The Discourse of Poverty as Psycho-Healing Ethos

Obama's discourse of urban poverty, as psycho-healing ethos, is structured as sociospatial spectacle. It is enacted through two identifiable phases: social fall and rootedness in malfunction (Fairclough 1992; Ehrenhaus 1993; Wilson 2004). The discourse's voice chronicles these stages via a time-tested positioning: as an attuned, benevolent observer (Fairclough 1992; Mumby 1993). The voice, made to relentlessly reveal truth from falsity, fixates on the onerous reality of a central object: a problematic "ghetto poverty." The public is provided an evolving melodrama, complete with stereotyped people, extreme states of being, fast-paced action, and the vindication of virtue over vice. On the one hand, contradictory fragments render this population in need of therapeuticizing: as pathetic, recoverable, culturally marginal, socially distinctive, best vocally contained, and with valid claims to the social centre. On the other hand, the other key object, society, is rendered in need of rehabilitation (morally and ethically). Caricature, in the end, makes this therapeutic movement simple, protective of existing power arrangements, and easily accomplished.

Social Plunge
The beginning of Obama's narrative is typically dominated by the exposition of the plunge phase. Descriptions reveal a population's dramatic plunge down a path of self- and community-afflicting deprivation. In the description, lives become increasingly distanced from the social and

cultural mainstream as people are increasingly ensnared in a new world: "ghetto living". But this poor, illuminated as central objects of concern, are also made markers for America's character and constitution, what Obama calls "society's ways" and "the American... economic agenda" (in Obama 2007; Sullivan 2007). The psycho-healing ethos, put into play in this phase, thus initiates the trend of the ethos throughout speaking about two central things: the nature of the population in question (the poor) and the essence of American society (its levels of health, inclusiveness, and mode of operation). Both are addressed as an inseparable unity, each always constitutes the other. Like other past prominent discourses on poverty (Peck 2001), a group's plight is made to speak about their predicament but also about a system's orientations, proclivities, possibilities, and capabilities. To illustrate, Obama declares at a public rally (Obama 2008):

> Two hundred and twenty-one years ago, a group of men gathered and... launched America's improbable experiment in democracy... It was stained by the nation's original sin of slavery... Of course, the answer to the slavery question was already embedded in our Constitution—a Constitution that had at its very core the ideal of equal citizenship under the law; a Constitution that promised its people liberty, and justice, in a union that could be and should be perfected over time. [Now we must] narrow that gap between the promise of our ideals and the reality of their time. [For] pockets of poverty... persist in so many of today's urban and rural communities. All helped create a cycle of violence, blight, and neglect that continue to haunt us.

Obama reinvents the central character in his narration of the plunge: the urban poor. He rejects neoliberal doctrine and asserts a new side to them: a group similar to other people in their goals and strivings and who are potentially recoverable in an economic and social mainstream. In the Bush years, the poor had been all but refused the possibility of middle-class, mainstream exploration and recapture; they were purportedly too culturally damaged (Kelley 1997). Obama situates this population within the turf of mainstream strivings. As a stylized cultural construction, the poor acutely eye and stay attuned to the mainstream; it is where they want to be. Their eyes and heads, immersed in the "ghetto" everyday, nevertheless read the broader society's realities and expectations. Thus, to Obama, poor people's engagement in any moral and ethical transgression (e.g. crime, drug-dealing, gang-banging), is both heinous and inexcusable but also expressions of unrealized symbolic and material acquisition. In Obama's oratory, the urban poor intensely desire to emulate the lives of the more well-to-do.

Yet, this poor emerges as an ambiguous population, also rendered different and distinctive via absorbing Obama's "ghetto realities" (in Obama 2009a). Working through American anxieties, sensibilities, and imagined spatialities, Obama situates the poor to relentlessly absorb the ills of a dysfunctional social terrain: the ghetto. Obama describes these terrains as "neighborhoods [where]... role models are few... the streets are cancerous... and there is little contact with the normalcy of life outside these streets" (In Obama 2007). Through a purported absorption of a decrepit landscape, this population is marked as socially and culturally distinctive. They typically desire a place in the mainstream, but profoundly absorb the ills of their class and place realities. The poor emerge as place-seared, searching souls emptied of something mainstream America covets: a normative daily round. As we chronicle shortly, this tension between mainstreaming and otherizing the poor becomes more pronounced in narrations of the next stage of the therapeutic motif.

The mode of presentation is also important in shaping this depiction of a socially distinctive urban poor. Put to work is a potent stylistic element, melodrama, which codes the plunge.

A mix of spectacle, human peculiarity, and tragic eclipse are set within offers of provocative spatial imaginaries. The motif of melodrama, Walkowitz (1992) notes, seamlessly otherizes subjects as they are placed on stages of fast-paced, amazing action. No other style of depiction, to Walkowitz, so effortlessly accomplishes this. For starters, the poor's fall is opened up as a public event for all to "see" and interrogate. As Obama puts it, "we all bear witness to... the shame and suffering of poverty... [Where] the anger is real; it is powerful...." Obama, here, invites the public to be voyeurs into his labyrinth of the "dark inner city" (Obama 2009b). In this context, Obama gives the public a tragic and pitiable fall. It is one that "sadly shows a horror seared into my genetic makeup that this nation is more than the sum of its parts" (Obama 2008). Here, adults and kids are dragged through a horrific barrage of jarring events (e.g. losing jobs, being evicted from homes, having to hustle to survive). In narrations, tragedy and pity ooze out of each trend. As Obama narrates:

> Those "quiet riots" that take place every day are born from the same place as the fires and the destruction and the police decked out in riot gear and the deaths. They happen when a sense of disconnect settles in and hope dissipates. Despair takes hold and young people all across the country look at the way the world is and believe that things are never going to get any better... If we have more black men in prison than are in our colleges and universities, then it's time to take the bullet out. If we have millions of people going to the emergency room for treatable illnesses like asthma; it's time to take the bullet out... If we keep sending our kids to dilapidated school buildings [...]. (In Sullivan 2007)

This stage of social fall is pivotal to the discourse because it establishes the objects which supposedly need to be therapeuticized, American society and the poor. American society, made fundamentally benevolent and fluid in its history of race and class relations, becomes strategically situated as a site for moral and ethical rehabilitation. In assertion, American society has fitfully moved towards inclusiveness of the poor amid bouts of reactionary policy and belief. The move, to Obama, has been slow and fitful, but inexorably toward a progressive pole that America's founders codified in the constitution. At the moment, to Obama, America is coming out of a reactionary time, an era of enhanced racial and class divisiveness, that most now find unacceptable. Currently, a rooted, democratic nation desires to shed reactionary values, move forward, and renew its historic commitment to helping the poor. As Obama (2008) notes:

> [There was a time] when segregation was still the law of the land and opportunity was systematically constricted. This [is] one of the tasks we set forth: to continue the long march of those who came before us, a march for a more just, more equal, more free, more caring and prosperous America... This belief comes from my unyielding faith in the decency and generosity of the American people... For as long as I live, I will never forget that in no other country on Earth is my story even possible... Now, we will move forward... spurred by the beliefs of our people, and move to eradicate poverty.

But Obama's malleable America is a curious offering: he serves up a kind of uncritiqued-critiqued object. While dissecting America, the country's ills are confined to national attitudes and views that locate the nation within what Anthony Giddens (1984) terms a terrain of brightness-darkness. This stroke, anything but new, has continuously infused mainstream constructions of American society post 1945 (Anderson 1984; Harvey 2005). It sets up the nation to be critiqued but cushions the intensity of the charge.

America, then, is found to be merely momentarily deficient; that is, periodically exclusionary in its predilections and policies due to a momentary attitudinal aberration. A structurally inclusive society is always inferred. Obama's centring of a societal anger and ignorance here, following Anderson (1984), becomes a terrain of protection. America gets hermeneutically sealed from serious criticism and reform as it is critically analyzed. Underneath calls for progressive change, it follows, is the careful choreographing of the gaze and the critique.

Similarly, the urban poor become situated as prime objects of therapy in this phase of the psycho-healing ethos. A heterogeneous population (Obama variously identifies them as the working poor, the unemployed poor, the hopeless poor), offered as entrapped in a slide, still deeply desires a place in America's mainstream. But now, they are being pushed into a state of deepening psychic and emotive damage. As Obama notes, "in our cities... poverty is not just a crisis that hits pocketbooks, but a disease that infects every corner of the community" (in Obama 2009a). In the process, to Obama, they increasingly absorb the ills of neglect and punitiveness in their demeanour, outlook, and acts. While Obama spurns any imagery that suggests society's establishing a hierarchical-custodial relation here, he sets up this poor as in need of healing and nourishing. As Obama (in Obama 2007) comments:

> If you had gone to any street corner in Chicago or Baton Rouge or Hampton—you would find the same young men and women without hope, without miracles, and without a sense of destiny other than life on the edge—the edge of the law—the edge of the economy—the edge of family structures and communities... [So], we need to give our young people some real choices out there so they move away from gangs and violence and connect them with growing job sectors... [We need to] bring hope and real job opportunities to our young people...

As now revealed, evocative spatial imaginaries "shoot out" and anchor this rendition of the urban poor's social fall. There are two repeatedly invoked discursive constructions: the falling-into-disrepair poor community ("the ghetto") and the increasingly isolated human life path. The imaginary of the ghetto darts in and out of narrations, appearing, disappearing, and re-appearing as a continuous evocation to bind presentations of urban poverty with imaginary space. This space encompasses the ills—bad schools, dangerous streets, decrepit housing, fallen-into-disrepair social relations—that seamlessly shape the everyday lives of the poor (on the role of spatial imaginary in marginalizing discourses, see Gönen and Yonucu, as well as Tomiak, both in this volume). As Obama's "contemporary cancer," no resident can avoid it. This space, in Obama's words, has "mayhem and violence… [These] were not phenomena created by the [Katrina] disaster… They have existed in inner cities across the country." To Obama, "The violence has always been there. It just wasn't on your television screen because it wasn't spilling out onto the lives of the rest of us" (In Jan 2005). Within these spaces "a sense of disconnect settles in and hope dissipates. Despair takes hold and young people all across this country look at the way the world is and believe that things are never going to get any better…" (In Sullivan 2007). No little girl's future should be confined to the neighborhood she is born into…." (Obama 2007).

Invoking the second identified imaginary space we identified, the increasingly isolated human life-path, is also methodical and strategic. Its contents—the streets, the journey to school, the ghetto block, the public housing project, the trip to the store, the local retail spine—appear at telling moments in narrative to capture the imaginary of an accelerated human plunge into isolation and discordance. The poor, immersed in these grim nodes and links, prove the "reality" of an ongoing human plunge into decay and despair. Here are Obama's "echoes on the streets of Compton and Detroit... It lingers... where every other child... lives below the poverty line." Within these isolated life paths, to Obama, "too many do not graduate and too many more do not find work. Some join gangs, others fall into... gunfire" (in Obama 2007). This life path, served up in frequently colourful, terse oratory, becomes the chain-link fence of isolation without the chains. "The streets" in Washington D.C. "are close to our capital, but far from the people it represents. Poverty is not just a function of simple economics. It's also a matter of where you live" (in Obama 2007).

Such use of spatial imaginaries is not unique to Obama's discourse on poverty. This usage permeates many policy discourses (see Wilson 2005; Lawson, Jaroscz, and Bonds 2008). Bonding subjects and ideas to imagined landscapes, this spatializing becomes a potent constitutive tool of knowledge. Such made and deployed space, in this sense, is inseparable from a field of strategies (statements, views, concepts, objects of analysis, and their interrelations) which creates and perpetuates narrow visions for comprehension. Obama's use of spatial imaginaries, anything but dispassionate "mental maps," are a complex textual politics: a graphical content propelling visions of reality and social commentaries as it works through traces of common understanding. It ultimately anchors a project: to illuminate one way of seeing contemporary poverty in America (and America itself) and to purge alternatives. Without the use of this activist space, we suggest, the ability of the discourse in this phase to be coherent and persuasive is doubtful.

Dilemma and Malfunction

The dilemma-malfunction phase of the discourse follows the social plunge phase, narrating a full-fledged rise of individual poverty and dysfunction and community decline. Obama, with rhetorical flourish, narrates a central object—ghetto realities—with passion, pity, and remorse. A therapeutic crisis is invoked—of discordant or hopeless people substantially removed from mainstream society—which is placed in an everyday human struggle to keep mainstream society's norms and values in sight. The urban poor, posited as near- or fully-bottomed out and typically scarred by despair and suffering, are people in need of economic, social, and psychic centring. "Ghetto realities", to Obama, easily overwhelm this most vulnerable and troubled population. Here, to Obama, are "dashed hopes, unfulfilled promises, and human suffering flowing from a fortress-like confinement in torn-apart neighborhoods" (in Obama 2009c). Dilemma and malfunction is ultimately read through the register of blocked possibilities, a perverse attitudinal compensation, and human suffering. "Denied opportunities… and pushed to the wall" (in Obama 2009b)—these people too often adjust and create their own alternative (and emotively and materially destructive) modes of survival and symbolic status.

Again, a spatialized melodrama bolsters the sense of a necessary therapeuticizing. This stage of the psycho-healing ethos, even more than in the previous one, becomes spatialized theatre. Searing heartbreak, emotive-drenched realities, and poignant human rumination is placed in a luminous spatial imaginary: "the ghetto." Reflected in an incendiary ghetto is something ominous: searing psychic and emotive states of people. But, here, the crisis is typically narrated in a different way: by brief bursts of evocative phrases set in offerings of ghetto space. Rejecting any detailed exposés of falls or squalid lives, Obama relies on the luminous qualities of phrases strung together—"a human story of misery", "the poor mired in despair", "the tortured realities of a despondent poor"—to take listeners to an imagined spatiality of fully fallen-into-disrepair people mired in grim neighbourhoods. The lives of the urban poor become reduced to improvisational sites for strange encounters and relations. Set in bizarre ghettos, the poor are posited to carry and reflect its mysteries and traps in their conduct and ways.

Even more than in the discourse's previous stage, the poor here are ambiguous beings. Obama's full-fledged poverty population combines the seemingly incompatible sensibilities of ordinary people with out-of-order, socially afflicted beings. He narrates self-reflexive, thoughtful people bent on re-locating into society's mainstream, but also socially wounded and emptied beings. Again, two goals drive this discrepancy: the desire to demonstrate possibilities for society to eradicate poverty, and to alert the American public to the ills of its past exclusionary acts. These themes are not inherently paradoxical as Obama creates a contradictory sense of who these poor beings are. Thus, in narratives, the poor angle to locate in America's "social epicentre", which displays possibilities for Obama's "recapture in the societal centre". But, they are also configured as grotesquely stark, larger-than-life symbols of emotive instability to reveal what a morally and ethically maladroit America can produce. The sense of the poor in this stage of the motif flickers dramatically across these poles. One sentence's struggling average person seamlessly slides into a next sentence's destroyed and distanciated person. This heightened ambiguity reflects a recurring reality of this discourse: objects and processes narrated across the three stages (e.g. "the poor", "the government", and "the downward spiral") are anything but fixed unities. They are, rather, changing, unstable, and sometimes contradictory elements set up to play distinctive roles in the stages; that is, to help produce coherent stories specific to a phase of the therapeutic motif.

This shifting, contradictory depiction of the bottomed-out, in-need-of-therapy poor is nothing new. It also marks a spate of previous bourgeois narratives on this topic (hooks 1993). The poor in America, to Piven and Cloward (1978), have always been ambiguous, complex symbols in the common consciousness typically set up to be therapeuticized for some ill or flaw. To Piven and Cloward, at issue has been the desire to "same them" and be inclusive at an abstract level versus the practical sense of desiring to otherize and segregate them (i.e. to create an "Other" and constitute the identity of the privileged middle). Similarly, Joseph (2002) describes America's poor as America's ultimate ambiguous fixation, a mirror onto the public's contradictory obsessions with inclusion, exclusion, class and racial difference, multi-cultural implementation, community divides, and democratic practice. Through the mirror of the poor, to Joseph, America has revealed its deepest contradictions and ambiguities. Such contradictory understandings acquire form in Obama's rendition of the poor in this stage: as different and feared, caricatured and reviled, suffering and pitiable, and culturally different but culturally recoverable (see Walkowitz 1992; Murji and Solomos 2005).

This dilemma and malfunction phase, like the previous phase, also directly narrates the other central object supposedly in need of therapy: American society. This object in Obama's poverty discourse, essential for his unveiling of a "comprehensive policy agenda to fight poverty," receives careful attention in this phase of the motif. In this context, Obama deepens a strategic concession: that society has destructively marginalized the urban poor. Through this offering, Obama serves up the need for a comprehensive rehabilitation of society. He suggests something supposedly vital—a "cleansing" of society in the realm of attitudes and behaviours—which would be cathartic to a values-faltering America. To Obama, an ebb and flow of unevenly treating the urban poor by society and public policy has gone on for too long. At issue is the fundamental proposition of equity and justice for all. In this context, a paralleling notion becomes crucial: Obama clings to the proposition of a fundamentally benevolent, easily transformed America. To induce progressive change, the country's moral and ethical compass simply needs to be adjusted. This theme poignantly emerges in his recent discussion of poverty and controversial pastor Jeremiah Wright of Chicago:

> The profound mistake of Reverend Wright's sermons is not that he spoke about racism in our society. It's that he spoke as if our society was static; as if no progress has been made; as if this

country—a country that has made it possible for one of his own members to run for the highest office in the land and build a coalition of white and black; Latino and Asian, rich and poor, young and old—is still irrevocably bound to a tragic past. But what we know—what we have seen—is that America can change. That is the true genius of this nation. What we have already achieves gives us hope—the audacity to hope—for what we can and must achieve tomorrow. (Obama 2009a)

But this phase, like before, offers a limited conception and appraisal of society. The discourse asks people to recognize poverty, but also to confine understanding to a grieving population and a sorrowful nation temporarily gone astray. Offered is recognition of the poor's plight, a sense of collective empathy for their traumas, and an apology to them. Silenced here are two potentially incendiary issues: any meaningful interrogation of poverty's causes and any substantive sense of societal culpability beyond transitory societal attitudes and predilections. In this way, Obama's crisis of poverty becomes something easily supportable and non-disruptive: a fixable, momentary lapse in a society's willingness to absorb and assimilate. The psycho-healing ethos in this phase, placing the poor's grief and society's bad values at the issue's core, ultimately silences the poverty-stricken as a dissident source of knowledge about poverty's multi-textured relation to society. Subverted is something we believe to be important: the potentially resonant challenges that have been issued by the poor about society's structural role in poverty (Lefebvre 1991; Mitchell 2003). The poor are to speak their truths about poverty, but only as it is manifest as an aspiration-blocked, hurtful reality. In both cases, scrutiny of American society is ultimately contained and managed.

It follows that the complex human accomplishment of the psycho-healing ethos fulfills a difficult task: it separates America's most vulnerable and potentially incendiary population from their structural circumstances. This rendition ultimately partitions and separates the poor from any sense of historically persistent, pervasively rooted forces that sustain poverty. What American society is, and how the poor are situated in relation to this, is ultimately reduced to the terrain of values and attitudes. This way, the poverty issue is collapsed into a politically simplistic, non status-quo threatening turf. Only cognitive error is made to exist, not structurally inflected outcome. Poverty becomes a correctible mental slippage, something reduced to a fluid, epiphenomenal issue.

Conclusion

This study suggests that Obama's rendition of contemporary urban poverty should be seen as a complex formation that defies the simple labels of "progressive" or "reactionary". This contradictory and turbulent piece of policy hybridity speaks to conflicting societal concerns: the poor's welfare, fear and revulsion of the poor, consternation about a faltering America, and desires to manage and control outcomes from "democratic" participatory processes. This hybrid formation, ironically, both challenges and maintains this poverty. It challenges its existence at an ethical level: its moral right to exist, its repugnance as a lived reality, and its efficacy as a societal outcome. But it also maintains this poverty at an epistemological level: as a pervasive human construct whose structural basis is left unexplored and intact. Urban poverty, sheared from its roots as a multi-scaled societal production, is offered as a tragic and unacceptable reality of struggling poor people which a central ameliorative agent—society—can and should eradicate.

We conclude that Obama's notion of urban poverty in America is problematic. Under the guise of a new progressive vision, there lies a solid core of historically retrieved assumptions and beliefs that intimately tie this conception to previous regressive notions. This is where Obama's poverty policy fails. Reliance on notions of momentary lapses in societal morals and ethics, coupled with suggestions of failed individual and household initiative, is a recipe for one more poverty-policy failure. Here, we believe, purportedly innovative social policy will suffer the same fate of its predecessors and further muddy the integrity of "the progressive political agenda." This, we fear in our darkest moments, could strengthen something pernicious: the neoliberal political agenda applied to domestic issues. Our task, then, must be to illuminate—for all to see—Obama's discourse on poverty for what it really is: a deeply ambivalent, neo-conservative anchored formation. Clearly, there is much work to be done.

References

Amin, Ash, and Nigel Thrift, eds. 2004. *Cultural Economy Reader.* Oxford: Blackwell.

Anderson, Benedict. 1984. *Imagined Communities: Reflections on the Origin and Spread of Nationalism.* London: Verso.

Barraclough, Laura. 2009. "South Central farmers and Shadow Hills homeowners: Land use policy and relational racialization in Los Angeles." *Professional Geographer* 61(2):164-186.

Bauder, Harald. 2001. "Agency, place, scale: Representations of inner city youth identities." *Journal of Economic and Social Geography* 92:279-291.

Berry, Kate, and Martha L. Henderson. 2002. *Geographical Identities of Ethnic America: Race, Space, and Place.* Reno: University of Nevada.

Bourdieu, Pierre. 1977. *Outline of a Theory of Practice.* Cambridge: Cambridge University.

Brenner, Neil, and Nik Theodore. 2002. *Spaces of Neoliberalism: Urban Restructuring in North America and Europe.* London: Blackwell.

Cara Community. 2008. Accessed October 3, 2010. http://caracommunity.com

Collins, Sheila. 1996. *Let Em Eat Ketchup: The Politics of Poverty and Inequality.* New York: M.E. Sharpe.

Cornfield, Daniel. 2009. "Ending poverty in America: How to restore the American dream." *Social Forces* 87(4):2203-2205.

Davies, Gower. 1972. *The Evangelistic Bureaucrat.* London: Tavistock.

Davis, Angela. 2003. *Are Prisons Obsolete?* New York: Seven Stories.

Davis, Angela, and Cassandra Shaylor. 2001. "Race, gender, and the prison industrial complex: California and beyond." *Meridians* 2(1):1-25.

Ehrenhaus, Peter. 1993. "Cultural narratives and the therapeutic motif: The political containment of Vietnam veterans." In *Narrative and Social Control: Critical Perspectives*, edited by D.K. Mumby, 77-96. California: Sage.

Fairclough, Norman. 1992. *Discourse and Social Change.* Oxford: Polity.

———. 2000. "Discourse, social theory, and social research: The discourse of welfare reform." *Journal of Sociolinguistics* 4(2):163-195.

———. 2001. *Language and Power.* London: Longman.

Foreclosuredata. 2009. Accessed October 3, 2010. www.foreclosuredata.com.

Gans, Herbert J. 2010. "Concentrate poverty: A critical analysis." *Challenge* 57(3):82-89.

Giddens, Anthony. 1984. *A Contemporary Critique of Historical Materialism*. New York: Polity.

Gorski, S. 2009. "Dungy declines spot on Obama's faith-based panel." *Eyewitness News*, April 7.

Harvey, David. 1989. *The Condition of Postmodernity*. London: Verso.

———. 2005. *A Brief History of Neoliberalism*. Oxford: Oxford University Press.

Heilbroner, Robert. 1995. *Visions of the Future*. New York: Oxford University.

hooks, bell. 1993. *Outcast Culture*. London: Routledge.

Jakle, John, and David Wilson. 1992. *Derelict Landscapes: The Wasting of America's Built Environment*. Lanham: Rowman & Littlefield.

Jan, Tracy. 2005. "Obama urges alumni to help fight poverty." *Boston Globe*, 18 September. Accessed August 31, 2011. http://www.boston.com/news/local/massachusetts/articles/2005/09/18/obama_urges_alumni_to_help_fight_poverty/

Johnson, Heather. 2006. *The American Dream and the Power of Wealth: Choosing Schools and Inheriting Inequality in the Land of Opportunity*. New York: Routledge.

Jonas, Andrew E.G., and David Wilson. 1999. *The Growth Machine: A Critical Appraisal Two Decades Later*. Albany: SUNY Press.

Jones, Peter E. 2004. "Discourse and the materialist conception of history: Critical comments on critical discourse analysis." *Historical Materialism* 12(1):97-125.

Joseph, Miranda. 2002. *Against the Romance of Community*. Minneapolis: University of Minnesota.

Kelley, Robin D. G. 1997. *Yo' Mama's Disfunktional! Fighting the Culture Wars in Urban America*. New York: Wiley.

Kiely, Kathy, and James Stinson. 2008. "Candidates make their case." *USA Today*, November 9.

Lawson, Victoria, Lucy Jaroscz, and Anne Bonds. 2008. "Building economics from the bottom-up: (Mis)representations of poverty in the American Northwest." *Social and Cultural Geography* 9(7):737-753.

Lefebvre, Henri. 1991. *The Production of Space*. London: Wiley-Blackwell.

Leitner, Helga, Jamie Peck, and Eric Sheppard, eds. 2007. *Contesting Neoliberalism*. Oxford: Blackwell.

Logan, John, and Harvey Molotch. 1987. *Urban Fortunes: The Political Economy of Place* Berkeley: University of California.

MacGillis, Alec. 2007. "Obama says he, too, is a poverty fighter." *Washington Post*, July 19. Accessed October 3, 2010. http://www.washingtonpost.com/wp-dyn/content/article/2007/07/18/AR2007071802529.html

Marshall, Ray. 2000. *Back to Shared Prosperity: The Growing Inequality of Wealth and Income in America*. Armonk: M.E. Sharpe.

McCarthy, Cameron. 1995. *Fear in the Suburban-Zone*. Unpublished manuscript, available from author, Department of Educational Policy Studies: University of Illinois.

Mitchell, Don. 2003. *The Right to the City: Social Justice and the Right for Public Space*. New York: Guilford.

Morford, Mark. 2009. Accessed October 3, 2010. www.markmorford.com

Mumby, Dennis K. 1993. *Narrative and Social Control: A Critical Perspective*. Newbury Park: Sage.

Murji, Karim, and John Solomos. 2005. *Racialization: Studies in Theory and Practice*. Oxford: Oxford University.

Nation. 2009. "Obama's fateful choice," *Nation* editorial. Accessed October 3, 2010. http://www.thenation.com/article/obamas-fateful-choice

Obama, Barack. 2007. "Changing the odds for urban America." Text from speech in Washington D.C., 18 July 7, Transcript for Organizing for America.

———. 2008. "Obama Race Speech." *Huffington Post* 18 March 2008. Accessed August 31, 2011. http://www.huffingtonpost.com/2008/03/18/obama-race-speech-read-th_n_92077.html

———. 2009a. "Barack Obama's inaugural address." Transcript from the Obama Re-Election Committee, January 20.

———. 2009b. "Obama address on America's domestic realities." *C-Span*. February 15.

———. 2009c. "Speech on the State of America." *C-Span*. November 8.

Palast, Greg. 2004. "No child left behind: the new educational eugenics in George Bush's State of the Union." *Common Dreams.org*. Accessed September 5, 2011. http://www.commondreams.org/views04/0122-08.htm

Peck, Jamie. 2001. *Workfare States*. New York: Guilford.

Pieterse, Jan. 2008. *Is There Hope For Uncle Sam?* London: Zed Books.

Piven, Frances Fox, and Richard Cloward. 1978. *Poor People's Movements: Why They Succeed, How They Fail*. New York: Vintage.

Potter, Jonathan. 1996. *Representing Reality: Discourse, Rhetoric, and Social Construction*. Thousand Oaks, CA: Sage.

Reese, James. 1986. "Policing the violent society: The American experience." *Stress Medicine* 2(3):233-240.

Rizvi, Fazal. 2008. Conversation with author, Department of Educational Policy Studies, University of Illinois at Urbana-Champaign, April 4.

Schorr, Daniel. 2009. "Little mention of poverty in public discourse."

National Public Radio. Accessed October 3, 2010. http://www.npr.org/templates/story/story.php?storyId=100831097&ps=rs

Smith, Neil. 2002. "New globalism, new urbanism: Gentrification as global urban strategy." *Antipode* 34(3):427-450.

Sobel, Robert. 1968. *Panic on Wall Street: A History of America's Financial Disasters.* New York: Macmillan.

Stein, Sam. 2009. "Barack Obama's innovative war on poverty." *Huffington Post.* Accessed October 3, 2010. http://www.huffingtonpost.com/2008/10/13/barack-obamas-innovative_n_134162.html

Sullivan, Andrew. 2007. Obama and Poverty. *The Daily Dish*, June. 7. Accessed August 31, 2011. http://andrewsullivan.thedailybeast.com/2007/06/obama_and_pover.html

Talbott, John. 2008. *Obamanomics: How Bottom-Up Economic Prosperity Will Replace Trickle-Down Economics.* New York: Seven Stories.

Thabit, Walter. 2003. *How East New York Became A Ghetto.* New York: New York University.

Tsoi-A-Fatt, 2009. *Keeping Youth Connected.* Accessed October 3, 2010. http://www.clasp.org/admin/site/publications/files/Cleveland-Profile.pdf

U.S. Department of Labor. 2009. Data obtained from monthly unemployment press releases. Available from federal agency. Washington, D.C.

Wacquant, Loïc. 2008. *Urban Outcasts: A Comparative Sociology of Advanced Marginality.* Cambridge: Polity Press.

Walkowitz, Judith. 1992. *City of Dreadful Delight.* Baltimore: Johns Hopkins.

Walsh, David. 2005. "Nearly one-third of Detroit's population lives below poverty level." *World Socialist Website.* Accessed October 3, 2010. http://www.wsws.org/articles/2005/sep2005/detr-s02.shtml.

Wilson, David. 2004. "Toward a contingent neoliberalism." *Urban Geography* 28(3):61-79.

———. 2007. *Cities and Race: America's New Black Ghetto.* London: Routledge.

Wilson, David, and Dennis Grammenos. 2005. "Gentrification, discourse, and the body: Chicago's Humboldt Park." *Environment and Planning D: Society and Space* 23(2):295-312.

Wilson, David, Dean Beck, and Adrian Bailey. 2009. "Neoliberal-parasitic economies and space building: Chicago's southwest side." *Annals of the Association of American Geographers* 99(3):604-626.

Wilson, D, and C. Sternberg. Forthcoming. "The new neoliberal growthocracy: Chicago." *Urban Geography*, Special Issue: New Trends in Governing Western Cities.

Chapter 3

Legitimizing Violence and Segregation
Neoliberal Discourses on Crime and the Criminalization of Urban Poor Populations in Turkey

Zeynep Gönen and Deniz Yonucu

Since the 1980s, neoliberalism has shaped capitalist accumulation, urban processes, and the state in Turkey in conjunction with transformations of the global political economy. As in the other geographies of the South, the neoliberal transformation of Turkey has been put in place through IMF and World Bank-led Structural Adjustment Programs. Agricultural deregulation erased government support through pricing, while the elimination of subsidies and loans destroyed rural economies, and created dependence on agricultural imports from the core capitalist countries. Deregulation of the labour market reduced the power and living standards of workers. Sharpening regional and class inequalities, poverty, unemployment, and destruction of social safety nets set the background for the emergence of thriving luxurious lifestyles, and new consumption and leisure patterns of the rich urban populations (Yeldan 2001; Köse, Şenses and Yeldan 2003; Buğra and Keyder 2003; Balkan and Savran 2003). Turkey's experience in this period was also shaped by the war in the Kurdish region against the PKK guerrillas.[1] The widespread destruction of Kurdish villages during the war and the already weak local and regional economies forced many Kurds from their lands to the cities between 1986 and 1995. Poverty and marginalization became the rule for the newcomers, as the new Kurdish migrants found no easy entry into urban economic life in contrast to former generations of migrants. This new wave of migration further contributed to class polarization and sharpening antagonisms in the large cities.

Crime is amongst many other consequences of these processes of polarization and growing antagonisms, as by the late 1990s crime became a focal issue in Turkey as evident in the discursive sphere. In this chapter, we discuss contemporary discourses on crime produced by media sources and criminological studies, and examine their ideological effect.[2] First, we will focus on the discursive processes of criminalization since the late 1990s that constitute the urban poor as "dangerous criminals" as opposed to the "innocent citizens". We argue that "criminals" are characterized as "abjected"[3] bodies with "animalistic" behaviours in the Turkish mainstream media. Second, we show how criminalizing discourses legitimize both civilian and state violence against the "criminals", associated primarily with urban poor populations (see O'Connor, in this volume, on the criminalization of sex workers in Machala, Ecuador). Fears of the criminal threat supposedly posed by an animalized and racialized class of "criminals" substitutes for the feeling of insecurity and precariousness caused by social, political, and economic transformations. This replacement produces ideological effects "especially in terms of provoking and legitimating a coercive reaction by both the public and the state" (Hall et al. 1978:224).

Furthermore, we argue that the association of crime with the urban poor legitimizes segregation practices and a remaking of urban space in accordance with neoliberal urbanism.[4] The urban poor are increasingly seen as a "race apart" and their particular culture as productive of "degeneracy" and "criminality" concentrated in the neighbourhoods in which they reside. The media are not alone in associating poor neighbourhoods with crime. Criminologists and urban planners in Turkey have been increasingly engaging with the spatial relations of crime, and have insinuated the "criminality" of particular neighbourhoods. The discourses they produce are aligned with the aim of reconstructing the metropoles of Turkey as "non-antagonistic" financial, business, and cultural centres attractive to foreign capital and global investment, "secured" and "freed" from crime and/or urban poor. Such "non-antagonistic" cities and/or the fantasy of non-antagonistic cities in Turkey are facilitated mainly through the *Urban Transformation Projects*, large scale housing developments in place of poor shantytown neighbourhoods.

The willingness of some academics to lend their discourses of crime to the project of creating "non-antagonistic" cities in Turkey urges us to see the place of scientific knowledge production in processes of domination and relations of power. While mainstream academic crime discourses in Turkey have joined the media in the legitimization of segregation and violence, our aim here is to provide a critical perspective. This critique aims to problematize crime and criminality by reframing the "problem" and thus intervene in the ideological processes of criminalization. In arguing against the marginalizing discourses of crime, we follow Wacquant's (2007:8) suggestion that scholars should give "particular attention... to the critical examination of the categories and discourses (including those produced by social science) that under cover of describing marginality contribute to moulding it by organizing its collective perception and its political treatment." We suggest that critical research is necessary for altering the terms of discourse, an engagement which in turn can lend itself to activist struggles.[5] Our attempt here is to discursively contribute to struggles against the "collective perception and political treatment" of "criminals" in Turkey.

Part I: Constructing Crime and Fear in Urban Turkey

Garland (1996, 2001) argues that contemporary discourses about crime are shaped through two kinds of criminological knowledge: "criminology of the other" and "new criminologies of everyday life." The latter perceive crime as a normal element in late-modern society; crime is a rational choice of normal individuals, or a result of opportunities to engage in criminality. In contrast, the "criminology of the other" is based on the idea that criminals are inherently dangerous "Others", abnormal people who "have no call on our fellow feeling." Accordingly, "there can be no mutual intelligibility, no bridge of understanding, no real communication between 'us' and 'them'" (Garland 2001:184). The "new criminologies of everyday life" propose interventions in the different aspects of everyday life, such as the conduct of individuals, daily routines, architecture, and buildings that would prevent victimization and opportunities for crime. The "criminology of the other", on the other hand, is a marginalizing discourse through which criminals are represented as inherently "evil", "wicked", and completely different from "us." It reduces "criminals" to a subhuman category, thus legitimizing punitive responses against "them" (Garland 1996).

The Turkish media have long had an interest in crime stories, producing criminological knowledge in their representations and interpretations. "The third-page news" composed of daily crime stories, has regularly provided curious details of acts of violence and drama, mostly of the lower classes. But, by the late 1990s, mainstream media headlines and columnists started to focus on urban crimes and their random violence. Robbery, theft, street gangs, school violence, beggars, and glue-sniffing street children—rather than domestic feuds or infanticides—occupied the media. Different from "the third-page news," reporting featured urban crime stories and news about an urban crime wave, stressing the extension of violence in the urban space and declaring a state of emergency demanding the immediate concern of the public. Moreover, they engaged in an animalistic depiction of criminals, thus producing a vehement "criminology of the other."

Mugging (*kapkaç*) incidents and glue-sniffers (*tinerci*) were of particular concern in the construction of this new crime wave. The media depicted *kapkaç* incidences as exhibiting a strange mix of violence and greed, and its perpetrators as "dangerous" "crime machines", directed by "psychopathic individuals" (see *Sabah,* September 26, 2003; *Sabah* September 23, 2003; *Yeni Asır*, June 6, 2006; *Yeni Asır*, June 23, 2006). According to the mainstream media, society was faced with "*kapkaç* nightmare" and "*kapkaç* terror" (see *Hürriyet,* June 6, 2007; *Hürriyet*, November 16, 2004; *Sabah*, November 8, 2004; *Yeni Asır,* February 24, 2006; *Star*, November 9, 2004). Stories told of glue-sniffing street children who randomly "terrorized" the citizens and created "disturbing scenes" of drug-addicted youth. Reproducing popular discourses of crime, the big metropoles of Turkey were represented as vulnerable places under the "invasion" of criminals. Many commentators, claiming to represent the views of the urban middle classes, contributed to the creation of a feeling of emergency and fear. In this process, the big cities of Turkey, especially Istanbul, were defined as "crime heavens" and "cities of fear," while particular neighbourhoods associated with crime were referred to as the "Harlems of Turkey" (*Sabah,* January 23, 2005; *Vatan*, June 18, 2004; *Sabah,* July 27, 2003). One widely-read columnist wrote, for instance: "Do you realize Istanbul is becoming intolerable! Streets are controlled by muggers, and the pavements by pickpockets. The glue-sniffers are the sovereigns of back alleys" (*Sabah,*

November 14, 2004). Ertugrul Özkök of *Hürriyet* alarmed readers: "Thieves go even into the bedrooms; people get robbed in front of their homes; people cannot get out in their neighbourhoods; people are mugged in the bus, metro, train. As if Istanbul has become the New York of the 1960s. Harlems are established in the midst of the city. What happened to us?" (*Hürriyet*, February 6, 2005).

In November 2005, three teenage boys attacked a teacher in Istanbul and nearly killed him. The Turkish media picked up this event, representing it as the new criminal norm in Istanbul. While the victim's life-story, particularly his innocence, occupied a central role in the newspapers' depictions, the criminals' stories were entirely ignored. *Sabah*, one of the most influential newspapers in Turkey, ran this headline about the incident: "the arena is usurped by the dogs"[6] (November 9, 2005), which offers a good example of the Turkish media's approach to the crime issue. Three of the newspaper's columnists declared that they completely agreed with the headline. One of these journalists, Sarıer, went further to say that there is no psychological, sociological, or material explanation of this act and other criminal incidences that recently took place in Istanbul. For him, the petty criminals of Istanbul were not human beings, but had the souls of dogs. He added that there is no way to explain their criminality, "since humans would not do the things they have done; their being uneducated and unemployed cannot be an explanation". Another journalist titled his article "Transition to savage society," and asserted that this incident is proof that the people of Istanbul are living with savages (*Sabah*, November 9, 2005).

This animalistic portrayal of criminals is not unique to Turkey. In fact, it is one of the major characteristics of neoliberal crime discourse (Doyle 2003; Garland 2001; Mauer 1999; Neocleous 2008; Rimke 2010; Wacquant 2002). Siegel (1998:75), for instance, in his study on the emergence of a new criminal type in Jakarta, describes the construction of the unfathomable criminal "who is, ipso facto, a monster, the sadist [...] who responds to something no one can recognize." In a similar vein, Wacquant (2002:11) points out that when attempted, explanations usually reflect a "pseudo-scientific discourse couched in genetic terminology and animalistic imagery." Representations of "criminals" as "dogs", "sadists", "psychopaths"[7], and "monsters" (see Neocleous 2005), naturalizes and de-socializes the crime issue, concealing the power relations and structural inequalities underlying the criminal incidences. In other words, this naturalization of crime has an ideological function as it detaches crime from its social and material context and "translate[s] a *political* issue into a criminal one" (Hall et al. 1978:224, emphasis in original). This translation, as the Comaroffs (2006:213) argue, "displaces attention away from the material and social effects of neoliberalism, blaming its darker undersides on the evils of the underworld." In a study which underlines the links between race, crime, and the criminal justice system in the United States, Mauer (1999:216) points out the animalistic imagery of the criminals that is invoked and argues that "[t]o many Americans, some combination of bad family, bad culture, or bad genes created this young thug whose behaviour is presumably beyond the capacity of modern law or social science to improve." In turn, as Garland (2001) explains, in place of the rehabilitative ideal of the welfare state, a new criminology of punishment that is decidedly anti-modern takes hold.

In Turkey, the self-defence of the victim has emerged as one of the most acceptable responses. The violence of victims and potential victims is increasingly becoming legitimate. As we discuss below, the neoliberal discourse on crime and security is, indeed, a call for violence. The killing, shooting and injuring of criminals is no longer unusual. There are many stories in the newspapers about how "innocent citizens" killed burglars who entered their homes, or about people who gathered to lynch thieves or burglars.[8] For example, the house of Özcan Deniz, a famous pop star, was robbed in February 2005. The burglars entered his bedroom and stole his laptop. The next day, the famous victim was on television arguing that it should be legal to kill these people who entered his bedroom, his "most private sphere." While there were no negative reactions in the media to his statements, in the following days different lawyers participated in news programs on TV to enlighten "innocent citizens" about how they could exert violence against burglars without being found guilty. Such views from lawyers expressing approval and legitimizing the murdering or wounding of criminals also found a place in newspapers (*Milliyet*, February 15, 2005; *Vatan*, February 17, 2005).

In December 2005, four people (two of them security guards) attacked a young man, who was standing in the garden of a building, and killed him. The reason they gave for this murder was that they thought he was a thief. Some columnists' interpretations of this event were even more terrifying than the event itself. According to one, the man who died was an innocent person and the people who killed him "probably had not thought of killing anyone before, and who had not injured anybody before" (*Tercüman*, December 16, 2005). For her, thieves and burglars were responsible for this event because if they had not been so dangerous, these four people who had not injured anyone before would not have killed the young man, an "innocent citizen". On the very same day, two people shot and injured a police officer who was not in his official clothes for the same reason: they thought that he was a thief (*Milliyet*, December 12, 2005). In this respect, the constitution of "unfathomable crime" (Siegel 1998) and the process of detaching the crime from its social and material context leads to the emergence of violent "victim-citizens" and contributes to the construction of "criminals" as abjected bodies that can and should be annihilated. In other words, dehumanization and/or animalization of "criminals" provoke "innocent citizens" and legitimize their violence against criminals.

It is not only the victims' or potential victims' violence that neoliberal crime discourses legitimizes. The neoliberal era has been marked by an expansion and centrality of the security apparatus of the state, unleashing its "sanctioned" violence against "criminals". The multiplication of penal and crime control facilities, the expansion and militarization of police forces, and increased surveillance technologies—accommodated by "law and order" paradigms—are major elements of the neoliberal security apparatus evident around the world (Davis and Shaylor 2001; Van Swaanigen 1995; Sudbury 2005; Wacquant 2003). On the recent transformation of public order policing in Izmir, Turkey's third largest city, Gönen (2010) explains the expansion of the security apparatus over "criminal" populations. Deriving its legitimacy from the growing panic about crime, the Izmir Police creatively adopted Giuliani's zero-tolerance policies from New York, incorporating new technologies, equipment and policing strategies in its "war on crime". In its own version of zero-tolerance policing, Izmir police engages in continuous harassment of "target populations", a category which include the "dangerous Others", such as the so-called "psychopaths", thieves, transvestites, and prostitutes, who together constitute the "lumpenproletariat" of a city.[9] Unprecedented use of stop-and-frisk, violent and aggressive handling of the "target populations", and continuous patrol and surveillance of the spaces that "target populations" inhabit are important elements of this new policing. Police officers are directed to employ physical power over the "target" persons, while they are advised to be gentle and professional with "respectable citizens". Hence, the new public order policing in Izmir depends on the clear separation between "dangerous Others" and "respectable citizens."[10]

As Bauman (2004:86) puts it, during the neoliberal period, "the social state is gradually, yet relentlessly and consistently, turned into a 'garrison state'," which is concerned with the security of its citizens and elimination of its "dangerous populations". Criminal justice institutions have become more violent and aggressive in the social regulation of the poor. Even though the history of Turkish police and prisons is replete with cases of brutality and torture of political dissidents, the extension of disproportionate police violence beyond the political realm is a new process. Current developments in policing are expanding the web of militaristic policing beyond dissidents to "common criminals" (see Berksoy 2007; Gambetti 2009; Uysal 2006).[11] A recent legal change offers an example of the increasing institutional and political power of the Turkish police and the emergence of this new kind of security/ "garrison" state in Turkey. In June 2007, the Turkish parliament passed the new *Police Duties and Powers Act*. The new regulations extend the powers of the police against suspects, especially in the use of force and guns. The police, in their "fight against criminals," retain a legal basis for expanding their use of force and violence. The new police act had almost instantaneous effects. According to a press release by *Turkish Human Rights Foundation* in June 2009, police brutality and torture cases rose rapidly after the introduction of the *Police Duties and Powers Act*. Between June 2007 and June 2009, a total of 416 police brutality and torture cases were recorded and 53 people were killed by the police.[12]

While the Turkish media's "criminology of the other" legitimizes the violence of citizens and of state-sanctioned violence by the police and other criminal justice institutions, the same discourses are utilized in the re-making of cities as "non-antagonistic unities" stripped of their undesirable "lumpenproletariat" or "dangerous criminals". But, before we explain the link between criminalization and the *Urban Transformation Projects*, we will discuss the processes through which the urban poor and their habitats were criminalized.

Part II: Who Are the "Criminals"?

As studies on the link between crime and poverty point out, the "old marginals of society", such as the black working class, rural migrants, and (post)colonial migrants, who were once deemed necessary as potential labour power to be exploited—but whose labour is no longer needed—are now, under the sway of neoliberalism, being criminalized, "re-marginalized" and redefined (Bauman 1997; Balibar 2004; Caldeira 2000; Wacquant 2002). Bauman (1997) argues that "dangerous classes" are redefined as "classes of criminals" in neoliberal society. At the same time, criminality of the poor is closely linked to spatial indicators. Ghettos, favelas, projects where the urban poor reside, are constituted as hotbeds of criminality. In Turkey, crime is being associated with *gecekondu* neighbourhoods, which are shelters for the country's old organized labour force and racialized poor (displaced Kurdish migrants, Roma people, etc.). In fact, *gecekondu* neighbourhoods[13] have always been regarded as the places of the marginal in Turkey and *gecekondu* people have never been regarded as citizens or "proper" citizens. Different from the emerging "citizen versus criminal" division of today, the division in the past was "citizen" versus "people". While the "citizen" implies middle and upper class urbanites, the "people" refers to rural migrants. A very well-known newspaper headline written fifty years ago represents this tension clearly: "The *people* rushed onto the beach, so that c*itizens* could not swim" (Akçay 2005). The article explains that citizens who are "civilized" and "modern" urbanites did not want to swim at the same beach as rural migrants because of their "uncivilized" habits. The citizens, of course, not only did not want to swim at the same beach as the people, but they also did not want to live in the same city with them. Hence, *gecekondu* populations of the big cities of Turkey were, since the establishment of the *gecekondu* neighbourhoods, subjected to exclusivist discourses of civilization and modernization. However, they were needed as a cheap labour force to be exploited for the "development" of the country. Due to the increasing need for cheap labour, and thanks to *gecekondu* people's struggle to stay in the city, *gecekondu* neighbourhoods became an integral part of the city by the mid-1950s (Aslan 2004; Yonucu 2009).[14]

However, by the 1980s the economic and the social structure of the country began to be reorganized according to the demands of neoliberalism. Economic liberalization and structural adjustment policies introduced in 1980 aimed at Turkey's full integration into global capitalism (Sayarı 1992; Öniş 1992). By the late 1980s, Istanbul especially became a symbol of Turkey's neoliberal policies. Turning the city centre into a hub of service and consumption to attract tourists, businessmen, and weekend visitors, was a principal policy measure of the city's governments during the early 1980s (Keyder 1996, 1999; Öktem 2005; Yonucu 2009). In this process, large-scale factories around the *gecekondu* neighbourhoods moved to peripheral areas and most of their residents were increasingly excluded from work and wage processes. Now, *gecekondu* neighbourhoods are predominantly residential districts whose inhabitants consist of workers who are employed in informal small-scale workshops, unemployed jobseekers and the permanently unemployed who have lost hope of finding jobs. More and more, some members of the latter group are moving towards another side of the "informal economy" as petty criminals and drug dealers (Yılmaz 2008; Yonucu 2009). Furthermore, during the 1990s, several hundred thousand Kurdish people migrated to Istanbul due to the forced displacement policies of the Turkish state.[15] These populations were comprised of poor peasants who ended up as tenants in the older *gecekondu* neighbourhoods (Şenyapılı 2004; Keyder 2005). They experienced greater obstacles and difficulties in the process of inclusion in the urban economies.

During this period, the *gecekondu* neighbourhoods were renamed and redefined. *Gecekondu* can be translated to English as "settled at night" or "perched on at night." The term came from the *gecekondu* people themselves and came to define the way in which they were naming, describing, and hence owning their new settlement experiences. By the 1990s, the term *gecekondu* began to be replaced by *"varoş."* The concept of *"varoş"* was first used and largely shaped by the mass media and it has strong pejorative and racist connotations. Briefly, *"varoş"* implies that the urban poor are both culturally and politically marginal people; they are not able to modernize and pose a threat to the state with their support of radical political organizations (Demirtaş and Şen 2007).

The emergence of *"varoş"* and its widespread use coincides with the important events that took place in the mid-1990s. In March 1995, there had been clashes between the police and *Alevi* demonstrators in the Gazi neighbourhood of Istanbul, where mostly low-income *Alevi* people live. In the evening of March 12, unknown gunmen riddled five coffee houses which the *Alevi*s frequent with bullets, killing one and wounding numerous people. The next day, young people of the Gazi neighbourhood took to the streets in protest, and they were soon reinforced by different groups that came to support the people of Gazi. That night the police shot one demonstrator. The rioting continued in the following days and the police, who lost control, shot into the crowds and killed another 15 people (Dural 1995). The streets of Gazi turned into a war zone, a war between its residents and the police. The riot was represented in the media as the riot of the "Other Turkey", the "unruly", "wild" urban poor who are totally different from the "normal Turkey". The following year, on May Day of 1996, there was tension between the members of radical Marxist groups and the police in Istanbul. The police killed three young men before the demonstration started. After this event, the clash between police and the people spread to the whole demonstration area. In spite of the murder of three young men and the clashes between the police and the people, the young people who shattered the windows and destroyed the tulips in the demonstration area became the major image of May Day 1996 in the Turkish media (Akçay 2005). The pictures of these young people from the *gecekondu* neighbourhoods, who were destroying the tulips and throwing rocks, were used as the images that symbolized the "Other Turkey".

After these two events *"varoş"* began to be represented in the media as a destructive and "dangerous bomb" that will explode and damage the entire city. News about *"varoş"* included melodramatic, incendiary headlines such as: "Ümraniye exploded," "Pendik may explode," *"Varoş:* Bombs that are ready to explode," *"Varoş* said I will explode" (Aksoy 2001). A newspaper warned that *"varoşes* [were] coming down to the city" (*Yeni Yüzyıl,* May 2, 1996). According to this new discourse, the danger did not come from "dangerous" *classes*—with whom the state could negotiate—but it was the monstrous result of the encounter between the city and its losers, between civilians and violent "barbarians" who do not know how to behave in a city. The changing ethnic composition of the western cities and poor was influential in these discourses. The long-term stigmatization of Kurds as "mountain savages" helped construct the urban poor's unrest as "barbarian" riots threatening the civilized order of the city.

According to the discourses of *"varoş"* and of "Other Turkey", the urban poor are harmful to city culture and to state ideology (Aksoy 2001). The terms *"varoş"* and "Other Turkey" do not only stigmatize the urban poor populations as the "Other", but also implies that there is a normal and/or real Turkey which, of course, includes neither the *gecekondu* people nor the other "marginalized" populations such as Kurds, *Alevis*,[16] or Islamists. This way, the *"varoş"* discourse and its accompanying discourse of "Other Turkey" give rise to the fantasy[17] of the city as a non-antagonistic unity, which legitimizes the exclusivist policies and discourses against the *gecekondu* populations. These discourses, emphasizing the differences between the "Other" and the "normal",[18] strengthen the boundaries between the middle and upper class urbanites, who supposedly deserve to live in the city, and the marginalized urban poor populations. For instance, a famous journalist, Yalçın Doğan, in his article on his visit to a *"varoş"* tells readers in an astonished way that *"varoş"* is not and/or cannot be a part of Istanbul: "Varoş is a different world. When I came here, I realized that this place is a different world. Is it Istanbul here? Is this the place that will be integrated into Europe? Is this place part of Istanbul?" (*Milliyet,* March 15, 1995). In a similar fashion, Baydar (1997), a well-known sociologist who celebrated the *gecekondu* neighbourhoods of the 1960s as working class districts, defined *"varoş"* in her article titled "Ötekine Yenik Düşen İstanbul" ("Istanbul defeated by the Other"): "*Varoş* as the buzzword of the recent years[...] has come to denote the residential areas that are established in the city or at its periphery but that are at the same time, with their rural identity, separated from the city by psychological, social and cultural boundaries" (1997:79, emphasis added). She further says:

> [A]s we approach the year 2000, what is bewildering, scary and new is that the urban cultural identity is almost erased by the *'Other' Istanbul*, and that for the first time, rather than coming up with a new synthesis, two alien structures, having completely closed the doors and sealed themselves off from one another, are trying to exist by destroying each other.

Gecekondu neighbourhoods are currently under-going a redefinition process. They are no longer represented with reference to their cultural and political identity as they were in the 1990s. Instead, they are associated with crime and violence. According to the records of the National Security Administration widely circulated in 2005, while crime rates rose 86 percent in Istanbul in the last ten years, they rose 285 percent in the 14 *gecekondu* neighbourhoods of Istanbul.[19] The increasing crime rates of Istanbul are being explained with reference to the "criminality" of the people who live in *gecekondu* neighbourhoods. Writer and columnist Mehmet Altan claims that the young people of *"varoş"* who want easy money are exclusively responsible for the rising crime rates in Istanbul (*Sabah*, December 7, 2005). In other articles, *gecekondu* areas are defined as the "viruses" that surround Istanbul and it is being asserted that the people of the *gecekondu* do not have any "moral or humane values," thus making them crime prone (*Türkiye,* March, 26, 2004; *Yeni Asır,* November 9, 2005; *Sabah,* November 22, 2003; *Radikal,* January 30, 2005; *Sabah,* May 19, 2004). In one of the discussions at the Turkish National Assembly on the issue of crime, it was argued that the *"varoş"* youth emulate those who are living in high standards and engage in crime in order to live like them.[20] In effect, poor people's assumed desire to be rich and their "moral depravity" and "degeneracy" have become the sole explanation of the rising crime rates.

The arguments about "moral depravity" and "degeneracy" were also linked to the new demography in the western cities. According to media representations, Kurdish migrants and their "violent" culture are largely responsible for the growing crime rates. In particular, Kurdish children of migrant families were implicated in increasing crime. A newspaper report provided the statistical "evidence" that 46.8 percent of street kids who committed crime had migrated from Eastern and South Eastern Anatolia, regions that predominantly consist of Kurdish populations (*Hürriyet*, February 20, 2008). Rising mugging incidences were an especially indispensable discursive source for the delineation of the criminality of Kurdish populations.[21] "Mugging migration is starting," warned a newspaper, describing Diyarbakir, the largest city in the Kurdish region, as the centre of mugging gangs (*Sabah*, April 9, 2005). Diyarbakir's poor neighbourhoods constituted the pool of mugger children to be transported to big cities (*Radikal*, November 9, 2004; *Sabah,* September 25, 2003; *Sabah,* April 9, 2005). The Kurdish families were depicted as immoral people who rented or sold their children to mugging gangs (*Sabah,* September 25, 2003; *Sabah,* December 9, 2004; *Hürriyet,* December 2, 2005; *Sabah,* December 9, 2004).

Part III: "New Criminologies of Everyday Life" in Turkey

While media in Turkey produce a "criminology of the other" that criminalizes and racializes the urban poor populations as the "dangerous Others", there is also scholarly literature which produces studies that quantify, categorize, and find patterns and causes of crime (İçli 1993, 2003; İçli and Özcan 1992; Yılmaz and Günayergün 2006; Çevik 2002; Hancı 1995; Cömerterler and Kar 2007). Especially since the 1970s, urban space and urbanization have received increased attention in Turkish criminology. *Gecekondu* neighbourhoods constituted a fruitful field where Turkish criminologists could investigate the relationship between urbanization and crime. As one criminologist suggested, *gecekondu* areas characterized by "accumulation of population, [...] congestion, informal relations, lack of informal regulation mechanisms," would be potentially productive of crime (Gürelli 1973:123). However, *gecekondu* areas remained relatively safe and secure until the late 1990s. Since the safeness and secure-ness of the *gecekondu* areas did not support the criminologists' assumptions, migrants were depicted as *potential* criminals rather than actual criminals up until the 1990s (Gürelli 1973; Gökçe 1976). Migrant workers who resided in *gecekondu* areas were more a part of the organized working-class struggles rather than a criminal culture. Yet, for these criminologists, their political struggles could easily be a precursor to common crimes with their defiance of state authority.

A shift occurred during the 1990s as criminological studies began to associate the habitats of migrants with a "culture of criminality" (İçli and Özcan 1992; Hancı 1995), which was transforming the children into "criminals." For instance, through a study of court files of 3327 juvenile offenders in Izmir Juvenile Court, Hancı (1995) concluded that the problem of *gecekondus* was not just about "crooked" urbanization but their effect in the formation of potential criminals from childhood. Similar to the methodology of early ecological criminology, Hancı (1995) traced the addresses of the juveniles and found a pattern that implied a link between *gecekondu* areas and criminality. Not unlike the media discourses, criminological studies treated child criminality as a subject through which the culture of the migrant family—the "culture of criminality"—could be deciphered.

While these studies show the interest of criminology in migrants and *gecekondus,* the field of city planning has recently become a powerful contributor to contemporary Turkish criminological literature. City planners and architects are increasingly concerned with issues of crime, producing "new criminologies of everyday life" for the neoliberal cities of Turkey. They produce theses, working papers, and publications investigating the relationship between crime and built environment, as well as the territorial distribution of crime, to show the "close link between crime ratios and the physical, socio-demographic characteristics and economic structures of settlements" (Ergün and Yirmibeşoğlu 2007:436; see also Ünlü and Edgü 2001; Ünlü, Erkut and Ocakçı 2001; Ünlü 2005). They are involved in the theorization and production of securitized space and quality of life of the middle classes, both of which were closely tied to the elimination of crime (Pulat 2005; Beşe 2006). Interested in building a relationship between the quality of life and (lack of) crime in urban settings, they seek to both theoretically and empirically locate criminal elements and spaces within the city. This knowledge provides the foundations for projects aimed at producing personal security from criminal victimization as well as secured buildings through architectural design. The fierce engagement of policy-makers with such criminologies has manifested in the transformation of Turkey's large urban areas, which are represented as "infested" with "*varoş*" and "criminal populations". The interventions of "criminologies of everyday life," in turn, coincide with the neoliberal *Urban Transformation Projects* which "cleanse" problem areas, "*varoş*" neighbourhoods, the habitats of the poor. The following section will discuss the *Urban Transformation Projects*, which are fostered by such interventions of scholars alongside the media's marginalizing discourses.

Part IV: Fantasizing the Non-Antagonistic City: The Urban Transformation Projects

As is argued, cities are one of the sites in which neoliberal policies, implementations, and regulations emerge most concretely (Harvey 2005, 2006a; Smith 1996, 2002; Brenner 2004; Brenner and Theodore 2002). During the neoliberal era, cities are being re-designed and re-imagined as commodities for global investment and consumption (Mbembe 2004; Zukin 1995; Sassen 2001; Hackworth 2007; Murray 2008). Commodification of the city goes hand-in-hand with the intensification of segregation, polarization, and fragmentation of urban space. Urban working- and under-class neighbourhoods are gradually being turned into stigmatized and pathologized places, symbols of violence and danger (Bourgois 2003; Caldeira 2000; Maskovsky 2006; Smith 1996; Wacquant 2007). Furthermore, this pathologization of the working class neighbourhoods legitimizes gentrification processes— "the middle class takeover of the city" (Smith 1996).

The association of crime with urban poverty is integral to the current attempt of the middle class takeover of the city in Turkey. Fear of crime and the criminalization of the racialized urban poor have facilitated urban segregation.[22] As the cities become associated "with more danger than safety" (Bauman 2005:73) spatial segregation between urban working classes and middle and upper classes is sharpening. The fantasies of the urban elite that "the city is an unpredictable and dangerous site of survival" (Diken and Lausten 2005) or that "the city is stolen from us" (Smith 1996) go hand in hand with the fantasies of the city as a non-antagonistic unity. As Diken and Lausten (2005:92) argue, in the contemporary whole and non-antagonistic city fantasy, the ghettos and ghetto-like places are regarded as the holes that prevent the city from being a city:

> [t]he fantasy created thus is: if the hole [...] did not exist, the city would have been a whole. The camp[23] in this sense is the "contingent" space that hinders the urban order that would have been if, that is, the camp that did not exist. What this fantasy hides is of course that the camp is a "necessary" effect of existing power relations. And precisely as such, the camp participates actively in the construction of the contemporary urban reality. Paradoxically, thus, the camp is what holds the city together: thanks to it, one can fantasize a non-antagonistic city!

These fantasies legitimize the "re-taking" of the city by the middle class and the exclusivist policies against the city's marginalized populations (Smith 1996; see also Tomiak, this volume, on the relationship of spatial imaginary and marginality). In effect, the current government in Turkey seems determined to turn the fantasy of the non-antagonistic city into reality, engaging in a basic form of gentrification and neoliberal urbanism: the *Urban Transformation Projects*. Istanbul Municipality aims to demolish the *gecekondu* neighbourhoods and re-design the city as a "modern", "civilized", and "secure" world city. According to statements by Istanbul's mayor, the first and most important thing to be done to "re-create" Istanbul as a world city is to demolish *gecekondu* neighbourhoods.[24] *Gecekondu* neighbourhoods are described as enemy lands[25] in the prime minister's declarations, as he frequently emphasizes how determined the government is in its "struggle" against *gecekondus* to create a "modern" city (*Turkiye,* April 13, 2006; *Turkiye,* October 3, 2004; *Sabah,* July 16, 2005; *Yenisafak*, November 30, 2005). According to the policies of the current government, there is no place for the marginalized urban poor populations in Istanbul. As Arif Hasan, who visited Istanbul in June 2009 as a member of the *UN Advisory Group on Forced Evictions*, observed, the scope and brutality of the Istanbul urban transformation project can only be compared to the case of post-apartheid Johannesburg.[26]

With the *Urban Transformation Projects*, *gecekondu* houses will be demolished and the urban poor who are living in *gecekondu* neighbourhoods will be moved out of the cities, to distant housing projects. Among the already demolished neighbourhoods' residents, those who managed to move to the new project housing built on the outskirts of the city are now in debt as they found themselves unable to keep their jobs due to the long and expensive commute into the city where employment opportunities exist. To make things worse, those who moved to the new projects are in debt mainly because they were forced to purchase or rent unaffordable apartments (Baysal 2009). For instance, the first *gecekondu* demolitions began in the Sulukule and Ayazma-Tepeustu neighbourhoods in 2006 and 2007. Sulukule is a Romani neighbourhood. Around 700 families had to leave Sulukule and moved to housing projects located at the outskirts of the city. However, because of the high rent only 20 families could stay in these new housings.[27] Ayazma-Tepeustu is predominantly inhabited by Kurdish people who were forced to leave their villages in the 1990s. Demolitions began in February 2007 in this neighbourhood. As Karaman (2008) shows, among the 396 house-owners who moved to their new homes from Ayazma, 123 received evacuation notices for failing to pay their monthly instalments only five months after they moved in.[28] Moreover, no compensation scheme was offered to tenant families who now have to pay $250 in monthly rent, whereas they used to pay $70 a month (see Karaman 2008). Hence, while the municipality claims that they offer new houses for the *gecekondu* people within new housing projects, these places are not affordable.

The *Urban Transformation Projects* have been a project of marginalization and exclusion. Those who have already been deemed redundant in the neoliberal economy are being pushed away from the cities.[29] Today, elimination of the *gecekondus* of urban poor through urban transformation projects has gained support from many different actors. Members of the Turkish National Police, for instance, are in favour of such projects, as they believe that these are the best way to eliminate the "criminal populations". For instance, a high level captain in the General Directorate of Security of Preventive Policing Subdivision, in his interview with Gönen, argues that "it is necessary to cooperate with the municipalities in policing of those areas, and better yet demolish the areas where criminals inhabit. We support the demolishment of the *gecekondu*s."[30] Accordingly, the urban transformation is also a project of the elimination of crime, and thus derives its legitimacy claims partly from the crime discourses that we have deconstructed in this chapter.

Conclusion

In this chapter we have critiqued contemporary discourses on crime and criminality in the Turkish media and in criminological studies, identifying their ideological effects in the legitimization of violence and spatial segregation in the big cities of Turkey. The mainstream media construct widely circulating representations of crime; in doing so they produce and inform public attitudes about crime, and thus are an indispensable part of the construction of popular discourses with ideological effects about crime and "criminals". Media do not simply represent but also produce reality in their selection, depiction, and analysis of news. As we point out, news about crime and criminals are not just objective descriptions of what has happened, but they coordinate opinion about criminality and criminals while facilitating certain policies such as urban segregation and an increased use of police violence (see Bauman 2004; Ericson 1995; Cohen and Young 1973; Comaroff and Comaroff 2004, 2006; Hall et al. 1978).

Engaging in a "criminology of the other," the Turkish media's representation of "criminals" contributed to the creation and exploitation of the fear of crime. Turkey's big cities and migrant neighbourhoods were discursively constructed as "crime heavens," and the racialized urban poor were depicted as "dangerous criminals". Such discourses, we argue, have legitimized citizens' violence as well as expansion of state violence against the "criminals". What is more, the cities are now being "cleaned up" of their "criminal spaces" through the urban transformation projects. The neoliberal media discourses of crime not only legitimize urban segregation but also conceal the real social antagonisms. Hence, the naturalization of crime and the denial of the social and material reasons underlying the crime issues silences the political voices of the disadvantaged people who are excluded from the wage and labour processes and may, therefore, turn to crime in order to survive.

Criminological studies also contribute to criminalizing discourses with their claims to "scientificity". As David Garland (1997:12) suggests, criminology is not simply a science of the ills of society, but "an administrative task" with "pragmatic, policy oriented, administrative projects, seeking to use science in the service of management and control." The "new criminologies of everyday life" in Turkey, as we argue, lend themselves to the legitimization of the segregation practices in the neoliberal city and partake in the construction of a fantasy of the "non-antagonistic city". In these "new criminologies", crime constitutes a threat to the fantasy of secure cities which are central to neoliberal processes.

In turn, there is a dire need for producing critical discourses of crime against these neoliberal criminologies, both of the media and of the criminologist. Throughout this chapter, we have contributed to the project of generating critical discourses, and altering the terms of debate on crime and criminals in Turkey. To this end, we have problematized the existing literature and crime discourses and discussed their effects. A necessary step, alongside the exposition of the effects of neoliberal crime discourses, is the engagement of activist and critical research in producing analyses of crime as a social, political, and economic category that can be utilized within the struggles against the neoliberal marginalization and segregation processes in Turkey. This way, crime can be un-translated from a criminal issue to a political one.

References

Akçay, Eylem. 2005. "The end and the beginning of politics: The case of Istanbul." Paper presented at *The Beginnings and Ends of Political Theory Conference,* UC Berkeley, May 27-28.

Aksoy, Asu. 2001. "Gecekondudan varoşa dönüşüm: 1990'larda 'Biz' ve Öteki' Kurgusu." In *Dısarida Kalanlar/Birakilanlar,* edited by Aliye F. Matarcı, 39-53. Istanbul: Baglam.

Aslan, Şükrü. 2004. *1 Mayıs Mahallesi: 1980 Öncesi Toplumsal Mücadeleler ve Kent.* Istanbul: İletişim.

Auyero, Javier. 1997. "Wacquant in the Argentine slums: Comment on Loïc Wacquant's 'Three pernicious premises in the study of the American ghetto'." *International Journal of Urban and Regional Research* 21(3):508-511.

Balibar, Etienne. 2004. *We, the People of Europe?* Princeton, NJ: Princeton University Press.

Balkan, Neşecan, and Sungur Savran, eds. 2003. *Sürekli Kriz Politikaları. 2000'lı Yillarda Turkiye 1.*Istanbul: Metis.

Bauman, Zygmund. 1997. *Postmodernity and Its Discontents.* New York: New York University Press.

———. 2004. *Wasted Lives: Modernity and its Outcasts.* Oxford: Polity Press.

———. 2005. *Liquid Life.* New York: Polity Press.

Baydar, Oya. 1997. "Oteki'ne yenik dusen Istanbul." *Istanbul* 23:78-82.

Baysal, Cihan. 2009. "Barinma bir haktir." *Radikal 2* 178:2.

Berksoy, Biriz. 2007. "Neo-liberalizm ve Toplumsalın Yeniden Kurgulanması: 1980 Sonrası Batı'da ve Türkiye'de Polis Teşkilatları ve Geçirdikleri Yapısal Dönüşüm." *Toplum ve Bilim* 109:35-65.

Beşe, Ertan, 2006. "'Kırık Pencereler' Teorisi Bağlamında Kentsel Yaşamda Suç ve Güvenlik." *Polis Bilimleri Dergisi* 8(1):1-24.

Bourgois, Philippe I. 2003. *In Search of Respect.* New York: Cambridge University Press.

Brenner, Neil. 2004. *New State Spaces: Urban Governance and Rescaling of Statehood.* New York: Oxford University Press.

Brenner, Neil, and Nik Theodore. 2002. "Cities and the geographies of 'actually existing neoliberalism'." *Antipode* 34(3):349-379.

Buğra, Ayşe, and Çağlar Keyder. 2003. *New Poverty and Changing Welfare Regime of Turkey.* Ankara: UNDP.

Butler, Judith. 1993. *Bodies That Matter.* London: Routledge.

Caldeira, Teresa. 2000. *City of Walls: Crime, Segregation, and Citizenship in São Paulo.* Berkeley: University of California Press.

Cohen, Stanley, and Jock Young, eds. 1973. *The Manufacture of the News: Social Problems, Deviance, and the Mass Media.* London: Constable.

Comaroff, Jean, and John L. Comaroff. 2004. "Criminal obsessions, after Foucault: Postcoloniality, policing, and the metaphysics of disorder." *Critical Inquiry* 30:800-24.

———. 2006. "Figuring crime: Quantifacts and the production of the un/real." *Public Culture* 18:209-246.

Çankaya, Dilek. 2003. "Migrants in poverty in Istanbul and education for them." Accessed January 15, 2010. http://74.125.155.132/scholar?q=cache:4RNpQkH0aOUJ:scholar.google.com/&hl=tr&as_sdt=2000

Çevik, Dolunay Şenol. 2002. "Türkiye'de Çocuk Suçluluğu." *Polis Dergisi* 31:17-22.

Cömerterler, Necmiye, and Muhsin Kar. 2007. "Economic and social determinants of the crime rate in Turkey: Cross section analysis." *Ankara Üniversitesi SBF Dergisi* 67(2): 37-57.

Davis, Angela Y., and Cassandra Shaylor. 2001. "Race, gender, and the prison industrial complex: California and beyond." *Meridians* 2(1):1-25.

Demirtaş, Neslihan, and Seher Şen. 2007. "Varoş identity: The redefinition of low-income settlements in Turkey." *Middle Eastern Studies* 43(1):87-106.

Diken, Bülent, and Carsten Bagge Laustsen. 2005. *The Culture of Exception.* New York: Routledge.

Doyle, Aaron. 2003. *Arresting Images: Crime and Policing in Front of the Television Camera.* Toronto: University of Toronto Press.

Dural, Tamaşa. 1995. *Aleviler...Ve Gazi Olayları....* Istanbul: Ant.

Ergün, Nilgün, and Funda Yirmibeşoğlu. 2007. "Distribution of crime rates in different districts of Istanbul." *Turkish Studies* 8(3):435-455.

Ericson, Richard Victor 1995. *Crime and Media.* Aldershot: Dartmouth.

Gambetti, Zeynep. 2007. "Linç girişimleri, neo-liberalism ve güvenlik devleti." *Toplum ve Bilim* 109:7-34.

———. 2009. "İktidarın Dönüşen Çehresi: Neoliberalizm, Şiddet ve Kurumsal Siyasetin Tasfiyesi." *İ.Ü. Siyasal Bilimler Fakültesi Dergisi* 40:143-164.

Garland, David. 1996. "The limits of the sovereign state: Strategies of crime control in contemporary society." *British Journal of Criminology* 36(4):445-471.

———. 1997. "Of crimes and criminals: The development of criminology in Britain." In *Oxford Handbook of Criminology*, edited by Mike Maguire, Rod Morgan, and Robert Reiner, 11-56. Oxford: Clarendon Press.

———. 2001. *The Culture of Control: Crime and Social Order in Contemporary Society.* Oxford: Oxford University Press.

Gökçe, Birsen. 1976. *Gecekondu gençliği.* Ankara: Hacettepe University Press.

Gönen, Zeynep. 2010. "Criminalization in the neoliberal era and restructuring of Izmir public order police." *Toplum ve Kuram* 3:55-79.

Gürelli, Nevzat. 1973. "Şehirleşme ve Suç." Şehirleşmenin Doğurduğu Ceza Adaleti Sorunları Sempozyumu, Istanbul Üniversitesi Hukuk Fakültesi Ceza Hukuku ve Kriminoloji Enstitüsü, December 17-19, Istanbul:121-128.

Hackworth, Jason R. 2007. *The Neoliberal City*. Ithaca: Cornell University Press.

Hall, Stuart, Chas Critcher, Tony Jefferson, John Clarke, and Brian Robert. 1978. *Policing the Crisis: Mugging, the State, and Law and Order*. London: Macmillan.

Hancı, Hamit. 1995. "Gecekondulaşma ve çocuk suçluluğu." *Adli Tıp Dergisi* 11:22-62.

Harvey, David. 2005. *A Brief History of Neoliberalism*. Oxford: Oxford University Press.

———.2006a. *Spaces of Global Capitalism*. New York: Verso.

———.2006b. "Neo-liberalism as creative destruction." *Geograpika Annuler Series B* 88 (2):145-158.

Hunt, Alan, and Trevor Purvis. 1993. "Discourse, ideology, discourse, ideology, discourse, ideology…" *The British Journal of Sociology* 44(3):473-49.

İçli, Tülin. 1993. *Türkiye'de Suçlular Sosyo Kültürel ve Ekonomik Özellikleri*. Ankara: Atatürk Kültür Merkezi.

———. 2003. "Toplumdan kopuş: Suç ve şiddet." In *Sosyolojiye Giriş*, edited by İhsan Sezal, 511-523. Ankara: Martı Yay.

İçli, Tülin, and N. Özcan. 1992. "Türkiye'de Ekoloji Suç İlişkisi Üzerine Sosyolojik Bir Çalışma." *H.Ü Edebiyat Fakültesi Dergisi* 9(1-2):27-53.

Karaman, Ozan. 2008. "Urban pulse-(re)making space for globalization in Istanbul." *Urban Geography* 29(6):518-525.

Keyder, Çağlar. 1996. *Ulusal Kalkınmacılığın İflası*. Istanbul: İletişim.

———. 1999. *Istanbul: Between the Global and the Local*. Lanham, MD: Rowman & Littlefield.

———. 2005. "Globalization and social exclusion in Istanbul." *International Journal of Urban and Regional Research* 29(1):124–134.

Köse, Ahmet H., Fikret Şenses, and Erinç Yeldan, eds. 2003. *Küresel Düzen: Birikim, Devlet ve Sınıflar.* Istanbul: İletişim.

Low, Setha. 2001. "The edge and the center: gated communities and the discourse of urban fear." *American Anthropology* 103(1):45–58.

Maskovsky, Jeff. 2006. Review article on "Pathologies of power: health, human rights, and the new war on the poor." *American Anthropologist* 107(2):283-284.

Mauer, Marc. 1999. *Race to Incarcerate*. New York: New Press.

Mbembe, Achille. 2004. "Aesthetics of superfluity." *Public Culture* 16(3):373-405.

Murray, Martin J. 2008. *Taming the Disorderly City*. Ithaca: Cornell University Press.

Neocleous, Mark. 2005. *The Monstrous and the Dead: Burke, Marx, Fascism*. Newport: University of Wales Press.

———. 2008. *Critique of Security*. Edinburgh: Edinburgh University Press.

Öktem, Binnur. 2005. "Küresel kent söyleminin kentsel mekanı dönüştürmedeki rolü: Büyükdere-Maslak aksı." In *Istanbul'da Kentsel Ayrışma*, edited by Türkün A. and Hatice Kurtuluş, 25-76. Istanbul: Baglam.

Önis, Ziya. 1992. "Redemocratization and economic liberalization in Turkey: The limits of state autonomy." *Studies in Comparative International Development* 27(2):3-23.

Parenti, Christian. 2000. *Lockdown America: Police and Prisons in the Age of Crisis*. New York: Verso.

Peck, Jamie, and Adam Tickell. 2007. "Conceptualizing neoliberalism, thinking Thatcherism." In *Contesting Neoliberalism*, edited by Helga Leitner, Jamie Peck, and Eric S. Sheppard, 26-50. New York: Gulford Press.

Pulat, Gülçin. 1995. "Konut ve yakın çevresinde Kalite Unsuru olarak Güvenlik Konusu." *Mimari ve Kentsel Çevre Kalite Arayışları Sempozyumu Bildiriler Kitabı*. İstanbul: ITU Mimarlık Fakültesi, ITU Çevre ve Şehircilik Uyg-Ar Merkezi, Cenkler Matbaası.

Rimke, Heidi. 2010. "Consuming fears: Neoliberal in/securities, cannibalization, and psychopolitics." In *Racism and Borders: Representation, Repression and Resistance,* edited by Jeff Shantz, 95-112. New York: Algora Publishing.

Samara, Tony Roshan. 2010. "Order and security in the city: Producing race and policing neoliberal spaces in South Africa." *Ethnic and Racial Studies* 33(4):637-655.

Sassen, Saskia. 2001. *The Global City*. Princeton: Princeton University Press.

Sayari, Sabri 1992. "Turkey: The Changing European Security Environment and the Gulf Crisis." *Middle East Journal* 46(1):9-21.

Schneider, Cathy. 2007. "Police power and race riots in Paris." *Politics & Society* 35(4):523-549.

Siegel, James. 1998. *A New Criminal Type in Jakarta: Counter-Revolution Today*. Durham, NC: Duke University Press.

Smith, Neil. 1996. *New Urban Frontier: Gentrification and Revanchist City*. London: Routledge.

———. 2002. "New globalism, new urbanism: gentrification as urban strategy." In *Spaces of Neoliberalism: Urban Restructuring in North America and Western Europe*, edited by Neil Brenner and Nik Theodore, 80-103. United Kingdom: Blackwell.

Sudbury, Julia. 2005. *Global Lockdown: Race, Gender, and the Prison-Industrial Complex*. New York: Routledge.

Sumer, Asuman. 2003. "White vs. black Turks: The civilizing process in Turkey in the 1990s." Unpublished MA thesis, Middle East Technical University, The Department of Political Science and Public Administration.

Şenyapılı, Tansu. 2004. *Barakadan Gecekonduya*. Istanbul: İletişim.

Terrio, Susan. 2003. "You'll get your day in court: judging delinquents at the Paris Palace of justice." *Political and Legal Anthropology Review* 26(2):136-164.

Ünlü, Alper. 2005. "İstanbul'un Görünmez Merkezi Tarlabaşı'nın Görünenleri." *Mimarist* Winter:48-52.

Ünlü, Alper, and Erincik Edgü. 2001. "Kent Merkezlerindeki Konut Alanları ve Suç." *İstanbul* 38:86-89.

Ünlü, Alper, Gülden Erkut, and Mehmet Ocakçı. 2001. "Evaluation of crime profile in İstanbul." *Trialog* 70:30-34.

Uysal, Ayşen. 2006. "Cop Gölgesinde Politika: Türkiye'de Toplumsal Olay Polisliği ve Sokak Eylemleri." *Mülkiye Dergisi* 253:79-94.

Van Swaanigen, René. 1995. "The Dutch prison system and penal policy in the 1990s: From humanitarian paternalism to penal business management." In *Western European Penal Systems: An Anatomy,* edited by Vincenzo Ruggiero et al., 38- 51. London: Sage.

Wacquant, Loïc. 2002. "Deadly symbiosis: Rethinking race and imprisonment in twenty-first-century America." *Boston Review* 27(2):23-31.

———. 2003. "Towards a dictatorship over the poor? Notes on the penalization of poverty in Brazil." *Punishment & Society* 5(2):197-205.

———. 2007. *Urban Outcasts: A Comparative Sociology of Advanced Marginality*. London: Polity Press.

Yeldan, Erinç. 2001. *Küreselleşme Sürecinde Türkiye Ekonomisi*. Istanbul: İletişim Yayınlari.

Yılmaz, Ali, and Semra Günayergün. 2006. "Türkiye'de şehir asayis suçlari: Dagılış ve başlıca özellikleri." *Milli Egitim* 170:230-249.

Yılmaz, Bediz. 2008. "Entrapped in multidimensional exclusion: The perpetuation of poverty among conflict-induced immigrants in an Istanbul neighbourhood." *New Perspectives on Turkey* 38:205-235.

Yonucu, Deniz. 2009. "A story of a squatter neighbourhood: From the place of the 'dangerous classes' to the 'place of danger'." *The Berkley Journal of Sociology* 52:50-72.

Zizek, Slovaj. 1997. *The Plague of Fantasies*. London: Verso.

Zukin, Sharon. 1995. *The Cultures of Cities*. Oxford: Wiley-Blackwell.

Chapter 4
Homelessness as Neoliberal Discourse
Reflections on Research and the Narrowing of Poverty Policy

Mark Willson

A guiding premise of this chapter is that the problem of homelessness tells us much more about contemporary social anxieties, ethical ambiguities, and economic imperatives than it does about the "homeless" that are often taken as the object of study or concern. To say this is not to minimize the fact that, since the 1980s, a growing number of individuals are finding themselves without social supports and forced to live in precarious conditions, including life on the streets. It also is not to suggest that popular discussions, academic studies, activist engagements, and policy responses have not succeeded in addressing aspects of these conditions in various ways. Instead, the aim is to highlight how the problem of homelessness, as a distinct object of popular and professional knowledges and practices, has come to exist and, perhaps more importantly, how this problem has come to be understood in terms antithetical to social justice claims for safe and secure housing and adequate social benefits for all (see Hulchanski 1987:17-18). The idea here is that a clearer understanding of how contemporary discourses regarding homelessness condition the articulation and uptake of social justice claims may allow those of us who identify as scholars, as activists, as engaged citizens, as "poor", as "homeless", or any combination of these, to develop better strategies of engagement with social struggles centred on homelessness, and about the possible effects of the language used in these struggles.

Writing as both a scholar-in-training and as an aspiring community organizer, I have two aims in this chapter. The first is to investigate how the problem of homelessness has come to be understood almost exclusively as a problem of a specific, narrowly circumscribed marginalized population, and how expert and popular knowledge (academic, media-based, governmental, or activist) has, even if inadvertently, re-enforced this narrow "framing" of the problem of homelessness. This approach expands on other scholarly critiques of the limits of the concept of homelessness (Hulchanski 1987; Hoch and Slayton 1989; Wright 1997; Blasi 1994; Marcus 2006; Stern 1984; Lyon-Callo 2004; Hopper and Baumohl 1994) by highlighting the limiting effects of inherited meanings of the term homeless, and of broader shifts in understandings of citizenship, for social justice struggles that take place through and about discourses of homelessness. This approach has been spurred by my experiences in several years of anti-poverty advocacy and activism in Victoria, British Columbia, which have led me to wonder whether there may be even less potential for discursive struggles through and about homelessness than suggested in existing critiques. As outlined below, inherited discourses regarding the "homeless" have proven well-suited to a configuration of homelessness through individual problems and highly targeted services, particularly as these have developed alongside increasingly sedimented neoliberal visions of citizenship (James 2007; Brodie 2002, 2007).

My second aim is to offer a few reflections on how this type of work relates to existing academic discussions about the relationships between scholarly and activist labour. I took up this approach to the discursive production of homelessness in a context where an intensive amount of social scientific research is already trained on the homeless as a marginalized, excluded or vulnerable target group, and where ongoing debates about the character of this target group have arguably served to further re-enforce the given-ness of the distinctiveness of this group. These considerations point to a highly contingent relationship between scholarly and activist labour, shaped by the particularities of political struggles and by shifting conditions for research within the university.

Some Thoughts on Methods and Marginalized Groups

My interest in the problem of homelessness stems from several years of research and advocacy on poverty-related issues which took place around the time of two landmark instances of "homeless" activism: a Charter case concerning the rights of Victoria residents lacking shelter to camp in public spaces (2005-2008),[31] and the three-month occupation of Vancouver's landmark abandoned Woodwards building and tent-city actions in Vancouver's Downtown Eastside (2002-2003).[32] My initial work on the problem of homelessness involved an exploration of claims emerging from homeless encampments in Victoria and Vancouver, with an aim of highlighting how these claims were effaced, co-opted, misread, or rejected as they were interpreted and represented in popular discussions about homelessness. It seemed, however, that this representational work, while ostensibly critical, risked re-enforcing dominant assumptions about the homeless as an identifiable and knowable group that can be characterized by a distinctive set of identities, cultures, and claims. On top of this, this type of research fits within a growing trajectory in neoliberal social governance towards knowledge about, and regulation of, vulnerable populations (Murray 2004), in which university resources and university-community partnerships are playing an increasingly important role (DeFilippis, Fisher, and Shragge 2010; see also Bourke, this volume).

My response to these reservations has been to turn my attention to dominant representations of homelessness, with the aim of teasing out the conditions that have made knowledge about homeless individuals the imperative it has come to be. This discursive analysis of the framing of homelessness as a problem is intended as a form of reflexive critique: as a supplement to, and not an attempt to replace, criticize, or disavow the important academic and activist work of, with, and alongside those who endure very real injustices—including daily deprivation, paternalism, and criminalization as targets of various policing and homelessness initiatives.

The methods used in this research are a discursive analysis attuned to the roles of language and context in setting out the truth of a given object of study (framing); in part through directing attention to the effects of logics and imperatives of contemporary governance (governmentality) on what can be known or intelligibly said about such an "object". The approach to discourse here is a delineated one, looking primarily at the forms of meaning that have been produced by the uses of particular words in particular historical contexts. This approach draws primarily upon *Interpretive Policy Analysis* (IPA) (Stone 1988; Fischer 2003)—which pays close attention to the ways narrative, uses of metaphor, the meanings attributed to particular words, and how these words are weighed and valued relative to one another, all play a role in the "framing" of an issue in a way that can "bestow the appearance of problematic on some features of a discussion while others seem proper and fixed" (Fischer 2003:85). Recognizing that the way words are weighed and valued is heavily dependent on historical contexts which set out the criteria by which truth claims are asserted and assessed, this framing of homelessness is thereby located in relation to a broader "regime of truth" with regards to proper forms of contemporary governance (Foucault 2008): that of neoliberal sensibilities regarding individual responsibility, active civil society, and minimal state (Dean 1999; Rose 1996; Banting 2005; Brodie 2007).

The story addressed in what follows concerns the relationship between pre-1980s uses of the term "homeless"—as victims of natural disaster, and as deviant men of skid row—as they have been deployed in the context of these changing conceptions of citizenship in Canada, and is laid out as three moments in the discovery of the problem of homelessness in Canada: a first moment focused on structural failure in the 1980s, a second moment focused on national disaster in the 1990s, and a third moment focusing on medical models of treatment through the 2000s.

Some Discursive Conditions of Possibility for the Problem of Homelessness

In the years immediately prior to 1981 the term homeless had three primary referents. A quick survey of Canadian media[33] suggests that "homeless" was most often used to describe a status of deprivation on an international scale, either of the condition of statelessness suffered by refugees, or of the literal loss of housing experienced by victims of natural disasters. As David Hulchanksi (2009) points out, homeless was also one of several terms used in policy reports through the 1960s and 1970s to describe the older men living in the single-residential occupancy hotels in the skid rows of Canadian cities. Homeless, in these instances, referred to the transient lifestyles of these men, who lacked the stable housing and family ties taken to be primary characteristics of having a home (Hulchanksi 2009:2; Sommers 1998). This meaning is also evident in newspaper coverage through the early 1980s—often in reference to conditions in the United States—where homeless is used interchangeably with terms such as vagrant, derelict, urban nomad, and down-and-out drifter (e.g.

Lurie 1982:1; Cuff 1981:F2). The language of "the homeless" thus carried two primary connotations in its take-up in the 1980s: of persons who lacked the normal goods of citizenship such as housing, income, and the communal bonds of family or nation, either due to external conditions (statelessness or natural disaster) or due to specific lifestyles characterized by deviance and difference. A classic character distinction between the passive victim and the wilful deviant is evident here, with all of the inherited associations with regards to the deservingness and agency of those addressed (Feldman 2004:6). While these homeless referents differ to varying degrees in the forms of innocence, agency, and deservingness attributable to them, Kathleen Arnold offers a way of understanding at least one shared characteristic: each of these homeless targets, and the forms of aid offered to them, tend to fall outside the contours of what Arnold describes as the entitlements due to the national citizen (Arnold 2004:133). Inasmuch as international disaster relief or sanctuary are offered on terms other than those of the duties of the state to provide specific social goods to citizens, and inasmuch as the homeless of skid row were deemed a problem that exceeded the redistributive approach to poverty that prevailed during the 1960s and 1970s, this otherness might be further specified as an outside to the universal provisions and social citizenship rights characteristic of idealized visions of the welfare state (Marshall 1950).

"The homeless" began to be accorded new meaning as a result of changing social and economic conditions in the early 1980s. Media accounts, beginning in 1981, point to a rising public awareness and anxiety with regards to increased pressure on Toronto's shelter and hostel services, and increased visibility of noticeably destitute persons throughout the city. Part of this anxiety had to do with the perceived newness of these conditions, as much of the media attention was focused on the increased visibility of women on the city's streets and a severe shortage of city support services, such as hostels. As with debates regarding the "new homeless" occurring at this time in United States, the problem was in ascertaining the extent to which these targets of attention were deserving of aid; a deservingness that was largely understood through contrast with conceptions of the undeservingness of the skid row bum (Hoch and Slayton 1989:199). This interpretive work of assessing the extent to which targets were "normal" citizens due aid or unworthy deviants was complicated by the loss of clear markers regarding the entitlements due the normal citizen, of which disenchantment with Marshallian notions of the social citizen and the undermining of social services which had acted as the foundation for post-war conceptions of social solidarity are emblematic. Uncertainty concerning obligations towards the "new homeless," as inside or outside the terms of citizen entitlements, then, might be seen as reflecting a broader uncertainty regarding the character of contemporary citizenship rights and obligations.

That the bag-lady came to be one of the early focal points for contemplating such obligations in Canada speaks to some of these uncertainties. One Toronto journalist lays out these ambiguities quite clearly, as the bag-lady is addressed as different from old notions of the homeless as poor male drunk, yet also distinct from the mainstream citizen:

> Whatever the reason, the homeless are everywhere in the downtown core...On any cold or rainy day, they can be seen huddling at the entrance to the Eaton Centre, at the bus terminal or in the main reference library at Yonge and Bloor...Winos are familiar, albeit unpleasant fixtures on the cityscape, but most of us find them easy to ignore. Bag ladies, on the other hand, are different somehow, at once more picturesque and inexpressibly sad. (Cuff 1981:F2)

The heavily aestheticized manner in which the question of ethical responsibility towards the "bag lady" is laid out here indicates instabilities in distinctions between a new and old homeless, as justifications for aid (that those on the streets and seeking support services were, perhaps, victims of circumstances outside of their control) ran up against public interest in individuals identified by their distinctive physical comportment and appearance (in popular imagery of rags, shopping carts, etc.). While this ambiguity might be attributed to the lack of a clear social imaginary for conceiving the relationships of rights and solidarity between citizens, or identifying the boundaries between citizen and non- or second-class citizen, the language of homelessness itself also posed a distinct obstacle here. The attention accorded the bag-lady is illustrative of the productivity of the language of homeless, as its use involved an engagement with past uses, in this case the homeless as the old men of skid row. Even in instances where these comparisons were explicitly addressed as a means of distinction, the act of comparison seems to have reproduced much of these inherited meanings, linking the "bag-lady" to the "wino" in popular conceptions of who is to be understood as the "homeless".

The failure of a first short-lived wave of attention to homelessness, as an area of focus for research and expert knowledge in Canada, might be understood within this context of uncertainty regarding the new and old homeless, and regarding the social model by which this new target was to be interpreted and addressed. Canada's first conference on the problem of domestic homelessness, in 1987, took place in the context of the introduction in the United States of the *McKinney-Vento Homeless Assistance Act*, the *UN Year of Shelter for the Homeless*, and the first attempt at enumerating the homeless in Canada.[34] The *Canadian Agenda for Action on Housing and Homelessness through the Year 2000* (1988), emanating from the *Canadian Conference to Observe the International Year of Shelter for the Homeless* (Lang-Runtz and Ahern 1988), carries a characterization of homelessness emphasizing unemployment and the "chronic set of conditions that continue to place the majority of the housing stock out of the reach of low-income persons" (121). Borrowing from United Nations definitions,[35] use of the terms "homelessness" and "the homeless" were deployed in accordance with a postwar social policy paradigm keyed towards structural inequalities and the redistributive failures of housing policy. Notably, this approach rejected the sense of newness that was a defining feature of popular attention to homelessness as a public problem, and the languages of deviance and difference popularly used to make sense of who the homeless person was. Making a distinction that would in later years be referred to as the difference between "absolute" and "relative" homelessness, narrow understandings of homelessness according to "housing crisis" or the "deficiencies of individuals" were explicitly rejected in favour of an approach to homelessness as a long-term issue of the state's role in housing provision, and an explicitly non-identarian definition of the homeless as all persons whose rent exceeded 30 percent of their income or whose housing was insecure, inadequate, or unsafe (117-121).

While this approach failed to capture the attention of the Canadian public and policy-makers, a similar failure in defining the meaning of homelessness along the lines of the welfare state paradigm had already been noted in the United States several years earlier. As Mark Stern pointed out in 1984, attempts by advocates to "draw continuities between the homeless and the explanation of poverty in the 1970s" were muted by a massive public response that saw the homeless in a wholly differing manner, a resistance he interpreted in terms of political shifts and social anxieties geared towards a reintroduction of relations of charity that clearly distinguished between the poor and non-poor (Stern 1984:118-120). It is also notable, though, that such attempts to describe homelessness in terms of structural analyses of poverty failed to clearly articulate poverty with inherited meanings of homelessness, or to address popular anxieties arising from the ambiguous social position of the figure of the homeless person. In terms of language, the problem might be set out as one of making use of language which was already keyed towards notions of aid external to both the rights of citizens and to the redistributive responsibilities of the state. To the extent that the structural analysis of poverty aimed to challenge perceptions of homelessness rooted in crisis or deviance, it did so using a language that served to invoke these same images. In terms of context, one of the barriers faced by the structural interpretation of the problem of homelessness was that the socio-economic conditions Stern describes as having induced the replacement of the language of poverty by that of homelessness also mitigated against the successful framing of homelessness as an issue of structural inequality. These early structural interpretations of homelessness, then, seem to have been limited both by their inability to find a compelling way of addressing popular uncertainty or disenchantment with the Marshallian story regarding desirable relations between citizens and state, and by a difficulty in working through and rearticulating inherited meanings associated with the term "homeless".

While this first period of struggle over the meaning of homelessness can be characterized in terms of its relation to inherited notions of the skid row drunk, and the failure of structural approaches to displace this story, a second period can be identified for the way homelessness is taken up according to the inherited language of crisis, in the context of a developing neoliberal social regime.

National Disaster: The Discovery of Homelessness

The freezing deaths of Eugene Upper, Mirsalah-Aldin Kompani, and Irwin Anderson on Toronto streets in 1996, and the coroner's inquest which followed, marked the beginning of the discovery of homelessness in Canada on a national scale (Layton 2000:12; Crowe 2007:13). The very conditions of this discovery, though, would have a significant impact on how this problem would be taken up in public debate. The discursive force of homelessness as national disaster served to articulate notions of the scope and deservingness of the homeless, and the nature of the problem of homelessness, in ways that were distinct from both the structural approaches pursued a decade earlier and punitive and space-clearing approaches gaining ground in public debate and provincial and municipal policies through the 1990s.[36]

In response to the ongoing failure of governments in Canada to take formal measures to address homelessness, the *Toronto Disaster Relief Committee* (TDRC) was formed in the spring of 1998 to declare homelessness a national disaster. The original declaration reads, in part:

> **We call on all levels of government to declare homelessness a national disaster requiring emergency humanitarian relief. We urge that they immediately develop and implement a National Homelessness Relief and Prevention Strategy using disaster relief funds both to provide the homeless with immediate health protection and housing and to prevent further homelessness... Despite Canada's reputation for providing relief to people made temporarily homeless by natural disasters, our governments are unwilling to help the scores of thousands of people in Canada condemned to homelessness... (Toronto Disaster Relief Committee 1998a)**

Governments were thus called to act by a framing of homelessness along the lines of emergency relief programs addressing victims of natural disaster. As Cathy Crowe, a co-founder of the TDRC explains, "[w]e asked that the disaster of homelessness be dealt with in the same manner and spirit as other Canadian disasters such as floods and ice storms" (Crowe 2005). The success of this framing was immediate and widespread. A "Disaster Declaration" was taken up by the Big City Mayors' caucus of the Federation of Canadian Municipalities (FCM) and other Canadian municipalities in the fall of 1998, followed by a host of endorsements from Canadian professional associations, unions and community organizations, and accompanied by extensive media coverage (Crowe 2007:24). This attention to homelessness as national disaster prompted the first instances of federal attention to homelessness, with the creation of the *National Homelessness Secretariat* and appointment of a Federal Coordinator on Homelessness in the spring of 1999, and the announcement of a $700 million-range *Federal Homelessness Initiative* in December 1999 (Weldon 2005).

If homelessness had become a legitimate social problem worthy of government attention, though, it had become so as a different type of problem than that envisioned a decade earlier by researchers and advocates deploying a postwar social policy framework. While both the TDRC's and FCM's campaigns highlighted long-term problems of affordable housing—in, for instance, the TDRC's "1% Solution" campaign calling on all levels of government to allocate an additional one percent of their budgets to affordable housing (Toronto Disaster Relief Committee 1998b)—these concerns sat uneasily with the targeted forms of short-term relief carried by the metaphor of disaster. Ambiguities with regards to the sameness or difference of the homeless and with regards to the scope of homelessness as a problem of relatively inadequate housing or as an absolute lack of housing, which had been opposing discourses in the 1980s, were carried together here in the language of disaster. Homelessness as emergency or disaster was useful, for instance, in asserting the deservingness of those addressed. Insofar as emphasis could be placed on domestic rather than international forms of disaster relief, the aid offered these innocent victims of circumstance could be understood as the entitlements of citizens to redistributive state resources. While aid was re-envisioned here on the model of citizen entitlement rather than that of charity towards the dispossessed, this entitlement was afforded in a language of emergency susceptible to narrow interpretations of the scope of disaster, and of the types of persons impacted by this disaster. Though the TDRC's campaign addressed the need for both short and long-term housing measures, the logic of the disaster frame may have been less amenable to considerations of affordable and adequate housing for a broad spectrum of poorly-paid Canadians than it was to emphasis on acute short-term need, and targeted aid towards specific populations. Because popular attention was already trained on the differences exhibited by a highly visible street population, this selectivity would continue to act as a basis for popular anxieties and uncertainties with regards to this target group, which seemed to resist interpretation as wholly same or different from "normal" citizens, or as recipients of aid clearly based on either entitlement or charity. The successful reinterpretation of homelessness as a problem worthy of concerted state intervention, then, seems to have involved a de-accentuation of elements of the social welfare orientation towards structural inequalities, as both difficult to clearly articulate in the language of national disaster, and too easily amenable to popular interests in the most visible forms of poverty.

While this rise in attention to the problem of homelessness could be attributed to an effective playing of inherited languages of the homeless as victims of disaster alongside those of the homeless as deviant, it is also important to recognize the extent to which the terrain for understanding social solidarity in Canada had shifted in the decade following the attempts of researchers in the 1980s to define homelessness in terms of structural poverty and inequality. As Matt James points out, Canadian federal disaster compensation and disaster response saw a remarkable rise through the 1990s, accompanied by a rise in the legitimacy and significance accorded these responses, in the form of official visits to disaster sites and the amount of funding allocated to respective instances of crisis (James 2007:337). To the extent that the rising significance of disaster relief can be interpreted as a means of enacting social bonds that had been rendered ambiguous with the retrenchment of welfare state services (James 2007:338-9), orientations towards the homeless as disaster victims might be interpreted less as an abandonment of those addressed as homeless from the stable ground of citizenship than as an attempt to make claims about ethical responses to homelessness through reference to norms of Canadian citizenship that were themselves in flux. To this extent, inherited languages regarding the figure of the homeless may have become productive as an effect of—and as part of—a reconfiguration of the terms of Canadian citizenship, while also acting as a concrete testing-ground for increasingly narrowed and targeted approaches to social policy engendered by this reconfiguration. Part of this testing-ground has involved an ongoing reformulation of the identities attributable to "homeless" and the logic by which aid is to be offered. One way of tracing these reformulations is through the evolving relationship between policy orientations towards housing and individual pathologies, as an industry of homelessness policy and research developed in Canada alongside government deployment of neoliberal "policy templates" oriented towards social inclusion, the voluntary sector, and vulnerable populations (Orsini and Smith 2007:2).

The Medicalization of Housing as the Sedimentation of a Discourse of Homelessness

Canadian literature on social policy has identified the Canadian state's deployment of Third Way rhetoric and policy to mediate the social disruptions caused by two decades of neoliberal socio-economic policies (Brodie 2007; Banting 2005). Such approaches to social governance have been read along the lines of a coercive imperative to individual "autonomization and responsibilization" among a citizenry with decreasing social security and supports, and a heightened state role in facilitating and enabling social bonds and community self-management among an increasingly insecure citizenry (Rose 2000:1400). One example of such a policy discourse can be seen in a focus on "vulnerable populations", which became explicit in Federal policy around 2002 (Murray 2004). As Murray points out, this has involved an emphasis on community service-delivery, in the form of federally funded voluntary sector initiatives, to address the individual failures or shortcomings of specific target groups who are seen as "disturbances to mainstream health, social and economic norms, and as threats to order and stability" (2004:52). If the problem of homelessness has been one testing-ground for this model of social policy, the changing relationship between policy orientations towards housing and individual pathologies offers a sense of how homelessness has evolved as a discourse well-suited to neoliberal imperatives of social governance.

With regards to housing and homelessness initiatives, Canada has largely followed US policy, from the adoption of "continuum of care" approaches which aimed to use the shelter system to "prepare hostel users for housing and employment" (City of Toronto 1999:43) to a contemporary shift in orientation towards a "housing first" approach where "homeless residents are provided immediate access to a place of their own without requiring treatment or sobriety as a precondition for housing" (City of Victoria 2007:18). Though both models take the homeless individual as their focus of attention, with the aim of addressing personal dysfunctions and training individuals as self-sufficient and self-reliant citizens, they differ in their approach to the provision of housing. Where the continuum approach saw outreach, treatment and transitional housing as pre-requisites for successful preparation of individuals for permanent housing, the "housing first" model marked a shift in medical knowledge which came to see stable housing itself as a necessary prerequisite for effective treatment and training (Tsemberis et al. 2004:651). Without broaching the question of the relative improvements or successes in service-delivery introduced by these models, the roles these approaches have played in contemporary discourses of homelessness are worth identifying.

Lyon-Callo (2004) offers one assessment of the impact of these models, suggesting that they be read as contributors to a "medicalization of homelessness" which has re-articulated interpretations of homelessness as a problem rooted in individual disease and dysfunction. Lyon-Callo's suggestion is that this medicalization has encouraged an interpretation of the behaviours of target populations solely on the grounds of personal pathology: "systemic inequities contribute to the production of many behaviors that are commonly read as pathological disorders among people without permanent shelter" (Lyon-Callo 2004:52). In addition to these narrow interpretations of the behaviours of this target population, it is also notable that this medicalization has supported a narrowing of the scope of policy in such a way that diagnosable individuals have become the primary target of attention. Examples of this narrowing of scope can be found in the differences in target populations addressed by Toronto's *Mayor's Homelessness Action Task Force Report* (City of Toronto 1999) and, a decade later, by Victoria's *Mayor's Task Force on Breaking the Cycle of Mental Illness, Addictions and Homelessness* (City of Victoria 2007). While Toronto's task force advocated for supportive housing aimed at the most visible homeless—understood as those most likely to suffer from mental illness and addiction—and for shelter allowances and new affordable housing to address financial strains faced by those described as the working poor (City of Toronto 1999:vii), Victoria's Task Force focused attention on those with "Severe Addictions and Mental Illness (SAMI)" (City of Victoria 2007:8). Calgary's *Ten-Year Plan to End Homelessness* (Calgary Committee to End Homelessness 2008) echoes this approach, by targeting only those dysfunctional individuals who are to "take personal ownership and accountability in ending their homelessness" through therapy and training aimed at "self-reliance and independence" (2008:10).

Attention to the discursive inheritances provided by prior understandings of "the homeless", as victims of disaster and as skid row deviants, offers a sense of the way a medical emphasis on pathology is less indicative of a shift in the meanings attributable to homelessness than it is of a continuity of a discursive tradition of selectivity and difference in approaches to the "homeless". While this selectivity and difference have largely come to be understood according to a medical logic, it might be more accurate to describe the remarkable shift in this period as the medicalization of housing: the language of housing, once closely associated with the rights of social citizenship, has come to be understood almost exclusively according to the targeted medical needs of a distinct homeless sub-population. This shift in the meaning of housing is identifiable in the uses of "housing and homelessness" to designate a distinct policy area from the 1980s through contemporary policy discussions.

The designation "housing and homelessness" was used in several Canadian conference publications in the mid-1980s, as an issue of both income inadequacy and secure, affordable housing (*Canadian Agenda for Action on Housing and Homelessness through the Year 2000*, 1988; Hulchanksi 1987). While housing served here to define the policy problem (of which homelessness was simply an effect[37]), policy literature over the following decades would come to more closely resemble public sensibilities and anxieties which took homelessness as a problem distinctive from that of housing. The first wave of homeless research had relied on a notion of structural failure and universal citizen entitlement to champion housing, thus failing to address discursive ambiguities regarding either the homeless (as victim or deviant; subject to inadequate housing or no housing; entitled to aid or subject to charity) or shifts in the rights and obligations of citizenship under an emerging neoliberal social paradigm. In the late 1990s Toronto's *Task Force* addressed these ambiguities by distinguishing two distinct groups of citizens to be addressed: the working poor, as undifferentiated citizen victims of structural conditions, and the mentally ill and addicted, as differentiated citizen victims of a more complex set of circumstances.[38] The tensions in "Housing and Homelessness" as a field of study in the late 1990s, then, seems to have been resolved somewhat through the de-linking of homelessness from its subordinate relationship as an effect of housing as a policy problem, allowing the unfettered identification and theorization of homelessness as a problem in its own right.

Without questioning the desirability or effectiveness of "housing first" approaches for those who are addressed by these initiatives, it is worthy of note that these approaches have contributed to the narrowing of contemporary meanings associable with "housing and homelessness" as a field of study. Housing, understood according to a post-war social paradigm orientated by the redistributive role of the welfare state and the rights of social citizenship, has never sat easily alongside inherited discourses of the homeless oriented towards specificity and difference. The risk is that the post-war language of housing becomes incomprehensible in these contexts, as it runs up against homelessness as an increasingly sedimented and autonomous component of neoliberal discourse.

Some Concluding Thoughts…

This brief outline of uses of the term "homeless" highlights various ways that homelessness as an interpretive framework has served to resist, and in some cases undermine, the conceptions of citizenship and social justice pursued by activists and researchers. The aim has been to draw attention to some of the constraints faced by scholars and activists when engaging with discourses of homelessness by sketching out how the contemporary problem of homelessness might be seen not just as the material product of neoliberal economic policies but, perhaps more importantly, as a distinct discursive component of a still-developing neoliberal social paradigm. This is to say that the material conditions understood as homelessness, and the discursive framework used to interpret and make sense of these conditions, can be seen as arising from the same context of social and economic turbulence. With regards to material conditions, an increase in the number of un-housed and precariously-housed persons over the past two decades can be attributed to a retrenchment of the Canadian welfare state—most notably in the demise of federal funding for social housing and the restructuring of social assistance and social insurance provisions.[39] With regards to interpretive frameworks, the stories that have come to be told about these conditions—as the "problem of homelessness"—have developed in the context of the end of the post-Second World War consensus regarding the redistributive role of the welfare state and the rights of social citizenship (Isin et al. 2008), and the ascendancy of neoliberal sensibilities regarding individual responsibility, active civil society, and minimal state (Dean 1999; Rose 1996; Banting 2005; Brodie 2002). As outlined above, a key problem with this problem-construction of homelessness is the limited scope of actors and remedies conceivable or articulable within what is essentially a neoliberal interpretive framework.

An underlying current of this paper is that the choice and use of words in political struggles matters. If these choices and uses of words are only one relatively small component in the construction of a "regime of truth" (Foucault 2008:19), they are also a relatively easy component of a discursive regime to challenge, alter, and contest. Recent uses of the term "precarious housing" (Wellesley Institute 2010) in Canadian policy literature offer one example of this type of discursive strategy, as precarious housing is put forward as a way of undoing conceptual divisions that have arisen between homelessness as a problem of individual failure on the part of a narrow sub-section of the population, and safe and secure housing as a problem of structural failure impacting a much broader number of people.[40] If such uses of language cannot in themselves alter the neoliberal discourses of social governance that make homelessness, and not affordable housing, a site of relevant public concern in the first place, such uses at least resist contributing to, or being easily subsumed by, these discourses. In a time when neoliberal visions of the social appear to be the only game in town, this type of discursive innovation may be more relevant than it would otherwise be for anti-poverty movement struggles to develop compelling claims for housing, income supports, and health services for all.

In terms of the relationships between scholarly research and activist practices, the approach pursued here points towards a reading of scholarly activist impulses and commitments amenable to methods emerging from fields, such as my own training in political science, that are oriented more towards dominant institutions and discourses than to those most affected by these forms of power (Calhoun 2008; see also Dafnos, and Kip, this volume). If this pushes at notions of activist scholarship defined through sole reference to direct scholarly engagement with a marginalized group (see also Pierre 2008), an additional push may be merited when it comes to the desirability or possibility of a unitary subject-position of activist scholar. On this front, my more intimate understandings of the changing social function and management of the university have led me to reconsider the possibilities of doing effective social justice work through university-based scholarship (Herman and Willson forthcoming). My experience has been that the most effective ways to engage in allied work with marginalized groups is to forgo the limitations of social-scientific research in favour of taking up and passing along community organizing skills, and of passing along university resources, as well as grants through the financial support that allows my engagement in unpaid forms of community organizing and allied work.[41] This is to say, I have felt most effective in my organizing work when it has been held separate from my scholarly writing and formal academic training. The flip-side of this is that I have appreciated the separation of my scholarly work from the organizations I work with, as this allows me space to reflect on and test thoughts that would be out of place in the concrete contexts of struggle.

James and Gordon's reflection on the "radical subject" is helpful in this regard, as they address the limitations of academic research by asking much more of the activist/ scholar concerned with struggles against social injustices:

> Once truly outside the academy, academic-bound radicals may be unmasked as "insiders" aligned with institutional power. Stable identity constructs as "transformative" or "activist" scholars crumble—except for those who can reconstitute themselves as practitioners outside the academic arena—This is one of the true hallmarks of the radical subject, a sign that distinguishes him or her from the activist scholar. (2008:370)

These questions, of the limits of intellectual labour within the university and the challenge to become "practitioners outside the academic arena," can only become more relevant as larger numbers of scholars-in-training find there are fewer spaces for us in the increasingly corporatized university.[42]

References

Arnold, Kathleen R. 2004. *Homelessness, Citizenship And Identity: The Uncanniness Of Late Modernity*. Albany: State University of New York Press.

Banting, Keith. 2005. "Do we know where we are going?: The new social policy in Canada." *Canadian Public Policy* 31(4):421-429.

Blasi, Gary. 1994. "And we are not seen: Ideological and political barriers to understanding homelessness." *American Behavioral Scientist* 37(4):563-586.

Brodie, Janine. 2002. "Citizenship and solidarity: Reflections on the Canadian way." *Citizenship Studies* 6(4):377-394.

———. 2007. "Reforming social justice in neoliberal times." *Studies in Social Justice* 1(2): 93-107.

Calhoun, Craig. 2008. "Foreword." In *Engaging Contradictions: Theory, Politics and Methods of Activist Scholarship,* edited by Charles R. Hale, xiii-xxv. Berkeley: University of California Press.

Calgary Committee to End Homelesssness. 2008. *Calgary's 10-year Plan to End Homelessness.*

Canadian Agenda for Action on Housing and Homelessness through the Year 2000. 1988. In *New Partnerships—Building for the Future: Proceedings of the Canadian Conference to Observe the International Year of Shelter for the Homeless,* edited by Heather Lang-Runtz and Doyne C. Ahern, 117-130. The Canadian Association of Housing and Renewal Officials.

City of Toronto. 1999. *Taking Responsibility for Homelessness: An Action Plan for Toronto*. Report of the Mayor's Homelessness Action Task Force.

City of Victoria. Executive Summary. 2007. *Mayor's Task Force on Breaking the Cycle of Mental Illness, Addictions and Homelessness.*

Connelly, J., Cecily Kelleher, Steve Morton, David St. George, and Paul Roderick. 1991. *Housing or Homelessness: A Public Health Perspective*, Faculty of Public Health Medicine of the Royal Colleges of Physicians of the United Kingdom.

Crowe, Cathy. 2005. *Cathy Crowe's Newsletter* 7. January. Accessed September 5, 2011. http://www.tdrc.net/resources/public/Crowe-Newsletter_01-05.htm.

———. ed. 2007. *Dying for a Home: Homeless Activists Speak Out*. Toronto: Between the Lines.

Cuff, John Haslett. 1981. "Life in the street." *The Globe and Mail*. August 1.

Dean, Mitchell. 1999. *Governmentality: Power and Rule in Modern Society*. London: Sage.

DeFilippis, James, Robert Fisher, and Eric Shragge. 2010. *Contesting Community: The Limits and Potentials of Local Organizing.* New Brunswick: Rutgers University Press.

Feldman, Leonard. 2004. *Citizens Without Shelter: Homelessness, Democracy, and Political Exclusion.* Ithaca: Cornell University Press.

Fischer, Frank. 2003. *Reframing Public Policy: Discursive Politics and Deliberative Practices.* Oxford: Oxford University Press.

Foucault, Michel. 2008. *The Birth of Biopolitics: Lectures at the College de France, 1978-79*, edited by Michel Senellart. New York: Palgrave Macmillan.

Herman, Tamara, and Mark Willson. Forthcoming. "Learning CBR through community organizing: reflections on struggles for essential health services for people who use drugs in a protracted policy context." In *Teaching Community Based Research: Linking Pedagogy to Practice,* edited by Catherine Etmanski, Teresa Dawson and Budd Hall. Toronto: University of Toronto Press.

Hoch, Charles, and Robert A. Slayton. 1989. *New Homeless and Old: Community and The Skid Row Hotel.* Philadelphia: Temple University Press.

Hopper, Kim, and Jim Baumohl. 1994. "Held in abeyance: Rethinking homelessness and advocacy." *American Behavioral Scientist* 37(4):522-552.

Hulchanski, David. 1987. "Who are the homeless? What is homelessness? The politics of defining an emerging policy issue." *UBC Planning Papers, Discussion Paper 10.* Vancouver: School of Community and Regional Planning.

———. 2002. "Housing policy for tomorrow's cities." Discussion Paper F27. *Canadian Policy Research Networks*, December. Accessed September 5, 2011. http://www.cprn.org/doc.cfm?doc=161&l=en.

———. 2009. "Homelessness in Canada: Past, present, future." Conference Keynote address, *Growing Home: Housing and Homelessness in Canada*, University of Calgary, February 18.

Isin, Engin, Janine Brodie, Danielle Juteau and Daiva Stasilius. 2008. "Recasting the social in citizenship." In *Recasting the Social in Citizenship*, edited by Engin Isin, 3-19. Toronto: University of Toronto Press.

James, Joy, and Edmund T. Gordon. 2008. "Afterword: Activist scholars or radical subjects?" In *Engaging Contradictions: Theory, Politics and Methods of Activist Scholarship,* edited by Charles R. Hale, 367-363. Berkeley: University of California Press.

James, Matt. 2007. "The permanent-emergency compensation state: A 'postsocialist' rale of political dystopia." In *Critical Policy Studies*, edited by Micheal Orsini and Miriam Smith, 321-346. Vancouver: UBC Press.

Layton, Jack. 2000. *Homelessness: The Making and Unmaking of a Crisis*. Toronto: Penguin/McGill Institute.

Lurie, Theodora. 1982. "Army of homeless haunts New York discharged mental patients, jobless left to scavenge among the garbage." *The Globe and Mail*. January 30.

Lyon-Callo, Vincent. 2004. *Inequality, Poverty, and Neoliberal Governance: Activist Ethnography in the Homeless Sheltering Industry*. New York: Broadview Press.

Marcus, Anthony. 2006. *Where Have All the Homeless Gone: The Making and Unmaking of a Crisis*. New York: Berghahn Books.

Marshall, Thomas Humphrey. 1950. *Citizenship and Social Class*. Cambridge: Cambridge University Press.

Murray, Karen B. 2004. "Do not disturb: 'Vulnerable populations' in federal government policy discourses and practices." *Canadian Journal of Urban Research* 13(1):50-69.

Orsini, Michael, and Miriam Smith. 2007. "Critical policy studies." In *Critical Policy Studies,* edited by Micheal Orsini and Miriam Smith, 1-16. Vancouver: UBC Press.

Pierre, Jemima. 2008. "Activist groundings or groundings for activism? A study of racialization as a site of political engagement." In *Engaging Contradictions: Theory, Politics and Methods of Activist Scholarship,* edited by Charles R. Hale, 115-135. Berkeley: University of California Press.

Rose, Nikolas. 1996. "The death of the social? Re-figuring the territory of government." *Economy and Society* 25(3):327-356.

———. 2000. "Community, citizenship and the third way." *American Behavioral Scientist* 43(9):1395-1411.

Sommers, Jeff. 1998. "Men at the margins: Masculinity and space in downtown Vancouver, 1950-1986." *Urban Geography* 19(4):287-310.

Stern, Mark J. 1984. "The emergence of the homeless as a public problem." *Social Services Review* 58:291-301.

Stone, Deborah A. 1988. *Policy Paradox and Political Reason*. New York: Harper Collins Publishers.

Toronto Disaster Relief Committee. 1998a. *The State of Emergency Declaration*. Accessed September 5, 2011. http://tdrc.net/index.php?page=state-of-emergency-declaration.

———. 1998b. *1% Solution*. Accessed September 5, 2011. http://tdrc.net/index php?page=1-solution.

Tsemberis, Sam, Leyla Gulcur, and Maria Nacae. 2004. "Housing first, consumer choice, and harm reduction for homeless individuals with a dual diagnosis." *American Journal of Public Health* 94(4):651-656.

Weldon, Jane [Director-General, National Secretariat on Homelessness]. 2005. *The Government of Canada's Response to Homelessness: Leading a Horizontal Response*. April 8.

Accessed September 5, 2011. http://www.powershow.com/view/204476-NjQ3M/The_Government_of_Canadas_Response_to_Homelessness_Leading_a_Horizontal_Response_flash_ppt_presentation.

Wellesley Institute. 2010. *Precarious Housing in Canada.* Accessed June 20, 2011. http://www.wellesleyinstitute.com/news/affordable-housing-news/new-report-precarious-housing-in-canada-2010.

Wright, Talmadge. 1997. *Out of Place: Homeless Mobilizations, Sub-Cities, and Contested Landscapes*. New York: SUNY Press.

Chapter 5

Samuel Delany's Lumpen Worlds and the Problem of Representing Marginality

Lisa Estreich

Since the publication of his first sci-fi novel in 1962, Samuel R. Delany has portrayed complex urban worlds in ways that counter oversimplified representations of the economic and social margins. Across Delany's body of work, which has taken a distinct autobiographical turn since the late 1980s, sexual relations with down-and-out men feature prominently. Delany provides an account of New York City's seedier gay spaces, and the men who participated in them, including clerical workers, poets, taxi drivers, food delivery men, construction workers, hustlers, artists, adjunct professors, runaways, and homeless men of varied racial and ethnic backgrounds. These scenes of encounter among men from all walks of life, but especially the lower social echelons, have largely escaped recording in any archive. For scholars and activists working in areas related to LGBTIQ issues and politics, Delany is important for mapping mostly lower-income worlds, foregrounding the ways sexuality and gender intricate with other vectors of class-based marginalization.

In *Times Square Red, Times Square Blue* (1999a), Delany has coined the phrase "'ethnographic' memoir" to describe his effort to capture those worlds he witnessed and participated in within the flickering dark of midtown's porn theatres, before they underwent the Forty-Second Street Development Project's wrecking ball in the mid-1990s. "Memoir", for Delany, runs counter to the continuous narrative form of "true biography", having instead the character of images flashed in darkness: "a collection of impressions and fragments" (Delany 1988:348). It is notable that, in this coinage, Delany puts the word "ethnographic" in scare quotes. I propose that this is not so much to indicate his status as sociological amateur (Delany avows "a commitment both to the vernacular and to the expert"), as it is to signal how his mode of social description and analysis diverges from ethnographic work based upon presumptions of ethnic or racial collectivity (Delany 1999a:xiv). Delany's methods and directions of inquiry defy comparison with the kind of scholarship that reinforces racialized "underclass" discourse in the United States. The latter, as one critic has put it, defines and explains its object of analysis through an impoverished "idea of race" (Jones 1998:382). But Delany's writing, registering ethnic and racial particularity within a fabric of interwoven gesture, event, and verbal exchange, documents his effort to find language for urban interactions that available codes (and presumptions of community) misrepresent or render invisible. His work runs counter to prevalent American imagery about "class", especially dominant representations of poverty as they are enmeshed in racial stereotype. In this essay, I locate Delany's mode of "ethnographic" memoir in relation to critiques of "underclass" discourse in the United States. I also map a trajectory from Delany's *The Mad Man*

(1994) to *Dark Reflections* (2007), considering how these two novels, both depicting a black gay writer's complex engagements with homeless people in ways we can take as quasi-autobiographical, illustrate Delany's insights into the relationship between discourses about poverty and structures of power in the United States at the advent of the twenty-first century.

Situating American "Underclass" Discourse

Surveying representations of poverty in the United States and Britain since the late nineteenth century, social historian John Welshman has noted the protean characteristics of "underclass" discourse, as well as its vampiric capacity for reinvention. He suggests that the very ambiguity of the idea of an "underclass" has lent to its successive reformulation (Welshman 2007). In its various incarnations—the "social residuum" (1880s), "unemployable" (1920s), "social problem group" (1930s), "problem family" (1950s), "culture of poverty" (1960s), "cycle of deprivation" (1970s), "underclass" (1980s), and "socially excluded" (1990s)—this discourse evokes a shadowy category of persons living perpetually off the labour of others, relegated to the social margins by their inability to acculturate to the work ethic (Welshman 2007:xix). But "underclass" discourse, for all its relative stability, has served to mask contingent, shifting contexts of political struggle under capitalism, serving a disciplining-and-dividing function with regard to more marginal factions of labour, not least by invoking the spectre of abject unemployment (Bourdieu 2010:155).[43] Following Loïc Wacquant (2009), who in turn draws upon Bourdieu's conceptions of symbolic power, we can understand "discourse" as a web of social representation which, by reinforcing tendencies to misrecognize the systemic origins of existing inequalities, has a role in perpetuating structures of power.[44] In Wacquant's view, it is not possible to comprehend America's transition from the more "communal" ghetto of the 1960s to the intensified poverty and violence of the American "hyperghetto" of the post-industrial era without taking into account the role of dominant representations of the urban poor in "legitimiz[ing] the state policy of urban abandonment and punitive containment" (Wacquant 2004:95).

Wacquant calls the idea of the "underclass" a "novel, yet pivotal, category of political and scholarly commonsense in the debate about the ghetto after the Civil Rights revolution" (Wacquant 2004:105). Replacing overt references to race with an emphasis on dysfunctional "behaviour" and "culture", scholarship on the "underclass" had attained the status of an "intellectual cottage industry" by the mid-1990s (Wacquant 2009:107). What is new, Wacquant observes, "is that the terminology of the "underclass" claims to be *race-blind*: it has this great virtue that it allows one to speak of African Americans in a superficially 'de-racialized' language" (Wacquant 2004:109). On the one hand, the loss of industrial jobs, state abandonment of poverty-stricken areas in the urban core, and punitive measures such as workfare and the "War on Drugs" targeting ghetto denizens "unknit the entire web of 'indirect social relations'" (Wacquant 2004:117). But these structural and political processes eroding the social fabric of the ghetto operated in tandem with rhetoric pathologizing those who bore the brunt of them. Wacquant (2004), therefore, has described these discursive and structural processes as interconnected and mutually reinforcing.

Historian Jacqueline Jones similarly emphasizes the extent to which rhetoric about the alterity of the poor is deeply rooted in American political culture and its racial fantasies (Jones 1998:382). According to Jones, the negative imagery of black family life and culture that characterized "underclass" discourse in the 1980s can be traced back to Reconstruction-era rhetoric that sought to control African American mobility and, above all, to justify a racial division of labour following the formal end of slavery. It is no coincidence, Jones notes, that this rhetoric was resurrected as labour unions declined in power and the racially-based division of labour "was fast succumbing to a new world economic order" (Jones 1998:382). Jones emphasizes not only the persistence of imagery invalidating black people's productive capabilities, but the American tendency to obfuscate class formation through racial representations. Thus, the national debates about poverty and economic opportunity which took place in the 1980s and early 1990s, obsessed with imagery of violent black young men in northern cities, rendered invisible the role of housing discrimination and real estate redlining in producing intensified levels of racial poverty and segregation after the 1960s (Massey and Denton 1993). Embraced by Democrats and Republicans alike, the "underclass" debates also subverted understanding of the larger history of dispossession and social inequality in the United States, in its demographic and geographic complexity (Jones 1992:9).

Place, Jones observes, "is a major theme in the history of poverty" (1992:5). More complex understandings of the relationship between place and lived experience can counteract stereotypes about the poor—as opposed to the invocation of sites in the national imaginary, such as the inner city, in which an idea of "race" supplants the analysis of convergent structural and subjective forces.[45] Racial and ethnic stereotypes, a staple of American political rhetoric regarding poverty, render invisible processes of economic marginalization, and also of cultural invention across social categories.

Like Jones, literary critic Hortense Spillers emphasizes the deep roots of "underclass" rhetoric in the language of racial representation in the United States. For Spillers, "underclass" discourse traffics in a notion of racial or ethnic collectivity that is fundamentally anti-historical, severing bodies from lived temporality. Spillers calls this the mode of "ethnicity" as myth. "'Ethnicity' perceived as mythical time", she suggests, "enables a writer to perform a variety of conceptual moves at once" (Spillers 2003:205; see also Tomiak's critique of "static Indianness", in this volume). She discerns these linguistic operations in sociological representations of the Negro Family, such as the Moynihan Report of the late 1960s. Representing "ethnicity" in the mode of an eternal present, these representations render black people into bodies, and make the body flesh, in a language descended from the "American grammar" of slavery (Spillers 2003:209). The human body, thus objectified, becomes "a resource for metaphor" and for "pornotroping", such that "we lose any hint or suggestion of a dimension of ethics, of relatedness between one human personality and another, between human personality and cultural institutions" (Spillers 2003:208; see also Wilson and Anderson, in this volume, on the representations of the poor in poverty discourse).

For Cornel West (1999), political discourse about race in "a twilight civilization," as he dubbed an increasingly class-polarized America entering the twenty-first century, renders invisible the "problem of black invisibility and namelessness" rooted in the dominant culture's undermining of black existence. This condition, writes West, "remains marginal to the dominant accounts of our past and present and is relatively absent from our pictures of the future", though it could be seen as increasingly relevant to the experience of poor people in the United States across racial and ethnic lines (West 1999:115). The obverse of such "invisibility and namelessness" is a hyper-visible image, mirroring the dominant culture's fantasy projections. American sociology since its inception, but especially the "neoromantic" vein of ethnography predominating since the 1990s (formed in the context of neoliberal ideology), has been criticized for colluding in such imagery (Wacquant 2002).[46]

In his essay "Looking for the 'Real' Nigga: Social Scientists Construct the Ghetto," Robin D. G. Kelley has observed that social scientists who take the black inner city as their object of study tend to use the terms "behaviour" and "culture" interchangeably, reinforcing stereotypes about the ways class, race, and sex are conjoined. The "ghetto authenticity" school privileges black male youth, and a certain notion of "soul", as the epitome of African American reality (Kelley 1997). This imagery erases the complex historical location of African American culture at the intersection of diverse cultural streams and identities, including sexual identities.[47] Kelley cites as typical a scholar who apparently regards rap music as the authentic expression of black youth. For him, Kelley (1997:37) comments, "the Hip Hop nation is the true voice of the black lumpenproletariat whose descriptions of street life are the real thing." Thus, the ghetto ethnographers invested in a heteronormative, masculinist image of black authenticity reduce African American cultural forms to an effect of the clash between a racist dominant culture and black male resistance:

> Without a concept of, or even an interest in, aesthetics, style, and the visceral pleasures of cultural forms, it should not be surprising that most social scientists [have] explained black urban culture in terms of coping mechanisms, rituals, or oppositional responses to racism. And trapped by an essentialist interpretation of culture, they continue to look for that elusive "authentic" ghetto sensibility, the true honest, unbridled, pure cultural practices that capture the raw, ruffneck "reality" of urban life. (Kelley 1997:35)

The spaces of sexual encounter described in Delany's writing, between men of various ethnic and racial backgrounds, many of them poor and homeless, defy such imagery. Perhaps the most striking aspect of these spaces is the extent to which they are dialogic. Amid the flicker and flash of images, on the screen and in the intermittent illumination of the men themselves, words and gestures are exchanged—sometimes surprising in their ordinariness, tenderness, generosity, and unanticipatibility. If Delany's places—among which the interior of the porn theatres serves as a kind of paradigm—testify to anything, it is to culture being made, not to a fixity of culture already given.[48] His "'ethnographic' memoir", the disjoint form of narrative flashing forth ephemeral social experience in its messy, compromised and sometimes disturbing particulars, would seem to answer to one contemporary ethnographer's call for "a politics of 'thick life'—in which the density of social representation is increased to meet the density of actual social worlds" (Povinelli 2006:21).

Alternative Models: Literature and Sociology

Marxist cultural critic Raymond Williams has observed that social analysis that would have any contemporary relevance "must now centrally involve place" (Williams 1982:243, cited in Merrifield 2002:15). But this is not an analysis of place that would be mindlessly empiricist. In an essay written a decade earlier, titled "Literature and Sociology", Williams emphasizes the importance of recognizing the formative role of individual consciousness in any given account of social reality. Such an emphasis on both place and consciousness corresponds to the aims of Samuel Delany's "'ethnographic' memoir". Reflecting on the divide between the disciplines of literary study and sociology, Williams observes that practitioners of the social sciences, despite their commitment to the empirically verifiable, "must deal with active values and with choices", not least including the historical formation of their own values (Williams 2005:15). Consequently, he implies that a more nuanced sociology must have a self-reflexive, indeed autobiographical dimension that remains responsible to the individual's lived experience of social reality: it must "answer... to our closest sense of our own living process."

In this regard, literature, Williams notes, can crucially supplement sociology, but not if literature is understood as merely furnishing life-stories to be decoded by "various empirical facts... about abstract groups" (Williams 2005:29). Instead, literature can be understood as the domain in which the formation of consciousness in relation to social processes, or the "sociology of knowledge"—which Williams calls the weakest area of the social sciences—is richly depicted and analyzed. Anticipating sociologist Pierre Bourdieu's concern with groupmaking processes, Williams identifies as "centrally necessary" the task of "extending" the material of literary study, "not simply to a background of social history or of the history of ideas, but to other active processes through which social groups form and define themselves" (Williams 2005:29).

It is important to note that Williams is far from celebrating literary studies as it exists within the academy. (Indeed, elsewhere he offers a critical account of the phenomenon by which the study of English became the centre of the humanistic project.) Rather, Williams is pointing toward a means of representing the social which cannot be confined to the self-consciously "literary". If social scientists may be criticized for neglecting the domain of consciousness, literary specialists tend to forget that they traffic in the end in a specific language that excludes as much as it accounts for. Williams advocates, by contrast, a form of writing that tracks the interface of subjective processes and social structures. This can be understood as precisely what Delany's mode of "'ethnographic' memoir" seeks to delineate.

Literature can supplement the sociological project by describing at capillary level processes of individual and group formation. Recording processes of personal formation in relation to the memory of specific places, the memoir in particular breaks down the rigid academic distinction between subjective experience and structural forces. In line with Rimke (2010:99), such recording can challenge the "psycho-centric" mode of representing human problems as innate pathologies of the individual. The emphasis in literary representation on the relation between consciousness and social process potentially relates to matters of social justice, though of course literature is only one subset of potential cultural resources for disclosing structures of symbolic violence and expanding the field of social representation.

Formation of a Black Gay Writer

Born in 1942, Samuel Delany grew up in Harlem during an era in which racial segregation still reigned in northern cities, as did—across the United States—a degree of homophobia that historian George Chauncey considers to be "mis-remembered" by gay advocates and opponents alike, both in its systematicity, reinforced by an "absolute ban on gay representation," and its historical specificity, which Chauncey characterizes as an "unprecedented and relatively short-lived development of the twentieth century" (Chauncey 2004:13). This period, by Delany's own account, was formative to his emergence as a writer. Deeply attuned to the ways categories can sever from context and "chop up reality", as he has vividly put it, Delany has pointed out that the words "black" and "gay" simply "did not exist" at the time in any way comparable to their present "meanings, usage, history" (Delany 1988:369). The early sixties, Delany recalls in his memoir *The Motion of Light in Water*,

> had still been, really, part of the fifties. The political consciousness that was to form by the end of the sixties had not been part of my world. There were only Negroes and homosexuals, both of whom—along with artists—were hugely devalued in the social hierarchy. It's even hard to speak of that world. (Delany 1988:369)

In one of the autobiography's key moments narrating his constitution as a writer, Delany realizes the given, public language can only negate and betray his experience. "Coming out" in a therapy group at New York's Mount Sinai hospital at the age of twenty-two following the publication of his first four science fiction novels and a nervous breakdown, Delany refers to his homosexuality as a "problem" he is "working on". No one seems to care much, least of all the group member whose reaction he had dreaded most— "Hank", the muscular guy with a propensity for cracking the occasional faggot joke. Lying in bed that night, Delany realizes his abject confession—formulated with "Hank" in mind—has done nothing to dislodge anybody's supposition as to what the experience of being a homosexual meant: primarily, nothing, since being a homosexual meant being severed by definition from all meaningful social context:

> [I]n the fifties—and it was a fifties model of homosexuality that controlled all that was done, by both we ourselves and the law that persecuted us—homosexuality was a solitary perversion. Before and above all, it isolated you. (Delany 1988:267-268)

The use of the given language, in other words, reinforces the prevailing "myth of the homosexual as outside society" (Delany 1988:267), colluding in a limited conception of the social whole that is not without systematic consequences. Delany's later fiction, as I will indicate later in this essay, is dedicated to understanding the fearsome power of such incomplete accounts of the "real" over those who, by their own account, are relegated to living "nowhere". In a critical connection central to all his subsequent work, Delany recognizes this myth of social unrelatedness as part of a larger myth of an "outside of language", fantasized as the domain of savagery and pure sexual instinct.[49] Against such an idea of the sexually marginal as outside the social, Delany's actual historical experience is that the sexual margins have an "astonishing social range", and have pioneered institutions offering "an extraordinary range of alternatives", even if unrepresented in dominant codes (Delany 1988:374).

It is the aftermath of the coming out scene, one focusing on a wholly other experience of marginality, that seems to provide the deeper imprint for Delany's subsequent preoccupations as a writer. An eighteen-year-old woman who was not part of the therapy group commits suicide, hanging herself from a bathroom shower pole using a stripped up towel. The rumour among the group members is that she was pregnant by another patient and had not been able to get an abortion. It is a moment that occupies just a few lines in the memoir, but that seems to provide the template for the central episode of his novel *Dark Reflections*, which I will consider later in this essay.

Samuel Delany on Language and Marginality

For Delany, a better word for margins is *context*: that which enables a shift in perspective upon the myths that the centre tells of itself. In "Aversion/Perversion/Diversion", a talk given at Rutgers in 1991, Delany observes, before an audience of academics invested in the study of gay culture, that he is compelled to tell stories that provide a glimpse of the "complex and worrisome" context without which Gay Studies would not exist, but which it seldom recognizes. These stories contradict "that wonderfully positive tale [of liberation] we all, perhaps, adore" (Delany 1996a:139). But he cautions his audience: if we disregard the troubling stories, if we insist on the narratives that confirm our happy notions of what gay subjectivity is, "we are betraying our object of study." Delany exhorts academics to consider the ways in which their own highly coded language, and perhaps also that of the literary texts they study, systematically omits from consideration entire terrains of social existence.

Language itself, he suggests, inevitably excludes: "what has been let into language has always been highly coded. That coding represents a kind of police action that, even while it is decried in the arena of politics, often goes, among us in the academic area of Gay Studies, unnoticed" (Delany 1996a:138). In effect, he observes the narrowness of the gay world as it is celebrated in the academy, and gestures toward a more expanded conception of queer existence, in terms of its non-elite institutions and cultures, that curricula delving into the worlds of Oscar Wilde and Virginia Woolf fail to recognize. This is one of Delany's major points: the narrowness of the exercise of textual study, and the considerable confines of what has been and can be represented in language.⁵⁰

Delany admits that the "specific and troubling tales" of the sexual and social margins are not easy to listen to: he wants to turn away from them himself. The story he "would very much like to tell" instead is more palatable. The fantasy protagonist of the more diverting tale "is without sex. He or she is wholly constituted by gender—female, male, gay male, lesbian. Furthermore, our protagonist is unaware of any contradictions in the constitutive process, so that his or her blissfully smooth, seamless self may be called 'natural', 'unalienated', 'happy'—or 'what-you-will'" (Delany 1996a:119). Above all, this hero of "that most glorious political comedy that we have yet been able to erect in the name of liberation" is the pilot of her destiny in matters of enjoyment and pleasure: "Our hero never does anything… that does not please her. The only unpleasant things that befall her inevitably originate outside the self. Whether she is defeated by them or triumphant over them, their external origin is a knowledge she is secure in" (Delany 1996a:120). Delany's purpose is to remind academics, in particular, of the incompleteness of their understanding of the social field within which the transformations of the 1960s took place, and the ways language—not just academic discourse, but language in general—systematically excludes, and fails to even recognize, "the bulk of the extraordinarily rich, frightening, and complex sexual landscape" (1996a:143).

From The Mad Man (1994) to Dark Reflections (2007)

Two novels by Samuel Delany set in New York City, *The Mad Man* (1994) and *Dark Reflections* (2007), explore the long aftermath of the 1960s for people toward the bottom of the social scale, focalized through the consciousness of gay black men at the margins of academe. The novels record the protagonists' efforts to understand and describe the marginal worlds with which they come into contact. In Raymond Williams' formulation, these novels can be seen as exemplifying the interpenetration of literary and sociological forms of inquiry, in their portrayal of the juncture of consciousness and social process (Williams 2005).

The Mad Man (1994)

Set in the 1980s, *The Mad Man* unfurls extravagant narratives of homeless gay encounter during the AIDS epidemic. Crossing the genres of murder mystery, academic satire, and gay pornography, the novel records the escapades of John Marr,[51] a philosophy graduate student in New York City who becomes sexually involved with men living on the streets as he attempts to unravel the mysterious death of a brilliant young philosopher years before. The dead man had also been involved with homeless men at the time of his murder—indeed, some of the very men Marr encounters. Marr's investigations become, more and more explicitly, an attempt to excavate the continuities as well as radical differences between the gay worlds (and wider social terrain) of the present, and of the era prior to AIDS. The novel functions as a kind of academic un-*Bildungsroman*, in which the narrator unlearns codes of representation in which he has been schooled, in order to render his experiences in a language that does not falsify them. The language of sociological and philosophical abstraction, by which the world is rendered purely in terms of "systems", is the first thing Marr jettisons.

Delany has described *The Mad Man* as a "pornotopia"—not, he emphasizes, a "porn-utopia", but a *pornos-topia*, or account of the place where the exchange of sex occurs. "Pornotopia", Delany has explained in an interview:

> is not the "good sexual place."[...] It's simply *the* "sexual place"—the place where all can become (apocalyptically) sexual. "Pornotopia" is the place where pornography occurs—and that, I'm afraid, is the world of *The Mad Man*. It's the place

where any relationship can become sexualized in a moment, with the proper word or look—where every relationship is potentially sexualized before it even starts. (1999b:133)

In this world of dissolved boundaries, such that the interpersonal is rendered instantaneously carnal, any axis of social difference is substitutable for another. It is also an exclusively male world, in which "race" and "ethnicity" outrageously transpose and replace other forms of difference—such as gender.

For example, in the lead-up to a sexual exchange on a park bench, the following dialogue transpires between the narrator and a homeless man in Riverside Park:

"Where'd you grow up?"

"In a orphanage," he explained. "Out in California—way down in the south. Below what they call Southern California. I mean where you can hardly tell it from Mexico no more. You ever heard of Brawley, California—in Imperial Valley, down south of Salton Sea?"

I shook my head.

"Well, that's the closest place with a name to where I come up." He added: "In the orphanage there—that's where I done learned about cocksuckers. And black people. See, in a' orphanage, the two sexes is niggers-Mexicans-n'-injuns—and whites. And in the orphanage where I was there weren't but about ten, twelve of us white guys out of about seventy or eighty kids. Man, by the time I got out of that place at seventeen, I had so much brown and black dick shoved up my fuckin' asshole, I was about almost likin' it, I tell you." (Delany 2002:26)

"Pornotopia", or we might say, "counter-pornotroping" to borrow Hortense Spillers' term, can be understood as the most obvious element of *The Mad Man* by which Delany opposes "underclass" discourse. The above story, making "niggers-Mexicans-n'-injuns" and "whites" the two sexes, and further effacing the distinction between consensual sex and rape, is certainly the domain of nightmare. Nevertheless, it happens to also be a story told by a friendly homeless man. While having sex in New York's streets and parks, Delany's conversationally and sexually obliging homeless men cheerfully recount scenes of compulsory homosexual initiation in places far from the city, in rural orphanages, or in an incestuous household in rural Appalachia. Thus, a curious "ghosting" effect is achieved: the book's pornographic scenes set in a *lumpen* New York "present" implode into fables of queer sex in non-urban American places with no name, between poor men and youth of varying racial and ethnic backgrounds, opening into an abyssal perspective upon American history in which sites of forced confinement have a pivotal role (and the line between force or compulsion and enjoyment is disturbingly blurred).

In and around the "pornotroping" nightmare/fantasy where race and sex converge is a very different narrative element: a fabric of observation on the part of the narrator recognizable as "'ethnographic' memoir". In a key sequence, Marr attempts to describe to a fellow graduate student, a recently married young white woman by the name of Sally May (a pun on the federal student loan acronym), the gay worlds he has been experiencing at the city's margins. The letter to Sally May amounts to a treatise on social representation occupying some sixty-five pages of this five-hundred-page novel. In the letter, Marr observes that his efforts to portray the men he has seen and had sex with in the city's public spaces are finally overshadowed by something abstract and terrible. In the margins of midtown, the single-room-occupancy hotels populated by the down and out, he observes that there is something "truly terrifying" that transcends the men's individual lives, which the "bourgeois visitor," in his "reports of this area's violence," tends to "repress all mention and memory of":

> The bourgeois visitor always goes home with reports of this area's violence, but that is to repress all mention and memory of what is truly terrifying here: the vast stasis, the pervasive immobility, the immense periods—hours, days, weeks—when nothing happens, when psychic paralysis reigns in the lives of those stalled here at an intensity people at jobs, people in families just cannot conceive of. (Delany 2002:131)

Interestingly, the narrator also associates what is "truly terrifying here"—the "vast stasis," "pervasive immobility," and "psychic paralysis"—with women, whose poverty and isolation, he notes, are often more hidden from view. "The women conduct us to the truly less comfortable pictures," graduate student John Marr opines in his letter to Sally May. One can understand Delany's sombre novel *Dark Reflections* (2007) as picking up from this point in *The Mad Man*.

Dark Reflections (2007)

Shadowy figures, often women, have long appeared at the sidelines of Delany's *Lumpen* cosmopolitan spaces; in *Dark Reflections*, one takes a more central role. An isolated, celibate, African American gay poet and a suicidal young white homeless woman are strangely paired at the heart of this novel. One could say that it explores more intimately the "vast stasis" or "psychic paralysis" glimpsed from the outside by the narrator of *The Mad Man*. In the process, it excavates a less familiar history of the aftermath of the 1960s, from the perspective of figures who seem to be marginal to liberatory trajectories.[52]

Dark Reflections can be understood as a darker, obverse reflection of Delany's luminous memoir *The Motion of Light on Water*, reinforcing the same core theme: that the full scope and history of the social terrain we occupy remain for the most part undisclosed. At the outset of the novel, sometime in the mid-1990s, we learn that Arnold Hawley (as the poet is named), aged sixty-eight, occupies the same Lower East Side rental into which he moved four decades ago; that he possesses a phone but no television; and that he is more isolated, as a result of the loss of friends who have died of AIDS. *Dark Reflections* is structured as a kind of reverse *Bildungsroman*, un-building the circumstances of the poet's precarious present to earlier formative moments, extending back to the middle of the twentieth century. Along the way it maps fragments of a less familiar American history, composed of networks of unrecognized bonds: linked, idiosyncratic lives that accord little with the group identities in terms of which that history is conventionally narrated.

The challenges facing the black creative artist living in America from the 1950s through the present constitute one important thread of the novel's narrative. *Dark Reflections* is honeycombed with Arnold Hawley's own encyclopaedic knowledge of less known literary history, such as Wallace Stevens' query, "Who let the coon in?" at the 1950 Pulitzer Prize banquet at which Gwendolyn Brooks won the award for poetry (Delany 2007:295). A prestigious but little known literary prize that Arnold wins, after decades of writing poetry, is shown to make an appreciable difference in his ability to pursue his art—not least because the small financial award enables him to subsist more comfortably on a part-time adjunct faculty position, a year after having quit a cubicle job with the city government. Meanwhile, his relation to his increasingly corporatized publisher is jeopardized when a supportive, think-outside-the-box editor—a young African American woman—is fired. Years down the road, still writing poetry and working as an adjunct with no benefits, Arnold fears homelessness as his retirement age approaches. Thus, the novel demonstrates some of the hazards for African American writers negotiating a still largely white literary and publishing world, as well as the critical importance of institutions supporting independent artists—an endangered breed in the post-1970s climate of funding cuts, a conservative movement turning arts grants by the National Endowment for the Arts into political fodder, and eroded environments for autonomous cultural production.

A self-taught intellectual with a vast range of aesthetic interests (including, late in life, a fascination with country western singers), Arnold Hawley is an iconoclast who has mostly chosen not to affiliate with the communities he might be part of—black, literary, or gay. The linkages he does form are not restricted in any straightforward way to those with whom he shares a common identity. It almost seems as if the price Arnold Hawley has paid for his intellectual and aesthetic autonomy, and deeply cosmopolitan ethos, is a life of isolation and profound personal compromise. But for all his idiosyncrasy, Arnold Hawley is perhaps best read not as exceptional, but rather as exemplary of the difficult position of the "black creative intellectual" (Spillers 2003:449) in an era of "paradigm shift," in which the old rhetorics of redemptive community seem somehow outmoded (Spillers 2003:449).[53]

The central section of the novel recounts the brief bond that arises sometime in the 1970s, between the poet when he is in his mid-thirties, and a grimy, barefooted young woman he meets in the park outside his Lower East Side apartment building. When Arnold Hawley asks where she lives, she responds: "I don't live nowhere" (Delany 2007:122). From this first chance meeting, a companionship ensues that ends in an abrupt and terrifying way: she hangs herself in the poet's bathroom, echoing the suicide of the unnamed woman in the asylum in Delany's autobiography. Perhaps even harder to explain, the two decide to get married within hours of meeting—after Arnold, hearing about the harassment she is subject to by family members regarding her unmarried status—"When ya' gonna get married? When ya' gonna get married?" (Delany 2007:132)—agrees, in a moment of extravagant generosity and camaraderie, to go to City Hall with her and get the paperwork done. It is she who pops the question. He guesses, from her intense quiet as he takes time to consider her outwardly casual question—"*You* ain't interested in gettin' married, are you?"—that probably no one has ever taken anything she actually wanted very seriously. And he also intuits a deeper yearning on her part, with which he identifies—not for an impossible "normalcy", but for a partner in a subversive parody of it. So, he says "Why not?" (Delany 2007:133), buys her a pair of shoes, and they head to City Hall to exchange vows, in a spirit of delirious conspiracy against the codes of a world in which they are relegated to a status outside "real" and valid modes of life: Arnold because he is gay, and the woman because she is homeless, and mentally ill.

That night, after a veal dinner prepared by her—"like real married people" she says with satisfaction, an instance of the awareness of the exclusionary "real" threading its way through her words (Delany 2007:148)—she insists that, since it is after all their wedding night, he should go to the park and get laid. While he, for once, indulges in the sexual carnival on his doorstep, she will, she announces—taking a book of his poems from the shelf—stay indoors for a change and enjoy a quiet night of reading (154). Arnold returns with a hustler he picks up in the park; it is the latter who discovers the young woman hanged in the shower, wrists sliced.

What ensues is a surreal, perverse, comic scene disclosing multiple processes of "misrecognition" at work. And these correct the presumption that, for all the reciprocal intuitions and recognitions that transpire between Arnold and the young woman, such acts at the margins and between marginals are sufficient to overcome systemic patterns of symbolic and structural violence. The hustler who finds the body, it turns out, was a sometime boyfriend of the dead woman and may have made her pregnant. Although it is Hawley who is apprehensive about his own safety in picking up a male prostitute, it is the hustler who is scared out of his wits upon finding the woman's bloody corpse in Arnold's shower—as he imagines he has stumbled into the apartment of a violent sexual predator. Then there is Arnold's dialogue, after discovery of the body, with a 911 operator who persistently calls him "Ma'am": only at the end of the call does Arnold realize that the operator has mistaken him for a woman because his voice has risen octaves above its usual pitch (Delany 2007:177). But the biggest "twist" to the narrative is the extent to which the police who descend on the apartment are entwined and implicated in this net of intimate violence. Several officers, it turns out, are familiar with the hustler, formerly a sometime drug dealer: not only have they dealt with him before, but at least one seems to have made use of his sexual services, though this is betrayed obliquely. Moreover, the suicide note which Arnold does not show the police discloses that the dead young woman was not only pregnant—but also that she may have been raped several months ago in an alley by a plainclothes detective. Because she is "just" a homeless psychiatric case, the police investigation is at best perfunctory. Arnold does not have to try to explain that he and the woman got married earlier in the day, though he does not even know her correct name.

What is disclosed in the woman's note is that she had a suicide pact with another young woman in the asylum, by the name of Kim—an African American woman, also barely twenty years old. Their joint commitment to death is, perversely, the "real" till-death-do-us-part contract, not the sham marriage in the court of law. The suicide note also discloses that she had vowed to marry before killing herself in order to prove to her psychiatrist in the asylum that she *could* get married—after the latter expressed the view that such an intention for the likes of her was "unrealistic" (Delany 2007:198). Finally, the note refers to a chain of female suicide in her family. An aunt just survived a third suicide attempt, and two sisters have already "done it." Indeed, her first stint in the asylum followed the death of one of the sisters: it was only then that she realized she "had to do it, too, and there wasn't any getting out of it" (Delany 2007:200).

Almost in a parody of notions of diversity, this multiracial female community of suicide, extending across traditional institutions of female confinement such as the household and the asylum, is the apparent obverse of the ethnically heterogeneous public and semi-public scenes of male sexual exchange so prominent in Delany's fiction. This glimpse of a world of death-bound female subalternity, which renders just about anyone still interested in living on the side of comparative normalcy, leaves Arnold with an uneasy feeling of complicity with the police and the male hustler crowding his apartment, for all their differences in social positioning. In its resistance to categorization or explanation, the episode with the homeless woman foregrounds questions central to Delany's work regarding the representation of marginalized experience. This can be said more precisely: in a terrifying flash, the suicide and its aftermath disclose the way symbolic violence and structures of power are conjoined. Arnold Hawley embroiders around the week's events, but does not describe them in a way that make them intelligible, in the book of poetry which he calls *Pretenses* (obliquely alluding to the sham marriage)— and which his publisher prefers to title *Dark Reflections*. Arnold's poetic response is thus implicitly juxtaposed with the more detailed account of event and consciousness provided by the form of the novel itself. As Delany handles the genre here, the *Bildungsroman*, or fictional narrative of individual formation, is a close cousin to the "'ethnographic' memoir" in its mode of witnessing. By contrast, Arnold's poems, described as "abstract and tasked constructions" (Delany 2007:201), render his experience opaque, covering over the track of possible social insight.

Judging from his own insightful criticism of the work of more hermetic writers, including early twentieth-century gay American poet Hart Crane,[54] Delany is by no means setting forth Arnold Hawley as a negative literary example who "should" be working in more directly referential forms of representation. But without question, Delany is making a didactic point here. In his autobiography, Delany refers to the fragmented, oblique forms of representation of gay existence available during the 1950s and early 1960s, which made apprehension of gay experience as a world, and as part of the larger world, virtually impossible. Above all, these representations were coy—as Arnold's poems apparently are (the poems are never actually displayed for our inspection). In his autobiography, Delany writes: "Only the coyest and the most indirect articulations could occasionally indicate the boundaries of a phenomenon whose centers could not be spoken or written of, even figuratively" (Delany 1988:268).

The episode with the homeless woman registers as such a dead centre, a kind of black hole or gravitational core of the book, potentially shifting how we read everything around it: namely, the life narrative of the poet, which occupies most of the novel's nearly three hundred pages. Foremost in this narrative is the problem of Arnold Hawley's consciousness, and how it has been constituted in such a way that his own representational choices collude in his self-thwarting.[55]

Sexuality, Symbolic Violence, and State Violence

Both novels by Delany that I have examined here, but particularly *Dark Reflections*, show at "capillary" level the role of symbolic violence in the reproduction of class structure in the United States. The police, the court system, and psychiatric and correctional institutions are shown to have extraordinary power over the lives of the poor. Indeed, the novel shows a society in which, across a period of decades, state and institutional forms of violence, far from diminishing, have if anything intensified for those at the social and economic margins. Yet Delany's emphasis is not on these more overt, spectacular forms of violence, but the micro-level of interpersonal relations, and processes of self-formation and self-destruction. In Bourdieu's conception of class, as summarized by Loïc Wacquant (2008:1):

> the stuff of social reality, and thus the basis for heterogeneity and inequality, consists of relations. Not individuals or groups, which crowd our mundane horizon, but webs of material and symbolic ties constitute the proper object of social analysis. These relations exist under two major forms: first, reified as sets of objective positions that persons occupy (institutions or "fields") and which externally constrain perception and action; and, second, deposited inside individual bodies in the form of mental schemata (whose layered articulation compose the "habitus") through which we internally experience and actively construct the lived world.

The novel *Dark Reflections* explores the installation of certain habituating schemata into poet Arnold Hawley's body and mind across a lifetime—a psycho-biographical account of a peculiarly immobilized man that amounts to a full-scale exposition of Bourdieu's concept of *habitus*. The child told by the kindly white doctor in the early 1950s that there are no black homosexuals, so he need not worry about becoming one, becomes the man who thinks along the following lines:

> [H]e was still unsure of what there was to be proud, in gay life. It was like celebrating the loosest and most lascivious behavior among black folk as the core of civil rights. It seemed some wholly and absurd internal contradiction that, if anyone really exposed it, would reveal all progress to be a sham and topple the entire liberatory project. (2007:285)

As a gay black man who came of age during the 1950s and 1960s, Arnold Hawley painfully inhabits the "wholly... absurd internal contradiction" between racial and sexual group politics. Arnold's lifelong repudiation of his own sexuality, and of any liberatory project involving sex, somehow has to do with a perceived schism between sexuality and rights: or, put more specifically, with a perceived incompatibility between civil rights and the liberatory project of a gay pride founded in the embrace of sexuality.[56] The passage suggests that part of Arnold's "problem" is his allegiance to an idea of the strivings of "black folk" that somehow entails repudiating anything that might have the taint of carnality, associated in "underclass" discourse with both blackness and the lower classes.[57]

The episode clinches the link between sexual, symbolic and structural violence in ways that the rest of the novel reiterates; this, indeed, can be understood as the central theme, even obsession, of the novel. And in Delany's writing, the violence of a system of representation enforcing social and sexual norms is shown to also relate to economic forms of marginalization. The novel shows the way in which the symbolic order, which leads Arnold to misrecognize these social encounters, is backed by institutions of power and punishment; and how, tragically, Arnold reinforces the symbolic violence from which he suffers, by his own writing. Yet it is in recognizing such systemic misrecognition—and the process of its reproduction, through the shaping of minds—that the possibility of political engagement lies. In this way, the novel is concerned with the domain, not of politics, but of its conditions of possibility. One might say that Delany is concerned with a politics anterior to what is recognized as politics as such—or the condition of possibility of agency, prior to anything like activism. This is writing which describes, documents, above all the relation between consciousness and environment; it is attuned to what is not yet recognized as knowledge as such.

Delany's novels *The Mad Man* and *Dark Reflections* are an effort to tell a swath of American social history from such a perspective, rather than in terms of the usual groups and identities. For all that Arnold Hawley may seem to be a peripheral figure, the narrative persistently points toward others who are *more* peripheral (such as the suicidal black young woman in the asylum), whose thoughts and experience and speech can only be guessed at, as the narrative captures only the faintest trace of their existence. None of these figures fit any stock imagery of poverty in the United States. Delany's portrayal of precarious urban American life thus points centrifugally, to the trace of singular and heterogeneous others, rather than to some core or essence of "culture."

History is also rewritten in Delany's work as a social web: in terms of bonds and mutual care-taking between outcasts, including unconventional interracial pairs, knit together by complex links and threads of encounter, and characterized by efforts to forge refuge from coercive institutions. This complex understanding of social being eschews simplistic division between subjective experience and "objective" social analysis, rendering the ethnographic project, far from having a set methodology, a task ever to be constructed. By foregrounding celibate African American subjects and interracial queer subcultures, Delany delineates fragments of socially and economically liminal existence that the glare of a hyperracialized and sexualized discourse about the poor erases from view. Finally, Delany's novels can be understood as showing some of the continuities between the "new regime of urban poverty" (Wacquant 2009:116)—associated with the neoliberal revolution and the end of the semi-welfare state—and earlier forms of marginalization, including the virulent discrimination against African Americans and gay people at mid-century. Wacquant states that he calls this new condition of insecurity "advanced marginality" because "it lies ahead of us: it is inscribed in the future of advanced societies subjected to the strains of capitalist deregulation" (Wacquant 2009:112). Delany's mapping of social transformation of the urban poor from the 1970s to the present anticipates some of the paradoxes of this condition, sketching its longer emergence in an American context.

Concluding Remarks

Samuel Delany and other African American writers foregrounding complex, gendered processes of individual formation provide a critical perspective on intertwined structural and discursive processes reproducing class division in the United States. Dominant trends in ethnography can be criticized for engaging overly head-on with hyper-racialized, hypersexualized "underclass" discourse—and not obliquely enough to portray the splintering of its effects across myriad contexts and subjectivities, within and outside the ghetto. Though not transpiring in the space of the black ghetto, the marginal life trajectories limned in *The Mad Man* and *Dark Reflections* can be understood as shadowed by "underclass" discourse—while reminding us that the shadows of such a normative moral economy refract far beyond their intended targets.

In closing, we might recollect Delany's address at Rutgers, in which he reminds academics of the role of scholarly discourse in reinforcing an incomplete understanding of the complexities of American social reality. "Underclass" discourse has a particular configuration and history within the United States, but also a floating, migratory power as a result of the global reach of the American pundits and academics who deploy it. Pierre Bourdieu and Loïc Wacquant have described "underclass" rhetoric as part of a "new planetary common sense" (Bourdieu and Wacquant 1999:47) or "neoliberal 'newspeak'" (Wacquant 2005:7) that, albeit formed within a specific American context, increasingly circulates widely outside the United States, superimposed on widely differing social realities. Thus, the lingo and perspective of a particular educated, mobile stratum of American society—academics, journalists, policymakers—now has the power to describe—and misrepresent—social inequalities across the globe:

> The terms, themes, and tropes of this emerging planetary lingua franca—"multiculturalism", "globalization", "fragmentation", "race", "underclass", "identity," and so on—tend to project and impose on all societies the concerns and viewpoints of the United States intelligentsia, thereby transfigured into tools of analysis and yardsticks for policy fit for naturalizing the peculiar historical experience of one peculiar society, tacitly instituted as a model for all of humankind. (Wacquant 2005:7)

Wacquant calls this "a particularly pernicious form of cultural imperialism" that renders us unable "to make out the limitations and possibilities of contemporary politics" (Wacquant 2005:7). And indeed, following riots in the UK in August 2011, a BBC news article titled "The Return of the Underclass" suggests that "underclass" discourse is far from dead. Instead, it assumes new forms, as it is applied to new contexts.

In concluding, I wish to emphasize the value of Delany's mode of "'ethnographic' memoir" in generating epistemic reflexivity with regard to the usual categories and concepts of social analysis. Delany's critique of US academic rhetoric as part of a systemic obfuscation of lived American social realities ties to Loïc Wacquant's reminder that American academe plays a role in cultural imperialism, as many of its concepts and presumptions, taken as universally applicable rather than originating in specific American historical and institutional configurations, are used to decode social terrains outside the United States. Reading Delany, I suggest, is relevant not just to understanding specific stigmatized American subcultures in more complex ways, but to grasping a wider implied critique of the more far-ranging effects of discursive violence.

References

Als, Hilton. 1996. *The Women*. New York: Farrar, Straus, & Giroux.

Bourdieu, Pierre. 2010. "The protest movement of the unemployed, a social miracle." In *Sociology is A Martial Art: Political Writings by Pierre Bourdieu*, translated by Priscilla Parkhurst Ferguson, Richard Nice, and Loïc Wacquant, edited by Gisèle Sapiro, 155-157. New York: The New Press.

Bourdieu, Pierre, and Loïc Wacquant. 1999. "On the cunning of imperialist reason." *Theory, Culture & Society* 16(1):41-58.

Chauncey, George. 2004. *Why Marriage? The History Shaping Today's Debate over Gay Equality*. Cambridge, MA: Basic Books.

Coetzee, J. M. 2003. *Elizabeth Costello: Eight Lessons*. London: Secker & Warburg.

Delany, Samuel R. 1988. *The Motion of Light in Water: Sex and Science Fiction Writing in the East Village, 1957-1965*. New York: Arbor House/W. Morrow.

———. 1996a. "Aversion/Perversion/Diversion." In *Longer Views: Extended Essays*, 119-143. Hanover, NH: Wesleyan University Press.

———. 1996b. "Atlantis Rose… some notes on Hart Crane." In *Longer Views: Extended Essays*, 174-250. Hanover, NH: Wesleyan University Press.

———. 1999a. *Times Square Red, Times Square Blue*. New York: New York University Press.

———. 1999b. *Shorter Views: Queer Thoughts & the Politics of the Paraliterary*. Hanover, NH: University Press of New England.

———. 2002. *The Mad Man*, 2nd ed. Ramsey, NJ: Voyant Publishing.

———. 2007. *Dark Reflections*. New York: Carroll & Graf Publishers.

Gilroy, Paul. 1993. *The Black Atlantic: Modernity and Double Consciousness*. London: Verso.

Hennessy, Rosemary. 2000. *Profit and Pleasure: Sexual Identities in Late Capitalism*. New York: Routledge.

Jones, Jacqueline. 1992. *The Dispossessed: America's Underclasses from the Civil War to the Present*. New York: Basic Books.

———. 1998. *American Work: Four Centuries of Black and White Labor*. New York: Norton.

Kelley, Robin D. G. 1997. *Yo' Mama's Disfunktional! Fighting the Culture Wars in Urban America*. Boston: Beacon Press.

Kusmer, Kenneth L. 1996. "African Americans in the city since World War II: From the industrial to the postindustrial era." In *The New African American Urban History*, edited by K. Goings and R. Mohl, 320-368. London: Sage.

Massey, Douglas, and Nancy Denton. 1993. *American Apartheid: Segregation and the Making of the Underclass*. Cambridge: Harvard University Press.

Melville, Herman. 1922. *John Marr and Other Poems*. Ithaca: Cornell University Library Press.

Merrifield, Andy. 2002. *Dialectical Urbanism: Social Struggles in the Capitalist City*. New York: Monthly Review Press.

Mosley, Walter. 2006. *Life Out of Context: Which Includes a Proposal for the Non-Violent Takeover of the House of Representatives*. New York: Nation Books.

Povinelli, Elizabeth. 2006. *The Empire of Love: Toward a Theory of Intimacy, Genealogy, and Carnality*. Durham: Duke University Press.

Rimke, Heidi. 2010. "Consuming fears: Neoliberal in/securities, cannibalization, and psychopolitics." In *Racism and Borders: Representation, Repression, Resistance*, edited by Jeff Shantz, 95-112. New York: Algora Publishing.

Spillers, Hortense J. 2003. *Black, White, and In Color: Essays on American Literature and Culture*. Chicago: University of Chicago Press.

Stoler, Ann Laura. 2002. *Carnal Knowledge and Imperial Power: Race and the Intimate in Colonial Rule*. Berkeley: University of California Press.

Timm, Annette F., and Joshua A. Sanborn. 2007. *Gender, Sex and the Shaping of Modern Europe: A History from the French Revolution to the Present Day*. Oxford: Berg.

Wacquant, Loïc. 2002. "Scrutinizing the street: Poverty, morality, and the pitfalls of urban ethnography." *American Journal of Sociology* 107(6):1468-1532.

———. 2004. "Decivilizing and demonizing: The social and symbolic remaking of the black ghetto and Elias in the 'dark ghetto.'" In *The Sociology of Norbert Elias*, edited by Steven Loyal and Stephen Quilley, 95-121. Cambridge: Cambridge University Press.

———. 2005. "Introduction: Symbolic power and democratic practice" In *Pierre Bourdieu and Democratic Politics: The Mystery of Ministry*, 1-9. Cambridge: Polity Press.

———. 2008. "On symbolic power and group-making: Pierre Bourdieu's reframing of class." Foreword to Pierre Bourdieu, *Et klassespørsmål*, Oslo : Forlaget Manifest.

———. 2009. "The body, the ghetto, and the penal state." *Qualitative Sociology* 32(1):101-129.

Welshman, John. 2007. *Underclass: A History of the Excluded, 1880-2000*. London: Hambledon Continuum.

West, Cornel. 1999. "Black strivings in a twilight civilization." In *The Cornel West Reader*, 87-118. New York: Basic Civitas Books.

Williams, Raymond. 2005. "Literature and sociology: In memory of Lucien Goldmann." In *Culture and Materialism: Selected Essays*, 11-30. London: Verso.

PART II
CONTESTED REPRESENTATIONS

Chapter 6
Indigeneity and the City
Representations, Resistance, and the Right to the City

Julie Tomiak

Contemporary Settlers follow the mandate provided for them by their imperial forefathers' colonial legacy, not by attempting to eradicate the physical signs of Indigenous peoples as human bodies, but by trying to eradicate their existence as peoples through the erasure of the histories and geographies that provide the foundation for Indigenous cultural identities and sense of self. (Alfred and Corntassel 2005:597-598)

The unrelenting project of erasing Indigenous[58] histories and geographies in relation to urban space, including Indigenous scales of governance, and the concomitant discursive marginalization of Indigenous peoples through the antithetical construction of Indigeneity and the city are the focus of this chapter. More specifically, this chapter explores how scholars have contributed to discourses that have marginalized Indigenous peoples, sovereignty, and nationhood by writing them out of urban spaces. The brief review of the literature presented here illustrates that these representations of Indigeneity as non-urban have been pervasive across a range of academic projects.

The analysis contained in this chapter forms part of a larger project that seeks to demonstrate how discursive and material strategies have been mutually reinforcing in recreating a racialized, colonial social order which aggressively erases and displaces Indigenous sovereignty, rights, and title through the neoliberal settler city. As such, my research aims to contribute to the decolonization of theory and praxis. It positions popular and academic discourse as among a range of interrelated technologies of power, including the law, private property, state policies, and population management, through which the settler city is re/produced. Attention to its central role in dispossessing and marginalizing Indigenous peoples brings the city into view as a linchpin of colonialism—and a crucial site of decolonization.

Discourse is here understood as relatively stable, yet mutable, sets of ideas, beliefs, and practices that co-constitute subjectivities and relations of power and inform the actions of the subjects it constructs. As Hall (1992:291) notes, "discourse is about the production of knowledge through language. But it is itself produced by a practice: 'discursive practice'—the practice of producing meaning. Since all social practices entail meaning, all practices have a discursive aspect." The historically and geographically specific production of meaning and ways of knowing are thus intricately connected to ways of governing and strategies of domination and resistance—and are constituted in and through the materiality of social relations. Discursive and material processes are thus seen as mutually constitutive insofar as the colonial imaginary of the settler city legitimates and is reinforced by the dispossession and displacement of Indigenous peoples.

Indeed, the construction of Indigenous and urban as mutually exclusive has been central to the production of city-space in what is now Canada and continues to structure dominant notions of where Indigenous peoples belong

(Peters 1996; Razack 2002a; Lawrence 2004; Proulx 2006; Borrows 2008). Despite historical trajectories and contemporary realities of cities as Indigenous places, this dichotomy has remained persistent (Wilson and Peters 2005:399), even in light of the fact that, according to the 2006 Census, 54 percent of Indigenous peoples in what is now Canada live in urban areas (Statistics Canada 2008).[59] In this chapter, I show that the socio-spatial order which marginalizes Indigenous peoples from city-life is premised on the settler fantasy of *terra nullius*[60] which requires the denial of the Indigenous past and presence, given that they invariably threaten to expose the self-serving fiction of white settler space (Razack 2009; Jacobs 1996; Shaw 2007).

Although it might be less difficult (or unsettling) to identify these processes as taking place in the historical past, it is important to note that this is an ongoing project carried out through narratives of erasure, active displacement, and the juridico-political containment of Indigenous nations and communities. These intertwined discourses and politico-administrative strategies have rendered Canadian cities seemingly exempt not only from Indigenous and treaty rights, but also Indigenous place-making more generally (on the imaginary of marginalized spaces see Wilson and Anderson, as well as Gönen and Yonucu, this volume). However, as this chapter seeks to illustrate, the geographies, including the imaginary and material, of urban spaces are highly contested. In addition to unmapping dominant representations, my aim is to highlight various forms of Indigenous resistance to this marginalization from and in urban space. Drawing on data from Ottawa and Winnipeg, I show how Indigenous peoples are seeking to destabilize the settler city by asserting symbolic space, reclaiming physical space, and carving out political space. Furthermore, I argue that the alternative histories and geographies on which these assertions of space are based open up possibilities for envisioning new urban and extra-urban politics and solidarities, along the lines of Lefebvre's (1996) notion of the right to the city.

Unmapping as a Decolonizing Methodology

The production of knowledge, under the guise of universal truth claims, about Indigenous peoples has been central to colonial projects and state strategies of control and coercion (Smith 1999; Henderson 2000). Academic knowledges, in particular, have re/produced deeply Eurocentric ontologies and epistemologies to the exclusion of Indigenous knowledges and in the service of multiple systems of domination (Smith 1999). Indeed, for Indigenous peoples, "the term 'research' is inextricably linked to European imperialism and colonialism" (Smith 1999:1), as scholars have constructed Indigenous peoples invariably in contradistinction and as inferior to Europeans (Hall 1992). The racialization of Indigenous peoples and their framing as inferior was a central structuring principle through which the colonial matrix of domination has operated in Canada. Coinciding with the formation of these racialized knowledges are classifications of space and spatialized representations aimed at asserting and controlling space—and dispossessing Indigenous peoples of their territories. In this sense, the racialized social order of a settler society like Canada is also a spatial order (Razack 2002a; Anderson 1991).

Contrary to mainstream scholarship, anti-colonial and Indigenist research encompasses a broad range of methodologies which share a commitment to producing knowledge that benefits Indigenous peoples and destabilizes colonial knowledge/ power regimes. As Rigney (1999:116) points out, "resistance is the emancipatory imperative in Indigenist research." Research within this philosophy of decolonization privileges Indigenous perspectives and stresses relationality and context (Smith 1999; Rigney 1999; Wilson 2007). This also entails a different spatial conceptualization of social relations and the transcendence of settler state mappings and boundaries (Forbes 1998).

By unmapping the transparent space[61] of settler cities and shedding light on Indigenous geographies of resistance, this chapter shows how cities are terrains of struggle over Indigenous access to rights, representation, and urban space itself. Unmapping is a method that seeks to denaturalize spaces by tracing the social construction of space and subjectivities (Razack 2002a:17). As Razack (2002b:128) notes, "to unmap means to historicize". This meshes well with Indigenist research paradigms committed to projects of decolonization and "writing back" within Indigenous historiographies that challenge mainstream accounts which leave out Indigenous peoples or represent them based on Eurocentric assumptions and racist ideologies (Miller 2009). Using the method of unmapping, the next section provides an account of the production of city space through the lens of coloniality.

The Spatial Logic of Coloniality: Re/Producing the Settler City

The concept of coloniality refers to a form of domination that includes the pervasive and invisible epistemic power and privilege of the colonizer.[62] The usefulness of this concept lies in its assertion that even in the alleged post-colonial era, coloniality, as a framework through which power operates, remains a central social, political-economic, and cultural organizing principle (Quijano 2007:171). Constitutive of modernity, the logic of coloniality has been central to the formation of new social classifications along racialized lines, as well as the emergence of capitalism, nationalism, and liberalism. Among its key elements are the appropriation of land, the control of authority, and the control of knowledge (Quijano 2007; Mignolo 2007; Moraña et al. 2008). The re/production of the settler city illustrates the intertwined nature of these elements, as land theft, state repression, and settler understandings have kept Indigenous peoples (in and) out of place and legitimized a property regime that is premised on the dispossession of colonized peoples. For instance, the incommensurability of settler and Indigenous notions of territoriality and ownership necessitated the closely linked fictions of *terra nullius* and Crown sovereignty.

Looking at the neoliberal settler city as a process helps to de-naturalize the work that goes into "settler colonialism's ongoing project of reterritorialization" (Edmonds 2010:246). In Canada, the construction of the settler city as modern required the deterritorialization of Indigenous peoples and their relegation to reserves, or "zones of exclusion" (Thobani 2007:48). This entailed a radical reconfiguration of space through a series of violent processes in the 1800s and early 1900s: the denial of Aboriginal title, the entrenchment of a private property regime from which Indigenous peoples were excluded, and the creation of the reserve system (Blomley 2003, 2004; Harris 2002, 2004; Wilson and Peters 2005). The large-scale remaking of geography and property has required both "historical amnesia" (Blomley 2004:106)—conveniently forgetting that settler cities are on Indigenous territory, often in locations of pre-existing Indigenous settlements (Pitawanakwat 2008:169)—and the removal of Indigenous peoples. As a result of these strategies, Indigenous peoples were deliberately and systematically pushed into the margins of the emerging settler society.[63] These historical practices continue to affect Indigenous peoples in that, as McKittrick points out (2006:95), "historical practices, of vanishing, classifying, objectifying, relocating, and exterminating subaltern communities, and desiring, rationally mapping, and exploiting the land and resources, are ongoing, firmly interlocked with a contemporary colonial agenda, which has material consequences." The material consequences are evident across all social, economic, and health indicators for Indigenous peoples.

The dispossession and displacement of Indigenous peoples have been legitimized by representations that depict Indigeneity as the constitutive outside of the "civilized" space of the settler city (Blomley 2004:119; Barman 2007:5; Razack 2002a; McClintock 1994; Prout and Howitt

2009). Within the logic of coloniality, space and time are activated to construct Indigenous populations in contradistinction to modernity. Mignolo (2007:470-471) traces the way in which, initially, temporal and spatial difference were expressed through the notions of "primitives" and "barbarians", respectively. These figures were later conflated with "the primitive" who is associated with "tradition", both, of course, appearing "as 'objects' outside Europe and outside modernity" (Mignolo 2007:472). The "frontier complex" described by Furniss (1999) or the "pristine myth" identified by Sluyter (1999:379) show how these discourses of dispossession are depicted as "progress", operating along oppositional binaries, such as civilized versus savage, and social versus natural. The expulsion of Indigenous peoples from urban spaces was legitimized through the construction of spatial *and* temporal difference with reserves imagined "as existing in another time frame" (Peters 2001:69).

As Fanon notes (1963:29-30), the division of space is crucial to the colonial project. In the case of project Canada, it was a division into Indigenous and settler space, the reserve and the city, and no property and private property (Blomley 2004). Since colonialism is centrally about "the transfer of land from one people to another" (Harris 1997:xxi; see also Smith and Godlewska 1994:2), space is acutely implicated in the settler project of colonial domination. However, given its inescapably social constitution, space is always contested (Lefebvre 1991). Furthermore, the object of struggle is not solely physical space. Contestations are "also about ideas, about forms, about images and imaginings" (Said 1994:7).[64]

Projected as "new", "modern", "civilized", and "innocent"[65], the settler city enabled settlers to imagine themselves as the original inhabitants. The dominant narrative thus "produces European settlers as the bearers of civilization while simultaneously trapping Aboriginal people in the pre-modern" (Razack 2002a:2). This Euro-Canadian invention of "static Indianness" continues to bolster the territorialization of the settler nation in contemporary discourses in relation to

Indigeneity and the city (Peters 1996; Razack 2002a; Proulx 2006; see also Estreich's discussion of "mythical time", in this volume), as we shall see in the next section.

Inventing "the Indian" was central to the colonial project of disconnecting Indigenous peoples from their land and relegating them to small and scattered reserves. In order to circumscribe Indigeneity in ways that served the purposes of re-settlement, a range of legal processes variably constructed Indigenous subjects as outside the law or as wards of the state, with tightly circumscribed rights restricted to spatio-temporal zones of exclusion (Monture-Angus 1999:30, 52; Thobani 2007). Consolidated in the *Indian Act* of 1876, federal Indian policy was driven by racist and paternalistic notions of Indigenous peoples as in need of being segregated from settler society and thus "protected" from "modern" society, until they could be "civilized" through an aggressive program of assimilation (Peters 2001:58; Tobias 1991). The *Indian Act* created racialized non-citizens on the basis of restrictive and gendered criteria of settler state recognition which, by 1985, had rendered an estimated two thirds of Indigenous peoples in Canada landless (Lawrence 2003:6). How the logic of elimination, which Veracini (2010) identifies as the central dynamic of settler colonialism, figured as a goal of state policies was perhaps most vividly expressed by Duncan Campbell Scott, an influential bureaucrat in the Department of Indian Affairs in the early 1900s, who stated that "our objective is to continue until there is not a single Indian in Canada that has not been absorbed into the body politic, and there is no Indian question, and no Indian Department [...]" (cited in Titley 1986:50). The initial state logic of the reserve system was one of eventual extermination, but, as Thobani (2007:62) points out, "the zones of exclusion mapped out by the sovereign, marking out the actual sites for the extinction of Aboriginal peoples, have been transformed by the resistance of these peoples into the sites of their survival and renewal, into the sites of the reproduction of their socio-cultural practices."

Until the 1940s, the state actively removed Indigenous peoples from settler cities. One of the strategies to accomplish this was the pass system which required First Nation people to secure the permission of the Indian Agent when leaving the reserve (Dickason 2006:357). After the Second World War, there was a shift in the strategies employed by the Department of Indian Affairs to accomplish the persistent goal of policies—the eradication of Indigenous peoples as peoples and as nations—from aggressive assimilation to integration. From the Second World War until 1966, Indian Affairs was a branch of the Department of Citizenship and Immigration, and, as Bohaker and Iacovetta (2009) point out, policies constructed Indigenous peoples as immigrants in need of Canadianization programs. In the 1950s and 1960s, urbanization was widely heralded (e.g. in the Hawthorn report) as a solution to First Nations poverty. The Citizenship branch of the federal government launched its Indian Integration program in the mid-1950s (phased out in the 1970s), appointing placement officers to help with finding employment in cities (Peters 2001). The federal government also began supporting the Friendship Centre movement. Friendship Centres emerged as important urban Indigenous institutions in the 1950s, initially as a referral service. Seen as agents of integration by the federal government (see Lagassé cited in Peters 2001:76), Friendship Centres, however, followed a very different logic based on self-determination and community-building. Bohaker and Iacovetta (2009:448) point out that:

> a long-standing cornerstone of government policy towards status Indians specifically was to encourage relocation from reserve communities to urban centres. Such a policy was attractive for three reasons. First, income earned off-reserve is generally taxable, especially if the employee also lives off-reserve. Second, off-reserve employment was preferable to and easier than encouraging economic development on often

isolated reserves. Third, off-reserve employment increased the likelihood that people would meet and marry non-status people and stay put in urban centres, and thus they (or their children) would no longer be the financial responsibility of the federal government.

The evasion of the state's fiduciary duty has undoubtedly been an important driver of policies with respect to Indigenous peoples. While it is beyond the scope of this paper to provide a further discussion on current policy initiatives, most notably the Urban Aboriginal Strategy, it should be noted that the focus is on the marketization of individuals and the responsibilization of communities, not on the implementation of Indigenous rights, jurisdiction, and treaties.

Narratives of Erasure and Containment

Based on a textual analysis, I sketch how settler discourses have imagined Indigeneity as incompatible with and at a perpetual distance to the city.[66] I demonstrate that this discursive marginalization is recursively linked to the state practices briefly touched upon in the previous section. I argue that the images and discourses that have constructed Indigeneity in contradistinction to the urban continue to structure contemporary realities. That is, settler representations shape expectations of Indigenous authenticity and ways of knowing and seeing Indigenous peoples in relation to the city through a racialized lens of invisibility and hyper-visibility (Proulx 2006). This colonial lens has a significant bearing on the dominant conceptualization of Indigenous and treaty rights, and, to a great extent, determines the material realities of Indigenous individuals and communities.

While the focus here is primarily on the discursive dimensions of how the settler mind has spatialized—or de-spatialized—Indigenous peoples, it is also important to examine "the diverse, on-the-ground workings of colonialism in colonized spaces" (Harris 2004:166), as well as the impacts of the "new regime of urban inequality and marginality" (Wacquant 1999:1640) which disproportionately affects Indigenous peoples. However, given that discursive and material practices are mutually constitutive of contemporary geographies of domination, narratives of erasure are integral to maintaining the colonial order and insulating city-space from Indigenous claims to sovereignty, title, and citizenship.

When Indigenous peoples are not completely written out of the story of cities, they are only briefly mentioned as a relic of the distant past, before the Indigenous presence fades from view around the time of "contact". Historical accounts tend to depict emerging settler cities, such as Winnipeg, as frontier towns, claiming that the historical geography of the city is "young" (Healy 1927:9). In a history of Ottawa published in 1896, the author asserts that "few traces remain of them; Algonquins, Hurons, Senecas have almost disappeared or at least greatly diminished, so that little reliable can be written of them" (Gourlay 1896:3). In a similar vein, *The Ottawa Country: A Historical Guide to the National Capital Region* acknowledges archaeological evidence of Algonquin presence in the region, but goes on to assert that "all these traces, however, were located upwards of a hundred years ago; little or nothing remains of them today" (Bond 1968:13). In this account, members of the Algonquin nation who reside in the region and the fact that Ottawa is on unceded Algonquin territory are erased.

Another facet of this discourse of erasure is the claim that Indigenous peoples "roamed" the land. Intended to disavow the notion of Indigenous title, this explains the assertion that "[t]o the hereditary wanderers the desolate forests were valueless" (Gourlay 1896:4). As noted by Blomley and Pratt (2001:158-9), colonial descriptions of Indigenous territories have consistently drawn on tropes of mobility, emptiness, and transience. However, while the mobility of Indigenous peoples was seen as a legitimate excuse for their expropriation, state policies and practices were simultaneously focused on restricting the movement of Indigenous peoples and keeping them in designated spaces, primarily through the reserve and pass systems (Dickason 2006).[67]

Popular and academic interest in urban Indigenous peoples began to pick up throughout the 1970s (Peters 1998), but, quite ironically, they came to be framed as the "most recent arrivals in Canadian cities" (Nagler 1973:1, 63), transient strangers who are not at home in the city (Brody 1971; Dosman 1972; Krotz 1980). A number of Indigenous persons, primarily First Nations, migrated to cities from reserve communities and homelands in the 1950s and 1960s. However, other Indigenous peoples and entire communities became urban by virtue of being engulfed by expanding cities. These Indigenous peoples can hardly be dismissed as "newcomers".

In asserting that "[…] the city involves a milieu for which he [sic] is not qualified. The city is the very Heart of the industrial ethic, and the location for the kind of employment for which the Indian feels in every way unqualified" (Brody 1971:27), writers have constructed the city as "modern" and "industrial" in contradistinction to Indigenous peoples who are depicted as "in every way unqualified". Due in part to essentialist settler notions of Indigeneity as incompatible with and at a perpetual distance to "civilization", "progress", and "modern life" with which city-life is generally associated, Indigenous people living in Canadian cities also came to be framed as a problem (Peters 1996, 1998).

Representing Indigenous peoples as a threat to the city, a recurring theme equates Indigenous peoples with existing or imminent ghettoization. Disregarding the structural forces that have marginalized Indigenous peoples, the Indigenous presence itself often came to be linked to the deterioration of inner cities (Peters 1998:250). For instance, in 1972, Dosman claimed that "the Indians' move to the city is a case history of an urban slum-in-making"

(1972:10; see also Nagler 1973:20). And Brody warns that "the swollen Indian skid row populations will be in danger of developing into squalid urban ghettos" (1971:4). More recently, Cairns attests to the "depressing reality of ghetto conditions [...] especially in several of the major cities in the prairie provinces" (Cairns and Flanagan 2001:111). While socio-spatial stratification along racialized and classed lines has produced spaces of marginality to which many Indigenous people in cities across Canada have been relegated (Peters 2005; Cardinal 2006; Cardinal and Adin 2005), Indigenous people are not homogeneously disadvantaged (Wotherspoon 2003). In addition, as Groves points out (1999:29-30), "[t]he social disadvantages and marginalization facing many Aboriginal people in urban areas is not, of course, unique to urban areas or uniquely caused by urbanity," but must be seen in the context of the historical and ongoing processes of dispossession and domination. Furthermore, while residential patterns of Indigenous peoples in cities vary across Canada, Indigenous residents, overall "may be more evenly distributed overall than some other ethnic groups" (Maxim, Keane, and White 2003:88). That is, residential concentration is, generally, low to moderate (see also Graham and Peters 2002:13).

The lens of poverty through which Indigenous peoples tend to be viewed often results in selective visibility. To illustrate, in 1971, Brody wrote that "one *sees* very few Indians in the city outside skid row" (1971:4, emphasis in original). It seems that Indigenous people who live in parts of the city other than the most marginalized areas and who do not conform to settler expectations of an Indigenous lumpenproletariat were simply overlooked. In this sense, a highly classed and racialized settler perception, to a large extent, determines who can be seen as Indigenous. An Indigenous resident of Toronto explains that "[t]he drunken Indian is ten feet tall, but a sober one is invisible. No one notices all the ones that they pass, that are on their way to work, on their way home, on their way to committees, whatever. No one notices those ones, but everybody notices the one that is drunk on the street" (Proulx 2006:414). This binary is further illustrated by Dosman's observation that Indigenous peoples have always been present in Saskatoon. Yet, he qualifies this by saying that the "Metis families [who] had taken up residence in the city early in its century-old history […] had long lost a consciousness of, and pride in, native ancestry" (Dosman 1972:4). In fact, as noted by Proulx (2003, 2006) and Lawrence (2004), disavowals of "authentic" Indigeneity have been a constant in the literature on urban Indigeneity.

In addition, tensions appear to exist between (earlier) assertions of an Indigenous inability to assimilate and the (more recent) claim that assimilation is an unavoidable effect of urban life (see RCAP 1996:519; Andersen and Denis 2003). Cairns reinforces this notion by stating that "[w]e agree that the Aboriginal future is within Canada, for both Aboriginal peoples living in cities and those living in organized communities" (Cairns and Flanagan 2001:111). According to this logic, Indigenous peoples living in cities do not form organized communities. Instead, they are conceptualized as atomized individuals, who are easily, if not already, assimilated (Flanagan 2000; Cairns and Flanagan 2001).

Thus, Indigenous people who reside in cities have been erased by persistent settler claims that they are not "real" (Lawrence 2004; Proulx 2006:413). This is a form of displacement which has made it possible to avoid engagement with urban Indigenous communities and people as citizens of Indigenous nations with inherent rights to self-determination, land, resources, and sovereignty. Community is certainly a more complex reality in urban settings because of the dispersed and diverse nature of local Indigenous populations (Lobo 2001; Proulx 2003, 2006), but assertions, such as in a 2001 report, that "there really is no such thing as an urban Aboriginal community" (Hanselmann 2001:20) are misguided. Together with state practices, these discourses of erasure and containment have marginalized Indigenous peoples from the benefits of city-life by confining them to constructions of degenerate space (Razack 2002b)—as well as from the benefits of inherent Indigenous and Treaty rights.

Indigenous Geographies of Resistance: "It's Like We're Coming Home"

> For a colonized people the most essential value, because the most concrete, is first and foremost the land: the land which will bring them bread and, above all, dignity. (Fanon 1963:34)

Indigenous peoples have always transgressed the boundaries imposed by the settler state and "engaged in a virtually constant micropolitics of resistance" (Harris 2004:179-180) to what Shaw describes, drawing on data from Australia, as the racialized "entitlement to urban space that has built on a history of actively excluding indigenous peoples" (2007:175). This has included forms of resistance that have sought "to occupy, deploy, and create alternative spatialities from those defined through oppression and exploitation" (Pile 1997:3). Indigenous resistance can be found in a wide range of practices, discourses, initiatives, movements, and organizations. While the focus in this chapter is on counter-discourses and institution-building, important movements have formed that connect the struggles of Indigenous peoples at and across multiple scales. Many urban First Nation, Métis, and Inuit who have moved to cities continue to be politically active and engaged in their home communities. Most importantly, many Indigenous peoples have continued to live in or moved, and, in some instances, returned to cities (Lawrence 2004; Harris 2002; Anderson and Jacobs 1997:19), and have reclaimed cities as Indigenous places (Borrows 2002; Peters 2006; Tsawwassen First Nation 2007).

This section looks at Indigenous re-territorialization and place-making and illustrates how Indigenous peoples are asserting the right to the city in Ottawa and Winnipeg, in the sense of a transformative agenda that hinges on "the freedom to make and remake our cities and ourselves" (Harvey 2008:23). The examples I draw on to explicate alternative accounts of Indigeneity and the city are informed by interviews with 31 key informants in Ottawa and Winnipeg.[68] Reflecting the primary research interest to examine changes in urban Indigenous governance under neoliberalism(s), interview participants were selected based on their professional roles in Aboriginal service agencies, community organizations, political advocacy bodies, and First Nation, federal, provincial, and municipal governments.

What emerged very clearly from these interviews is that contemporary struggles over access to Indigenous rights and the right to the city are not only about geography, but also fundamentally about different versions of history. In fact, these struggles are simultaneously about space, time, scale, boundaries, property regimes, and the meanings that are inscribed in them. That is, they are not confined to the urban; they are multi-scalar and, to some extent, confound the physical and representational boundaries of the city. In effect, it comes down to competing versions of what kind of city and whose city it is, as highlighted in the following excerpt from an interview with a community leader in Ottawa:

> The irony is that [...] major cities, towns, villages in this country were urban areas for Aboriginal peoples for thousands of years. I mean Ottawa, this was a major trading intersection, because of the rivers. And Toronto, Montreal, Winnipeg, all the major cities, they were all urban areas that, you know, *it's like we're coming home*. And we just don't have a tendency to necessarily think that way, but again, they were our urban areas, and they still are. (Interview, October 3, 2008)

In a similar way, a Métis leader asserts the continuity of Métis urbanness by drawing attention to the historical geographies of cities in Ontario:

> I think for many people when they hear the term urban Aboriginal, what's implied by virtue of what they know about First Nations is people have now moved into urban settings and they're transient [...]. Whereas for Métis it's different, it doesn't reflect us [...]. So if you look at the make up of Sault Saint Marie as an example which plays itself out many times across Ontario and Canada, very often you see communities that currently exist established on these Métis communities. Those original people, their descendants are still there. And so again in the case of Sault Saint Marie that historical community existed there, and the contemporary community continues to exist today and people in the contemporary community have a direct connection to the historic community. So the conflict of an urban community, the way the language is used doesn't recognize those historical communities and the towns and cities that Ontario now has are, in fact, in many cases historic Métis communities that grew up around them. (Interview, October 29, 2008)

This emerging counter-discourse re-asserts cities as Indigenous places by collapsing the false binary between Indigeneity and the urban. Contesting the urban/ rural divide plays an important role here, as illustrated in the following quote by a representative of a national Aboriginal organization in Ottawa:

> I think there's this growing sense of an urban identity. I'm from Ottawa. I think there's this myth that Aboriginal people come from reserves and Métis settlements and Inuit homelands to cities

and that's how we come here. That's how we have, but, at the same time, there's multiple generational people being born urban [...]. You see this urban identity emerge which is new and distinct I think. You know, I hate to put too much emphasis on it right now, because I don't think it would stand tremendous scrutiny, but I think it's a trend and we're seeing it across the country. (Interview, October 23, 2008)

Arguably, the most powerful way in which Indigenous peoples are reclaiming cities is through the reclamation of land and place-making projects. By bringing territoriality into the equation, Indigenous nations in Canada have problematized entrenched settler notions of cities as inherently non-Indigenous spaces. In the remainder of this section, I discuss the Algonquin land claim which covers Ottawa and the Aboriginal Centre of Winnipeg as important examples of reclaiming physical and institutional space in cities.

The Algonquin land claim encompasses an area of 36,000 square kilometres on the Ontario side of the Ottawa River (Ontario Ministry of Aboriginal Affairs n.d.). The Algonquin have persistently asserted that they never surrendered their territory by treaty, sale, or conquest. Petitions to remove settlers from their lands and to have Aboriginal title recognized date back to at least 1772 (Steckley and Cummins 2007; Richardson 1993).[69] As a result of litigation, the federal government created a process through which First Nations can reclaim land. The Algonquin of Pikwàkanagàn presented their claim to title to the Government of Canada in 1983 and to the Government of Ontario in 1985. In 1991 and 1992 the Algonquin land claim was formally accepted as a comprehensive claim by the provincial and federal governments, respectively.[70]

In 2008, the Algonquin of Ontario released an Economic Development Plan outlining the goals related to the successful implementation of a land claim settlement agreement. The plan stated that one of the criteria with respect to the selection of lands is "to ensure the survival of the Algonquins by providing high profile and historically meaningful locations for the establishment of 'signature' projects that will support and enhance the rejuvenation of Algonquin history and culture" (Tanakiwin n.d.). Ottawa will be an important location for these place-making projects. As an interviewee points out:

> There are hopes that there would be some recognition of Algonquins in the Ottawa area and we have met with Ottawa City Council members and staff and there have been some discussions around the recognition of Algonquins and some role, maybe an employment centre, within the Ottawa area. […]. There should be something in Ottawa for the members. There was some plan of a centre, not just a Friendship Centre, but something like a service centre. There's little I can say at this point, but I'm sure there should be and there will something in Ottawa […]. We are going to negotiate some properties for housing, economic development, for people in the Ottawa area. (Interview, January 6, 2009)

Although the comprehensive claims process is highly contested, because it is entirely on settler state terms and inevitably results in surrender of Aboriginal title (Lawrence 2009),[71] a settlement of the Algonquin land claim could potentially entail a reclamation of Ottawa, albeit partial, in physical, symbolic, and political terms.

Another important aspect of Indigenous place-making in cities is the creation of institutional spaces. The Aboriginal Centre of Winnipeg represents such a collective effort to re-assert urban space. It grew out the philosophy of the Neeginan project, which was an unsuccessful proposal to create an Aboriginal village and service centre in Winnipeg in 1970 (Bileski 2006). In December 1992, the Aboriginal Centre of Winnipeg Incorporated (ACWI) purchased the

CP Station based on the premise that "all ACWI member organizations needed proper space to deliver their services effectively and efficiently" (Bileski 2006:1). After the restoration process was completed in 1998, the Aboriginal Centre became home to a range of community organizations and service providers. One of the rationales for the Centre was to increase inter-agency collaboration and to pool scarce resources (interview, May 15, 2008). As an interview participant explains:

> The role of the Aboriginal Centre, again, was, like I said, to provide space and training, really space. But the Aboriginal Centre has really become more than that, than just a building. It's kind of a focal point in the city. I mean you hear a lot… a taxi driver will tell that someone will come off the reserve and say I want to go to the Centre, to the Aboriginal Centre […]. I think that we're a good example of an Aboriginal organization that was able to pull together enough resources to buy something for themselves that makes them independent. (Interview, May 15, 2008)

The Aboriginal Centre has transformed the North Main Street/ Higgins Street area and has given the Aboriginal community in Winnipeg a flagship place-making project which is expanding and linking up with other projects in the area. For instance, the proposed addition of housing units adjacent to the Centre will add to the benefits for the local community. In combination with the headquarters of the Manitoba Métis Federation (MMF) and Thunderbird House, a cultural centre, across from the Aboriginal Centre, it has created a strong Aboriginal presence in downtown Winnipeg. And, for the Aboriginal organizations housed in the Centre, it has created a self-determined space.

Conclusion: The Right to the City

In addition to Indigenous discourses which have stressed the right to self-determination as an inherent right, the notion of the right to the city offers a normative framework for urban-focused activist research that captures the demands and aspirations of Indigenous peoples on their own terms, as well as in a broader context of social struggle. In Henri Lefebvre's words, "[t]he *right to the city* cannot be conceived of as a simple visiting right or as a return to traditional cities. It can only be formulated as a transformed and renewed *right to urban life*" (Lefebvre 1996:158, emphasis in original). Lefebvre conceptualized the right to city as "a cry and a demand" for social justice, entailing not only the appropriation of existing, but also the re-structuring and re-creation of social, political, and physical spaces by marginalized populations (Gilbert and Dikeç 2008). For Lefebvre, social justice requires *autogestion*, or collective self-management, a notion that resonates with Indigenous struggles for self-determination.

Indigenous collectivities have asserted the right to the city in various ways, often extending beyond city limits and effectively contesting the territorialization and scales imposed by the state. Thus, Indigenous resistance to an array of social formations produced by colonialism, capitalism, and neoliberalization underscores, as Purcell suggests (2002:103), that the right to the city, in practice, translates into a "multi-facetted politics of scale." This is particularly relevant given that this "call for a radical restructuring of social, political, and economic relations" (Purcell 2002:101) is not restricted to the territorial boundaries of the city, but, in an increasingly urban world, encompasses the right to reorganize and shape the social system of production, more generally (Lefebvre 1996; Dikeç and Gilbert 2002:65). Given the centrality of cities in capitalist systems of accumulation, the right to the city is essentially aimed at structural changes concerning the ways in which cities are re/produced (Harvey 2008), including their racialized foundations.

Similar to Indigenous rights, the right to the city also transcends the individualistic, liberal trajectory of juridical rights (Mayer 2009:367; Marcuse 2009:192-193).[72] And whereas, in mainstream discourses, the right to city is often framed as, above all, a vehicle for inclusion (Mayer 2009; see Brown and Kristiansen 2008), it must be conceptualized in tandem with the right to difference, as Lefebvre (1996:34) stressed (see also Dikeç and Gilbert 2002:71; Gilbert and Dikeç 2008). With respect to Indigenous peoples, difference forms the basis of efforts to decolonize social relations and spatial structures and to remake the real and imagined geographies of what is now Canada.

Cities have been vital to the colonial project in Canada, as they were predicated upon the displacement and dispossession of Indigenous peoples, and have functioned as the nerve centres and primary beneficiaries of the colonial-capitalist system of accumulation by dispossession (Gordon 2006, 2010; Harvey 2003). In settler states, the right to fully participate in the life of the city and to shape its future continues to be constructed as an inherently non-Indigenous prerogative. Given that historical and ongoing processes of colonization have marginalized Indigenous individuals and collectivities, it is important to think about the right to the city in relation to Indigenous sovereignty and to, thereby, reframe Canadian cities as crucial sites of decolonization. In order to de-link what are, in fact, polysemic and highly contested urban spaces from the logic of coloniality, the suppressed histories and geographies of Indigenous peoples are integral to disrupting settler myths and colonial domination and connecting struggles for freedom, land, and life. In this way, struggles to substantiate Indigenous rights, including the right to the city, not only represent profound contestations of city spaces across Canada, but also challenge the very idea of the settler city itself.

References

Alfred, Taiaiake. 1999. *Peace, Power, Righteousness: An Indigenous Manifesto*. Don Mills: Oxford University Press.

———. 2005. *Wasàse: Indigenous Pathways of Action and Freedom*. Peterborough: Broadview Press.

Alfred, Taiaiake, and Jeff Corntassel. 2005. "Being Indigenous: Resurgences against contemporary colonialism." *Government and Opposition* 40(4):597-614.

Andersen, Chris, and Claude Denis. 2003. "Urban natives and the nation: Before and after the Royal Commission on Aboriginal Peoples." *Canadian Review of Sociology and Anthropology* 40(4):373-390.

Anderson, Kay. 1991. *Vancouver's Chinatown. Racial Discourse in Canada, 1875-1980*. Montreal: McGill-Queen's University Press.

Anderson, Kay, and Jane M. Jacobs. 1997. "From urban Aborigines to Aboriginality and the city: One path through the history of Australian cultural geography." *Australian Geographical Studies* 35(1):12-22.

Asch, Michael, and Norman Zlotkin. 1997. "Affirming Aboriginal title: A new basis for comprehensive claims negotiations." In *Aboriginal and Treaty Rights in Canada: Essays on Law, Equity and Respect for Difference*, edited by Michael Asch, 208-229. Vancouver: UBC Press.

Barman, Jean. 2007. "Erasing Indigenous Indigeneity in Vancouver." *BC Studies* 155:3-30.

Bileski, Bern. 2006. *The Aboriginal Centre of Winnipeg: Impact Analysis*. Winnipeg: Aboriginal Centre of Winnipeg.

Blomley, Nicholas. 2003. "Law, property, and the geography of violence: The frontier, the survey, and the grid." *Annals of the Association of American Geographers* 93(1):121-141.

———. 2004. *Unsettling the City. Urban Land and the Politics of Property*. New York: Routledge.

Blomley, Nicholas, and Geraldine Pratt. 2001. "Canada and the political geographies of rights." *The Canadian Geographer / Le Geographe canadien* 45(1):151-166.

Blunt, Allison, and Gillian Rose. 1994. "Introduction: Women's colonial and postcolonial geographies." In *Writing Women and Space. Colonial and Postcolonial Geographies*, edited by Allison Blunt and Gillian Rose, 1-25. New York: Guilford Press.

Bohaker, Heidi, and Franca Iacovetta. 2009. "Making Aboriginal people 'immigrants too': A comparison of citizenship programs for newcomers and Indigenous peoples in post-war Canada, 1940s-1960s." *Canadian Historical Review* 90(3):427-462.

Bond, Courtney C. J. 1968. *The Ottawa Country. A Historical Guide to the National Capital Region*. Ottawa: Minister of Public Works.

Borrows, John. 2002. "'Landed' citizenship: An Indigenous declaration of interdependence." In *Recovering Canada. The Resurgence of Indigenous Law*, 138-158. Toronto: University of Toronto Press.

———. 2008. *Seven Generations, Seven Teachings: Ending the Indian Act*. Research Paper prepared for the National Centre for First Nations Governance. West Vancouver: National Centre for First Nations Governance.

Brody, Hugh. 1971. *Indians on Skid Row. The Role of Alcohol and Community in the Adaptive Process of Indian Migrants*. Ottawa: Minister of Indian Affairs and Northern Development.

Brown, Alison, and Annali Kristiansen. 2008. *Urban Policies and the Right to the City. Rights, Responsibilities and Citizenship*. New York: UNESCO.

Cairns, Alan, and Tom Flanagan. 2001. "An exchange." *Inroads* 10:101-122.

Cardinal, Nathan. 2006. "The exclusive city: Identifying, measuring, and drawing attention to Aboriginal and Indigenous experiences in an urban context." *Cities* 23(3):217-228.

Cardinal, Nathan, and Emilie Adin. 2005. *An Urban Aboriginal Life: The 2005 Indicators Report on the Quality of Life of Aboriginal People Living in the Greater Vancouver Region*. Vancouver: Centre for Native Policy and Research.

Dickason, Olive Patricia. 2006. *A Concise History of Canada's First Nations*. Oxford: Oxford University Press.

Dikeç, Mustafa, and Liette Gilbert. 2002. "Right to the city: Homage or a new societal ethics?" *Capitalism Nature Socialism* 13(2):58-74.

Dosman, Edgar. 1972. *Indians: The Urban Dilemma*. Toronto: McClelland and Stewart.

Edmonds, Penelope. 2010. *Urbanizing Frontiers: Indigenous Peoples and Settlers in 19th Century Pacific Rim Cities*. Vancouver: UBC Press.

Escobar, Arturo. 2007. "Worlds and knowledges otherwise. The Latin American modernity/ coloniality research program." *Cultural Studies* 21(2):179-210.

Fanon, Frantz. 1963. *The Wretched of the Earth*. Harmondsworth: Penguin Books.

Fernandes, Edésio. 2007. "Constructing the 'right to the city' in Brazil." *Social and Legal Studies* 16(2):201–19.

Flanagan, Tom. 2000. *First Nations? Second Thoughts*. Montreal: McGill-Queen's University Press.

Forbes, Jack D. 1998. "Intellectual self-determination and sovereignty: Implications for Native Studies and for Native intellectuals." *Wicazo Sa Review* 13(1):11-23.

Furniss, Elizatbeth. 1999. *The Burden of History. Colonialism and the Frontier Myth in a Rural Canadian Community*. Vancouver: UBC Press.

Gehl, Lynn. 2005. "'Oh Canada! Your home is native land': The Algonquin land claim process." *Atlantis* 29(2):1-4.

Gilbert, Liette, and Mustafa Dikeç. 2008. "Right to the city: Politics of citizenship." In *Space, Difference, Everyday Life. Reading Henri Lefebvre*, edited by Kanishka Goonewardena, Stefan Kipfer, Richard Milgrom, Christian Schmid, 250-263. New York: Routledge.

Gordon, Todd. 2006. "Canada, Empire, and Indigenous peoples in the Americas." *Socialist Studies* 2(1):47-75.

———. 2010. *Imperialist Canada*. Winnipeg: Arbeiter Ring Publishing.

Gourlay, J. L. 1896. *History of the Ottawa Valley. A Collection of Facts, Events and Reminiscences For Over Half a Century*. Ottawa: s. n.

Graham, Katherine, and Evelyn Peters. 2002. *Aboriginal Communities and Urban Sustainability*. Ottawa: Canadian Policy Research Networks.

Groves, Robert. 1999. *Urban Aboriginal Governance in Canada: Re-fashioning the Dialogue*. Ottawa: National Association of Friendship Centres.

Hall, Stuart. 1992. "The West and the rest: Discourse and power." In *Formations of Modernity*, edited by Stuart Hall and Bram Gieben, 275-331. Cambridge: Open University/Polity Press.

Hanselmann, Calvin. 2001. *Urban Aboriginal People in Western Canada: Realities and Policies*. Calgary: Canada West Foundation.

Harris, Cole. 1997. *The Resettlement of British Columbia*. Vancouver: UBC Press.

———. 2002. *Making Native Space. Colonialism, Resistance, and Reserves in British Columbia*. Vancouver: UBC Press.

———. 2004. "How did colonialism dispossess? Comments from an edge of Empire." *Annals of the Association of American Geographers* 94(1):165–182.

Harvey, David. 2003. *The New Imperialism*. Oxford: Oxford University Press.

———. 2008. "The right to the city." *New Left Review* 53:23-40.

Healy, W. J. 1927. *Winnipeg's Early Days*. Winnipeg: Stovel Company.

Henderson, James Sákéj Youngblood. 2000. "Post-colonial ghost dancing: Diagnosing European colonialism." In *Reclaiming Indigenous Voice and Vision*, edited by Marie Battiste, 57-76. Vancouver: UBC Press.

Hessel, Peter. 1993. *The Algonkin Nation. The Algonkins of the Ottawa Valley: An Historical Outline*. Arnprior: Kichesippi

Books.

Huitema, Marijke. 2000. *"Land of Which the Savages Stood In No Particular Need": Dispossessing the Algonquins of South-Eastern Ontario of Their Lands, 1760-1930*. MA Thesis. Kingston: Department of Geography/ Queen's University.

Jacobs, Jane M. 1996. *Edge of Empire: Postcolonialism and the City*. London: Routledge.

King, Anthony. 1990. *Urbanism, Colonialism, and the World-Economy. Cultural and Spatial Foundations of the World Urban System*. London: Routledge.

Krotz, Larry. 1980. *Urban Indians. The Strangers in Canada's Cities*. Edmonton: Hurtig Publishers.

Lawrence, Bonita. 2003. "Gender, race, and the regulation of Native identity in Canada and the United States: An overview." *Hypatia* 18(2):3-31.

Lawrence, Bonita. 2004. *Real Indians and Others: Mixed-Blood Urban Native Peoples and Indigenous Nationhood*. Lincoln: University of Nebraska Press.

———. 2009. "Fractured homeland: Federal recognition, land and Algonquin identity in Ontario." Lecture at Carleton University, March 13.

Lefebvre, Henri. (1974) 1991. *The Production of Space*. Oxford/ Cambridge: Blackwell.

———. 1996. *Writings on Cities*, Translated and edited by Eleonore Kofman and Elizabeth Lebas. Cambridge: Blackwell Publishers.

Lobo, Susan. 2001. "Is urban a person or a place? Characteristics of Urban Indian Country." In *American Indians and the Urban Experience* edited by Susan Lobo and Kurt Peters, 73-85. New York: Altamira Press.

Marcuse, Peter. 2009. "From critical urban theory to the right to the city." *City* 13(2):185-197.

Mawani, Renisa. 2005. "Genealogies of the land: Aboriginality, law, and territory in Vancouver's Stanley Park." *Social & Legal Studies* 14(3):315-339.

Maxim, Paul S., Carl Keane, and Jerry White. 2003. "Urban residential patterns of Aboriginal people in Canada." In *Not Strangers in These Parts: Urban Aboriginal Peoples*, edited by David Newhouse and Evelyn Peters, 79-91. Ottawa: Policy Research Initiative.

Mayer, Margit. 2009. "The 'right to the city' in the context of shifting mottos of urban social movements." *City* 13(2-3):362-374.

McClintock, Anne. 1994. *Imperial Leather: Race, Gender and Sexuality in the Colonial Context*. New York: Routledge.

McKittrick, Katherine. 2006. *Demonic Grounds. Black Women and the Cartographies of Struggle*. Minneapolis: University of Minnesota.

Mignolo, Walter. 2007. "Delinking: The rhetoric of modernity, the logic of coloniality, and the grammar of de-coloniality." *Cultural Studies* 21(2):449-514.

Miller, Susan A. 2009. "Native historians write back: The Indigenous paradigm in American Indian historiography." *Wicazo Sa Review* 24(1):25-45.

Monture-Angus, Patricia. 1999. *Journeying Forward: Dreaming First Nations Independence*. Halifax: Fernwood.

Moraña, Mabel, Enrique Dussel, and Carlos A. Jáuregui, eds. 2008. *Coloniality at Large: Latin America and the Postcolonial Debate*. Durham: Duke University Press.

Nagler, Mark. 1973. *Indians in the City. A Study of Urbanization of Indians in Toronto*. Ottawa: Saint Paul University.

Ontario Ministry of Aboriginal Affairs. n.d. "Algonquin Land Claim". Accessed July 16, 2009. http://www.aboriginalaffairs.gov.on.ca/english/negotiate/algonquin/algonquin.asp.

Peters, Evelyn. 1996. "'Urban' and 'Aboriginal': An impossible contradiction?" In *City Lives and City Forms: Critical Research and Canadian Urbanism*, edited by Jon Caulfield and Linda Peake, 47-62. Toronto: University of Toronto Press.

———. 1998. "Aboriginal people in urban areas." In *Visions of the Heart: Canadian Aboriginal Issues (Second Edition)*, edited by David Long and Olive Patricia Dickason, 237-270. Scarborough: Thomson/Nelson.

———. 2001. "Developing federal policy for First Nations people in urban areas: 1945-1975." *The Canadian Journal of Native Studies* 21(1):57-96.

———. 2005. "Geographies of urban Aboriginal people in Canada: Implications for Urban self-government." In *Canada: The State of the Federation 2003. Reconfiguring Aboriginal-State Relations*, edited by Michael Murphy, 39-76. Montreal: McGill-Queen's University Press.

———. 2006. "'[W]e do not lose our treaty rights outside the... reserve': Challenging the scales of social service provision for First Nations women in Canadian cities." *GeoJournal* 65:315-327.

Pile, Steve. 1997. "Introduction: Opposition, political identities, and spaces of resistance." In *Geographies of Resistance*, edited by Steve Pile and Michael Keith, 1-32. London: Routledge.

Pitawanakwat, Brock. 2008. "Bimaadzwin Oodenaang: A pathway to urban nishnaabe resurgence." In *Lighting the Eighth Fire. The Liberation, Resurgence and Protection of Indigenous Nations*, edited by Leanne Simpson, 161-173. Winnipeg: Arbeiter Ring Publishing.

Proulx, Craig. 2003. *Reclaiming Aboriginal Justice, Identity, and Community*. Saskatoon: Purich Publishing.

———. 2006. "Aboriginal identification in North American cities." *The Canadian Journal of Native Studies* 26(2):405-438.

Prout, Sarah, and Richard Howitt. 2009. "Frontier imaginings and subversive Indigenous spatialities." *Journal of Rural Studies* 25:396-403.

Purcell, Mark. 2002. "Excavating Lefebvre: The right to the city and its urban politics of the inhabitant." *GeoJournal* 58:99-108.

Quijano, Aníbal. 2007. "Coloniality and modernity/ rationality." *Cultural Studies* 21(2): 168-178.

Razack, Sherene, ed. 2002a. "Introduction: When place becomes race." In *Race, Space, and the Law. Unmapping a White Settler Society*, 1-20. Toronto: Between the Lines.

———, ed. 2002b. "Gendered racial violence and spatialized justice: The murder of Pamela George." In *Race, Space, and the Law. Unmapping a White Settler Society*, 121-156. Toronto: Between the Lines.

———. 2009. "Death worlds where bad things happen: Contemporary settler violence against Aboriginal peoples." Lecture presented to Canadian Association for Commonwealth Literature and Language Studies (CACLALS), May 25.

Richardson, Boyce. 1993. *People of Terra Nullius. Betrayal and Rebirth in Aboriginal Canada*. Vancouver: Douglas and McIntyre.

Rigney, Lester-Irabinna. 1999. "Internationalization of an Indigenous anticolonial cultural critique of research methodologies: A guide to Indigenist research methodology and its principles." *Wicazo Sa Review* 14(2):109-121.

Said, Edward. 1994. *Culture and Imperialism*. New York: Knopf.

Shaw, Wendy. 2007. *Cities of Whiteness*. Malden: Blackwell Publishing.

Sluyter, Andrew. 1999. "The making of the myth in postcolonial development: Material-conceptual landscape transformation in sixteenth-century Veracruz." *Annals of the Association of American Geographers* 89(3):377-401.

Smith, Linda Tuhiwai. 1999. *Decolonizing Methodologies. Research and Indigenous Peoples*. London: Zed Books.

Smith, Neil, and Anna Godlewska. 1994. "Introduction: Critical geographies of Empire." In *Geography and Empire,* edited by Anna Godlewska and Neil Smith, 1-8. Oxford: Blackwell.

Statistics Canada. 2008. *Aboriginal Peoples in Canada in 2006: Inuit, Métis and First Nations, 2006 Census* (Catalogue no. 97-558-XIE). Ottawa: Statistics Canada.

Steckley, John, and Bryan Cummins. 2007. *Full Circle. Canada's First Nations*. Toronto: Pearson Prentice Hall.

Tanakiwin—Algonquin Nation. n.d. "Economic development plan." Accessed April 4, 2009. http://www.tanakiwin.com/treaty_economic.htm.

Thobani, Sunera. 2007. *Exalted Subjects. Studies in the Making of Race and Nation in Canada*. Toronto: University of Toronto Press.

Titley, Brian E. 1986. *A Narrow Vision: Duncan Campbell Scott and the Administration of Indian Affairs in Canada.* Vancouver: UBC Press.

Tobias, John L. 1991. "Protection, civilization, assimilation: An outline history of Canada's Indian policy." In *Sweet Promises. A Reader on Indian-White Relations in Canada*, edited by J. R. Miller, 127-144. Toronto: University of Toronto Press.

Tsawwassen First Nation. 2007. "Making History. Tsawwassen First Nation. First Urban Treaty in Modern-Day British Columbia." Accessed September 5, 2011. http://www.tsawwassenfirstnation.com.

Veracini, Lorenzo. 2010. *Settler Colonialism: A Theoretical Overview*. Basingstoke: Palgrave Macmillan.

Wacquant, Loïc. 1999. "Urban marginality in the coming millennium." *Urban Studies* 36(10):1639-1647.

Wilson, Kathi, and Evelyn Peters. 2005. "'You can make a place for it': Remapping urban First Nations places of identity." *Environment and Planning D: Society and Space* 23:395-413.

Wilson, Shawn. 2007. "Guest editorial: What is an Indigenist research paradigm?" *Canadian Journal of Native Education* 30(2):193-195.

Wotherspoon, Terry. 2003. "Prospects for a new middle class among urban Aboriginal people." In *Not Strangers in These Parts: Urban Aboriginal Peoples*, edited by David Newhouse and Evelyn Peters, 147-165. Ottawa: Policy Research Initiative.

Chapter 7
Palestinian Refugees and Citizens
Trajectories of Group Solidarity and Politics

Silvia Pasquetti

Political economy analysis is not a panacea to compensate for individualistic, racist, or otherwise judgmental interpretations of social marginalization. In fact, a focus on structures often obscures the fact that humans are active agents of their own history, rather than passive victims. Ethnographic method allows the "pawns" of larger structural forces to emerge as real human beings who shape their own futures. Nevertheless, I often caught myself falling back on a rigidly structuralist perspective in order to avoid the painful details of how real people hurt themselves and their loved ones in their struggle for survival in daily life.

(Philippe Bourgois, *In Search of Respect,* 1996:17)

For a Comparative Ethnography of Social Marginalization

Students of social marginalization[73] face the dilemma of studying the structural forces that produce and manage marginalized populations or exploring the subjective and experiential dimensions of social marginalization. Both approaches run the risk of reproducing the marginalizing practices that they study. A focus on the (political, economic, and discursive) structures of marginalization can reduce human beings to "pawns" or passive victims if it neglects their specific adaptations to and contestations of their state. A focus on the daily experiences of marginalization can reinforce already existing negative stereotypes about destitute populations. Battling negative stereotypes in public opinion, scholars might also try to sanitize their data, which in turn would preclude a better understanding of how individuals and collectivities negotiate social marginalization.

However, structural reductionism, "voyeuristic" representations, or sanitized accounts of marginalized people are not inescapable outcomes; those who study social marginalization can avoid these pitfalls by analytically focusing on the linkages between structures and experiences of marginalization. Ethnography, moreover, is a mode of inquiry particularly apt for shedding light on how seemingly abstract forces work at the ground level and how marginalized people experience and act upon these forces.[74] Ethnographers have highlighted both the nexus between structural violence and intimate experiences of suffering under various conditions of marginalization (Scheper-Hughes 1992; Bourgois 1996; Bourgois and Schonberg 2009; Bourdieu 1999; Wacquant 2004, 2008; Allen 2008; Auyero and Swistun 2009; Perlman 2010; see Estreich, in this volume, on the difficulty of representing marginalized experiences) as well as the forms of politics that marginalized people pursue under different structural constraints (Bayat 1997; Auyero 2001; Gutmann 2002; Arias 2006).

In this chapter, I draw attention to comparative ethnography as a methodology that can shed light on how structures and experiences of social marginalization co-vary across place: how distinct regimes of social control shape subjective experiences of marginalization, impact interpersonal relations, and influence social organization among dispossessed populations.[75] Comparative ethnography is a methodology well-suited to interrogate, rather than reproduce, the distinct logics and effects of marginalizing institutional policies and to debunk assumptions about the "natural proclivity" of marginalized populations for specific, often harmful, behaviours.

This chapter draws on a comparative study of two Palestinian populations across the Green Line[76]: refugee camp dwellers in the West Bank (residents of Jalazon camp) and urban minorities inside Israel (residents of the Mahatta district in Lod).[77] These two populations have similar cultural, religious, and ethnonational characteristics; indeed, their members are all Muslim Palestinians. Furthermore, the occupational structures of Jalazon and the Mahatta district in Lod—as those of the broader Palestinian populations in the West Bank and in Israel—have been historically affected by the Israeli state's regime of restrictions over Palestinians' mobility and policies of control over the land, which have usually had priority over the economic exploitation of Palestinian workers. Thus, many camp dwellers, who in the 1970s and the 1980 worked as day labourers in Israel's construction industry, have lost their jobs due to the Israeli policies of "closure" which since the 1990s have introduced a system of permits for West Bank Palestinians working in Israel. Thus, the release and denial of work permits have become political tools for the management of Palestinian lives. At the same time, since the 1990s, the Israeli state has stepped up the construction of Jewish settlements in the West Bank and has redirected part of the Palestinian labour force, especially from refugee camps to construction jobs in the settlements (Farsakh 2002, 2005). The vulnerability of refugees to the

Israeli policies of land and population management has also led to high levels of unemployment.[78] Alternatives to the Israeli low-skill employment market are unsteady service and construction jobs in the weak Palestinian economy of the West Bank, as well as temporary jobs inside the camps, financed by international donors in periods of Israeli policies of curfews and "closures" (Hass 2002).

For urban residents of the Mahatta district, their Israeli citizenship is a legal layer that protects them from the mobility restrictions that are imposed on West Bank Palestinians. Yet, the state's "security" discourse against Palestinian citizens, who are seen primarily as a "security threat" because of their ethnonational identity, as well as the state's active role in maintaining spatial segregation between Palestinian and Jewish citizens of the state and in directing resources towards all-Jewish towns and cities, have greatly limited the employment opportunities of Palestinian citizens. For example, Palestinian citizens are exempt from serving in the Israeli military on the basis of their ethnonational membership; this exemption bars them from a wide variety of jobs, which, even when unrelated to the military apparatus, require military experience. In general, Palestinian citizens are under-represented among professionals, academics, and public employees (Adalah 2011).[79] Living in under-serviced segregated districts with overcrowded and neglected schools, residents of the Mahatta district are mainly employed as unskilled waged workers in Lod or in the nearby city of Tel Aviv's low-wage service industry. They have also sought alternative sources of income in the informal and illegal economies.

Despite these similarities between refugees and "minority" citizens in terms of cultural and ethnonational characteristics, as well as in terms of their fluctuation inside and outside the Israeli low-skill employment market (a fluctuation which is particularly erratic for the refugees), my research shows that, due to being submitted to distinct regimes of sociolegal control, they differ strikingly in terms of their internal solidarity and political practices. Specifically, I highlight how refugee camp dwellers display a strong degree of social cohesion, which facilitates collective forms of politics. In contrast, in the urban district, internal fragmentation and mutual distrust push residents to exhaust all their political energy into defensive and individualistic strategies of exit without mounting a collective reaction against the institutional sources of their marginalization.

Two caveats are in order. First, this chapter gives glimpses into how institutional policies work at the ground level in the camp and the city; a thorough demonstration of the link between the two regimes of sociolegal control and the practices on the ground that they generate is beyond its scope. I include here a simplified account of my argument about the distinct logics of the two regimes in order to emphasize that the differences between the camp and the district cannot be explained in terms of the individual characteristics of the two populations but, rather, in terms of larger institutional forces. In my broader study, I demonstrate that the camp and the urban district are managed by two different regimes of sociolegal control, both of which contain elements of coercion, though each is driven by a different logic: intermittent military repression by the Israeli army within an institutional context mainly informed by humanitarian practices and discourses in the refugee camp versus the continuous intrusion of the Israeli police and security agencies in all realms of life in the urban district and a dominant discourse of criminalization of Palestinians in Lod. I argue that the military arrests by the Israeli army and the humanitarian approach promoted by the United Nations Relief and Work Agency (UNRWA)[80] generate a strong social cohesion among camp dwellers who perceive themselves as victims of military repression entitled to humanitarian support. This strong social cohesion supports mechanisms of conciliation and prevention of infighting inside the camp, collective pride in the camp, and collective forms of politics. By contrast, the continuous intrusions of both Israeli police and security agencies in the lives of the urban residents produce social fragmentation and mutual distrust among residents. The extensive use of police informers to gather information not only on specific criminal activities, but on a broad range of peoples and local initiatives, weakens the internal cohesion among residents while strengthening strategies of individual exit that are at times detrimental to other residents.[81]

Thus, while both Palestinian refugees and citizens are perceived as "security threats" by the Israeli state, there are different state coercive logics at work in the camp and in the urban district. Furthermore, in the case of Palestinian refugee camps, refugees have recognized the threat of pacification via humanitarian aid and have succeeded in transforming the UNRWA from a tool used by international (especially Western) states to depoliticize the roots of their dispossession to an institutional arena, in which they have articulated and defended their demands for political recognition (Al-Husseini 2000:53-54; Peteet 2005:64-65).[82]

The second caveat is that, far from standing in a political vacuum, the practices of resistance and survival pursued by Palestinian refugees of Jalazon and citizens of Lod belong to a broader range of forms of politics among different segments of Palestinians under Israeli rule. These forms of politics range from popular uprisings among Gaza and West Bank Palestinians to mass demonstrations and legal mobilization for cultural and national autonomy among Palestinian citizens of Israel. Specifically, in the period between 1987 and 1993, Gaza and West Bank Palestinians started a popular uprising (*Intifada*, "shaking off") against the Israeli military rule, which had been imposed on them in 1967 after the Israeli occupation of the West Bank, the Gaza Strip, and East Jerusalem (Lustick 1980; Hiltermann 1985, 1991; Lockman and Beinin 1989; Nassar and Heacock 1990).[83] As a response to the uprising, the Israeli army relocated outside the main urban centres of the Occupied Territories. Furthermore, an entity of self-rule (the PA, Palestinian Authority) was given limited powers in small and territorially non-contiguous areas of the Occupied

Territories. However, despite the presence of the PA, the Israeli authorities have continued to dictate the everyday lives of Palestinians from movement to marriage practices, to changes in place of residence, to access to land (Zureik 2001). The establishment of Israeli military checkpoints on many West Bank roads and the construction of by-pass roads to connect Israeli settlements to the Israeli territory have intensified this process of territorial fragmentation. In October 2000, Gaza and West Bank Palestinians started a new uprising (the Second Intifada). Unlike the first uprising, this uprising quickly lost its popular nature and was militarized (Johnson and Kuttab 2001; Hammami and Tamari 2001). However, forms of popular protests against Israeli military rule have continued to the present. Thus, for example, at least for five years now, West Bank villagers have been engaged in a sustained campaign of weekly demonstrations against the ongoing construction of a fortification system including fences and concrete walls, which has further restricted their movement and their access to cultivated land (Weizman 2007).[84]

As for Palestinian citizens of Israel, they have protested their marginalization with different tools, from the mass protests against land confiscation in the 1970s to the current court-based mobilization against state discrimination, promoted by a new generation of educated Palestinians (Rouhana 1989; Yiftachel 1996; Payes 2005; Rekhess 2007; Haklai 2009). In October 2000, Palestinian citizens mounted mass demonstrations in solidarity with Gaza and West Bank Palestinians.[85] Israeli security and police forces repressed these protests with the use of live ammunition resulting in the killing of thirteen unarmed protestors. The deadly repression of these protests has deepened Palestinian citizens' estrangement from the Israeli state (Bishara 2001; Rouhana and Sultany 2003; Blecher 2005; Peled 2005; Rabinowitz and Abu-Baker 2005; Pappé 2011).

Thus, while this chapter focuses on forms of politics at the local level in the camp and in the urban district, it is important to emphasize that camp dwellers of Jalazon connect their struggles for UNRWA services to the broader political struggle in the West Bank and consider their group solidarity as a fundamental ingredient of this struggle. By contrast, urban residents of Lod remain at the margins of the political organizing efforts among Palestinian citizens of Israel, especially those efforts centred on a direct engagement with the Israeli courts and civil society.

The data presented here illustrate the importance of long-term immersion amidst marginalized populations in order to observe patterns of behaviour and see the social world through their eyes. This is particularly important for investigating both the potential for and the limits of collective action within different contexts of marginalization. My ethnographic immersion in the lives of refugees and urban residents took strikingly different forms, which in itself reveals the distinct structural logics of their respective predicament of marginalization. Building on Venkatesh's argument (2002:91) that "reconstructing the informants' point of view can aid the researcher in determining patterns or structure and meaning," I briefly discuss how refugees and urban residents perceived my presence and my research initiative.

In their everyday lives, camp dwellers encounter a broad range of international and local "humanitarian" actors (UNRWA personnel, NGOs staff, foreign volunteers, and foreign delegations of politicians, journalists, architects, and lawyers). In this setting, my explicit intention of living in the camp for at least eight months and, then, my constant presence in the camp, pushed camp dwellers to categorize me in an ad-hoc role vis-à-vis other "information-seekers." Although I was a foreigner like most visitors of the camp, camp dwellers routinely asked me to be present at their formal and informal meetings with other foreigners. They presented me as "a student from Italy who speaks Arabic and lives with us." The routine performance for foreign visitors at the camp included a short presentation about my life in the camp. This became an occasion for me to "give back" to those who were helping me and to show my gratitude to them. Camp dwellers also actively sought my help to write grants for several cultural centres inside the camp, to encourage foreign delegations to support some of the camp institutions, and to photographically document various cultural and social activities inside the camp and write reports to foreign donors and supporters. Additionally, from the very first week of fieldwork, some camp dwellers were already teaching me the ABCs of ethnographic fieldwork. A couple of students in social work approached me to discuss my techniques of participant observation and then regularly scrutinized (and critiqued) my fieldwork. In light of the energy that many camp dwellers invested in assuring "the success" of my presence and project in the camp, I consider my ethnographic fieldwork a collaborative project. The widespread perception among refugees that my fieldwork was a shared project is the main reason why I was allowed to join and record the weekly meetings of the camp popular committee (a non-elected, interfactional administrative body inside the camp).

Unlike in the camp, where most "information-seekers" fall within the category of humanitarian aid workers, in the urban district the dominant typology is tied to repressive local and state agencies. Within the Palestinian population of the city, there was a mostly homogenous reaction to my presence among them: a mixture of curiosity for an unknown category (the foreign researcher) and suspicion as to my possible connection with the Israeli security agencies. My thick Italian accent, my connections with reputable people in the West Bank, and my Italian passport all made this second option quite unlikely in their eyes. Yet, while my role as police informer was quite implausible, residents never felt totally relaxed around me. A young man clearly explained his distrustful attitude towards me:

> If every day you are served hot tea, you get used to blowing the cup of hot tea before drinking it... So you can't possibly be from the *Shabak*[86] but to my lips you are hot tea no matter what.

Many residents also saw me as a disturbed young woman possibly in search of drugs or a local boyfriend. But this scenario was quickly belied by my banal routine and conservative behaviour. The category of "researcher" gradually became the prism through which residents related to me, though they remained puzzled by my interest in their current lives rather than historical events (for example, the 1948 Arab-Israeli war). Internalized racism and stigma circulated among the residents who often expressed their frustration at my study of everyday life in the district: "What do you want? There are only Arabs here" or "We had a history, now we have the cocaine." Along similar lines, they regularly scheduled interviews on my behalf with "the elderly" who could tell me about Arab history and traditions. Unlike camp dwellers, most residents voiced concerns and doubts about my research on the urban district, which they perceived as an unworthy, stigmatized location of neglect and danger.

The ethnographic dissection of the effects of institutional practices at the ground level generates insight into the specific logic of these practices while at the same time highlighting how marginalized people perceive and experience their distinct predicament. This is equally true when the effects under investigation deal with the capacity for collective action (or lack thereof). Far from denying the political agency of urban residents, this chapter documents how Palestinians living in the urban district find it difficult to act collectively as a social group and thus spend much of their political energy in the pursuit of defensive, individualistic problem-solving activities. By contrast, refugees successfully deactivate internal lines of division and engage in collective forms of politics.

The ethnographic perspective on social cohesion and collective politics (or lack thereof) developed in this chapter resonates with the new interest in "political ethnography" among sociologists and political scientists (Joseph, Mahler, and Auyero 2007; Schatz 2009). Political ethnographies shed light on aspects of politics that often remain invisible in non-ethnographic studies, including everyday encounters with street-level state agents (Ismail 2006), political apathy (Eliasoph 1998), and experiences outside the realm of formal politics (Mahmood 2005).

I suggest that, through a comparative approach, political ethnographers can shed light on the co-variation of structures and experiences of social marginalization. By doing so, they can explain the plurality of meanings and experiences of politics among dispossessed populations not in terms of the individual characteristics of these populations, but, rather, in terms of larger institutional forces. Along these lines, my comparison between the refugees and the urban minorities operates as antidote against essentialist explanations of the lack of collective action in the Mahatta district, and draws attention to the different structures of marginalization that operate in the camp and the city. To sum up, I support "comparative political ethnography" as a methodology well-suited to explore how marginalized individuals and collectivities engage into politics.

Jalazon Refugee Camp and the Mahatta Urban District: History and Structure

The 1948 Arab Israeli war led to the establishment of the Israeli state and the dispersion of the Palestinian population. Most Palestinians (about 800,000) became refugees while a minority (150,000) were able to remain in the newly created Israeli state (Morris 1987). Palestinian refugees settled in the West Bank, the Gaza Strip, Jordan, Syria, and Lebanon. Palestinians who remained inside the Israeli state were given Israeli citizenship but were placed under military rule for two decades (Lustick 1980; Leibler and Breslau 2005). Within this broader experience of destruction and displacement, the history of the Palestinian town of Lydda became intertwined with the creation of the refugee camp of Jalazon. During the 1948 war the Israeli army occupied Lydda and expelled most of its inhabitants (Munayyir 1998; Yacobi 2009). Most refugees who arrived in the refugee camp of Jalazon came from Lydda (renamed Lod by the newly created Israeli state) and 36 rural villages around the city (Yahya 2006).

From 1948 to 1967 the refugee camp, like the rest of the West Bank, was under the control of the Jordanians. After the 1967 war, the Israeli state extended its rule to the West Bank but did not give citizenship to its inhabitants. In other words, since 1967 both the Palestinian minority in Lod and the camp dwellers in Jalazon have been under Israeli rule, the former as citizens and the latter as stateless subjects (see map 1).

Jalazon camp is one of the 19 refugee camps in the West Bank. The West Bank has a total population of about 2.4 million and about one quarter of them are registered as refugees. About 20 percent of the registered refugees in the West Bank live in camps. With a population of about 8,000 inhabitants (on 0.25 square kilometres), Jalazon is a camp of medium population size.[87]

According to the Israeli Bureau of Statistics, in 2008 Lod had 67,484 inhabitants, including 16,800 "Arabs", 45,500 "Jews", and 5,184 "others".[88] The city includes a large contingent of recent migrants from the former Soviet Union and Ethiopia and for some of them the official recognition as "Jewish" is a difficult process. Palestinians live in three segregated areas of the city: the Mahatta district,[89] around the old city, and the Northern part of the city.

The comparison between these two populations highlights distinct trajectories of internal cohesion or fragmentation. Both localities have internal lines of division, including place of origins, membership in extended families (*ḥamā'il*), political affiliation in the camp, and ethnic categorization and the divide between old timers and newcomers in the urban district.

The camp has several village and town associations (*jam'īyāt*) which comprise only refugees (and their descendants) who come from specific villages and mobilize resources along their places of origins. Interconnected with village affiliation, kin-based ties also constitute important

Israel, the West Bank, and Gaza Strip

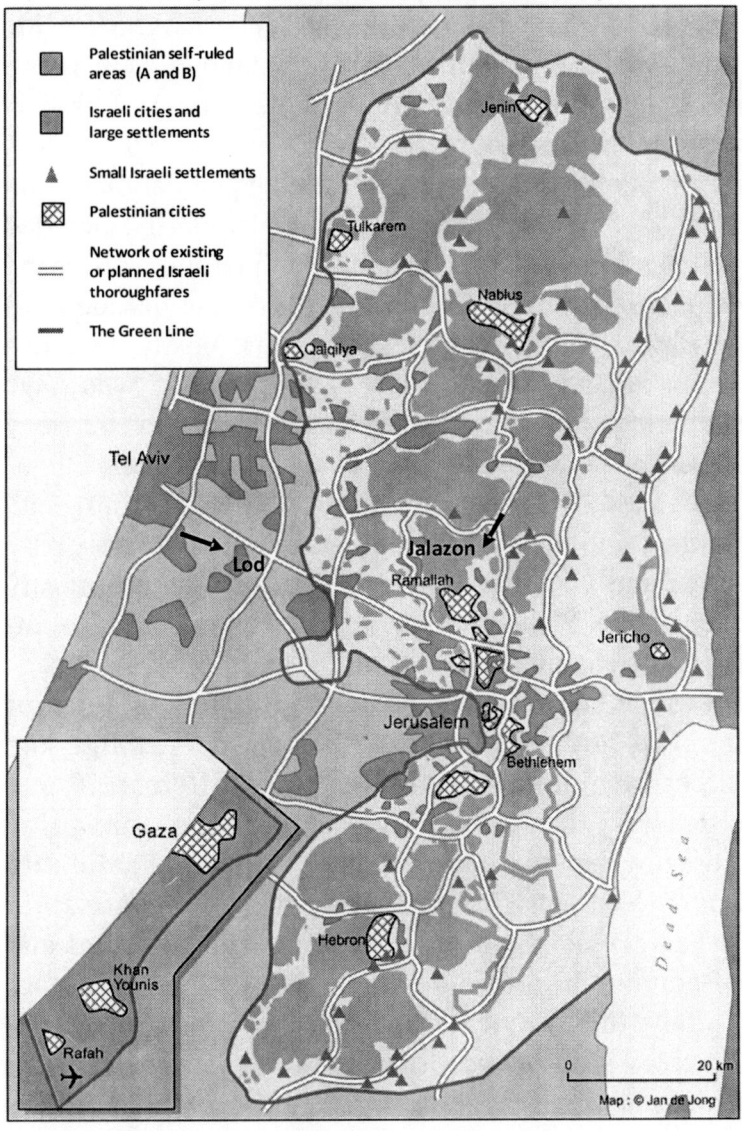

Source: Palestinian Academic Society for the Study of International Affairs

Map 1: Across the Green Line: Lod (Israel) and Jalazon (West Bank)

lines of solidarity and support. Further, political factions organize a wide range of cultural and social activities inside the camp (from graduation awards to summer camps) and measure their relative strength in terms of rates of participation among dwellers.

The recomposition of the Palestinian population in Lod after the 1948 war, this time as an official minority, included remaining urbanites, descendants of internally displaced Palestinians who relocated to the city in the decade after the 1948 war, and other internal migrants, mostly Bedouins from the Southern desert area of the Negev,[90] who have settled in the city since the late 1960s. The divide between old timers and newcomers intersects with three main ethno-religious categories: Muslim Arabs, Christian Arabs, and Bedouins (who are all Muslims). Old timers include only Muslims and Christians, while new migrants are mostly Bedouins. The Mahatta urban district comprises (Muslim) Arabs and Bedouins.[91]

However, despite the presence of internal lines of division in both locales, their effects on feelings and practices of internal solidarity are different. Camp dwellers are able to deactivate potentially paralyzing fractures to develop a high degree of internal solidarity and pursue collective forms of politics. By contrast, in the urban district the divide between Arab Bedouins and non-Bedouins becomes a salient line of fracture. More accurately, the fragmentation that urban residents experience goes well beyond this divide to permeate social relations among neighbours regardless of their ethnic categorization.

Internal Cohesion and Collective Protest in Jalazon

In July 2007, when I started my fieldwork in Jalazon camp, the Palestinian Occupied Territories were experiencing a period of acute political crisis due to the ongoing factional infighting between Fatah and Hamas, the two main Palestinian political groups. Moreover, Israeli policies such as curfews, travel permits, and checkpoints had contributed to the vulnerability of Palestinian workers and widespread unemployment by drastically reducing the number of Palestinians from the Territories allowed to work inside Israel and by severely limiting the freedom of movement of Palestinians between the Gaza Strip and the West Bank as well as within different areas of the West Bank.

In Jalazon, the political tensions were palpable and the official unemployment rate reached 25 percent. Furthermore, UNRWA had decided to cut some basic services usually available to all camp dwellers to focus on food distribution to the poorest families. Within this context of acute deprivation, political violence, and the Israeli army's raids and arrests, I was surprised by the vivacity of the people I first met in the camp. Gradually, I came to interpret the daily cheerfulness and warmth that characterized social relations and the ongoing collective contestation of UNRWA's plans for service cuts as two sides of the same coin: a defensive stance against the external forces that threatened to penetrate the camp as well as the reinstatement of a sense of a membership to something larger than political affiliation or other internal divisions: the Jalazon people (*ahl al-Jalazon*). This is not to say that the camp is not traversed by internal fractures. On the contrary, I witnessed many instances in which political affiliation or family ties operated as fissure lines. Yet, despite the existing cleavages, camp dwellers express a shared sense of membership and establish relations of mutual trust.

The camp protests against UNRWA are an example of the consolidation of social cohesion among camp dwellers under external pressure. These protests were coordinated by the popular committee, an organization of self-government inside the camp. Formed mainly by unelected representatives of the different political factions, the popular committee of the camp holds weekly meetings in a building that, opposite to the main mosque, overlooks the central square of the camp.[92] While the discussions between members of the committee often reflect their factional affiliations, the committee is responsive to pressure from ordinary camp dwellers to act and make decisions. I argue that far from being naively blind to the attempts of political manipulation—especially by representatives of the dominant political faction (*Fatah*)—camp dwellers are deliberate and purposeful in protesting the UNRWA; therefore, we cannot easily dismiss their protests as evidence of top-down political manoeuvring. While the camp protests took many forms, I will focus on two episodes to discuss the dynamics of solidarity and politics in the camp: the suspension of the "Emergency Job Creation Program" (JCP) and the one-day occupation of two UNRWA buildings in the nearby city of Ramallah.

The Suspension of Emergency Job Creation Program (JCP)
The JCP is an emergency program run by the UNRWA that offers short-term contracts to refugees for jobs in the camp institutions and clinics. A system of three-month rotation funded by international donors,[93] the JCP is managed in each camp jointly by the UNRWA and the popular committee. Extremely popular among the thousands of unemployed in the camps, the selection process used by the camp director in coordination with the camp popular committee is fraught with expectations and anxieties, and recriminations and despair among those who were not selected, once the list of the lucky ones is released.

In mid-October 2007, the camp popular committee suspended the program to protest what they considered a low number of positions (75) given by UNRWA to Jalazon in comparison to the number of jobs granted to other camps. The goal of the suspension was to pressure UNRWA to obtain a higher number of positions. While waiting for the UNRWA reaction, the popular committee also worked on a list of requests about other services, such as cash and food distribution, which had been frozen by UNRWA. Meanwhile, a certain set of arguments became quite common in conversations on the question of the JCP (and especially its risky suspension) at the dinner table as well as in the streets. For example, during a conversation, two elderly refugees made the following comments:

> "Unlike other camps in the North, Jalazon people didn't use violent pressure to obtain more positions. This is why we were discriminated against."

> "We didn't invent jobs and we presented a list of positions that are really available at our institutions."

> "We need jobs, how long would the suspension last?"

In late October, the popular committee held a meeting with the JCP coordinator, a European who was assisted by a translator. The conversation between three members of the popular committee and the JCP coordinator was fraught with tension and frustration. The program coordinator focused on two things: the immense gap between the number of applicants from all camps and the funding for the JCP; and the exact match between the number of jobs that the camp had asked and what it had obtained (75 jobs). While acknowledging that they had initially requested 75 positions, the members of the popular committee were interested in other things. One member of the popular committee explained why they wanted more JCP positions in these terms:

> "We didn't like that other camps made pressure to increase their beneficiaries."

> "We are dealing with an increase in the price of

food and I give you an example, we were forced to go to the shopkeepers in the market [inside the camp] to tell them to keep the prices down, so the people and the children can buy falafel and sandwiches."

During the three hours-long meeting, there were times when the program coordinator showed signs of boredom, reeled off a list of numbers from the JCP budget, or made remarks such as "What can we do? There are as many applications as families in each camp!" Moments of tension between the members of the popular committee and the JCP coordinator would ensue with members of the popular committee reacting with statements such as "You are a guest here," "What is your salary?" or "Don't complain, you are the strongest side here." Eventually, after three hours of negotiations between the popular committee and the JCP coordinator, Jalazon camp obtained 25 additional jobs immediately, followed by a renegotiation of the number of jobs after three months. In the subsequent renegotiation, UNRWA, once again, reduced the number of positions granted to Jalazon to 75. The camp protests against UNRWA continued unabated during 2008.

The One-Day Occupation of Two UNRWA Offices in Ramallah

As every Wednesday, tonight there was the meeting of the popular committee. Tonight they discussed two things: they agreed to organize a one-day occupation of the UNRWA Area Office in Ramallah. They are afraid that there are plans to reduce the services provided by the agency (*wakala*). They also refused access to an international organization that wanted to carry out a survey in the camp. Most of them were troubled with some of the questions about religion (how many times do you pray per day?), wealth

(your monthly income), and politics (support for different political figures or movements). Others were simply tired of surveys: "We have already done one like this," "Do we need more statistics?"
(Fieldnotes, March 12, 2008)

About ten days after the meeting, I was on a bus with about a hundred women on my way to the main UNRWA area office in Ramallah. Another bus full of men from the camp followed. Most women and men were in their thirties, forties, and fifties. While the men remained outside the building, the women entered and occupied all of the rooms, sitting on chairs, desks, and the floor. I sat with other women on the floor of the main office of the UNRWA building, just in front of the area officer's desk. He was a Palestinian who visited the camp once in a while. He was almost frozen behind his desk, with a grin on his face. He told us "I am also a refugee (*āna kamān lāji'*)" and he tried to move from behind his desk to reach a map on the wall with the names of the Palestinian villages destroyed during the 1948 war. He most likely wanted to show his place of origin. A tiny woman with piercing eyes, who was sitting on the floor, told him "You have just to listen (*inte lāzem bass tisma'*)." He remained where he was, behind his desk. Other women directly addressed him: "The food prices are going up and you [UNRWA] stop food and cash distribution to camps, do you want to starve us?" After thirty minutes, about twenty men also entered the office, members of the camp committee as well as a group of elderly. Still behind his desk, he clearly showed respect to them, took out a notebook and a pen as if to say: I hear you and I want to write down all of your requests. After lengthy monologues of elderly leaders and members of the popular committee, a sudden and unplanned idea developed (when I later asked several people who had come up with the idea, nobody really knew): why don't we go to the UNRWA office that runs the JCP?

Again on the bus, most women looked outside the windows to search for this other UNRWA office that they were not familiar with. As soon as they saw some parked cars with the acronym UNRWA on the doors, they screamed to the driver to stop the bus in front of the cars to block the exits for the employees (*muwaẓẓafīn*). The driver did as he was instructed. This time, the confrontation between the refugees and the UNRWA personnel was quite heated. In the JCP office there were a couple of men who were born in the camp but had left it to relocate in the city; they tried to mediate but they were visibly embarrassed. I myself avoided interactions with some employees who had always been very nice to me during their visits to the camp. With what appeared to be a sense of cheerful complicity, a group of women approached a truck in the parking lot; I followed them while they tried to open the back of the truck to check "if they hide food from us." While I was with them in the parking lot, I saw a group of men from Jalazon coming out of the building pushing an employee. There was a scuffle outside the office. Later on I was told that the employee did not want to let them in his office and told them they were "animals (*ḥayawānāt*)." I heard this story for weeks inside the camp.

Analysis: Social Cohesion and Collective Politics

Internal fractures in the camp—factional affiliation, place of origin and clan membership—could potentially paralyze collective action, especially under the tremendous pressures of scarce resources internally, and political polarization and social fragmentation externally. The two episodes recounted above show how camp dwellers are able to deactivate internal lines of division and engage into collective forms of protest. Although the UNRWA area officer is also a refugee, the class distinction between him and the camp dwellers becomes the most salient principle of division during their interactions. The slur "animals" launched by an UNRWA employee against the men from

Jalazon, who wanted to enter his office, not only causes a scuffle between the refugees and the employees but more importantly becomes a subject of conversation among those who did not participate in the one-day occupation of the UNRWA offices. The suspension of the JCP emerges in the context of Jalazon against other camps, which had, allegedly, obtained more jobs through threats. Camp dwellers do not take into consideration that unemployment is higher in the Northern camps, which, unlike Jalazon, do not benefit from the spatial proximity to Ramallah, the de-facto "capital" of the Territories. The suspension of the JCP is a source of collective pride, because it proves that the camp dwellers can stand together against injustices and violations. The disdain that most members of the popular committee express for surveys and questionnaires reflects their feelings of exasperation against the transformation of the camp into a "laboratory" for researchers and policymakers. The heated discussion between some members of the camp's popular committee and the European coordinator of the JCP program is revealing of how refugees relate to humanitarian aid as an instrument to keep their cause alive in the international arena. In other words, their understanding of humanitarian aid does not obfuscate their view of the complex political terrain on which they move and the powerful forces that aim to silence them. A similar argument animates Peteet's (2005:82) historical and ethnographic study of Palestinian refugee camps in Lebanon:

> The Palestinian case underscores the cross-cultural, historical and political variability of the meaning and effects of aid. Palestinian voices were disqualified and marginalized less by aid regimes and more by the silencing impulses of the U.S. and Israeli diplomatic and scholarly communities.

In this sense, the Palestinian case draws attention to how military, diplomatic, humanitarian (and scholarly) interventions interact within broader political projects of domination. Neocleous (2010:9) highlights how the blurring between "war" and "peace" is not a new phenomenon but "was part and parcel of an ascendant liberalism which found an important political use for the language of peace within the context of international law." Malkki (1996:378) contends that humanitarian interventions transform political actors into "mute victims." My field-materials draw attention to how, despite their marginality, dispossessed populations can attempt to subvert the logic and goals of the humanitarian interventions directed towards or against them.

To sum up, these episodes of collective mobilization build on and reinforce the self-identification of the camp dwellers—including those who did not board the two buses to Ramallah—as members of a social group, their pride in Jalazon as a place, and their defenses against hopelessness.

Atomization and Distrust in Mahatta

In late March 2008, I moved from Jalazon to the city of Lod, which is a fifteen minute-drive from Tel Aviv and a ten minute-drive from the Israeli international airport. A series of articles on the Israeli "mixed cities"[94] published in the Israeli newspaper *Ha'aretz* defined Palestinian urban minority districts, including the Mahatta district, as "refugee camps in the heart of Israel" (Galili and Nir 2000). However, during my first visit to the Mahatta district in Lod, I noticed a striking difference between the district and Jalazon camp:

> The district is really in poor condition: I crossed the eight train tracks (no bridge or tunnel for people and/or cars) and entered the district on foot: unpaved roads, pools of sewage water, mounds of trash, a combination of big cement houses (some resemble villas) and shacks with zinc roofs. One could almost say that the Mahatta resembles the

camp but there is a striking difference: the lack of external symbols of collective cultural and institutional life in the district. The camp is full of flags and graffiti, and signs, flags of political factions as well as national flags, and there are signs everywhere to mark the various local institutions: the popular committee, the village societies, the children's center, the center for disabled people, the youth center, etc., you walk around and there are signs on the walls everywhere. Here, by contrast, the street walls are bare, no writing, no graffiti; one looks around and sees houses and shacks, a few small mini markets, a lot of vacant lots (and often big rocks in the middle of empty spaces [later on I learned that the role of these rocks is to prevent the illegal building of other houses on state-owned land]. (Fieldnotes)

Most Palestinian citizens of Israel live in all-Arab cities, towns, and villages.[95] Only ten percent of them (around 100,000) live as urban minorities in cities with a Jewish Israeli majority. Scholars know little about the lives of Palestinian minorities inside Israeli cities (on Lod see Yacobi 2004, 2006, and 2009). According to geographer Yacobi, around 50 percent of Palestinians in Lod "live in 'illegal' structures." Yacobi also refers to a survey of 500 Palestinian households showing that "28 percent of the houses are marked for demolition and 26 percent are used for dwelling although unfinished" (2004:60).

While precarious and hazardous living conditions are a central concern for Palestinians in Lod, another factor deeply affects their everyday lives: the continuous interferences of the Israeli police and security apparatuses. Scholars have conducted archival work on the phenomenon of "collaboration" of Palestinian citizens with Israeli authorities (Sa'di 2003; Cohen 2010).[96] Making use of unprecedented access to Israeli police files, Cohen has studied "the networks of informers" created by the Israeli security agencies in Arab villages and towns in the period 1948-1967. He argues that the state security agencies drove the decision to use "informers" among Palestinian citizens of Israel as part of an overall "system of control" (Lustick 1980):

> The bodies that coordinated the activities of the security forces in Arab settlements were the Regional Committees on Arab Affairs, which were subordinate to a Central Committee composed of senior representatives of the GSS, the police, the army (the Israel Defense Forces—IDF), and the prime minister's adviser on Arab affairs. The three regional committees—the Galilee (northern), the Triangle (central), and the Negev (southern)—were composed of field personnel from the same agencies. (Cohen 2010:8)

Cohen (2010:235) also addresses how "the informers" operated within this larger structure:

> One of their [the informers'] central missions… was to report all nationalist sentiments they heard expressed in their villages and cities…The result was a comprehensive system of reports from informers…Security agencies found ways to strike at Arabs who took nationalist positions, especially by blocking their professional advancement. It was a carefully calculated system through which the security agencies tried to "educate" Arab citizens in what they were permitted and what they were forbidden to say. In other words, the system established the boundaries of Arab discourse in Israel.

Today the Palestinian minority inside the state remains a source of security concerns for Israeli authorities. However, an analysis of how the Israeli security agencies' involvement in Palestinian lives today compares to what Cohen has documented for the period 1948-1967 remains beyond the scope of this chapter. Rather, I would like to draw attention to how ubiquitous discussions of "informers" and "the Shabak" are in the everyday lives of residents of the Mahatta district. My field notebooks are full of instances in which I was warned not to speak with a certain person or to say certain (misleading) stories if that person asked me about my research. A typical entry reads:

> Today I told Ahmed[97] [a resident of the district] that this morning I got to know a taxi driver who approached me to ask me what I was doing in the neighborhood. I described the taxi driver and where he lives; Ahmed made a wry face and told me: "He is not clean (*huwa mish ndīf*), don't speak with him, don't tell him about the camp [Jalazon], you are a woman, just tell people here that you want to write a book on the Arab marriage traditions." (Fieldnotes, April 15, 2008)

Residents also discuss their actual interactions with Israeli security agents in ambiguous terms. Yusef, a man who tried to set up a local committee to represent the residents of the district, complained that three neighbours circulated rumours about him; they told people that "he works with the police":

> The spies (*jawāsīs*) think that all people are spies like them…At that time I had troubles with Samir, Hassan and Nancy [the three neighbors who, according to him, had circulated rumors about him]…And I cannot remember who told my wife that [I] was talking with the police and that [I] wanted to establish the committee because the police asked me to do that.

Yusef also described how he cleaned up a vacant house to run cultural activities and amusingly spoke of his contacts with the Israeli security services:

One day, in July during the [school] holidays while I was working to fix the place, I saw a man nearby; he came to speak with me and told me that he wanted to build a small playground to give the children an opportunity to play so they wouldn't be interested in drugs. So I started to laugh and he asked me "why are you laughing?" I told him "I am thinking to help the kids in their studies in the afternoon… I want to help them by opening this place." He told me that he would clean this place and that we would get donors for both my place and the playground…Thus after a while I asked him: Who are you? And guess who he was? He was the head of the *Shabak* [Israeli security agency]!?! [We laugh together].

Silvia: The head of the *Shabak* in Lod?

Yusef: Not in Lod! He was the head for the whole district!!

Silvia: How did you feel?

Yusef: I don't know. I thought he was someone from the municipality (*al-baladia*) [He laughs].

Silvia: What did you think?

Yusef: So I thought that this is not important. The important thing is to develop our goal not the other thing, so I didn't care.

The question of "collaboration" also emerges from Yusef's discussion of who actually funded his project.

He [the donor] was always in contact with the police, that was known…But…I have a goal to help those kids, I don't care where the funding comes from Azrael [the angel of death] or anywhere [else] (*ījī min 'izrā'īl, ījī min hīkī*).

Analysis: Fragmentation and Distrust in Lod

Residents of the district share a similar predicament of social marginalization and ethnonational exclusion; yet they struggle to recognize their shared interests and develop social networks of solidarity. The question of "who is an informer" shapes social relations in the district. In their everyday lives, residents deal with crucial dilemmas such as accepting the support of Israeli security agents for an afterschool program or providing information to the police in exchange for a shop license. Rumours are circulated about those individuals who have obtained a teaching job, opened a mini-market, or secured the early release of a relative from prison. Yusef has renounced the idea of setting up a local committee but he defends his decision to accept the support of an Israeli security agent. Sure of his good intentions, he draws a line between "collaborators" (those who actively give information to the police) and his acceptance of support from the Israeli security forces.

In his study of marginalized squatters in Iran, Bayat argues that, through the medium of "common space", the squatters are likely to recognize their shared interests: "even when they do not know each other, [they] may act collectively because common space makes it possible for them to recognize their common interest and identity." He also states that "a common threat" activates this recognition of shared interests: "the threat of eviction brings many squatters together immediately, even if they do not know each other" (1997:17).

The view from Lod shows that, even in the case of a common threat, we cannot take for granted the recognition of shared interests among individuals who live in a common space and share a similar predicament. By contrast, the recognition of a common threat relies on a process of group formation.

Conclusion

This chapter has drawn attention to comparative ethnography as a method that can identify and explain how structures and experiences of marginalization co-vary across places. I have argued that comparative ethnography can shed light on the conditions under which marginalized populations direct their political energy towards collective forms of protest against the institutional sources of their marginalization or towards internal infighting and individualistic problem-solving activities. If political ethnography can study political subjectivities and practices that remain invisible to other methodologies, *comparative* political ethnography can take a step further in explaining the plurality of forms of politics among marginalized populations. Comparative political ethnography can study how distinct forms of sociolegal control manifest themselves at the ground level and can trace their different effects on political consciousness and action of dispossessed populations.

Empirically, I have documented how refugee camp dwellers and urban residents differ in terms of their internal solidarity and political action: refugees display a high level of solidarity and pursue collective forms of claim-making while residents have a low level of social cohesion and mainly engage in practices of individual exit. I have argued that these differences can be explained in terms of the institutional policies at work in the management of these two marginalized populations: the practices and discourse of humanitarianism and rehabilitation in the camp and the interferences of state security forces in the urban district.

The relevance of this study for understanding social marginalization is twofold. First, I aim to develop an analytic framework that compares and contrasts phenomena that are not often studied together: criminal violence and political violence; urban ghettos in industrial cities and refugee camps; state penal policies and humanitarian interventions of international agencies. I suggest that a comparative perspective on social marginalization can shed light on both the effects of increased surveillance and policing in the Global North (Goffman 2009) and the effects of humanitarianism as a privileged form of management and reproduction of marginalized populations in the Global South (Feldman and Ticktin 2010). Furthermore, a comparative perspective on forms of sociolegal control of marginality can lead to a better understanding of the conditions under which humanitarianism depoliticizes political struggles, and the conditions under which dispossessed populations use the presence of humanitarian agencies to their favour within highly disadvantageous relations of power.

Second, I mobilize group formation as an analytic link between forms of sociolegal control from above (by the state or other ruling agencies such as international organizations) and the development of subjective meanings and pursuit of political actions. By doing so, I emphasize the formation of group identity and solidarity as a central arena of struggle between the institutional forces that re-produce marginalization and those who resist it.

References

Abu-Saad, Ismail. 2008. "Spatial transformation and indigenous resistance: The urbanization of the Palestinian Bedouin in Southern Israel." *American Behavioral Scientist* 51(12):1713-1754.

Adalah. 2011. *The Inequality Report: The Palestinian Arab Minority in Israel*. Adalah, The Legal Center for Arab Minority Rights in Israel. Accessed August 24, 2011. http://www.adalah.org/upfiles/2011/Adalah_The_Inequality_Report_March_2011.pdf.

Al-Husseini, Jalal. 2000. "UNRWA and the Palestinian nation-building process." *Journal of Palestine Studies* 29(2):51-64.

Allen, Lori. 2008. "Getting by the occupation: How violence became normal during the second Palestinian Intifada." *Cultural Anthropology* 23:453-487.

Arias, Desmond Enrique. 2006. *Drugs & Democracy in Rio de Janeiro: Trafficking, Social Networks, & Public Security*. Chapel Hill: The University of North Carolina Press.

Auyero, Javier. 2001. *Poor People's Politics, Peronist Survival Networks & the Legacy of Evita*. Durham, NC: Duke University Press.

Auyero, Javier, and Debora Swistun. 2009. *Flammable: Environmental Suffering in an Argentine Shantytown*. Oxford: Oxford University Press.

Bayat, Asef. 1997. *Street Politics: Poor People's Movements in Iran*. New York: Columbia University Press.

Bishara, Azmi. 2001. "Reflections on October 2000: A landmark in Jewish-Arab relations in Israel. *Journal of Palestine Studies* 30(3):54-67.

Blecher, Robert. 2005. "Citizens without sovereignty: Transfer and ethnic cleansing in Israel." *Comparative Studies in Society and History* 47(4):725-754.

Bourdieu, Pierre. 1999. *The Weight of the World: Social Suffering in Contemporary Society*. Stanford: Stanford University Press.

Bourgois, Philippe. 1996. *In Search of Respect: Selling Crack in El Barrio*. Cambridge/New York: Cambridge University Press.

Bourgois, Philippe, and Jeff Schonberg. 2009. *Righteous Dopefiend*. Berkeley: University of California Press.

Cohen, Hillel. 2010. *The Israeli Security Agencies and the Israeli Arabs, 1948-1967*. Berkeley: University of California Press.

Eliasoph, Nina. 1998. *Avoiding Politics: How Americans Produce Apathy in Everyday Life*. Cambridge: Cambridge University Press.

Farsakh, Leila. 2002. "Palestinian labor flows to the Israeli economy: A finished story?" *Journal of Palestine Studies* 32(1):13-27.

———. 2005. *Palestinian Labour Migration to Israel: Labor, Land, and Occupation*. New York: Routledge.

Feldman, Ilana, and Miriam Ticktin. 2010. *In the Name of Humanity: The Government of Threat and Care.* Durham, NC: Duke University Press.

Galili, Lily, and Ori Nir. 2000. "Refugee camps in the heart of Israel." *Ha'aretz*, December 11.

Goffman, Alice. 2009. "On the run: Wanted men in a Philadelphia ghetto." *American Sociological Review* 74(June):339-357.

Gutmann, Matthew. 2002. *The Romance of Democracy: Compliant Defiance in Contemporary Mexico.* Berkeley: University of California Press.

Haklai, Oded. 2009. "State mutability and ethnic civil society: The Palestinian Arab minority in Israel." *Ethnic and Racial Studies* 32(5):864-882.

Hammami, Rema, and Salim Tamari. 2001. "The second uprising: End or new beginning?" *Journal of Palestine Studies* 30(2):5-25.

Hass, Amira. 2002. "Israel's closure policy: An ineffective strategy of containment and repression." *Journal of Palestine Studies* 31(3):5-20.

Hiltermann, Joost R. 1985. "Mass mobilization under occupation: The emerging trade union movement in the West Bank." *MERIP* 136/137:26-31.

———. 1991. *Behind the Intifada: Labor and Women's Movements in the Occupied Territories.* Princeton, NJ.: Princeton University Press.

Ismail, Salwa. 2006. *Political Life in Cairo's New Quarters: Encountering the Everyday State.* Minneapolis: University of Minnesota Press.

Johnson, Penny, and Eileen Kuttab. 2001. "Where have all the women (and the men) gone? Reflections on gender and the Palestinian second Intifada." *Feminist Review* 69(winter):21-43.

Joseph, Lauren, Matthew Mahler, and Javier Auyero. 2007. *New Perspectives in Political Ethnography.* New York: Springer.

Kedar, Alexandre. 2003. "On the legal geography of ethnocratic settler states: Notes toward a research agenda." *Current Legal Issues* 5:401-441.

Leibler, Anat, and Daniel Breslau. 2005. "The uncounted: Citizenship and exclusion in the Israeli census of 1948." *Ethnic and Racial Studies* 28:880-902.

Lockman, Zack, and Joel Beinin. 1989. *Intifada: The Palestinian Uprising against Israeli Occupation.* Boston: South End Press.

Lustick, Ian. 1980. *Arabs in the Jewish State: Israel's Control of a National Minority.* Austin: University of Texas Press.

Lybarger, Loren. 2007. *Identity and Religion in Palestine: The Struggle between Islamism and Secularism in the Occupied Territories.* Princeton, NJ: Princeton University Press.

Mahmood, Saba. 2005. *Politics of Piety. The Islamic Revival and the Feminist Subject.* Princeton NJ: Princeton University Press.

Malkki, Lisa. 1996. "Speechless emissaries: Refugees, humanitarianism, and dehistoricization." *Cultural Anthropology* 11(3):377-404.

Morris, Benny. 1987. *The Birth of the Palestinian Refugee Problem, 1947-1949*. Cambridge: Cambridge University Press.

Munayyir, Isbir. 1998. *Lydda During the Mandate and Occupation Periods*. Beirut: Institute for Palestine Studies (in Arabic).

Nassar, Jamal, and Roger Heacock. 1990. *Intifada: Palestine at the Crossroads*. New York: Praeger.

Neocleous, Mark. 2010. "War as peace, peace as pacification." *Radical Philosophy* 159:8-17.

Pappé, Ilan. 2011. *The Forgotten Palestinians: A History of the Palestinians in Israel*. New Haven: Yale University Press.

Payes, Shany. 2005. *Palestinian NGOs in Israel: The Politics of Civil Society*. London: Tauris Academic Studies.

Peled, Yoav. 2005. "Restoring ethnic democracy: The Or Commission and Palestinian citizenship in Israel." *Citizenship Studies* 9(1):89-105.

Perlman, Janice. 2010. *Favela: Four Decades of Living on the Edge in Rio de Janeiro*. Oxford: Oxford University Press.

Peteet, Julie. 2005. *Landscape of Hope and Despair: Palestinian Refugee Camps*. Philadelphia: University of Pennsylvania Press.

Rabinowitz, Danny, and Khawla Abu-Baker. 2005. *Coffins on our Shoulders: The Experience of the Palestinian Citizens of Israel*. Berkeley: University of California Press.

Rabinowitz, Danny, and Daniel Monterescu. 2007. *Mixed Towns, Trapped Communities: Historical Narratives, Spatial Dynamics, Gender Relations and Cultural Encounters in Palestinian-Israeli Towns*. Aldershot: Ashgate.

———. 2008. "Reconfiguring the 'mixed town': Urban transformations of ethnonational relations in Palestine and Israel." *International Journal of Middle East Studies* 40:195-226.

Rekhess, Eli. 2007. "The evolvement of an Arab-Palestinian national minority in Israel." *Israel Studies* 12(3):1-28.

Rempel, Terry. 2010. "UNRWA and the Palestine refugees: A genealogy of 'participation' development." *Refugee Survey Quarterly* 28(2-3):412-437.

Rouhana, Nadim. 1989. "The political transformation of the Palestinians in Israel: From acquiescence to challenge." *Journal of Palestine Studies* 18(3):38-59.

Rouhana, Nadim, and Sultany, Nimer. 2003. "Redrawing the boundaries of citizenship: Israel's new hegemony." *Journal of Palestine Studies* 33(1):5-22.

Sa'di, Ahmed. 2003. "The incorporation of the Palestinian minority by the Israeli state, 1948-1970: On the nature, transformation, and constraints of collaboration." *Social Text* Summer:75-94.

Schatz, Edward. 2009. *Political Ethnography: What Immersion Contributes to the Study of Power*. Chicago: University of Chicago Press.

Scheper-Hughes, Nancy. 1992. *Death without Weeping: The Violence of Everyday Life in Brazil*. Berkeley: University of California Press.

Schiff, Benjamin. 1995. *Refugees unto the Third Generation: UN Aid to Palestinians*. Syracuse: Syracuse University Press.

Venkatesh, Sudhir. 2002. "'Doin' the hustle:' Constructing the ethnographer in the American ghetto." *Ethnography* 3:91-111.

Wacquant, Loïc. 2003. "Ethnografeast: A progress report on the practice and promise of ethnography." *Ethnography* 4(1):5-14.

———. 2004. *Body & Soul: Notebooks of an Apprentice Boxer*. Cambridge: Polity Press.

———. 2008. *Urban Outcasts: A Comparative Sociology of Advanced Marginality*. Cambridge: Polity Press.

Weizman, Eyal. 2007. *Hollow Land: Israel's Architecture of Occupation*. London: Verso.

Yacobi, Haim. 2004. "In-between surveillance and spatial protest: The production of space of the 'mixed city' of Lod." *Surveillance & Society* 2(1):55-77.

———. 2006. "From Rakevet to the neighborhood of Neve-Shalom: Planning, difference and the right to the city." *Makan* 1:25-39.

———. 2009. *The Jewish-Arab City: Spatio-Politics in a Mixed Community*. London: Routledge.

Yahya, Adel. 2006. *The Story of Jalazon Refugee Camp*. Ramallah: PACE (in Arabic).

Yiftachel, Oren. 1996. "The political geography of ethnic protest: Nationalism, deprivation, and regionalism among Arabs in Israel." *Transactions: Institute of British Geographers* 22(1):91-110.

———. 2006. *Ethnocracy: Land and Identity Politics in Israel/Palestine*. Philadelphia: University of Pennsylvania Press.

Zureik, Elia. 2001. "Constructing Palestine through surveillance practices." *British Journal of Middle Eastern Studies* 28(2):205-227.

Chapter 8

Sexual Violence and the Creation of a Postcolonial Ordinary

Engagements Between Street-Based Sex Workers and the Police in Machala, Ecuador

Karen O'Connor

A faint hum overpowered people's fast-paced bartering, relaxed gossip, and invitations to make a purchase. This low sound intensified, as if coming from multiple directions at once. Nervousness rippled through Machala's downtown market. Eyes darted, backs stiffened, and many sex workers and informal labourers subtly moved toward the narrow alleyways and away from the busy intersection. Suddenly the sound became visible as multiple police officers on motorcycles sped through the crowded market streets and converged at the intersection. Many sex workers, informal labourers, and shoppers fled. The last police raid and accompanying arrests of sex workers in the market occurred two weeks prior and had been followed by speculations about when the next anticipated raid would unfold.[98] These four officers, shrouded in an aura of exhaust and dust, watched as people disappeared into the crowded market streets, and they leaned back on their motorcycles, slowly dismounted, and laughed.

They parked their motorcycles at the corner beside a vendor selling coconut milk, where a group of sex workers normally wait for and flirt with their clients. They purchased milk and stood laughing, talking, and smoking in that space. In all of my discussions with sex workers and informal labourers about police violence, these taunting mock raids had never been mentioned. There seemed to be something disturbingly thrilling for these police officers when they received such a strong reaction to their arrival and watched people run away. This essay will illuminate the many inequitable social and cultural relationships that are articulated through everyday engagements between sex workers and the police.

My MA fieldwork, conducted from June to August of 2006, focused on police violence against sex workers during an urban regeneration campaign in the coastal city of Machala, Ecuador, as street sweeps against sex workers and informal labourers gained momentum (see O'Connor 2007; see also Gönen and Yonucu, in this volume, on the process of marginalization through urban transformation campaigns). Many anthropologists who research violence insist that anthropologists must double as advocates and activists in the field in order to support peoples who are negatively affected by violence (Scheper-Hughes and Bourgois 2004; Scheper-Hughes 1992; Taussig 1987). However, the delicate decision-making of anthropologist-activists as they attempt to decide if and when violence can be clearly labelled as oppressive or liberatory and which forms of activism and intervention are (or are not) appropriate in certain situations is often understated in these texts.

I was working in awkward collaboration with several sex workers' rights organizations which competed with one another to service increasingly fragmented groups of sex workers, while attempting to organize against heightened state regulation and violence. Activism, in this context, became an increasingly problematic practice, as it was often unclear who to advocate for and how, or to foresee the possible outcomes of such activist work. My attempts to "give back to the community" by locating and bringing free condoms from different organizations and NGOs in Canada to sex workers' rights groups in Machala at the request of many sex workers who do not have access to free condoms, erupted in competing claims and disputes over these resources, with complicated and sometimes negative effects. Perhaps the largest benefit of my fieldwork for the sex workers I was working with was unintended. The police never raided the market while I was there, either out of fear that I might be hurt in the process and there would be consequences for individual officers or due to nervousness about the negative international attention that might occur if a raid happened before my eyes or involved me.

Producing and Reconsidering Testimony

I did not intend to conduct my fieldwork on police raids against sex workers in the downtown market. After volunteering with a sex workers' rights NGO in Machala for four months as a part of a study abroad program in Ecuador in 2005, I was interested in mandatory health care services for sex workers and the implications of the state's regulation of sex workers' bodies, labour, and sexuality.[99] I planned to conduct my fieldwork in the waiting room in front of the mandatory gynecological exams for sex workers at a downtown hospital. However, tensions within and between the Sex Workers' Union, various sex workers' rights organizations, and feminist organizations transformed the waiting room of these health care services into a deeply contested space where various spokespeople for the sex workers' rights movement were struggling to maintain their political clout with many fractured communities of sex workers.[100] After realizing that my research site was becoming increasingly fraught with conflict in ways that made it difficult to work, I changed my research topic to a study of sex work in the downtown market.[101] One week after I began my fieldwork in the market, the National Police, working with the Provincial Health Commissioner and Machala's mayor, began a series of police sweeps to arrest sex workers in the market.

My intent at the time of my fieldwork was to compile sex workers' testimonies of police abuse and brutality, in part to provide local social justice organizations with documents that could be used to resist the implementation of the current urban regeneration campaign and violence against sex workers. Many of my interviews included what I now realize were somewhat scripted questions about violence during the urban regeneration campaign and tended to yield formatted answers denouncing police beatings, insults, arrests, and rapes.[102] It strikes me now, as I reflect back on my fieldwork, that my interviews may not have generated a space to discuss the many ways that inhabitants of Machala coexist with violence, the extent to which violence is experienced as emotionally and viscerally charged, or to question the problematics of testimony, and the standardization of "victim's narratives".

Violent Designs: Escalating Violence During an Urban Regeneration Campaign

Many of my participants noted that intermittent police sweeps and state violence against sex workers in marginalized urban spaces have long histories in Machala and other cities in Ecuador.[103] The street sweeps intensified during July of 2006 and focused on sex workers working in Machala's central streets as part of a contingent and sometimes uncoordinated municipal and provincial urban renewal campaign that attempted to regulate, tax, relocate, and eliminate sex workers and informal labourers from Machala's downtown core.[104] During my fieldwork, the municipality of Machala was attempting to force sex workers into managed and enclosed brothels on the city's fringes. The municipality was also in the process of relocating informal labourers to a market enclave on the outskirts of town where they now pay for space to sell their merchandise.

These "regeneration" and relocation projects seemed to encourage and intensify police violence against the urban poor in Machala. The threats and enactments of violence between police officers and groups being displaced sometimes assumed a taunting, "playful" edge. Disturbing linkages between uneven power relationships, unconsensual violence, and pleasure have been documented and theorized by anthropologists working in diverse contexts (e.g. Appadurai 1998; Das 2006; Goldstein 2004; Hunt 2008; Nelson 2009). Nancy Rose Hunt, writing about histories of sadistic rape and violence in the Democratic Republic of the Congo, apprehends engagements with violence as tactile, acoustic, and affective. She elaborates:

> [t]he complex relationships among laughter, domination, pleasure, anguish, and frenzy are worthy of further exploration, especially as they relate to fields of vision and sound—capacities and incapacities for observation, silence, and controlling and modulating sound—in situations of sadism and torture. (Hunt 2008:236)

Hunt's emphasis on the ways that sensual bodies enact and encounter violence and their affective relationships with frenzy and domination may gesture towards the articulation of pleasure during police sweeps against sex workers in Machala. These raids are experienced as sensation and sound, through the approaching hum of police vehicles coming from multiple directions in an attempt to seal off the area in order to make arrests, the casual (and possibly nervous) laughter and joking as officers occupy the street corner, the scathing sting of gas which some officers cruelly aimed at the face to render someone senseless, or, as one participant described, aimed at exposed flesh which burns and shrivels as the pepper spray penetrates into layers of tissue, the insults and shoves, the sharp constriction of handcuffs which often mark a sex worker's entrance into the back of a police vehicle, and the blinding flash from the camera of one of the local reporters. I spoke with sex workers after raids and arrests or while visiting them in jail accompanied by other sex workers in the market after bribing the police to enter and bring food. Many described their physical pain and discomfort, and frequently displayed their bodily wounds, such as bruises, burnt skin, and damaged clothing as a kind of physical testimony to violence.

Hunt also notes that sadistic violence may assume a tenor of "sport, like hunting" (Hochschild 1988:166, quoted in Hunt 2008:236). I noticed certain officers pleasurably threatening sex workers immediately after the first raid in early July of 2006, when the police presence in the market increased. More officers walked the beat through the market and an officer was almost always stationed at the particular intersection where I was conducting fieldwork, watching and monitoring the sex workers who worked there.[105] One officer stationed himself on the corner in the market several days after the raid, and stood watching myself and several sex workers with a grin while he mockingly flashed his baton and aimed it at us and jerked his shoulders as though he felt the strain of the rifle kickback, pretending he was shooting us.

Steven Gregory describes the enjoyable dimensions of hierarchical encounters between military officers and sex workers. As he writes about US military officers flirting with under-aged sex workers in the Dominican Republic, he explains that "[o]ne might say that in the cult of imperial masculinity hierarchy *feels* good" (Gregory 2007:133, emphasis in original). I do not believe that officers' subjectivities are easily summed up by generalizations of imperial masculinity. However, during the urban regeneration campaign certain officers flaunted their pleasure during their hierarchical encounters with sex workers. Arresting, beating, or threatening sex workers was not solely a sterile bureaucratic practice, but an affective process whereby inequalities, enactments of violence, and articulations of power were sometimes marked by taunting or thrilling gestures.

As bored officers walk the beat in the market, performing low paying and potentially dangerous forms of labour and surveillance, some officers seem to seek out any experience that yields a thrilling sense of power. A sex worker who has sold sex in the market for fourteen years explained that she has been arrested more than twenty times.[106] She notes that often, after a police raid, "[w]e would get out [of jail] in the middle of the day on Monday and the police would return that day to put us back in jail." Some officers flaunt their power to play games of cat and mouse with sex workers, who are free for a few moments, only to be arrested again when they return to the market to work.

Taussig (2004:150) writes of state and para-state violence in Colombia, "... humour is actually very close to violence, as in cartoons, and there is nothing more chilling than absurdly blended with terror." In these strange, taunting moments, kinds of chilling state power seep into daily life and fill it with absurd and uncanny charges. Following Taussig's explorations of the fetishization of state power in *The Magic of the State* (1997), these charged encounters seem to suggest an extra-official, immanent state corruption with contradictions that feed and reinforce state power.[107] These strange textures and gradations of power ground threats of violence within the corrupt practices that both blur the boundaries of, and reaffirm, postcolonial state power. Those who experience the brutal and absurd tenor of state violence may be shocked by the swift and jolting shifts in posture, as some officers who are supposedly "keeping the peace" or "instilling justice" suddenly alter their form to enact sadistic forms of corruption and misconduct.

Forms of sinister play are fashioned alongside articulations of state power and masculinity in ways that sexualize threats and enactments of violence. Fantasies of sexual violence are embodied literally and figuratively within some officers' daily routines and constitute bodies, communities, states, and nations. Feldman describes police interrogations in Northern Ireland as ritualized performance through which statehood emerges. He writes:

> The analysis of arrest and interrogation forces one to read the state not only as an instrumental and rationalized edifice but as a *ritual* form for the constitution of power; in turn, one is led to the central role that arrest and interrogation play in the performative construction of state power in Northern Ireland. (Feldman 1991:86)

As some officers interrogate, harass, arrest, and rape sex workers, a sexually potent and virile state emerges through the enactment of officers' sadistic sexual misconduct. Threats of violence and arrest in the market suggest the constant possibility of rape by the National Police which frequently occurs when sex workers are interrogated or incarcerated. Raids and arrests are frequently publicized in the Machalan press and widely discussed in Machala. However, police sexual misconduct and rape are often unreported and unacknowledged, and surface through sex workers' gossip, silences in conversations, suggestions, metaphors, and clinical-sounding testimonies.

In these moments, the state is often encountered with brutal intimacy, as its power is "experienced close to the skin" (Aretxaga 2003:396). Aretxaga (2001:8) analyses the gendered state practice of strip searching incarcerated women in Northern Ireland as prison guards lay their hands on and interrogate women's bodies in ways that animate gendered state technologies of control. These violent enactments of strip-searching pleasurably cluster around nodes of difference as these powerful relationships enact and recreate sexual and ethnic differences through fantastic and sexually charged performances of state governance of the body (Aretxaga 2001; Feldman 1991).

Ambiguous Interrogations: Multiple Investments in Identity Documents

Many violent interactions between police officers and sex workers begin as police interrogations as officers demand that sex workers hand over the mandatory state documents which they are expected to carry with them while working. However, mandatory health documents and citizenship papers assume a complicated presence in many sex workers' daily lives. These documents are demanded and utilized in diverse situations and sometimes in surprising ways. These interactions suggest theoretical questions that some conceptualizations of top-down state formation, understandings of embodiments of nationalism and postcoloniality, and discussions of sex workers' agency may fail to consider.

Health and citizenship documents are not demanded solely by the police. They are distributed and required in sex workers' mandatory health care services, where sex workers are supposed to receive high quality and free state-sponsored health care. These mandatory exams (once bi-weekly, now monthly) include pelvic exams, pap smears, and blood tests. The results of these tests are stamped onto sex workers' health documents to ensure and "prove" sex workers' sexual health. Many sex workers complained about the frequent disrespect and abuse from some doctors, rough handling during gynaecological exams, and fees added to supposedly free services by corrupt doctors or requested from the underfunded public hospital. While most of the sex workers I spoke with articulated their discomfort and ambivalence with state-imposed health care, some preferred mandatory, problematic health care to no health care at all. Several feminist NGOs run by Machalan sex workers advocated for quality health care for sex workers and approached different levels of government health bureaucracies in order to defend sex workers' dignity and rights to health care.

Some sex workers found their mandatory health cards to be useful when negotiating with clients, as they provide proof that the cardholder does not have sexually transmitted infections (STIs). Some sex workers offered to show clients their health and citizenship documents as an incentive to purchase their "risk free" services as opposed to their competitors' presumably less certain services. Some sex workers noted that this guarantee of good health gave them leverage to secure a higher price and to demand that clients wear a condom. Clients also sometimes demand to see a sex worker's papers as a kind of "consumer's entitlement" to quality services while sometimes attempting to establish a power dynamic whereby sex workers must satisfy their demands. Constructions of biopolitical sexual health and risk (see writings on biopolitics, such as Agamben 1998; Biehl 2007; Fassin 2007; Foucault 1978; Petryna 2002; Rabinow [1982] 1992; Rabinow and Rose 2006) seem to merge with gendered and sexualized capitalist logics of entitlement, as both sex workers and clients articulate the unequal footing of their relationships through demands and displays of paperwork during negotiations on the street.

Mandatory health and citizenship documents are also demanded between sex workers, as some attempt to police the health and citizenship of others working in their vicinity in the market. Near the end of my fieldwork, an older woman who had sold sex in the market for many years approached me, visibly upset, and explained that a group of sex workers were attempting to force her out of the market because she did not attend the mandatory health services or carry a health card. She explained that she did not go to the mandatory health services because they made her uncomfortable. A group of sex workers who sold sex near her accused her of having AIDS and were attempting to humiliate and bully her out of the market. I also heard stories of "documented" sex workers organizing against "undocumented" sex workers to force them off of street corners with, among other things, threats to involve the authorities. These practices of internal policing were sometimes framed by both a disdain for foreigners and an awareness that "illegal" sex workers would bring greater state surveillance and police violence for everyone working in the area. These internal divisions sometimes also assumed violent and taunting forms. However, some "documented" and "undocumented" sex workers did not approve of internal policing and would attempt to disrupt sex workers who were interrogating one another over "appropriate documentation". Such disruptions included everything from counter-accusations, telling someone to "shut up and mind their business," and discussions about the value of the documents and the reasons why sex workers migrate to work elsewhere, or avoid or delay trips to the health facilities.

However, one sex workers' rights NGO asked sex workers to present their documentation and "register" in order to access the NGO's resources at the insistence of its international funding organization which demanded a record of all sex workers who were using the NGO. These uncomfortable encounters seemed to recall other occasions when sex workers are asked or expected to display their paperwork, and many sex workers who worked in the market complained bitterly about the disrespect they felt was implicit within this "forced registration". I also spoke with a friend who worked in this office who expressed her discomfort at "registering" her friends and acquaintances at her funding organization's request. These demands for paperwork resulted in the NGO's brief exclusion of sex workers without documents, although I do not think that the funding company foresaw these effects when it made these requests and asked this particular NGO to authenticate their office and work in this way. At certain moments, bureaucratic state practices were reproduced within organizations that represent and work for sex workers and exist in somewhat compromising relationships with their funding organizations.

Sex workers' rights activists and NGO workers in Machala are divided about the benefits and drawbacks of mandatory health care services and the accompanying paperwork. Some activists and NGO workers are deeply invested in health care services as a way to combat stigmatizing stereotypes about sex workers as so-called carriers of disease. Many feel that it is important that the state acknowledge sex workers as legitimate citizens as an important step away from criminalization and as an assurance that sex workers (however, only those with citizenship) receive free health care. Within this logic, it is important that sex workers are understood as equal citizens with the rights and entitlements that they deserve through their legitimate relationships with the state. However, these activists are also aware that sex workers only gain partial inclusion within state bureaucracies that subject sex workers to increased surveillance, making them easier to locate and identify, and perhaps more and not less "vulnerable".

Other sex workers' rights activists and NGO workers oppose forms of state regulation and stress their many drawbacks while attempting to imagine forms of health care that are open to sex workers, with or without citizenship, and do not centre around the state regulation of sexual health. However, these activists and NGO workers must contend with sex workers who have some investments in government-issued documents and the acknowledgement of their citizenship, and who may not trust NGOs or activist groups to deliver a viable alternative that is free from forms of corruption. Many NGO workers and activists hold nuanced positions which exist somewhere between these poles and work in awkward and sometimes dissonant collaboration with funding organizations, other sex workers' rights groups, NGOs, state bureaucracies, and fragmented "communities" of sex workers, while attempting to create more equitable futures.

Many of the sex workers who participated in my research engaged with intermingling transnational political designs that include NGO mandates, health and policing regulations, and urban regeneration schemes. Sex workers' concerns and agendas shape and are shaped alongside and through diverse political formations. It is important to consider both the radical possibilities implicit and explicit within some forms of political organizing, while also avoiding the romanticization of sex workers and sex work activism as inherently "oppositional". Political organizing involving sex workers in streets and brothels sometimes challenges broader governing logics, but may not be easily celebrated by the category "grassroots activism" or understood through a deterministic top-down understanding of NGO governance. The language and logics of human rights and NGO activism seem to place limits on the possibilities for political dissent while tethering people's struggles to neoliberal and state frameworks (see for example D'Souza 2007; Choudry 2008). However, confronting state violence and state regulation place activist groups in problematic relationships with the state, often working through statist languages of recognition and entitlement, and pre-existing formations of power.

Everyday relationships are forged through the exchange of state health and identity documents in ways that suggest that sex workers' engagements with the state are not always subversive or strategic. Sex workers' daily entanglements with the state pose challenges to humanistic understandings of agency and point towards Mahmood's exploration of agency "not as a synonym for resistance to relations of domination, but as a capacity for action that historically specific relations of subordination enable and create" (2001:203). Relationships between sex workers and the state do not necessarily spring from polarized enactments of state domination and sex workers' subversion, but from multiple nodes of power which converge around cultural forms, such as bureaucratic practices and identity documents, and constitute the diverse and inequitable relationships through which people live their lives.

Reconsidering Everyday Relationships with State Power

While these analyses of state power offer insights into the powerful relationships through which state violence occurs, they may not apprehend increasingly complex ambiguities and tensions that surface in relationships between police officers and sex workers in daily life. Amidst the proliferation of academic work on policing as a vague and wide-spread form of governmentality, texts that consider the complex practices and institutional formations of the police and their relationships with state power in diverse contexts is scant (Neocleous 2000:ix-x). Neocleous (2000:xi) utilizes an "expanded concept of the police" to think through the many diverse institutions through which policing occurs.

Policing is shaped through both diverse institutions and multiple social and cultural relationships. Members of the national police are also friends, neighbours, lovers, relatives, clients, and partners, and may be distinctly uncomfortable with their roles as interrogators, arresting officers, perpetrators of violence, or "state representatives".[108] In Machala, police examinations of sex workers' ID, police records, and mandatory health cards are often peppered with playful banter, questions about purchasing services after their shift is over, and comments that transgress the boundaries between flirtation and harassment. Extra-official state power is also sometimes enacted by "turning the other cheek", during moments when arrests are not made, bribes are not solicited, and neighbours and friends are granted impunity. However, some officers may allow personal disputes to seep into their policing, as familial or neighbourhood conflicts resurface in the market and become recast as an antagonism between officers and sex workers.

Kempadoo (2004:65) notes that many forms of sex work may "produc[e] situations where women are simultaneously bound and free, coerced and constrained, victims and agents." Likewise, police officers cannot always be categorized as perpetrators or protectors, or as embodiments of state ideology or personal motivations. Complex and inconsistent fields of power emerge, even between state representatives and marginalized subjects in contested urban spaces. Daily interactions between sex workers and the police are often confusing and include moments when it is unclear who supposedly holds power. The nuanced relationships between sex workers and police officers may encompass more than an assumed exercise of state power in ways that gesture toward open-ended, multi-layered forms of power that come into being amidst shifting and strained social relationships and roles, differing aims and agendas, and layered and contradictory contexts and temporalities which may not be obvious or easily taken-for-granted (see Young 1990).

These subtle terrains of power mark many interactions between officers and sex workers with heightened uncertainty. An approaching officer may flirtatiously express an interest in purchasing services, and, if he does not like the price he is offered, may demand to inspect a sex worker's documents. An officer's flirtatious interest can transform into sexual harassment infused with threats or enactments of violence, especially if his masculinity or sexuality are challenged through a sex worker's disinterest or request for a high price. Many jilted officers angrily demand bribes or free sex in exchange for not arresting a sex worker with "improper" paperwork. Sex workers are often tauntingly reminded that they cannot refuse to have sex with an officer without risking rape or arrest. An officer may arrest a sex worker after raping her or return to solicit free sex or a bribe again the following day. Multiple nodes of power converge and contract as intimate, social, cultural, and stately power are entwined ways that are both "official" and "extra-official".

These nuanced engagements destabilize and blur academic categorizations of violence. Many of the material, tactile, and affective relationships through which people live their lives do not neatly fit within supposedly separate forms of social, economic, and political violence.[109] These categories are useful as they illuminate that forms and enactments of violence are diverse and that experiences of violence are not easily shared between people in differing contexts. However, such categories may perpetuate flattening generalizations and deceptively shift people's focus away from the historically-specific conditions through which people coexist with many forms of violence, often simultaneously.

Assumptions about the spatialization of violence unravel as sex workers experience violence from different people in multiple spaces, including on market streets, in their neighbourhoods, in their homes, in jails, and working in clubs and brothels. At times, this violence is committed and/or witnessed by their romantic partners. However, violence is reterritorialized during the urban regeneration campaign as state bureaucracies attempt to relocate sex workers to the outskirts of town. During these territorializing practices, the police demand documents from sex workers working on downtown streets, arrests are made, and gendered and sexualized violence is enacted by police officers in jail (often with impunity).

The Influence of Colonial Processes in Daily Life: Beyond Historical Determinism

These enactments of power seem to build upon constructions of difference in ways that illuminate the multiple dimensions of *mestizo* nationalisms, which do not openly acknowledge cultural difference. Muteba Rahier (1998:421) asserts that Ecuador's "official imagination of national identity has been constructed since the colonial period by the white and white-*mestizo* elites around the notion of *mestizaje* (race mixing)" where "whiteness and moves towards whiteness are most valued" (Radcliffe and Westwood 1996:68). Radcliffe (1999:215) writes of Ecuadorian nationalisms that "[p]articularly in post-war development discourses, the *mestizo* category (broadly, persons of "mixed" indigenous / European ethnicity) became a marker of engagement in the urban, market-led and modernizing national society and an avenue for social advancement." Machala's urban regeneration campaign draws upon *mestizo* desires for so-called cultural and racial "improvement" in ways that tie racial and sexual "purity" with constructions of urban modernity. As *mestizo* nationalisms partially inspire the violence unfolding in Machala's altering downtown core, many Machalans, including members of the municipal bureaucracy and the police, emphasize sex workers' so-called contagion and racialized and sexualized differences while also denying the existence of those differences within Machala through attempted relocation projects.

As racialized and sexualized colonial categories of difference are reconstituted within the present, genocidal and ethnocidal urges resurface in subtle ways in the Machalan market. Walter Mignolo's (2000) discussion of "the coloniality of power" reveals the ways that the colonial past is entangled within unfolding, present formations of power. For Mignolo, constructions of difference and the power they come to assume in daily life must be historicized alongside colonial projects in order to think through the ways that colonial categories of difference are reworked within nation-states, modernizing projects, and universalizing global frameworks.

Police enactments of sexual violence against sex workers reverberate alongside memories of colonial rape. Diverse colonial projects were implemented in part through forms of gendered and sexualized control and violence. The power of sexual violence is mobilized for somewhat different purposes in Machala today, as powerful forms of community, municipality, nation, and state (among other formations) are constituted through the routinization of taunting, arresting, and raping sex workers. Benavides (2006:42) notes that in Ecuador, "the postcolonial native" was "only made possible by this rape context" of colonization. The *"mestizo"* is a product of colonial rape and unequal relationships between Spanish men and indigenous women. This supposedly ideal and nationalized subjectivity carries the weight of colonial memories of violation and power inequalities.

Rape and colonial categories of difference resurfaced during Machala's urban regeneration through municipal attempts to craft an ordered downtown centre, however, they emerged during interactions between police officers and sex workers in ways that are not necessarily rational, predictable, or focused on the fulfillment of specific agendas. The urban regeneration campaign (intentionally or not) propped up sex workers and informal labourers as supposedly "acceptable targets" for violence and hatred. Many of these unpredictable, unequal, and affective exchanges constitute surprising social and cultural relationships, such as diverse forms of community, nation, and state.

The violence that unfolded on the streets involved contingent networks of people and sometimes generated surprising responses, such as unsuccessful raids that enraged many people in the market, and inspired different affinities between sex workers, informal labourers, and officers. These raids initiated a strong, semi-organized response from sex workers in the market, sex workers working in other areas in Machala, activist groups, and many people living in Machala who do not agree with the municipality's methods and goals for so-called urban regeneration. Some sex workers banded together and began to stand defiantly and confront officers who arrived to raid the market. Such stand-offs were often confusing and fear-instilling. In the one instance that I witnessed, a sex worker was let off with a warning as a group of uneasy officers left the market without making any arrests.

Municipal projects mobilize forms of violence and colonial constructions of difference by drawing on particular pasts in order to imagine specific futures. Enactments of violence are deeply rooted to and erupt out of conflicts over specific places, communities, and urban sites situated uniquely within nationalistic and globalizing thrusts of place-making. Analyses of violence in urban spaces may seek refuge in archetypal, sweeping theoretical generalizations which fail to engage with the specificities of place, the particular histories which influence the present, and the ways that people engage and live through these complex fields of power (following Koonings and Kruijt 2007).

The city of Machala celebrates its largest export by declaring itself to be the "banana capital of the world". Many city spaces sport recent municipal murals which remind the city's diverse inhabitants that "Machala advances with you!" These murals exist as visible signs of the urban regeneration campaign which promotes tourism in order to create an alternative to the instability of the boom and bust banana economy. As the municipality attempts to cultivate different "tourist-friendly" sensibilities for inhabitants of Machala, they suggest that certain ways of life are incompatible with the supposedly progressive, current designs for the city. Various municipal bureaucracies and community groups are heavily invested in removing certain people and their lifeways from the urban landscape.

During my fieldwork, I passed time in Machala's market almost every day, and spent hours sitting near and walking past the market stands which swell and contract over the central streets. A walk through this space of informal vendors, makeshift stands, and tantalizing products is a sensory experience. This lively place is filled with heated bartering, invitations to make purchases, arguments, laughter, gossip, and daily conversations. The fast pace of much of the conversation is countered by the plodding steps of browsing customers and frustrated honks from halted taxis trying to manoeuvre through the streets filled with overflowing produce and products, shoppers laden with heavy purchases, and mobile vendors wheeling their carts along the road. The roar of aggressive traffic from the main streets outside of the market gives way to invigorating salsa beats from an informal music stand selling pirated CDs and DVDs near the edge of the market. Rows of worn wooden market stands are topped with corrugated steel roofs and filled with merchandise—fresh produce, plantain, trays of seafood and fish, clothes, toiletries, jewellery, baked goods. The enticing smell of freshly prepared food wafts down side streets, near the permanent businesses located behind the market stands.

Anxieties about race, class, gender, and sexuality mingle in discussions about the future of the market and the recreation of Machala's urban spaces. A journalist describes the night encroaching onto the market as a scene that is "full of prostitutes, homosexuals, thieves, a situation that impedes the normal and safe walkways for Machalans in these zones" ("Prostitución clandestina, lunar que afea la ciudad" *El Correo,* June 29 2006:1). Moral panics about sex work and crime on Machala's market streets situated sex workers as so-called social waste or vectors of disease to justify and escalate the erasure of the downtown market (see "A Las Autoridades no Les Importa: Trabajadoras Sexuales Tomadas Centro de Machala." *El Nacional,* March 18 2005:12B). These monstrous portrayals of sex workers in Machala relate to the many ways that constructions of "disorder" arrange dominant orders (see Neocleous 2000; Rimke 2010). Street-based sex workers are sometimes framed as a gnawing reminder of informal labour, underemployment, poverty, gender inequalities, and the so-called "immoral underbelly" of sexual exploitation that might rupture Machala's aesthetics of modernization during attempts at urban regeneration.

This municipal attack on sex workers and informal labourers in the market seems to draw on colonial constructions of indigeneity and fears of poverty and informality that resurface within *mestizo* modernizing projects. Koonings and Kruijt (2007:10) note that in Andean countries, informality is often racialized as an indigenous cultural tradition, and that in many Latin American countries "the informal economy has more to do with black people than the black market" in the popular imagination. In coastal Ecuador, a region of the country often racialized as "black" (Radcliffe and Westwood 1996:110-112), the market is often conceptualized as a "backward" and "unhygienic" indigenous tradition that shelters (black, indigenous, rural, or undesirable) underclass "delinquents" and needs to be eradicated, reformed, or relocated. Andean market spaces are also historicized as a pre-modern, rural tradition that is destructive to *mestizo* articulations of so-called urban progress.

These racialized and classed market landscapes are also tantalizingly gendered and sexualized. Mary Weismantel (2001:47) writes of Ecuadorian highland markets:

> The market woman is an indecent figure who arouses rumors of sexual anomaly: the sight of her muscular torso, or a glimpse of her naked legs under the big skirt, is invested with unsettling meaning. Like race, sex creates a geography of estrangement, the boundaries of which require their own forms of policing, to which the jostling bodies of the produce market offer an immediate challenge.

Charged and tactile bodily encounters between sex workers, informal labourers and other Machalan inhabitants are inflected with seductive and violent possibilities, as conceptualizations of dangerous femininity and uncurbed sexualities are perceived to encroach on the supposedly sterile order of nationalized, masculine spaces. Many people's ambivalence and disdain for market spaces and the people who inhabit them gain intensity through surges of negative feelings and dispositions about sex work, informal labour, indigeneity, and the migrants from Peru and Colombia who also work in these spaces.

I spoke with a Peruvian migrant worker selling small goods near the intersection where sex workers flirted with their clients. Our conversation unfolded several days after the first police sweep in July, during which he had fled alongside many sex workers as he was afraid of being questioned about his citizenship documents and was unsure about who the police were coming to arrest. His feelings about sex work in the market were ambiguous during this period of amplified violence, as he was friends with many of the women selling sex who sometimes helped him manage his stand. He told me that his uncle, who had been running the stand several years ago, had been arrested for being "illegal" and two sex workers saved his merchandise for him. His uncle bribed the police to return to the market the following day and continue working.[110] My participant did not seem to morally judge sex workers for selling sex and considered some to be loyal friends, but at times he also expressed frustration and resentment toward sex workers for the growing conflict on the street and the increasing stigmatization and thorough policing of informal labour and market spaces in general.

Reformulating Social and Cultural Relationships Within Urban Space

Veena Das (2006:1) describes the ways that a violent event "attaches itself with its tentacles into everyday life and folds itself into the recesses of the ordinary." Enactments and threats of violence against sex workers in the market steeped everyday routines with a kind of anxious energy as violence and arrests were continually anticipated. After the police raids began, a feeling of nervousness seemed to creep over the market. The laughter and light gossip that permeated many conversations among women[111] selling sex in the market seemed to dissipate and their often casual postures stiffened. One sex workers' rights NGO encouraged sex workers to continually walk back and forth or to circle the block, as they could be charged with loitering or soliciting by the police if they were caught standing still. Many sex workers repeated a kind of anxious pacing—scanning the streets for police or potential customers while they quickly circled the block. Others stationed themselves near the many small alleyways between market stalls and businesses, preparing for a stealthy exit in case the police arrived to perform a sweep. The continuous rumours speculating about the date and time of the upcoming police raids put many people on edge.[112] The raids seemed to animate some sex workers' lives with fear, anxiety, and a deep distrust of the police in ways that subtly altered the daily texture of life in the market. For some, these feelings were also accompanied by an intensified resolve not to be relocated to a mega-brothel and forsake the relative autonomy of street-based sex work.

A growing environment of nervous and pleasurable permissiveness seemed to thrive alongside many peoples' moral disdain for sex workers and their so-called responsibility for the criminalization of informal labour in Machala's market. Resentment and anger surged into the everyday relationships between sex workers and other vendors in the market. One sex worker bitterly described an incident when a fruit vendor punched her for standing too close to his cart. Differing forms of territoriality emerged during the street sweeps as complex mobilizations of anger, violence, and resentment intensified while more sex workers were relocated to the market and off of other street corners and parks in Machala. Shoving, painful insults, and fights became more common in the market. Relationships that did not seem to be marked by overt violence—such as friendships, some patron-client relationships, passing conversations, and daily banter—grew increasingly strained or came under different forms of tension.

Uneasy formations of expanding and contracting nodes of power well up in violent social relationships situated in deterritorialized and reterritorialized urban spaces. Diverse histories of migration across municipal, provincial, and national boundaries in search of better options for survival, labour histories performing various kinds of degraded and stigmatized work, and personal engagements with violence, poverty, race, gender, and informality may surface during engagements between police officers and inhabitants of the Machalan market.

Remembering Police Violence and Rape

Hunt (2008) notes that in violent contexts, non-sexualized violence is often photographed or given voice and sometimes endlessly proliferated as testimony or as humanitarian propaganda, while sexualized and gendered forms of violence are often brushed aside and rendered unfit for repetition. Many of my participants mentioned the frequent rapes by the police in jail in everyday conversations and several narrated their experiences of sexual violence at the hands of the police in a distant and somewhat clinical way. I did not ask what might be violating questions about bodily pain, suffering, and the specifics of how the rapes were carried out. While I do not pretend to know how this sexual violence unfolds or the charged bodily interfaces that sense or are numbed during these violent enactments, I would like to offer an anecdote that reveals complicated familial relationships with incarceration, sexual violence, legal bureaucracies, and fear.

I returned to Machala during the summer of 2007 with my mother to visit with friends and return my thesis to local activist groups. As we walked through the downtown market toward the intersection where many sex workers meet with their clients, we could see the rapid motion of several officers who were attempting to seal off the space as a strange silence descended on the area. Suddenly, the officers halted in the middle of their raid, seemingly unsure about what to do with the pair of *gringa* tourists who were watching them closely. As the officers slowly left the area, I approached startled friends and acquaintances who informed me that the raids had amplified during my absence and squads of officers visited the market routinely.

I was searching for one of my friends, Ana, who had sold sex in the market for many years. I had heard in an email from a mutual friend that she had suffered a heart attack while cooking with hot oil and had been hospitalized. As I approached her I saw that her leg was thickly scarred with white, raised veins of flesh that stretched around her calf and foot. The accident happened several months before, and Ana explained that business was especially difficult lately as the police raids had frightened many clients who were afraid of being arrested and humiliated, and that her scars made hustling in the market harder as she competed with younger women whose bodies may not reveal visible signs of trauma.

She dabbed her eyes with a handkerchief and explained that she was upset and worried about a more desperate problem. Her son had just been arrested. The police claimed that he was involved in a group mugging with a firearm. She asked me to go with her to speak with her former lawyer who now refused to help her. She was reluctant to elaborate further on what had transpired, so, in a state of confusion, I followed her to her former lawyer's office. As she sat in the waiting room heavy tears rolled down her face. "He's my youngest son. I am terrified of what might happen to him in jail." As a client left the lawyer's office, my friend approached her door. I was surprised to see this educated, well-dressed, *mestizo* woman physically block Ana from the doorway while a security guard rushed over to push her out of the office.

"No, señora," the lawyer forcefully insisted. "You lied to me and I won't help you anymore." Ana's distress heightened and she begged, explaining to the lawyer that she was her only option. "No," the lawyer firmly reasserted. "You're lucky I'm not having you arrested too, for forging documents." A mutual friend explained to me later that Ana had reportedly forged her 19-year-old son's identification to make it look like he was still a minor, in order to have him released from the provincial jail.

We moved away from the lawyer's doorway and Ana, my mother, and I sat down. I have never seen Ana weep in a way that seemed so thoroughly defeated. She spoke in choppy sentences between sobs. "He's so young and slight. He'll be violated in jail. What could I do? I had to try anything to get him out." She bent over in her chair and shook with convulsions. Ana has sold sex in the market for over sixteen years and has been arrested many times. I do not know how many times Ana has been raped by clients, partners, and the police, or the shock, jolt, and pain of those experiences, or how she carries those memories and sensations through her daily life now. However, grief, fear, and bodily registers of pain seemed to well up within her as she shook and sobbed while imagining the probability of her son being raped in jail.

While devastated to see Ana in such pain, I was uncertain if and how I should intervene. I was unclear as to what had or had not happened, and had difficulty keeping up with the dizzying veiling and unveiling of information as various stories about the son's arrest and paperwork circulated from sex workers, advocates, and other market regulars with a wide range of allegiances and vested interests. Compounding this confusion, the criminalization of sex work and informality in the Machalan market situated many sex workers in strained, complicated relationships with legal, government, and NGO bureaucracies—relationships which they (and I) often struggled to manoeuvre within. In this instance, I went with Ana to the lawyer's office, but was unable to speak with her lawyer before her security guard escorted us away. Several of the lawyers who worked for local NGOs seemed very reluctant to take the case. To my knowledge, Ana is currently volunteering in an office for sex workers' rights and her son is still in jail.

I worry that the ethnographer's task of charting the contours of processes that build inequitable worlds and writing about their daily lives does not necessarily inspire meaningful, long-term social change. In spite of its limitations, ethnographic work illuminates the need to forge different, less essentializing relationships with one another in order to pursue political goals (Haraway 1991). Openly fraught forms of affinity politics may link the ethnographer with their research participants without presuming to "share politics", close gaps in privilege, or to erase other differences. Many important social justice efforts initiated by the sex workers' rights movement struggle to hold together. Multiple differences erode attempts to forge agendas or visions based on supposedly unifying forms of oppression experienced as sex workers and women. It is becoming increasingly important to think through the situations of many people who are not easily inserted into activist agendas or legal frameworks and complicate our understandings of social justice. Activism that acknowledges uneven and contingent power in everyday interactions while avoiding victim-oppressor binaries and essentializing labels crafts a different starting-point from which to imagine and build equitable relationships and worlds.

References

Agamben, Giorgio. 1998. *Homo Sacer: Sovereign Power and Bare Life,* translated by Daniel Heller Roazen. Stanford: Stanford University Press.

Appadurai, Arjun. 1998. "Dead certainty: ethnic violence in the era of globalization." *Public Culture* 10(2):225-247.

Aretxaga, Begoña. 2001. "The sexual games of the body politic: Fantasy and state violence in Northern Ireland." *Culture, Medicine and Psychiatry* 25:1-27.

———. 2003. "Maddening states." *Annual Review of Anthropology* 32:393-410.

Benavides, O. Hugo. 2006. *The Politics of Sentiment: Imagining and Remembering Guayaquil.* Austin: The University of Texas.

Biehl, João. 2007. *The Will to Live: AIDS Therapies and the Politics of Survival.* Princeton: Princeton University Press.

Choudry, Abdul Aziz. 2008. *NGOs, Social Movements and Anti-APEC Activism: A Study in Power, Knowledge and Struggle.* Unpublished Ph.D. dissertation. Montreal: Concordia University.

Das, Veena. 2006. *Life and Words: Violence and the Descent into the Ordinary.* Berkeley: University of California Press.

D'Souza, Radha. 2007. "What's wrong with 'rights'?" *Seedling: Biodiversity, Rights and Livelihood.* October:17-20. Accessed July 10, 2011. http://www.grain.org/seedling_files/seed-07-10.pdf.

Fassin, Didier. 2007. *When Bodies Remember: Experience and Politics of AIDS in Post-Apartheid South Africa.* Berkeley: University of California Press.

Feldman, Allen. 1991. *Formations of Violence: The Narrative of the Body and Political Terror in Northern Ireland.* Chicago: The University of Chicago Press.

Foucault, Michel. 1978. *The History of Sexuality, Volume I,* translated by Robert Hurley. New York: Pantheon Books.

Goldstein, Daniel M. 2004. *The Spectacular City: Violence and Performance in Urban Bolivia.* Durham: Duke University Press.

Gregory, Steven. 2007. *The Devil Behind the Mirror: Globalization and Politics in the Dominican Republic.* Berkeley: University of California Press.

Haraway, Donna Jean. 1991. *Simians, Cyborgs, and Women: The Reinvention of Nature.* New York: Routledge.

Hunt, Nancy Rose. 2008. "An acoustic register, tenacious images, and Congolese scenes of rape and repetition." *Cultural Anthropology* 23(2):220-253.

Kempadoo, Kamala. 2004. *Sexing the Caribbean: Gender, Race, and Sexual Labor.* New York: Routledge.

Koonings, Kees, and Dirk Kruijt, eds. 2007. "Fractured cities, second-class citizenship and urban violence." In *Fractured Cities: Social Exclusion, Urban Violence & Contested Spaces in Latin America,* 7-22. London: Zed Books.

La Asociación de Trabajadoras Autónomas "22 de Junio" de El Oro. 2002. *Memorias Vivas: Trabajadoras del Sexo.* Machala: IMPSSUR.

Mahmood, Saba. 2001. "Feminist theory, embodiment, and the docile agent: some reflections on the Egyptian Islamic revival." *Cultural Anthropology* 16(2):202-236.

Mignolo, Walter D. 2000. "The many faces of cosmo-polis: Border thinking and critical cosmopolitanism." *Public Culture* 12(3):721-748.

Moser, Caroline, and Cathy McIlwaine. 2004. *Encounters with Violence in Latin America: Urban Poor and Perceptions from Colombia and Guatemala.* New York: Routledge.

Muteba Rahier, Jean. 1998. "Blackness, the racial/spacial order, migrations, and Miss Ecuador 1995-96." *American Anthropologist* 100(2):421-430.

Nelson, Diane M. 2009. *Reckoning: The Ends of War in Guatemala.* Durham: Duke University Press.

Neocleous, Mark. 2000. *The Fabrication of Social Order: A Critical Theory of Police Power.* London: Pluto Press.

O'Connor, Karen. 2007. *Nationalism and State Violence as a 'Moral' Practice: Sex Work and Urban Regeneration in Machala, Ecuador.* Unpublished Master's Thesis. Toronto: York University.

Petryna, Adriana. 2002. *Life Exposed: Biological Citizens after Chernobyl.* Princeton: Princeton University Press.

Rabinow, Paul. (1982)1992. "Artificiality and enlightenment: from sociobiology to biosociality." In *Incorporations,* edited by Jonathan Crary and Sanford Kwinter, 234-252. New York: Zone Books.

Rabinow, Paul, and Nikolas Rose. 2006. "Biopower today." *Biosocieties* 1(2):195-217.

Radcliffe, Sarah. 1999. "Embodying national identities: *Mestizo* men and white women in Ecuadorian racial-national imaginaries." *Transactions of the British Institute for Geographers* 24(2):213-225.

Radcliffe, Sarah, and Sallie Westwood. 1996. "Nationalized spaces?" In *Remaking the Nation: Place, Identity and Politics in Latin America,* 107-133. London: Routledge.

Rimke, Heidi. 2010. "Beheading aboard a Greyhound bus: Security politics, bloodlust justice, and the mass consumption of criminalized cannibalism." *The Annual Review of Interdisciplinary Justice Research* 1(Fall):172-192.

Scheper-Hughes, Nancy. 1992. *Death Without Weeping: The Violence of Everyday Life in Brazil.* Berkeley: University of California Press.

Scheper-Hughes, Nancy, and Phillip Bourgois, eds. 2004. *Violence in War and Peace.* London: Blackwell.

Taussig, Michael. 1987. *Shamanism, Colonialism, and the Wild Man: A Study in Terror and Healing.* Chicago: University of Chicago Press.

———. 1997. *The Magic of the State.* New York: Routledge.

———. 2004. *My Cocaine Museum.* Chicago: University of Chicago Press.

Weismantel, Mary J. 2001. *Cholas and Pishtacos: Stories of Race and Sex in the Andes.* Chicago: University of Chicago Press.

Young, Iris Marion. 1990. "The five faces of oppression." In *Justice and the Politics of Difference,* 39-65. Princeton: Princeton University Press.

Chapter 9

Making Sense of Failure

Why German Trade Unions Did Not Mobilize Against the Hartz-IV Reforms—Partisan Research in Frankfurt, Germany

Markus Kip

Probably the most controversial reform in social and employment policies in post-War Germany was the so-called "Hartz IV" laws which took effect in 2005. These reforms reinforced the workfare logic of social service provision in Germany (Wohlfahrt 2003) and essentially cut back social and unemployment benefits (Upchurch, Taylor, and Mathers 2009). Starting in 2003, proposals for these reforms were countered by broad protest, including controversies in the mass media, public demonstrations, and occupations of employment offices. However, it appeared that trade unions did not throw in their institutional weight in support of this emerging movement (Wompel 2006). It has even been argued that the conduct of the national leaderships of trade unions had a demobilizing effect on union involvement in this contestation (see e.g. Wompel 2006; Lahusen and Baumgarten 2006).

As Handler (2004) argues, major transformations of welfare regimes are first experimented with at the social margins before they encroach upon other social segments. Such dynamic suggests the potential to build broad alliances, even as cutbacks and punitive measures affect marginalized and relatively small populations at first. In my experience as an organizer with homeless and low-income labourers in the United States,[113] we faced ongoing clawbacks in housing provision, social assistance, and other services for the poor. The attacks could also be read as having potentially broader implications—only those who are successful in the labour market are cast as worthy of public support. Even though such discourse seems to fundamentally contradict the social democratic ethos of trade unions, I have found little support from trade unions for our struggles against welfare clawbacks and the subversion of labour rights. On the occasion of my move back to Germany, I was also disappointed with the weak trade union back up for the movement of the unemployed, even as the repercussions of the Hartz IV reforms would be felt beyond the group of the currently unemployed (Wohlfahrt 2003). Yet, before pleading with trade unions, my intuition was that this lack of response is not just a question of "insight" in their "best interest". In order to analyze this failure to mobilize in support of the movement of the unemployed, I chose to employ a "partisan research" approach in a case study in Frankfurt. This research renders problematic a tendency in literature on "social movement unionism" to focus on cases of trade union support for social movements which ended up being successful and were of mutual benefit. By contrast, in this case study, labour activism was up against formidable odds, such that the expectation of movement success was highly uncertain in the short-term. Nevertheless, such resistance remains indispensable as a condition of possibility for success in the long-term. The question that I therefore offer for activist reflection is to scrutinize what sources other than "success" might motivate activism if failure is a likely outcome in the near future.

Partisan Scholarship

The approach of partisan scholarship[114] that I present here builds on a Marxist attempt to establish a non-relativist notion of truth, to produce theory as a constitutive moment of social praxis, and to diminish the social division between theory production and its application. I will briefly outline these three aspects before applying them to my research case study.

First, in rejecting the notion of neutrality in research, both Horkheimer (1972) as well as Gouldner (1968, 1975) argue that research is inevitably interest-driven and political. These authors share commitments towards emancipatory aims—however, they do not propose truth to be a merely relativistic affair dependent on the wishes of a particular group (see Hammersley's 2000 critique). In this vein, Habermas (1987) argues that truth-claims in the social sciences imply communicative rationality—that is, an orientation towards interaction based on the better argument. Thus, the contribution of social scientific research to human emancipation is not in its potential to manipulate certain actors—even if it is for a "good" cause. Moreover, the assessment of research endeavours is not to be limited to their outcomes. Rather, the research process itself actualizes a form of emancipation to the extent that the relationships of research are guided by communicative rationality. This motive to foster communicative rationality through research is also found in Gouldner (1975:5), who proposed a notion of objectivity as a "critique of the cognitive vulnerabilities generated by people's struggle on behalf of their everyday interests" —a sense of "realism" that obligates researchers to "fac[e] the bad news and not exaggerat[e] the good news". Accordingly, Gouldner conceives of the researcher's task as "to help people to remain critical and sceptical of *good* news, to insist that even this be double-checked and, correspondingly, to help people to accept bad news and to *remember* it" (1975:7, emphasis in original).

Second, partisan research seeks to dialectically connect research to practice. Since this idea has also been pursued in many works of the Frankfurt School (see e.g. Horkheimer 1972; Habermas 1973), it should not come as a surprise that many proponents of action research have built upon their ideas (Kemmis 1988). As Horkheimer (1972:222) puts it, it is in "concrete historical activity" that "the truth [of social theory] must be decided." In being committed to an emancipatory praxis, partisan research takes as a starting point questions that emerge in the praxis of movements rather than those emerging from self-referential academic discourses (see Shukaitis, Graeber, and Biddle 2007).

While social scientific research unfolds its emancipatory potential in the form of communicative action, Habermas (1973:29-40) also considers the possibility for research and theory to contribute to reflections around strategic action. As the conditions for communicative rationality are structurally undermined by the influence of capital and the state in late modernity (Habermas 1989), strategic action might be necessary, for example, to initiate a public discussion around a conflict that has been silenced. In such a situation, activist politics need to act strategically in order to raise the issue to public awareness (see also Cohen and Arato 1992:492-563). However, theoretical reflection "does not contain any information which prejudges the future action…"—its "practical consequences… are changes in attitudes which result from insight into the causalities in the past" (Habermas 1973:39).

The third aspect of partisan research is the effort towards overcoming the division of theory production and its application. Partisan research addresses the division of material and mental labour that Marx considered fundamental to capitalist production (Marx 1998:50). Against such division, Marx posited the communist association of free individuals (Marx and Engels [1848] 2008:26) as one in which "nobody has an exclusive sphere of activity" (Marx 1998:53). Horkheimer (1972:221) states that "[i]t is the task of the critical theoretician to reduce the tension between his own insight and oppressed humanity in whose service he [sic] thinks." In working towards this, it is important to take practical problems as they appear for movement activists as a starting point. Moreover, the research should also become an opportunity to involve those affected by the researched problem, so that they too can shape and eventually appropriate the research process. Clearly, such interaction between "theoreticians" and "the rest of the class" can be conflict-fraught (Horkheimer 1972:215; on the problem of "worker education" see Bleakney and Morrill 2010). In such cases, it is important to heed Morgan's (1987) description of Gramsci's pedagogy, which advises the partisan researcher to appreciate the already existing intellectual activities of movement members and to build collaborative efforts upon them. To attain an understanding of such activities, the researcher should learn from them by partaking in the common practices of "the researched". Several works within the history of labour studies have adopted this insight and became known as "workers inquiries", "militant investigations", "conricerca", or "co-research".[115]

Given these ideas, partisan scholarship is not a clear-cut method, but rather an approach. Since it stresses the procedural character of research, rather than research-outcomes, multiple ways of conducting research can be imagined that could be subsumed as partisan, from "studying up" (see Dafnos, this volume), to participatory action research (see critique of this approach by Bourke, this volume), and discourse analysis (see e.g. Willson, this volume). In the following section, I will present and discuss my research as an example of partisan scholarship. Before I position this research in the contemporary conflict around welfare support for the unemployed, I will first offer a brief historical contextualization of this conflict by looking at the relationship between trade unions and the unemployed in Germany.

Trade Unions and the Unemployed: "No Right To Laziness!"[116]

Germany was among the first nation-states to institute national insurance schemes. Chancellor Bismarck pushed for health provision (1883), accident insurance (1884), as well as old age and disability insurance (1889), as a preemptive attempt to reduce the momentum the socialist movement was gaining at the time (Beck 1995). Soon thereafter, a major split within the socialist movement happened as a result of the Berlin riots of the unemployed in 1892. At the time of the uprising, the leadership of the social democratic workers' organization was concerned about demonstrating their loyalty towards parliamentary democracy. To do so, they denounced these protests and justified their brutal crushing by the state. Reflecting Marx's ambiguous conceptualization of those outside of formal employment (see introduction to this volume), Wilhelm Liebknecht declared with relief at the 1892 congress of the social democratic party: "In any case, our party comrades at the February riots have neither smashed windows nor pillaged shops. Whoever did that deserves the name lumpenproletarian in an even worse sense than Marx has used it" (quoted in Fröba and Nitsche 1983:60, my translation). Similarly, Friedrich Engels expressed: "I am content that the Berlin riots are over and that our people withheld from it so stalwartly" (quoted in Fröba and Nitsche 1983:61, my translation). The Berlin riots marked the beginning of the conflict-riddled history of the social democratic party and its associated trade unions with the movements of the unemployed (Rein and Scherrer 1993).

Fast forward to the 1980s.[117] This time, the welfare state was on the defensive. Welfare benefits became increasingly framed as contributing to, if not exacerbating, the problem of unemployment.[118] Trade unions also faced considerable challenges as membership numbers went on a sharp decline.[119] Resources were consequently focused on retaining members, but the unemployed were not considered a core constituency (Wolski-Prenger 1993:74). While several trade union initiatives of the unemployed were founded in the 1980s (starting with an initiative in Rosenheim in 1980), the national leadership of the German Trade Union Confederation (*"Deutscher Gewerkschaftsbund"*— DGB) remained suspicious of these initiatives. Several trade union leaders considered these initiatives as unruly or as "free-riders" (see also Wolski-Prenger 1993:76). As a reaction, several initiatives of the unemployed were founded in the organizational context of churches, or else independently.

In the late 1980s, the national leadership of the DGB reluctantly began to support certain initiatives of unemployed trade unionists. Unemployment activists in turn struggled within trade unions for recognition of the unemployed as a status group. Their intention was to ensure greater influence for unemployed trade unionists through the establishment of such a status group in the bylaws (for the debate within the DGB see Zinn and Steiner 2006; LabourNet.de 2011a; for IG Metall see LabourNet.de 2011b). Currently, the service sector union ver.di is the only union in which this has been successfully achieved so far.

The relationship between trade unions and initiatives of the unemployed became strained again as social-democratic Chancellor Schröder's (1998-2005) prepared his reform-program for social and employment policies called "Agenda 2010". Schröder's advance must be understood in the context of broader ideological shifts among several leading European social democratic thinkers who subscribed to the *Third Way* (Giddens 1998). In addressing a disenchantment with the Marshallian notion of citizenship based on rights, such thought reconceptualized citizenship to be dependent on labour market inclusion (see e.g. Schierup 2004). In emphasizing the moral virtues of work and the responsibility of the individual to insert herself into the labour market, these *Third Way* ideas reflect the transformation from *welfare* to *workfare*.

A central part of Schröder's "Agenda 2010" package was colloquially referred to as the Hartz reforms, named after Peter Hartz, head of the government-appointed "Committee for Modern Services in the Labour Market". These reforms were presented to provide greater flexibility on the labour market, thereby safeguarding economic competitiveness, high employment rates, and welfare supports.[120] Among the four parts of the Hartz package, the Hartz IV law unified the administration of social assistance and unemployment assistance for the long-term unemployed. Various public voices expressed hope that these reforms could offer solutions to an unacceptably high level of unemployment and an inefficient welfare bureaucracy. The *status quo* of social and employment policies had long been delegitimized by many powerful social actors, both on the left and on the right—by welfare activists and employers' associations (Wompel 2006:136). Most controversially, Hartz IV reinforced the principle of "Supporting and Demanding" (*Fördern und Fordern*) in the provision of welfare benefits for unemployed and social assistance recipients. In the view of many critics, this came down to cuts in unemployment assistance and a tightening of the eligibility criteria for unemployed persons to receive benefits. In this respect, Hart IV was an important piece in the efforts of the "Agenda 2010" to reduce the number of unemployed workers and to expand the low-wage sector (Henning 2005). Even though it represented only part of a broader reform effort, Hartz IV became emblematic to many for the paradigm shift from welfare to workfare in Germany (see also Wohlfahrt 2003).

Trade union representatives shaped these proposals through their participation in the Hartz committee, with leaders of the trade unions endorsing the direction of the reform. Generally, the trade union support for the proposed Hartz welfare reforms could be rationalized by referring to their structural interest in the maintenance of welfare systems. In particular, the Hartz reforms claimed to secure the financing of social security programs by addressing the mass unemployment that had become a top political priority since the 1990s. Early on, the president of the DGB, Michael Sommer, endorsed the committee's proposal as part of "socially just modernization" (*Die Welt*, October 21, 2002). The idea of cutting welfare benefits in order to "activate" citizens to work—as the new policy lingo expresses it (see also Wohlfahrt 2003)—had already gained currency among national trade union leaders. As an example, one could mention the president of German metal workers' trade union (*IG Metall*) Klaus Zwickel who, in 1999, infamously denounced the young unemployed who refused to participate in state apprenticeship programs and argued in favour of cutting their social assistance (Lüke 1999).

However, soon after the publication of the proposals, several labour activists denounced the Hartz-reforms as a punitive measure against the poor (for an extensive documentation of critical comments, see LabourNet.de 2011c). Sharp public criticism against the reforms by national representatives of ver.di and IG Metall already created much irritation within the trade union movement as to whether this would be a legitimate engagement with the trade unions' historic partner, the social democratic party (Hassel and Schiller 2010:265-270). Even so, the national representatives of ver.di and IG Metall were accused of not following through with their criticism. In particular, the role of two trade union representatives in the Hartz Committee (one from IG Metall and one from ver.di) was assailed for partaking in the design of the reforms (Wompel 2006:139; for a discussion, see LabourNet.de 2011d).

In June 2003, the rationale of keeping good relations with the social democratic government ultimately brought critical leaderships of trade unions like ver.di into a conciliatory course of "constructive dialogue" that the DGB and several individual trade unions had already favoured (Hassel and Schiller 2010:269). As national trade union leaderships were perceived to sell out the demands of the protest movement, a network against the Agenda 2010 was formed "from below" based on organizations of the unemployed, social assistance recipients, anti-globalization activists, as well as local trade unions (Rein 2008:608). On November 1, 2003, this network organized a mass demonstration of 100,000 people in Berlin. Trade union memberships, however, remained divided in view of addressing the Hartz IV proposals. In the end, the trade union congresses of the metal workers union (IG Metall) and the public sector union (ver.di) endorsed the call for the November demonstration a few days before it took place. Given the growing momentum of the rank-and-file movement to resist the Hartz IV reforms, the national trade union leaderships decided to take a more active role in the mobilizations that followed. In attempting to spearhead the protest movement, the DGB organized demonstrations in Berlin, Cologne, and Stuttgart on April 3, 2004 bringing a total of more than 500,000 participants onto the streets (see Lahusen and Baumgarten 2006:114). While unemployment activists saw themselves to be on an equal footing with trade unionists in the preparations for the demonstration in November, soon after that they felt pushed to the margins by the national leadership of trade unions (Lahusen and Baumgarten 2006:114; Rein 2008:608).

A decisive break in the conflict-fraught relationship between initiatives of the unemployed and national trade union federations occurred when in September 2004 the DGB leadership declared the reform process as irreversible (see Lahusen and Baumgarten 2010:87). Around the same time, Monday demonstrations[121] occurred in several cities, organized in decentralized fashion by local networks of activists. Rein (2008:593) reports that in August and September 2004 more than one million people participated in such Monday demonstrations. With the passing of the Hartz IV laws in 2005, however, the movement quickly receded.

Labour Research—Partisan Questions

While a look at history can show us patterns in the relationship between trade unions and the unemployed, an interesting question from an activist perspective is to draw lessons in view of developing alternative engagements. A challenge for trade unionists and activists in opposition to workfare is thus to understand the concrete obstacles as to why trade unions did not mobilize with more determination and endurance against Hartz IV. In this respect, my research intends to intervene in ongoing discussions of a small but critical group of trade unionists and activists in Germany (see Frankfurter Arbeitslosenzentrum 2005; Agenturschluss 2006; Lahusen and Baumgarten 2006; LabourNet.de 2011e). I argue that reinforcing these critical voices of trade unionists in academic debate is an important contribution in the battle for a more inclusive labour movement. While labour studies have been accused of marginalizing populations outside of the core constituency of trade unions through disregard and silence (see Hines 2002), it is an interesting field from the perspective of partisan scholarship: not only academics but also trade unionists and other labour activists shape discussions in the field. Although labour studies have been institutionalized under the auspices of the "social partnership" compound between state, capital, and labour—particularly in German post-war academia[122] (see also Kaufman 2004:435-488)—it has also been an arena for radical interventions (see Birke 2010; for Canada see Camfield 2011; Thomas and Tufts 2007; for the United States see Scipes 2010).

Engaging Disengagement: Social Movement Unionism

In reflecting on strategy, one framework often utilized by unemployment activists is the so-called "social movement unionism" (e.g. LabourNet.de 2011f). This framework commonly refers to forms of labour organizing with agendas oriented towards "social justice" rather than narrowly defined workplace interests of the trade union membership. Originally developed in the 1980s as an effort to understand militant labour activities in "newly industrializing" countries such as South Africa, Brazil, South Korea, and the Philippines (see Lambert 1990; Munck 1987; Seidman 1994), this approach has also been applied to "advanced industrialized countries" (see e.g. Waterman 1999; Lopez 2004; for discussions related to Germany see Birke 2010; Turner 2007). Works in this vein share the analysis that the predominant trade union model after World War II, mostly referred to as "business unionism", is part of the problem why organized labour has been on the decline. Trade unions acting as service-providers have too often sacrificed union democracy in favour of unaccountable leaders negotiating with representatives of state and capital (see McLennan, this volume, for an alternative account of union democracy in the Ottawa Panhandlers' Union). When faced with opposition of their leadership, rank-and-file initiatives have often been stymied due to their structural disadvantage in terms of the available resources (Piven and Cloward 1977; for a discussion on Frankfurt see Jacobi 2007). This structural imbalance is particularly pronounced in post-War Germany, as trade unions developed highly centralized structures in order to act with one voice in corporatist arrangements with state and capital (Schmidt 2005). Trade unions' embeddedness in corporatist arrangements has also led them to align themselves to the "national interest" of ensuring a competitive German economy (see also Hirsch 1995).

While the centralized trade union bureaucracy could be said to have increased bargaining efficiency for their employed union members during the three decades after the Second World War, groups that were not within its ideological scope were excluded. The prevalent model of trade unionism in post-War Germany is strongly related to Fordist production patterns that assumed a male, heterosexual, white breadwinner model in a full employment labour market (see e.g. Esping-Andersen 1999). In this regard, trade unions have often been reproached for advocating on behalf of their members at the expense of those who do not fit into the scheme, e.g. unemployed, women, and racialized groups (see e.g. Schierup, Hansen, and Castles 2006; Glover and Kirton 2006).

Given these organizational conditions, it might appear difficult to explain moments in which trade unions did, in fact, mobilize in alliance with groups outside of the conventional trade union model. Some labour scholars point to the emergence of political opportunities which could arise in the context of social conflict and crises (see e.g. McAdam 1996). Such moments of opportunity are characterized by a polarization of powerful actors, including political parties, trade unions, churches, and welfare organizations. Under such circumstances, a topic such as unemployment could be rendered a focal point of public attention and an arena for mobilization and the dispute of political ideas. Resource-weak unemployment activists may then be in a position to draw resources from other social actors and force the leadership of the trade union bureaucracy to heed their demands (for specific discussion related to unemployment protest in western European countries, see Baglioni et al. 2008).

Most works on alternative union strategies analyze labour campaigns that were successful in terms of gaining union recognition or improving wages, benefits, and working conditions (see e.g. Bronfenbrenner 1998). Scholars describe processes in which workers of diverse gender, race, occupation, or other differences overcome these divisions, realize their common interests and, in acting collectively, construct a sense of identity as workers (see also Fantasia and Voss 2004). Several authors have also specifically addressed the challenges and prospects of anti-racist (see e.g. Kelley 1997; Fletcher and Gapasin 2008) and anti-patriarchal politics (Chhachhi and Pittin 1999; Yates 2006) within this approach.

A common account of social movement unionism details a virtuous cycle of social movement unionism: the success of this model reinforces its legitimacy and serves as a major boost for further organizing campaigns (see e.g. Johnston 1994). The shared hope that collective action will be victorious is a key to such campaigns (Fantasia and Voss 2004:121). To be sure, this line of research of social movement unionism has its strengths in analyzing the possibility and feasibility of alternative trade union models. Although my key informants shared many convictions of the alternative unionism model, their organizing efforts were not successful in view of their demands. As this case study will show, the body of social movement literature is of little *practical* use when reflecting on "unpromising" (but nevertheless important) cases, such as the one in this study. In my case study, the undoing of the Hartz IV reforms was arguably the lowest common denominator among the anti-Hartz protestors. While activists widely agreed on protesting the reduction of benefit levels and the implementation of more restrictive eligibility criteria for the receipt of benefits, their goals otherwise differed considerably (Rein 2008:599). The mere undoing of Hartz IV leaves open the quest for political alternatives to the previous unemployment benefit system which was widely regarded as economically dysfunctional and unsatisfactory for recipients.

Method and Methodological Reflections

The question and intention of this research is partisan in the sense that it shares the premises and concerns of those activist-scholars with whose discussions it seeks to engage. Although I have tried to be clear with my informants about my intentions with the empirical research, it was my academic persona as "researcher" that they related to in the first place. My hope that this research engagement could develop into an unfolding dialogue with several labour activists whom I contacted for an interview, unfortunately, has not yet materialized as conversations were usually driven by my interests and questions.

Most of the fieldwork for this chapter was done during the summer of 2009, with some follow-up work conducted in the summer of 2010. There were two stages to my fieldwork. First, I contacted and informally spoke with twenty representatives of trade unions, labour activists, and local labour experts in order to gain a better understanding about the relationships in the field and political views of Hartz IV. Based on the suggestions and references from my informants, I identified actors suitable for in-depth interviews in the second stage of this research. For the purposes of this chapter, I found four organizations (which I will present below) to be relevant, as they have been pushing trade unions for greater critical engagement with the Hartz reforms. A few organizations or coalitions had only a brief existence during the height of the anti-Hartz mobilization and could not be contacted for an interview.[123] In the second stage of my fieldwork, I conducted semi-structured and open-ended interviews with key informants (i.e. local trade union activists and representatives, as well as unemployment activists). The analysis of the remained of this chapter will concentrate on these interviews in which I asked my informants about their experiences in view of the relationship between trade unions and unemployment. In particular, I confronted them with the question of how they understood the lack of trade union mobilization in the context of the Hartz-contestations. In essence, case study fieldwork was conducted as a way to understand how the local is embedded in extra-local and historical contexts (see Lehrer 1999; Yin 2003). To this end, a case study is suitable for partisan research since it takes the experiences of activists and trade unionists opposing the workfare reforms as a starting point.

Furthermore, a city such as Frankfurt is an appropriate site for a case study and the gathering of a rich description of mobilization efforts. Several authors claim that cities have increasingly become the site of managing and contesting labour market issues and experimentation with workfare programs (Peck 2001; see also Wohlfahrt 2003; Eick et al. 2004), even as the laws are determined at the federal level.

Case Study in Frankfurt

I chose Frankfurt/Main as my location since it is considered *the* global city in Germany (Hitz, Lehrer, and Keil 1995; Keil and Ronneberger 2006; Keil 2011). As the site of the German stock exchange, Frankfurt is a strategic node in articulating the German economy and global finance capital. It also has symbolic significance as the headquarter location for two large trade unions (IG Metall and the construction, agriculture, cleaning, and environmental workers' union IG BAU). The economic analysis of global cities (Sassen 2001) led me to expect a high potential for labour conflict centred on unemployment. First, as the political priorities shifted to develop the "command and control" function (Sassen 2001) of Frankfurt, processes of deindustrialization and the shift to the service-sector economy have been particularly pronounced. High numbers of stable, unionized jobs have been lost in the industrial sector, while precarious low-wage jobs have emerged in the service sector. Second, Frankfurt's exposure to global capital could be expected to foster the shift from managerialism to entrepreneurialism (Harvey 1989), leading the city to orient its social and economic policies towards competitiveness. Entering this global competition, cities prioritize spending money on incentives to attract capital investments, rather than budgeting subsidies for uncompetitive industries or social purposes (Jessop 2002). This political move away from the goal of social equilibrium further exacerbates the hardship of those threatened or affected by unemployment. Since these two aspects are particularly pronounced compared to other German metropolitan centres, Frankfurt can be considered an illuminating case to study resistance in the context of changing conditions for welfare regulation and the diminishing influence of traditional trade union strongholds (Mayer 2006).

In 1995, Noller and Ronneberger described the process of deindustrialization and the notable shift towards a service sector economy in Frankfurt. Since their publication, this trend has deepened. In the period between 1996 and 2004, the proportion of industrial employment in terms of total employment fell from 18 percent to 12.1 percent—compare this to other service centres in Germany such as Hamburg with 16 percent in 2005, and Munich with 19 percent in 2005. At the same time, the proportion of the service sector increased from 81.7 percent to 87.7 percent (Jacobs 2008:50-55). The changes of the unemployment rate in Frankfurt largely mirror, in an amplified way, developments at the national level. The rate fell from 11.2 percent in 1997 (Germany: 12.7 percent) to 7.3 percent in 2001, (Germany: 10.3 percent) and increased again to 12.7 percent in 2006 (Germany: 12 percent) (Jacobs 2008:62). In 2009, the unemployment rate was 8.3 percent in Frankfurt (Bundesagentur für Arbeit 2011a) compared to 8.2 percent in the rest of Germany (Bundesagentur für Arbeit 2011b).

Given the significant loss of jobs in the industrial sector in Frankfurt and its surrounding Rhine-Main region since the 1970s (see Noller and Ronneberger 1995:47-98), it should not come as a surprise that an initiative of unemployed trade unionists (*Metaller Arbeitsloseninitiative* (MAI)—Unemployed Metal Workers' Initiative) has formed in the context of the metal workers' trade union (IG Metall). Yet, it is currently the only initiative of unemployed trade unionists operating within the city of Frankfurt.[124] Aside from MAI, there are few and relatively small trade union-based efforts in Frankfurt addressing the question of unemployment. The Frankfurt regional office of the DGB has previously been sponsoring, for several years before the Hartz-controversies, a bureau to give advice to people on unemployment or social assistance (*Arbeitslosen- und Sozialberatung* (ALSO)—Counselling on Unemployment and Social Assistance). ALSO originally had two staff positions which were gradually reduced, leaving only one part-time position since 2005. Prior to this reduction, one staff person of ALSO, together with activists of MAI, would on occasion engage in outreach in neighbourhoods with high rates of unemployment. In Frankfurt, the DGB Hesse-Thuringia representative for employment and social policies also coordinates activities of the "Network of Hessian Unemployment Initiatives", whose primary purpose is to enhance the exchange of information between unemployment initiatives in the German federal state Hesse. At times, these trade union-based initiatives also collaborated with the independent Unemployment Centre Frankfurt (*Frankfurter Arbeitslosenzentrum* (FALZ)) which has been a major hub of unemployment activism, in addition to also offering advice to the unemployed and social assistance recipients.

Hartz Reforms and Protest in Frankfurt

Among my initial conversations with trade union representatives, labour activists and local labour experts, a broad sentiment in favour of the anti-Hartz protestors' cause was expressed. The interviewees stated that the level of trade union involvement in these contestations was low and not sustained enough considering the severity of the proposed changes. Overall, the level of trade union mobilization against the Hartz Reforms in Frankfurt largely reflected the cycle of activity at the national level. It peaked in 2004 and dwindled in 2005 as the Hartz laws were passed into law.

One of the first significant local contestations happened in November 2002 and illustrates a significant conflict within the trade union organization. Peter Hartz was invited by the leadership of IG Metall to speak at the national headquarters of the union. Taking this as an affront, MAI spearheaded a protest against the event. Notably, MAI's press release to this action was also endorsed by the local office of IG Metall. Heinz Klee from MAI argues that the invitation is indicative of the intention of the trade union leadership to keep good relations to the government. At the same time, however, the rank-and-file were left ill-informed about what the Hartz-proposals entailed and the consequences they would bring. While MAI had the support of several local trade unionists, Klee claims this conflict between national leadership and local activists left many rank-and-file confused. It was only after the concerted efforts of some concerned activists in Frankfurt that the specifics of the Hartz-committee proposals were reported to unionized workers, eventually leading several rank-and-file to take a stand against these proposals. This educational effort led by rank-and-filers, however, rested on few shoulders and was only able to reach a fraction of union members prior to the passing of the reform.

A similar incident that illustrated the growing conflict between national trade union leadership and local labour activists occurred in December 2004. When ver.di's representative in the Hartz commission defended the commission's proposal at a conference of the DGB, several activists in the audience became agitated and initiated a spontaneous demonstration in the city with approximately two hundred protestors.

In contrast to the national leadership, regional trade union representatives were commonly considered by my informants to be closer to the concerns of anti-Hartz activists. Several of these regional representatives helped to mobilize and contributed to the financing of buses bringing people to the large national demonstrations in November 2003 and April 2004. Moreover several regional representatives participated regularly in the local Monday demonstrations in summer and autumn 2004. However, conflicts also emerged between them and local labour activists. Harald Rein from FALZ gave the example of a local functionary who was active in these demonstrations and various other activities against Hartz IV, yet refused bring the protest into the local administration of the employment centre in which he represented the DGB. In Rein's assessment, this could have been a strategic position to further politicize the Hartz reforms. Instead, the administration of the local employment centre operated as an old boys club in which its various members knew each other well. Apparently, the DGB representative did not want to endanger these relationships by acting on behalf of the protestors.

Frustrated by such experiences, several activists preferred to rely on rank-and-file efforts. Arguably, the most significant event in this respect was the mobilization on the first day the Hartz reforms took effect, January 3, 2005. Roughly two hundred trade unionists and unemployment activists—including members from the organizations in this case study—participated in a demonstration-turned-blockade of one employment centre in Frankfurt. This demonstration was part of the nationally coordinated effort, *"Agenturschluss"* (translates roughly into "Closure of Job Centres"), in which more than seventy-five cities participated (for an overview of these activities, see LabourNet.de 2011g). Notwithstanding such demonstrations, such rank-and-file movements receded after this event.

These accounts indicate that protest against the Hartz reforms by rank-and-file trade unionists and labour activists were often at odds with the interests of trade union functionaries, particularly in the higher ranks of the bureaucracy. Protestors, therefore, only had few resources available for mobilization. In addition to adverse organizational conditions, the political opportunities for mobilization were largely constricted due to the fact that the social democratic party pushed these reforms. While these aspects can help us understand the low level of mobilization in this case study, they also leave open questions. On the one side, trade union history shows that rank-and-filers were successful in mobilizing even against the will of the leadership or other adverse organizational dynamics (see e.g. La Botz 1990). On the other side, we could ask why this movement was not stronger, even as there were signs that the political climate became more favourable to the anti-Hartz movement. In particular, the rise of the political party of the left, "Die Linke," as a result of its positioning in opposition to Hartz IV may be taken as an indication of the political opportunities for anti-Hartz protest.[125]

Besides organizational conditions and political opportunities, my interviewees have repeatedly emphasized the issue of political motivation in accounting for the low degree of trade union mobilization. I therefore wish to highlight motivation as an area for further reflection and strategizing. Harald Fiedler (DGB region Rhine Main and initiator of ALSO) laments the lack of desire to engage in political action:

> Employees are increasingly reserved [...] to organize, to contest, to stand up for their rights. And you can try to beat a path to their doors... it essentially won't lead to more success. ... It is necessary that people want [to organize]. [...] But if people prefer to go to the amusement arcade or the tavern, then you can't [force someone to come here]. [My translation]

Fiedler accounts for the decreasing willingness to engage in collective action as based on considerations of individual utility. Ironically, the advice provided by ALSO has, in certain cases, led members to cancel their membership. Since the support of ALSO is provided independently of trade union membership, some who seek support realize that they can save a few euro per month in union dues.

Heinz Klee refers to situations in which cost-utility-calculations pre-empt forms of oppositional activity. As employment conditions become increasingly precarious, labour activism becomes risky. He speaks of the *Bild*-newspaper campaign describing the miserable fates of Hartz IV recipients when the welfare reform took effect. Rather than denouncing the effects of welfare reform, the intention of this campaign, according to Klee, was to increase the fear of those who are employed:[126]

> The pressure is on the employees: "Hartz is coming—if you become unemployed, then you will be [at the bottom of society]. So better be quiet at your workplace, don't be recalcitrant, don't say anything against the company, better don't organize with the trade union...so nothing happens to you..." The fear was fuelled to lose one's job... [My translation]

Klee also mentions employer strategies that seek to foster a competitive outlook among its employees. For one, the increasing usage of temporary labour fuels the employed workers' fear of losing their job—as labour replacement is readily available. Furthermore, competition also emerges between "Germans" and "migrants" as employers play these groups against each another. One of the employers' tactics is to, more or less subtly, label work-crews or shifts as belonging to a certain ethnicity and then appeal to "national pride". However, the logic of competition does not stop at supposed borders of ethnic identity, since even members of the same (assumed) ethnic group enter in competition with each other in view of securing one's workplace.

In addition to the growing risks, welfare activism also seems to require additional commitment and effort. Growing complexities of welfare provision in a differentiated society necessitate serious study and communication regarding their consequences and desirable alternatives. In view of the Hartz welfare reform, Brigitte Baki from the DGB Region Hesse-Thuringia and coordinator of the "Network of Hessian Unemployment Initiatives" states:

> At the latest in 2005 with the introduction of [Hartz IV] those who until then had interest in labour market and social policy resigned... since it requires such an expertise in the debate... Nobody can [educate herself in these matters] on the side. [My translation]

Thus, according to Baki, activism in welfare contestations demands significant commitment to study, communicate, and negotiate—in other words, to engage in activities that do not readily produce results or success. In practice, these activities can be deeply frustrating, and particularly after the legislation of Hartz IV these reforms can assume the appearance of immutability. In such terms, Klee states that the thought "in the consciousness of most of our colleagues is: once a law is there, there is nothing you can do about it anymore."

In summary, most employed and unemployed workers reportedly opt for individual accommodations with the Hartz IV laws and disengage from activism because of its risks and difficulties—whether perceived or real. It is thus important to note that the reasons for abstaining from mobilization efforts do not necessarily reflect an agreement with the reforms. In fact, it can be assumed that there was a lack of mobilization *despite* wider discontent. However, highlighting the issue of political motivation and commitment, the interviewees also suggest that mobilization could be imagined even under disadvantageous organizational or political circumstances.

Conclusion

In view of strategizing for labour revitalization with more inclusive and democratic trade unions, it is one thing to analyze successful examples of social movement unionism. In such cases, victories render a certain legitimacy to the movement and suggest that further advances can be achieved. However, it is another thing to make sense of movements which are up against strong obstacles, as in this case the efforts against the Hartz IV reforms. In particular, the important question for the anti-workfare movement is how such experience of disappointment can be rendered productive. Clearly, the problem and discontent with Hartz IV persists, even if the circumstances have become more complicated with its passing into law.

This case study offers insights on the significance of motivation in political protest as another aspect in mobilization besides political opportunities and organizational conditions. Clearly, motivation needs to be understood in relation to such analytical frames, as political and organizational context may affect motivations by inciting, repressing, or relativizing them. However, the issue of motivation is not entirely subsumed under these frameworks, and should therefore be analyzed and discussed further. The trade unions' failure to establish a strong mobilization against the Hartz reform is not necessarily due to a disagreement of aims. Instead, the problem is how collaboration can be ensured in a situation in which individual accommodation strategies and "free-riding" appear to be the easier way.

Against such framing of the problem, it could be objected that the history of labour solidarity was never based on the presumption of *homines oeconomici*. Rejecting such economistic caricature of human behaviour, such critique contends that solidarity has been practiced by real people based on affects, values, and creativity. Despite such criticism, this case study calls attention to the problem of cost-utility calculation as an important factor in individuals' willingness to engage in collective action (see Olson 1965). For the organizing mantra of *realizing common interests through collective action* to be effective, having common interests is not a sufficient condition. The case study shows that for movement success it is indispensable that individuals act on these interests even as they face risks, difficulties, and the uncertainty of whether their commitment will accomplish anything. For example, organizing at different workplaces against Hartz IV was a crucial strategy for the movement, with dedicated rank-and-filers risking their jobs and spending time and energy in reaching out to their fellow workers.

In those cases that chances of short-term success are slim, it would make sense to reflect on what "utility" activist involvement might already yield in the process, that is, before goals might be achieved. Such consideration would depart from the experience of many activists who, in fact, experience the practice of solidarity as fulfilling—even in the context of seemingly lost causes. Obviously, in such cases "utility" is not restricted to material benefits or political recognition by the state. To the extent that our discussions are limited to such narrow conceptualization, we might lose sight of other "utilities" inherent in our struggles: the transformation of relationships (Thompson 2010).

While we should continue to celebrate victories, it is more urgent than ever before to reflect on motivations in the face of adverse conditions that might require individual sacrifices as a condition of possibility for long-term achievements. Extrapolating from the dizzying decline of organized labour in the past thirty or so years, we should expect that losing battles will remain a common experience for some time to come. Rather than giving up activism altogether, it is crucial for us to make sense of failure and to increase our capacity to act collectively in re-considering individual motivation and common interests as well as fostering trust among activists.

To be sure, the question, analysis, and conclusions of this research resonate with my experiences in other contexts, especially my involvement in day-to-day activist practice. In this case at hand, however, I have assumed a more scholarly role—as materially facilitated by my academic position—which has allowed me to research and write on this movement. How do I thus justify taking a certain distance to an issue that I care about, an issue that arguably requires accepting risks, overcoming difficulties and building trust? A certain distance, in fact, has helped me to heed Gouldner's principle of facing the bad news and not exaggerating the good news. However, for this piece of research to be partisan scholarship, the litmus test is whether it is of any use for activists—and whether it will involve the author further into this struggle.

References

Agenturschluss. 2006. *Schwarzbuch Hartz IV: Sozialer Angriff und Widerstand—Eine Zwischenbilanz.* Berlin: Assoziation A.

Baglioni, Simone, Britta Baumgarten, Didier Chabanet, and Christian Lahusen. 2008. "Transcending marginalization: The mobilization of the unemployed in France, Germany, and Italy in a comparative perspective." *Mobilization: An International Journal* 13(3):323-35.

Beck, Hermann. 1995. *The Origins of the Authoritarian Welfare State in Prussia: Conservatives, Bureaucracy, and the Social Question, 1815-70.* Ann Arbor: University of Michigan Press.

Birke, Peter. 2010. *Die große Wut und die kleinen Schritte.* Berlin: Assoziation A.

Bleakney, David, and Michael Morrill. 2010. "Worker education and social movement knowledge production: Practical tensions and lessons." In *Learning From the Ground Up: Global Perspectives on Social Movements and Knowledge Production*, edited by D. Kapoor and A. Choudry, 139-156. New York: Palgrave Macmillan.

Bronfenbrenner, Kate, ed. 1998. *Organizing to Win: New Research on Union Strategies.* Ithaca: Cornell University Press.

Brühl, A. 2004. "Florida-Rolf, Viagra-Kalle und Yacht-Hans" *info also* 1/2004. Accessed September 5, 2011. http://www.tacheles-sozialhilfe.de/aktuelles/2004/Florida-Rolf_Viagra-Kalle_Yacht-Hans.html

Bundesagentur für Arbeit. 2011a. "Presse Info 002/2010 der Agentur für Arbeit, Frankfurt/Main." Accessed June 7, 2011. http://www.arbeitsagentur.de/nn_169620/Dienststellen/RD-H/Frankfurt/Agentur/Presse/Presseinfo/2010/002-Arbeitsmarkt-Frankfurt-Dezember-09.html.

———. 2011b. "Presse Info 001/2010." Accessed June 7, 2011. http://www.arbeitsagentur.de/nn_27030/zentraler-Content/Pressemeldungen/2010/Presse-10-001.html.

Camfield, David. 2011. *Canadian Labour in Crisis.* Halifax: Fernwood.

Casanova, Ron. 1996. *Each One, Teach One: Up and Out of Poverty, Memoirs of a Street Activist.* Willimantic, CT: Curbstone.

Chhachhi, Amrita, and Renee Pittin. 1999. "Multiple identities and multiple strategies: Confronting state, capital, and patriarchy." In *Labour Worldwide in the Era of Globalization: Alternative Union Models in the New World Order*, edited by Ronaldo Munck and Peter Waterman, 64-79. New York: St. Martin's Press.

Cohen, Jean L., and Andrew Arato. 1992. *Civil Society and Political Theory.* Cambridge, MA: MIT Press.

Cohen, Roger. 2001. "Germany and its leader achieving new stature." *New York Times.* April 17.

DGB.de. 2011. "Die Mitglieder der DGB-Gewerkschaften". Accessed July 15, 2011. http://www.dgb.de/uber-uns/dgb-heute/mitgliederzahlen

Eick, Volker, Britta Grell, Margit Mayer, and Jens Sambale, eds. 2004. *Non-Profit-Organisationen und die Transformation Lokaler Beschäftigungspolitik.* Münster: Verl. Westfälisches Dampfboot.

Esping-Andersen, Gøsta. 1999. *Social Foundations of Postindustrial Economies.* New York: Oxford University Press.

Fantasia, Rick, and Kim Voss. 2004. *Hard Work: Remaking the American Labor Movement.* Berkeley: University of California Press.

Fletcher, Bill, and Fernando Gapasin. 2008. *Solidarity Divided: Union Crisis, Globalization, and a New Road to Social Justice.* Berkeley: University of California Press.

Frankfurter Arbeitslosenzentrum. 2005. *Arbeitsdienst—Wieder Salonfähig!: Autoritärer Staat, Arbeitszwang und Widerstand.* Frankfurt am Main: Fachhochschulverlag.

Fröba, Gudrun, and Rainer Nitsche. 1983. *'...ein bißchen Radau...' Arbeitslose machen Geschichte.* Berlin: Transit.

Giddens, Anthony. 1998. *The Third Way. The Renewal of Social Democracy.* Cambridge: Polity.

Glover, Judith, and Gill Kirton. 2006. *Women, Employment and Organizations.* London: Routledge.

Gouldner, Alvin. 1968. "The sociologist as partisan: Sociology and the welfare state." *The American Sociologist* 3: 103-116.

———. 1975. "The dark side of the dialectic: Toward a new objectivity." *Sociological Inquiry* 46(1):3-15.

Habermas, Jürgen. 1973. *Theory and Practice.* Boston: Beacon Press.

———. 1987. *The Theory of Communicative Action. Vol. 2. Lifeworld and System.* Boston: Beacon Press.

———. 1989. *The Structural Transformation of the Public Sphere: An Inquiry into a Category of Bourgeois Society.* Studies in Contemporary German Social Thought. Cambridge, MA: MIT Press.

Hammersley, Martyn. 2000. *Taking Sides in Social Research: Essays on Partisanship and Bias.* London: Routledge.

Handler, Joel. 2004. *Social Citizenship and Workfare in the United States and Western Europe: The Paradox of Inclusion.* Cambridge: Cambridge University Press.

Harvey, David. 1989. "From managerialism to entrepreneurialism: The transformation in urban governance in late capitalism." *Geografiska Annaler* 71B(1):3-17.

Hassel, Anke, and Christof Schiller. 2010. *Der Fall Hartz IV. Wie es zur Agenda 2010 kam und wie es weitergeht.* Frankfurt am Main: Campus.

Henning, Dietmar. 2005. "Germany: Hartz IV measures begin to bite: Cheap labour, harassment, massive cuts in jobless benefits." Accessed June 7, 2011. http://www.wsws.org/articles/2005/jan2005/germ-j21.shtml.

Hines, Gerald. 2002. *Armut—Pauperismus—Gewerkschaften: die Praxis der Deutschen Gewerkschaften, Sich Nicht mit der Armut zu Beschäftigen.* Leipzig: AVA, Akad. Verl.-Anst.

Hirsch, Joachim. 1995. *Der Nationale Wettbewerbsstaat: Staat, Demokratie und Politik im Globalen Kapitalismus.* Berlin: Edition ID-Archiv.

Hitz, Hansruedi, Ute Lehrer, and Roger Keil 1995. *Capitales Fatales: Urbanisierung und Politik in den Finanzmetropolen Frankfurt und Zürich.* Zürich: Rotpunktverlag.

Horkheimer, Max. 1972. *Critical Theory: Selected Essays.* New York: Herder and Herder.

Jacobi, Otto. 2007. "Restructuring without unions: The polycentric region of Greater Frankfurt" In *Labor in the New Urban Battlegrounds: Local Solidarity in a Global Economy*, edited by Lowell Turner and Daniel B. Cornfield, 224-234. Frank W. Pierce Memorial Lectureship and Conference Series, No. 12. Ithaca: ILR Press/Cornell University Press.

Jacobs, Herbert. 2008. *Frankfurter Sozialbericht Teil 8. Arbeitsmarkt und Beschäftigung in Frankfurt am Main.* Reihe Soziales und Jugend, 38. Frankfurt, M.: Dezernat für Soziales, Senioren, Jugend und Sport.

Jessop, Bob. 2002. *The Future of the Capitalist State.* Cambridge, UK: Polity.

Johnston, Paul. 1994. *Success While Others Fail: Social Movement Unionism and the Public Workplace.* Ithaca: IRL Press.

Kaufman, Bruce E. 2004. *The Global Evolution of Industrial Relations: Events, Ideas, and the IIRA.* International Labour Office.

Keil, Roger. 2011. "The global city comes home: Internalized globalization in Frankfurt am Main." *Urban Studies* 48(12):2495-2517.

Keil, Roger, and Klaus Ronneberger. 2006. "The globalization of Frankfurt am Main: Core, periphery and social conflict." In *The Global City Reader,* edited by Neil Brenner and Roger Keil, 288-295. London: Routledge.

Kelley, Robin D. G. 1997. *Yo' Mama's Disfunktional!: Fighting the Culture Wars in Urban America.* Boston: Beacon Press.

Kemmis, Stephen. 1988. "Action research." In *Educational Research Methodology and Measurement: An International Handbook*, edited by John P. Keeves, 42-49. Oxford: Pergamon.

La Botz, Dan. 1990. *Rank and File Rebellion: Teamsters for a Democratic Union.* Haymarket Series on North American Politics and Culture. London: Verso.

LabourNet.de. 2011a. "Auszüge der Tagesprotokolle des 18. Ordentlichen Bundeskongresses des DGB vom 22. - 26.05.2006 in Berlin." Accessed June 7, 2011. http://labournet.de/diskussion/gewerkschaft/debatte/alosdgb06.pdf.

———. 2011b. "IG Metall und Erwerbslose - Vorschläge für Anträge zum 20. ordentlichen Gewerkschaftstag der IG Metall." Accessed June 7, 2011. http://labournet.de/diskussion/gewerkschaft/igmetall.html.

———. 2011c "'Zusammenführung' von Arbeitslosen- und Sozialversicherung: Kommentare & Bewertungen." Accessed June 7, 2011. http://labournet.de/diskussion/arbeit/realpolitik/hilfe/kommentaralt.html

———. 2011d. "Hartz-Kommission: Infos und Kommentare." Accessed June 7, 2011. http://www.labournet.de/diskussion/arbeit/realpolitik/modelle/hartz/kommentare.html

———. 2011e. "Debatte der Gewerkschaftsstrategien." Accessed June 7, 2011. http://labournet.de/diskussion/gewerkschaft/debatte/index.html.

———. 2011f. "Social Movement Unionism." Accessed June 7, 2011. http://labournet.de/diskussion/gewerkschaft/smu/index.html

———. 2011g. "Berichte von der Aktion 'Agenturschluss'." Accessed September 5, 2011. http://www.labournet.de/diskussion/arbeit/aktionen/agenturschluss_berichte.html.

Lahusen, Christian, and Britta Baumgarten. 2006. "The fragility of collective action: Protests by the unemployed in Germany and France." *Zeitschrift Für Soziologie* 35(2):102-19.

———. 2010. *Das Ende des sozialen Friedens? Politik und Protest in Zeiten der Hartz-Reformen.* Frankfurt am Main: Campus.

Lambert, Rob. 1990. "Kilusang Mayo Uno and the rise of social movement unionism in the Philippines." *Labour and Industry* 3(2&3):258-80.

Lehrer, Ute Angelika. 1999. "Case+Study=Case Study? A methodological inquiry at image production at Potsdamer Platz." *Critical Planning* 6:36-50.

Lopez, Stephen. 2004. "Overcoming legacies of business unionism: Why grassroots organizing tactics succeed." In *Rebuilding Labor: Organizers and Organizing in the New Union Movement*, edited by Ruth Milkman and Kim Voss, 114-132. Ithaca: Cornell University Press.

Lüke, Ulrich. 1999. "Guter Vorschlag, Herr Zwickel!" *General Anzeiger.* February 23.

Marx, Karl, and Friedrich Engels. 1998. *The German Ideology, Including Theses on Feuerbach.* New York: Prometheus Books.

———. (1848)2008. *Manifesto of the Communist Party.* Oxford: Oxford University Press.

Mayer, Margit. 2006. "Urban social movements in an era of globalization." In *The Global Cities Reader,* edited by Neil Brenner and Roger Keil, 296-304. London: Routledge.

McAdam, Doug. 1996. "Political opportunities: Conceptual origins, current problems, future directions." In *Comparative Perspectives on Social Movements,* edited by Doug McAdam, John D. McCarthy, and Mayer N. Zald, 23-40 Cambridge, UK: Cambridge University Press.

Morgan, W. J. 1987. "The pedagogical politics of Antonio Gramsci: 'Pessimism of the Intellect, Optimism of the Will'." *International Journal of Lifelong Education* 6(4):295-308.

Munck, Ronaldo. 1987. *Third World Workers and the New International Labour Studies.* London: Zed Press.

Noller, Peter, and Klaus Ronneberger. 1995. *Die Neue Dienstleistungsstadt: Berufsmilieus in Frankfurt am Main.* Frankfurt: Campus.

Olson, Mancur. 1965. *The Logic of Collective Action: Public Goods and the Theory of Groups*, Harvard Economic Studies, v. 124. Cambridge, MA: Harvard University Press.

Peck, Jamie. 2001. *Workfare States.* New York: Guilford Press.

Piven, Frances Fox, and Richard A. Cloward. 1977. *Poor People's Movements: Why They Succeed, How They Fail.* New York: Vintage Books.

Rein, Harald. 2008. "Proteste von Arbeitslosen." In *Die sozialen Bewegungen in Deutschland seit 1945,* edited by Roland Roth and Dieter Rucht, 593-612. Frankfurt am Main: Campus.

Rein, Harald, and Wolfgang Scherer. 1993. *Erwerbslosigkeit und Politischer Protest: Zur Neubewertung von Erwerbslosenprotest und der Einwirkung Sozialer Arbeit.* Frankfurt am Main: P. Lang.

Sassen, Saskia. 2001. *The Global City: New York, London, Tokyo.* 2nd ed. Princeton, NJ: Princeton University Press.

Schierup, Carl-Ulrik. 2004. "Whither the social dimension? Citizenship, multiculturalism and the enigma of social exclusion." In *Perspectives of Multiculturalism—Western and Transitional Countries,* edited by Milan Mesić, 17-54. Zagreb: FF-press.

Schierup, Carl-Ulrik, Peo Hansen, and Stephen Castles. 2006. *Migration, Citizenship, and the European Welfare State: A European Dilemma.* Oxford: Oxford University Press.

Schmidt, Ingo. 2005. "Can Germany's corporatist labor movement survive?" *Monthly Review* 57(4):49-62.

Scipes, Kim. 2010. *AFL-CIO's Secret War Against Developing Country Workers: Solidarity or Sabotage.* Lanham, MD: Lexington Books.

Seidman, Gary. 1994. *Manufacturing Militance: Workers' Movements in Brazil and South Africa, 1970- 1985,* Berkeley: University of California Press.

Shukaitis, Stevphen, David Graeber, and Erika Biddle, eds. 2007. *Constituent Imagination: Militant Investigations/ Collective Theorization.* Oakland, CA: AK Press.

Strümpel, B., C. Nitschke and P. Pawlowsky. 1986. "Konflikt und Solidarität im Zeichen hoher Arbeitslosigkeit." *Aus Politik und Zeitgeschichte*, B17, 26(4):19-36.

Thomas, Mark P., and Steven Tufts. 2007. "Introducing 'New Voices in Labour Studies in Canada'." *Just Labour: A Canadian Journal of Work and Society* 11 Autumn:1-5.

Thompson, A. K. 2010. *Black Bloc White Riot: Anti-Globalization and the Genealogy of Dissent.* Oakland, CA: AK Press.

Turner, Lowell. 2007. "Introduction: An urban resurgence of social unionism." In *Labor in the New Urban Battlegrounds: Local Solidarity in a Global Economy*, edited by Lowell Turner and Daniel B. Cornfield, 1-20. Frank W. Pierce Memorial Lectureship and Conference series, No. 12. Ithaca: ILR Press/Cornell University Press.

Upchurch, Martin, Graham Taylor, and Andy Mathers, eds. 2009. *The Crisis of Social Democratic Trade Unionism in Western Europe: The Search for Alternatives.* Contemporary Employment Relations. Farnham, Surrey, England: Ashgate.

Waterman, Peter. 1999. "The new social unionism: A new union model for a new world order." In *Labour Worldwide in the Era of Globalization: Alternative Union Models in the New World Order,* edited by Ronaldo Munck and Peter Waterman, 247-264. New York: St. Martin's Press.

Wohlfahrt, Norbert. 2003. "The activating state in Germany: Beyond the Hartz Commission." In *From Welfare to Work: Nonprofits and the Workfare State in Berlin and Los Angeles*, edited by Volker Eick, Margit Mayer, and Jens Sambale, 12–20, Working Paper No. 1. Berlin: John F. Kennedy-Institute Department of Politics, Free University.

Wolski-Prenger, Friedhelm. 1993. *'Niemandem wird es schlechter Gehen...!': Armut, Arbeitslosigkeit und Erwerbslosigkeit in Deutschland.* Köln: Bund-Verlag.

Wompel, Mag. 2006. "Gewerkschaftsbewegung im Hartz-Dilemma." In *Schwarzbuch Hartz IV,* edited by Agenturschluss, 135-139. Berlin: Assoziation A.

Wright, Steve. 2002. *Storming Heave: Class Composition and Struggle in Italian Autonomist Marxism.* London: Pluto.

Yates, Charlotte. 2006. "Women are key to union renewal: Lessons from the Canadian labour movement." In *Paths to Union Renewal: Canadian Experiences*, edited by P. Kumar and C. Schenk, 103-112. Peterborough: Broadview Press.

Yin, Robert K. 2003. *Case Study Research: Design and Methods.* Thousand Oaks, CA: Sage.

Zinn, Carsten, and Andreas Steiner. 2006. "Erwerbslose in die Satzung!" *Neues Deutschland.* December 5.

PART III
METHODOLOGICAL REFLEXIVITIES

Chapter 10

Participatory Practices
Contesting Accountability in Academic-Community Research Collaborations

Alan Bourke

The rule I follow says that, if there is something systematically silenced in an area of discussion, it is the analyst's responsibility to bring it into focus. In this analytic, then, it is a critical theorist's special task to speak the bad news.

(Alvin W. Gouldner, 1980, *The Two Marxisms*)

Paradigms of participatory research have entered a time of great uncertainty. Currents of political conservatism have been actively enforcing "evidence-based", "scientifically-based", or biomedically-derived models of methodological practice (Boden and Epstein 2006; Denzin, Lincoln, and Giardina 2006). Beneath the auspices of "accountability", the perceived benefit of research is cast increasingly in terms of its practical utility wherein the semantics of social partnership, civic participation, and community collaboration are incrementally tied to research "deliverables", "outcomes", and "products". Commensurate with this process has been the pressure exerted upon universities to produce tangible evidence demonstrating how they are producing socially responsive research and contributing to the communities in which they reside. Although the university has long occupied a space of relative privilege in many urban regions, it has often been an institution lacking substantive ties with local communities. In Canada, as elsewhere, community-based research (CBR)[127] has emerged as a particularly salient paradigm of academic-community engagement. Experiencing considerable popularity in recent years—what Brydon-Miller, Greenwood, and McGuire (2003:19) have characterized as a "period of expanded legitimacy"—CBR approaches have been actively championed by university administrations as demonstrating tangible evidence of scholarly engagement in the community.[128]

For some, initiatives bridging the twin antagonisms of "town and gown" can produce a "win-win" situation for all (see e.g. Martin et al. 2005). As such, calls have increased from both inside the academy, and without, to greatly increase the degree of institutional recognition and support accorded to CBR practice (Israel et al. 1998; Chopyak and Levesque 2002; Savan et al. 2009). Others, however, have questioned the extent to which the rhetoric of community engagement has approximated to the reality, particularly in regard to whether or not such collaborations have increased the degree of dialogical engagement between the community and the university (Cancian 1993; Baum 2000; Dippo 2005; Jordan 2003; Roche 2008; Bourke and Jenkins Jayman 2011). At the level of individual faculty commitment—undoubtedly there are many scholars building genuine and lasting ties with community constituencies (Flicker et al. 2007; Minkler and Wallerstein 2003).[129] Furthermore, a range of institutional mechanisms has emerged with the explicit mandate of facilitating greater dialogue between the university and community (Roche 2008; OCBR 2009).[130] Notwithstanding the laudable achievements of such endeavours, concerns linger that the distribution of power and authority remains concentrated within the institutional confines of the university, serving to dictate and delineate the degree and scope of reciprocity (Cancian 1993; Elkeland 2006). As one of my respondents would note in regard to working with a disadvantaged community adjacent to their host institution—residents from the area would quite likely experience considerable difficulty finding an available parking space at the university, never mind a reciprocal space of dialogical inclusion.

The following discussion intends to address how the methodological orientations employed in contesting marginalization are themselves rendered complicit *as* marginalizing discourses. Ostensibly, my intention is to critically interrogate the means by which the use of participatory research methods in the social sciences are positioned as *reactive* in their practice; that is, how they are forced to twist and turn within the circumscribed methodological and political spaces they are accorded. Critically, therefore, and as we state in the introduction, the chapter is provoked by the Gramscian concern that scholars are experiencing more pressure than ever before to become the organic intellectuals of the status quo. In practice, this is evidenced by the incremental blunting of the critical force of inclusive, collaborative, and activist methodologies. Extrapolating from an opening, illustrative example of action research, the discussion will initially focus upon the coalescence of action-oriented and participatory approaches in contemporary paradigms of CBR. Drawing upon interview data, the remainder of the discussion critically and reflexively situates CBR discourse in the context of scholarly accountability, methodological conservatism, and the bifurcation of academic and activist identities.

(In)Action Research

In 2007, I was involved in an action research project evaluating the workings of an educational partnership program between a high school and a university in a Canadian metropolitan area (see Bourke and Jenkins-Jayman 2011). The high school in question is located adjacent to the university in an area widely represented in official discourse to be one of "concentrated disadvantage"—characterized by intensifying social and economic marginalization, precarious employment, chronic housing insecurity and poverty, the area is routinely constructed in the media as typified by youth delinquency, crime, and alcohol and drug abuse. Frequently cited concerns by community agencies in the area include insufficient support for recent immigrants coupled with a high degree of demographic transience, a lack of affordable housing and rental units, excessive policing, negative media stereotyping, insufficient address of linguistic barriers, and a disproportionately low percentage of students transitioning from high school to university.

The program we were evaluating was one in which selected high school students would take a first year level university course with the expectation of attaining advanced credit through its successful completion, thereby facilitating their transition to full time university study. Building participant confidence through a variety of supportive structures (e.g. mentoring, tutorials, campus work placement, and volunteer work in their own communities) the program is generally seen as eminently successful in giving students who may not otherwise have considered the option of pursuing a post-secondary degree the opportunity to sample university life.

As part of the research team I conducted interviews with individual students (collectively we conducted 25). Students spoke of their involvement in the program, of what worked well and what did not, and of the apprehensions they had held beforehand compared with their subsequent experience. An often-cited value attributed to the program was deemed to be its assistance in demystifying university life. Nearly all of the students we spoke with were first generation of immigrant families, a population statistically most susceptible to both educational and labour market vulnerability. Few had parents who had attended university, although many had an older sibling or close relative who had. Hard-working, diligent, and among the best performing in their peer group, by their own self-assessments the students were particularly well suited to the program. To this end, participation in what they had perceived to be an enrichment program presented a valuable opportunity to potentially secure a lucrative entrance scholarship, gain work placement experience, give something back to the community, enhance their résumés, and gain advanced credit for their first year of study.

It was with surprise, therefore, and considerable dismay, that several students later realized that the program had been described—by the university and in a media release—as targeting an "at-risk" student demographic. Indeed, it soon became apparent from listening to the emotionally wrought stories the students told that those students most genuinely "at-risk" of falling between the cracks of the Ontario educational system were most unlikely to be amongst those actively sought out and recruited into the program. Rather, it was the academically successful students, and those exhibiting the most enthusiasm that were encouraged by their teachers to apply (one student described this as being "head-hunted"). In addition to being presented to the university and area district school board, the report we compiled was also later included in a funding proposal as evidence of the valuable work being done by the university in the community.

The question troubling the program evaluation, however, and the one which continued to linger in my thoughts afterwards, remained that of whether it made any difference to those to whom it should be held most accountable—that is, to the students themselves. Had students found comfort in the fact that their comments and concerns had been included in our report? Did exposing the representational violence of being labelled "at-risk" make any degree of impact in terms of policy recommendation? More broadly, has the shift in educational research away from the critical interrogation of pedagogical ideals and practice and toward the purpose of serving policy entailed that we are now "living in a simulacrum of education constructed by the rhetoric of policy makers and reinforced by our own collusion as researchers and practitioners," as Atkinson (2004:113) contends? Arguably, the students were vulnerable given their residence in a chronically under-resourced and systemically disadvantaged area—but were they necessarily "at risk"?

The program was certainly successful—largely due to it being built upon strong foundations; namely, enthusiastic and high-scoring students, whilst also drawing upon existent long-standing historical links between the local community and university. But therein lay a problematic tension—as, arguably, the recruitment of students on a more precarious footing as regards their academic performance would have had significant impact upon the perceived "success rate" of the program. In the increasingly parsimonious fiscal climate within which higher education is forced to manoeuvre, such indicators of success are of paramount concern. As James and Haig-Brown (2001:248) note in regard to the administrative apparatus of the university, the ascription of credit for perceived success becomes necessary for public relations and ultimately for the continuation of funding, irrespective of any mandate the university may espouse in combating social inequalities. Although official policy is committed to facilitating an ideal of post-secondary education for all, statistical data indicates that the system has become more inaccessible than ever before (Campbell 2003:36)—the recognition of which is often lost amidst the administrative pressure felt by schools to demonstrate marked improvement in student and institutional performance (Ward 2006:65). As noted by one experienced and well-funded community-based researcher:

> Really, honestly—the university couldn't care less about what research you're doing. What they care about is whether you're bringing in dollars, whether you're building a reputation, that you're publishing and you're supervising students. Whether you're doing that research on chocolate, or HIV, or creating blue bananas... they don't care. I mean, they care, but they don't *really* care. The bottom line for a university administrator is... all about the bottom line.

Readers familiar with debates on the "entrepreneurial university" (see e.g. Slaughter and Leslie 1997) will, no doubt, find such sentiments entirely unsurprising. Nevertheless, the program was one of many community-university partnerships being fostered in the immediate area, the vast majority of which continue to be of great benefit to local residents and agencies. Irrespective of the critical tone of the discussion I wish to present here, it is not one which seeks to disparage the undoubtedly valuable and practical outcomes being achieved in such linkages. Rather, it is one which seeks to trace and interrogate specific discursive trajectories structuring and implicitly authorizing dominative modalities of "community engagement". In particular, these concerns have prompted me to contemplate if community-university partnerships more generally operate under similar contradictions—that is, whether they draw upon community organizations and agencies with existent research and programmatic capacity whilst inadvertently marginalizing those who would otherwise stand to have the most to gain by drawing upon university resources.

Methodological Engagements

Not withstanding the extent to which it may have ultimately contributed to a more effective and efficient model of program delivery, the above illustration of action research offered little in the way of challenging the exclusionary mechanisms it revealed. If, following Bourdieu (1977:487), the epistemological ambit of the social sciences is partially the requirement to determine the contribution made by the educational system to the reproduction of the structure of academic capital which exists between social groups—the question becomes one of what such revelation can achieve in effecting social change. What this would seemingly suggest is that, irrespective of proclamations often made to the contrary, not all action-oriented or participatory research is committed to a transformative praxis in terms of seeking to effect social change—with such research effectively serving to alleviate, rather that eradicate, the inefficiencies and inequities of the status quo. Contrary to their points of origin, furthermore, many paradigms of action-oriented or participatory research designed to account for a traditionally excluded experience are now instigated from within the university itself, thereby facilitating the means by which various conceptualizations of "engagement" and "participation" become operationalized. As Jordan (2003) has claimed in relation to participatory action research (PAR), paradigms of community-based research have gradually experienced a blunting of their critical and transformative potential as they succumb to a process of institutionalization by mainstream agencies and organizations acting to global concert. To this end, as claimed by de Sousa Santos (2006:87), the neoliberalization of higher education threatens to transform the university into a "global institution of action-research at the service of global capitalism."

Given this context, and assuming that they can be clearly differentiated paradigmatically, what exactly are the political effects of action research (AR) compared with participatory action research (PAR)? Ostensibly, the degree of participation varies widely between projects. Furthermore, can clear distinctions be drawn between action science, collaborative inquiry, participatory inquiry, participatory research, co-operative inquiry, and a range of similar approaches which have proliferated in the past three decades? Attempting to clearly demarcate the precise methodological coordinates of each approach would surely be to reify what each entails, especially given that such collaborative, cooperative, or participatory forms of inquiry find definitional and operational precision in the very context of their application. For my present purposes, and given that the two risk being confused or collapsed in practice, I intend to draw an analytical distinction between the respective traditions of AR and PAR before proceeding to explicate their mutual convergence in contemporary paradigms of CBR.

Drawing upon interview data with a range of CBR practitioners in Canada,[131] the discussion aims to trace a specific discursive trajectory of scholarly engagement, one in which the semantics of participation and partnership are evoked as legitimizing referents in research practice. In terms of community-university collaborations, this refers to the ways in which particular discursive frames (e.g. community "engagement", "participation", "advocacy", "social justice" and so on) are accepted or disqualified in relation to authorized knowledge (Murray's contribution to this volume attempts something not entirely dissimilar to this aim in interrogating how the fundamental tenets of institutional ethnography inadvertently re-inscribe the authoritative sovereignty of the researcher gaze). This concern evokes a further key feature of participatory methodologies; that is, they tend to be organized around specific practices of exclusion which maintain existing social relations—albeit often whilst utilizing the semantics of inclusion and social change. A challenge for the critique of CBR practice, therefore, is in discerning how community consultation and input may be partially co-opted or rendered passive in participatory discourse. To this end, the term "discourse" is employed here in a twofold manner. On the one hand, it is used to refer to the context in which knowledge is produced and structured—that is, in terms of what is "thinkable" or "do-able" in a given milieu. Following Foucault (2002:54), discourses thus exert "practices that systematically form the objects of which they speak." On the other hand, discourse is understood to be ideological in terms of its connection with systems of domination (Purvis and Hunt 1993). To this end, a critical analysis of the language enveloping community-university collaborations serves to reveal a variety of strategically employed symbolic and referential discourses which coalesce in constituting a hegemonic paradigm that reinforces a strict demarcation between community and university spaces (Fairclough 1992). As argued by Jordan (2003), the general effect of such hegemony has been to assimilate and reconstitute participatory methodologies within existing forms of social organization which conserves rather than contests existent relations of ruling. In their most extreme manifestations, such co-optation bears witness to the collusion of social scientists, including entire disciplinary specializations, with a state agenda of national security (Neocleous 2008:16), the pharmaceutical industry (Washburn 2005), or the transnational neo-imperialism of financial institutions (Miraftab 2004). Similarly, Feagin and Vera (2001:177) have claimed that participatory paradigms of development have been incrementally co-opted and domesticated in obeisance to the dictates of the status quo.

Research in Action

Despite not having a universally agreed upon definition, most conceptualizations of action research (AR) emphasize it to be a "community of practice" encapsulating elements of research, participation, and action (Whyte 1991; Greenwood 2008). The approach is credited as originating with the work of Kurt Lewin and generally attributed to practitioners of clinical research, social psychology, and management/organizational theory (Lewin 1946; Nelson et al. 1998:884; Flicker et al. 2007). An additional point of influence for AR, particularly in the field of public education, has been the American pragmatist tradition (Greenwood and Levin 2003:147). As its Lewinian origins would seem to suggest, the ideological postulates informing AR have been decidedly influenced by the "cultures of affluent nations with an emphasis on such concepts as efficient and effective task accomplishment, the centrality of individuals, and consensus theories of social change" (Khanlou and Peter 2005:2335). The collaborative dimension is often either client or consultant-driven, with the action component conducted explicitly within the spirit of a decidedly problem-solving utilitarianism (Flicker et al. 2007:241). Much AR is undeniably democratic in intent, particularly in regard to seeking to open a space of participation for the "non-scientific" community, and arguably represents the closest to an activist outlet for those disciplines not especially amenable to collaborative approaches. Nonetheless, the tradition is seen as significantly differing from that of Freirian approaches to research with regard to issues of power and conflict often concealed in the participatory process (Nelson et al. 1998:884; Flicker at al. 2007:249).

Participatory Action Research (PAR), by way of contrast, has originated in areas of adult education, international and community development, and has been particularly salient within the context of the social sciences (Fals-Borda and Rahman 1991; Feagin and Vera 2001). Drawing extensively upon various traditions of critical pedagogy, PAR orients towards a transformative research praxis incorporating elements of equity and resistance to societal oppression, a process Paulo Freire (1990) termed *conscientização* (usually translated from Portuguese as "conscientization"). Integral to this approach is the pedagogical principle of co-learning wherein community members acquire skills of critical consciousness so as to recognize and assume the roles they may take in affecting community change. Drawing upon the tools of critical theory, feminism, anti-colonial, anti-racist, and constructivist paradigms as a strategy by which to critique the epistemological rigidity of more positivist-inclined approaches to teaching and learning, PAR typically recognize the intrinsic value, validity, and veracity of indigenous knowledge claims and local experience. The affirmation of such knowledge claims implies a concomitant re-positioning of epistemological stance—signalling, in effect, a collapse of the traditional distinction between researcher and researched in which the de-colonization of knowledge stands as the pedagogical aim. Such critiques have led to the opening of innovative and experimental representational spaces in which the experiential and indigenous can be voiced.

Despite their differences, both action-oriented and participatory approaches to research arguably create a space of possibility for bridging the divide between academia and society. In addition, both are explicitly normative in tone, variously espousing a variety of underlying beliefs and values in regard to how and for whom research should be conducted. In this sense, both traditions stand in contrast to more traditional forms of research in which decisions regarding project design and implementation are made in advance of the data collection process. Nonetheless, the pragmatic/reformist impulse typical of action research approaches stand in somewhat stark contrast to its more radical/transformative and participatory variants. A further analytical point of distinction emerges when one considers that AR is generally attributed to the conservatively-inclined "Northern" tradition of "scientific" practice as opposed to the "Southern" PAR tradition of pedagogical empowerment and militancy (Chopyak and Levesque 2002; Khanlou and Peter 2005).

If both AR and PAR are positioned as representative of scholarly engagement in the community, paradigms of community-based research, or CBR, have been typically represented as providing an intermediate point of reconciliation between each—variously incorporating both problem-solving and emancipatory elements depending upon the context in question (Nelson et al. 1998). Within CBR practice, therefore, a range of complimentary action-oriented and/or participatory approaches is generally practiced. Notwithstanding the occasional simplistic equivocation made between positivist epistemology and quantitative methodology as voiced by critics of "traditional" methodological approaches, a range of both qualitative and quantitative approaches can be gainfully employed in CBR without compromising the participatory or collaborative component. Broadly speaking, CBR approaches acknowledge the politicized nature of the questions posed and methods used and attempt to "democratize" the research process by sharing capacity and resources with various community partners (Savan et al. 2009).[132] Given the current salience of CBR, there nonetheless remains considerable conceptual confusion which tends to collapse traditions of AR and PAR into a unitary approach, often resulting in studies identifying as inherently PAR when in practice they are closer in conceptualization and operationalization to the methodological and epistemological tenets of AR (Khanlou and Peter 2005:2339). The absence of a universally agreed upon definition of CBR in mainstream methodology textbooks arguably perpetuates such analytical confusion. Of course, it should also be noted that the inherently reflexive nature of CBR proves resistant to such definitional capture.[133]

Notwithstanding such differences, a reluctance to engage in the critical and reflexive evaluation of the methodological tenets of CBR remains endemic to the orientation (Roche 2008). According to one community-based researcher, the task of critically interrogating such research is often hindered by a tendency toward methodological dogmatism on behalf of its proponents:

> They treat it a bit like a religion... like there's one way and this is the only way. It depends, I think, on your goals. I think that people do delude themselves about whether or not they are really

engaging in participatory action research or just action research. I think community based research is not just community based *participatory* research. I think that there are benefits in engaging the community or engaging with the community even if it is not in a participatory manner. I think that one needs to be self-aware about what one is accomplishing and what the goals are. I'm not sure that everybody really reflects on how much critical thinking is going into community-based research projects and the absence of critical thinking often being the big piece that is missing from projects that think that they are doing participatory action research—when they're really doing just action research.

This lack of immanent critique in CBR practice further entails that researchers should remain cognizant of the degree to which an activist component is actualized. As I will explicate below, two factors mediating whether research is positioned as "activist", or not, are pressures requiring conformity to disciplinary protocol and institutional dictates serving to delimitate the scope of community "engagement". To this end, as stated by one community-based researcher,

> One of the things that has come out of couple of participatory action research projects that I have known about is that the final product is actually pretty lame in terms of activism. So, they've all engaged in critical thought, and they've all engaged in all of the processes that you're supposed to have engaged with in participatory action research, and then the final product is that they write a letter to somebody. Well, that's not going to change anything, and so their awareness of activist outcomes and their willingness to commit to activism can be quite constrained.

Such sentiments raise the question of whether critical thought is being substituted for a more radical and potentially transformative form of critical praxis. According to Greenwood (2008), a leading contemporary practitioner of action research, the "professionalization" of the social sciences in the United States occurred through the elimination of the reformist ideals that caused them to be founded in the first place. In such terms, the domestication of the social sciences that their newly acquired institutional strength entailed not only demanded the circumscription of their methodological and epistemological breadth, but also their compliance to government sanctioned regimes of research governance (Neocleous 2008:184). In the place of the collaborative research practices of, for instance, the Hull-House scholars of Chicago were embedded the "punishing dualisms" (Greenwood 2008) of theoreticism versus empiricism, basic versus applied research, and the displacement of collaboration by competition—the cumulative effect of which was to construe theory and practice in ever more antagonistic terms.

Holding the Academy to Account

A guiding contention of my discussion thus far has been to suggest that the eagerness with which universities are keen to capitalize upon their community linkages is being shaped by the increasingly entrepreneurial-tinged ethos influencing research on traditionally excluded social groups. Such populations have been particularly fertile ground for "top-down" methodological research designs, and I am concerned here with the complicity of "bottom-up" participatory approaches amidst currents of methodological conservatism. To this end, a key impediment to the forging of collaborative alliances has been the (arguably justified) legacy of mistrust which has characterized relations between the university and communities (Stoecker 1999:851; Day 2005:14). In the Canadian context, Aboriginal activists and advocacy groups for persons living with HIV/AIDS

(PHAs) have been particularly vocal in petitioning (with considerable success) for greater accountability from academic researchers and currently represent a prominent, and innovative, site of CBR activity.[134] To this end, Aboriginal scholars (and scholars of Indigeneity) have been to the forefront in challenging traditional methodological conservatism, variously calling for the dismantling, deconstruction, and decolonization of existent ways of doing research (Smith 1999). Indeed, one researcher interviewed cited how their Indigenous partners refused to even allow the word "research" to be associated with their project, such was their bad experience of past research practice. For many, and with considerable justification, the image of the "ivory tower" academic has become a tarnished and archaic motif. Indeed, as Rubin (1998) states, one reason for this refusal has been participant dissatisfaction with the characterization of their communities as a collection of pathologies requiring expert action and consultant-driven remedial intervention.

This brings me to the question of how political forces in the current neoliberal climate have impacted upon CBR practice. As CBR has gained traction as a "research strategy of choice" (Roche 2008:2), its proponents have suggested manoeuvring it closer to mainstream scholarly practice, with concomitant reforms implemented in the rewards culture of academia (Chopyak and Levesque 2002; OCBR 2009). In this sense, CBR has, arguably, moved from being a relatively marginal and largely experimental paradigm to acquiring a greater degree of mainstream acceptance. Yet, whereas CBR has long been denigrated as lacking in scientific rigour, as being methodologically suspect, or has stood accused of being politically partisan rather than "objective" scholarship, its current symbolic currency in institutional discourses of academic accountability is also problematic. On the one hand, this shift towards accountability is to be welcomed—too often in the past, for instance, has research been ruthlessly exploitative of vulnerable communities. This continues to be a concern for Aboriginal communities, particularly in regard to the threat of bio-piracy from multinational corporations which seek to exploit Indigenous knowledge for commercial gain (see Seccia 2010).[135] On the other hand, the drive toward accountability carries its own dominative logic, one with the potential to permeate the structuring of the research design at all stages of its implementation.

Of significance for my present discussion has been the question of how this shift toward accountability is linked with broader structural transformations taking place in the research landscape, one in which CBR risks being rendered complicit with de-politicized conceptualizations of community participation. Furthermore, as many of my respondents noted, a discrepancy has emerged between the promotion of community-engaged scholarship by the federal government, and the systematic erosion of community capacities through funding cutbacks at the provincial level. The following community-based researcher suggested that the structuring of funding mechanisms has had a detrimental impact upon the agency of community organizations with regard to their ability to collaborate as equitable partners in research:

> I've seen a systematic dismantling of the welfare state and if we keep this conservative government in power much longer and if we shift at the provincial level to an even more conservative government, we're basically seeing a stripping of our infrastructure for social change. A lot of the non-profits that I work with have fewer and fewer resources to put to anything but core services and are being asked to cut all kinds of other services. So I think that if the neoliberal strategy that we have been adopting stays the course it could be extremely tricky for social service organizations that really should be thinking about how to develop the knowledge landscape… they are being stripped of their capacities.

Another respondent expressed this in similar terms:

> What the government has done actually is, I think, a travesty. They've created small pots of money, usually "soft money" or what they call "research money," or "development money," and then organizations apply for it and government only fund a few, and that creates division in communities. It creates conflict and tension in the community. It really is the government driving wedges between people. So, people don't like each other, and rightly so, because they set up one organization to do something different from the other organizations—and that is all due to funding cuts.

As we state in the introduction to this volume, such dampening of community capacity is indicative of a new orthodoxy of essentially de-politicized conceptualizations of engagement and empowerment—as such concepts as civil society, social capital, participation, and so on, are operationalized within the ideological edifice of neoliberal governance (for example, as Dafnos notes in her contribution to this volume, participatory action research is being increasingly used in collaborations between academics and police services). To this end, Dippo (2005:91) discerns the presence of a "neoconservative fantasy" in which granting mechanisms and funding support are gradually being replaced by a culture of volunteerism at community level (see also Baum 2000). Whilst the legitimacy for the social accountability of much CBR research is ensured by the participation of members of the community, the fact that such projects cost considerably less than more traditional research practice is also surely a key source of their attraction for the state. Indeed, the very conditions facilitating potentially successful community empowerment initiatives are themselves premised upon the existence of previously established social and political capacities conducive toward such empowerment.[136] What this means is that community organizations and university researchers who are able to draw upon such existing networks and capacities are better positioned to capitalize upon participatory projects, whereas those without remain marginalized. To this end, a range of institutionalized gate-keeping mechanisms invariably deny assistance to those community agencies and organizations who would otherwise have much to gain from drawing upon the university resources in their midst.

Co-opting Collaboration

Following Fairclough (1992), the structuring of academic-community discourse entails a parallel structuring of knowledge and social practices in which community "partners" are positioned into roles through the discursive structuring of "authorized knowledge". As such, a key site of tension exists between the technocratic language of "users" and "beneficiaries" increasingly utilized and co-opted by social scientists in CBR practice, and the experiential dimension of the extra-academic constituency collaborated with in the research encounter. Fairclough (1992:3) notes how, in educational settings, considerable pressure is being placed upon researchers and educators to envelop existing activities and relationships in new discursive practice—in such terms, students become "clients", course modules and curricula become "packages", and research "subjects" become (re)positioned as "partners", and so on. Such discursive inculcation was suggested as follows by the following respondent:

> I think you are seeing, increasingly, people adopting the language, co-opting the language, and saying, okay, now I'm doing community-based research and I'm really doing it for the reasons of an action research kind of reasoning. So now I'm working with the community [as] there is money there and I want to follow it. I'm working with the

community and, lo and behold, my resistance is lowered and this is so much easier and better... but maybe [they're] not actually doing business all that differently. So I think there is a danger of that as well... If you throw money at something then people follow the money and change their language but they may not be actually changing anything about the way that they are doing business.

Another respondent situated the movement of CBR practice in terms of an incremental instrumentalism:

There have been folks doing feminist research and activist research for a very long time and there have been folks deeply committed to partnering with different communities and you can see the historical roots of activist research in the 50s, 60s, 70s. So is it a whole new way of doing things? I don't know. Is it a whole new lingo to talk about what it is we're doing? Perhaps. Are we living in an era of the bureaucratization of community-based research? I would say absolutely.

The predominance of such bureaucraticizing trajectories in turn implicates the encompassing "passion for accountability" (Atkinson 2004:114) and "tyranny of transparency" (Strathern 2000) characterizing contemporary higher education more generally. In the process of claiming relevance, the incorporation of the semantics of "knowledge users" in producing "value-added" research is thus of significant consequence for the selection of research methodologies employed, with corresponding consequences for the epistemological and political status of resulting knowledge claims. As Denzin, Lincoln, and Giardina (2006:774) suggest, the contemporary utilization of "evidence-based" approaches to research has been accompanied by the neutralization of critical intent. In this regard, the emphasis upon externally constituted evaluative judgments (e.g. performance indicators/research assessments) manifests itself as a "performance ideology" (Atkinson 2004:118) necessitating the construction of a "rhetoric of relevance" which scholars adopt as a purely pragmatic response to a situation which calls for such transparency and accountability (Rappert 1999:717).[137]

Perhaps more insidiously, the incorporation of marginal voices into the research agenda may represent more in the way of rhetorical manipulation rather than the cultivation of a sincere collaborative ethos, thereby furnishing research with a "delusion of relevance" which embalms mainstream CBR practices rather than interrupting, challenging, and transforming them in the name of equity and social justice (Smith 1996:84; Rappert 1999:714). One respondent expressed the following concern:

> The broad use of community-based research that is happening now is that it is taking away from participatory action research. What is happening is that people are paying lip-service to "community engagement" and they're doing at best action research, and at worst are really just using a couple of community residents as figureheads.

Another respondent spoke of their experience of serving on grant review panels:

> I was doing reviews for [...] grants in the 1990s and we were receiving some participatory research proposals and it was tricky because you had to figure it out... I know that there were instances where we received grant proposals from people who said they were doing participatory research processes and they didn't have a clue what they were talking about and their research was not appropriate.

What these quotes suggest is that university researchers gain funding legitimacy for their CBR projects when community organizations are listed as co-participants. In a political climate in which all post-secondary sectors are being cautioned to exercise budgetary restraint and demonstrate "value for money", universities are thus being encouraged to capitalize upon their links with extra-academic organizations. In such terms, the participatory aspect may well be conducted on an equitable basis, albeit within parameters which preclude the possibility of substantive social change occurring. The competitive entrepreneurialism that this encourages was suggested by one respondent's view that "my experience of going and seeking community partners was that almost any community organization that I approached had already been approached by someone else that was interested in community-university partnerships." This view was mirrored in discussions I had with individuals working in community agencies who commented upon the frequency with which they are approached by academics seeking to partner.

The above respondent was also emphatic in their contention that the emphasis being placed upon securing external funding should be seen as a troubling trajectory for scholarly practice:

> This preoccupation that we see with externally funded research as being the only thing that counts for anything in the university is to me a very troubling development... and I think that the teaching and service mandates of the university are being completely overshadowed with this preoccupation of bringing money into the university, and it is distorting the way that we think about our work and it is distorting the kind of lives academics are able to live in a university environment and it has put to me very significant barriers and obstacles in the way of thinking about how to make a better relationship between the university and the community.

Such claims suggest that the transition to a form of practice in which research is done *with* rather than *to* a community is more rhetorical than real. In such terms, it may be as plausible to suggest that certain forms of scholarly engagement contribute to the organizational relations of domination that researchers manifestly proclaim to challenge. To this end, Campbell (2009:5) suggests that individual researchers are notoriously poor at thinking outside of established frames (this is, arguably, bolstered by disciplinary norms and institutional protocol), whilst collectivities (e.g. disciplinary fields) are notoriously prone to conforming to the fads and foibles of convention.

Where does this leave the status of the researcher in the contemporary configuration of what Slaughter and Leslie (1997) have termed the "entrepreneurial university"? Are our academic callings inevitably compromised if we inadvertently, or even intentionally, distort our work so as to resonate with disciplinary norms and institutional dictates? Although traditional unidirectional research methodologies now stand less chance of successfully securing lucrative funding packages, several commentators have noted that the initiation and control of much community-based research has remained firmly within the university system (Cancian 1993; Baum 2000; Elkeland 2006). To this end, the community "partner" may act as a legitimizing tool in a mode of inquiry that is largely pre-defined for promotional purposes to funding agencies and university administrations. This is not to suggest that scholars and administrators are engaging in overtly manipulative or calculative strategies in order to retain the vestiges of power and privilege, but rather to suggest that a range of systemic gate-keeping mechanisms presently place serious impediments to the cultivation of a more inclusive and emancipatory scholarly practice. To this end, there is mounting evidence (see Polster 2004) which suggests that the pressure to compete for funding is having a decisive impact upon the strategic choices scholars make in choosing a research topic. As stated by Drakich, Grant, and Stewart (2002:255), "Gone are the days when the failure to obtain a research grant was simply a personal disappointment." In other words, contemporary modes of regulation and accountability in research have coalesced to constitute professional subjectivities which require scholars/researchers to add certain kinds of value to their professional selves (Walker and Nixon 2004). One respondent presented this in clear terms:

> What I have noticed without a shadow of a doubt—there are some scholars, and most of the ones I know are in [...] who are totally in tune to getting money and they will reshape their work to whatever the topic is, and I have to say that current interest in aboriginal education is phenomenal. People who have never looked in that direction are suddenly framing their work as "aboriginal education" or making themselves "experts" in aboriginal education. So, definitely, the naming of a particular thing and the funding attached to it in some ways draws out the worst in people. It draws out the people who are great grant writers and ambitious and opportunist. Oh, it's terrible to say that isn't it? At the same time its supports some people who are doing some very good work. But I do also know there are people, I've seen them, I've watched them over the years—they'll apply for whatever is going. I find it appalling what it does. It's not that they don't have the interest. It's that they don't have the expertise and they manage to make it look like they do.

Commenting upon scholars in the field of education, Howe (2006) suggests that a significant number of researchers have compromised to current political imperatives and become complicit in the implementation of conservative methodological orientations (Denzin,

Lincoln, and Giardina 2006). In such terms, it is hardly surprising that the ethos of entrepreneurialism permeating the university produces a highly competitive and distorted research landscape.

Academic/Activist Bifurcations

Notwithstanding the progress made in forging a participatory research practice, many academics with a commitment to social justice continue to experience a bifurcation of scholarly practice in regard to their "academic" and "activist" activities. Such demarcation is arguably influenced by both disciplinary norms (e.g. adherence to standards of "scientific" rigour) and institutional constraints (e.g. adherence to traditional criteria for evaluating candidates for tenure and promotion) which effectively promote and reward disciplinary specialization. Commenting upon this university-sanctioned academic/activist divide, one experienced CBR practitioner suggested:

> I think that is interesting from the university perspective, because the university doesn't want to be seen to be engaged in activism... [We] were talking with some administrators about community engagement and about activist scholars and they were actually quite put off by the term "activist scholars" because they don't wish to be engaged in activism. But many of people who are participating under the "knowledge mobilization" umbrella actually do see themselves as activist scholars. They actually see themselves as using research for activist aims and see them as intertwined. And I think that is a challenge to the institutions, because the institutions are... they're pretty conservative in many ways even when they're making an effort to be community engaged. They want to be community engaged in the safe ways and not in the activist ways.

Although respondents claimed that such tensions permeate all levels of academe, most suggested that younger scholars and those in contract and/or pre-tenure positions were rendered especially vulnerable. With regard to my own disciplinary affiliation—Michael Burawoy (2005:14), in his call for public sociology, has stated that "today careers in sociology are more heavily regimented than they were in Mills's time… It is as if graduate school is organized to winnow away at the moral commitments that inspired the interest in sociology in the first place." Burawoy's concern, however, is not in itself a new one—as Alvin Gouldner memorably wrote in 1968, "Sociology begins by disenchanting the world and it proceeds by disenchanting itself" (103). Such sentiments of disciplinary disaffection are unlikely to change as long as the award of funding, or the necessity to acquire the signifiers of academic legitimacy, is given a higher degree of recognition than the actual research they assist in producing. As stated by a community-based researcher in education:

> I think that the message that is sent—that is conveyed to graduate students from the get-go in doctoral programs is: start running now. Start chasing the money now, because this is your life and this is your future. It's all about chasing money. There's no other way to be an academic. There's no other way to get a job. Get external funding and you're home free. Do what you need to do to do that.

For any graduate student or junior scholar, such views reveal a dispiriting glimpse of what an academic career may hold. Such regimented practice, of course, is far from specific to those in the lower echelons of the academic hierarchy. As one senior scholar admitted, "I feel like I'm just sprinting to get the superficial bit of knowledge that I need to submit for grants."

Such views resonate with the school-university partnership program I was involved in evaluating. On the one hand, my identity as a white, Anglophone academic researcher, and outsider to the area in question, and the concomitant power relations these characteristics may espouse, may well have served to position me as eminently representative of the very structures of privilege that participants struggled against. On the other hand, the resulting "research outputs" of this research—i.e. conference presentations, academic publications, and the academic status one accrues through such activities—are greatly beneficial to someone seeking to forge an academic career. In terms of the beneficial flow of research, there thus exists a problematic tension as to who stands to gain from such research. Do such tensions accentuate, as Burawoy contends, a winnowing away of moral commitment? As critically-oriented scholarship it certainly reveals the limitations, if not the decidedly conservative effects, of conducting research deemed "relevant" to community needs. Yet, according to Appadurai (2001:6), the "research imagination" of critical scholarship is also the "faculty through which collective patterns of dissent and new designs for collective life emerge." As such, the potential of critical research works as a de-stabilizing force in revealing the disciplinary protocols and institutional pressures which systematically silence voices of critique, opposition, and dissent. The contributions in this volume, for instance, exhibit similar imagination in seeking to destabilize hegemonic regimes of research governance. If, as suggested by Gouldner (1980) in the quotation which begins this discussion, it is the responsibility of the critically-minded scholar to speak the "bad news", it is surely imperative that we seek to expand the vocabularies of scholarly-activism which will allow us to do so. Such may be a practice we could all participate in.

References

Appadurai, Arjun. 2001. *Globalization*. Durham, NC: Duke University Press.

Atkinson, Elizabeth. 2004. "Thinking outside the box: An exercise in heresy." *Qualitative Inquiry* 10(1):111-129.

Baum, Howell S. 2000. "Fantasies and realities in university–community partnerships." *Journal of Planning Education and Research* 20(2):234–246.

Boden, Rebecca, and Debbie Epstein. 2006. "Managing the research imagination? Globalization and research in higher education." *Globalization, Education and Societies* 4(2): 223-236.

Bourdieu, Pierre. 1977. "Cultural reproduction and social reproduction." In *Power and Ideology in Education*, edited by J. Karabel and A.H. Halsey, 487-511. New York: Cambridge University Press.

Bourke, Alan, and Alison Jenkins Jayman. 2011. "Between vulnerability and risk: Promoting access and equity in a school-university partnership program." *Urban Education* 46(1):76-98.

Brydon-Miller, Mary, Davydd Greenwood, and Patricia Maguire. 2003. "Why action research?" *Action Research* 1(1):9-23.

Burawoy, Michael. 2005. "Presidential address: For public sociology." *American Sociological Review* 70(1):4-28.

Campbell, Horace. 2003. "Is it possible to have access and equity in university education in the twenty-first century? Lessons from the Transitional Year Programme of the University of Toronto." In *Access and Equity in the University: A Collection of Papers From the Thirtieth Anniversary Conference of the Transitional Year Programme University of Toronto*, edited by Keren Brathwaite, 35-58. Toronto: Canadian Scholars' Press.

Campbell, Nancy. D. 2009. "Reconstructing science and technology studies views from feminist standpoint theory." *Frontiers: A Journal of Women's Studies* 30(1):1-29.

Cancian, Francesca M. 1993. "Conflicts between activist research and academic success: Participatory research and alternative strategies." *American Sociologist* 24:92-106.

Chopyak, Jill, and Peter Levesque. 2002. "Public participation in science and technology decision making: trends for the future." *Technology in Society* 24(1):155–166.

Day, Richard J. F. 2005. *Gramsci is Dead: Anarchist Currents in the Newest Social Movements*. Toronto: Between the Lines.

Denzin, Norman, Yvonne Lincoln, and Michael D. Giardina. 2006. "Disciplining qualitative research." *International Journal of Qualitative Studies in Education* 19(6):796-782.

De Sousa Santos, Boaventura. 2006. "The university in the 21st century: Toward a democratic and emancipatory university reform." In *The University, State, and Market: The Political Economy of Globalization in the Americas*, edited by Robert A. Rhoads and Carlos Alberto Torres, 60-100. California: Stanford University Press.

Dippo, Don. 2005. "Redefining community-university urban relations: A project for education facilities?" *Teaching Education* 16(2):89-101.

Drakich, Janice, Karen R. Grant, and Penni Stewart. 2002. "The academy in the 21st century—editors' introduction." *Canadian Review of Sociology and Anthropology* 39(3):249-260.

Elkeland, O. 2006. "Condescending ethics and action research." *Action Research* 4(1):37-47.

Fairclough, Norman. 1992. *Discourse and Social Change.* Cambridge: Polity Press.

Fals-Borda, Orlando, and Muhammad Anisur Rahman. 1991. *Action and Knowledge: Breaking the Monopoly with Participatory Action-Research.* New York: Apex Press; London: Intermediate Technology Publications.

Feagin, Joe R., and Hernán Vera. 2001. *Liberation Sociology.* Boulder, CO: Westview Press.

Flicker, Sarah, Beth Savan, Mary McGrath, Brian Koleda, and Matto Mildenberger. 2007. "If you could change one thing . . . what community-based researchers wish they could have done differently?" *Community Development Journal* 43(2):239-253.

Foucault, Michel. 2002. *The Archaeology of Knowledge.* New York: Pantheon Books.

Freire, Paolo. 1990. *Pedagogy of the Oppressed.* New York: Continuum.

Gouldner, Alvin. 1968. "The sociologist as partisan: Sociology and the welfare state." *The American Sociologist* 3:103-116.

———. 1980. *The Two Marxisms: Contradictions and Anomalies in the Development of Theory.* London: Macmillan.

Greenwood, Davydd. 2008. "Theoretical research, applied research, and action research." In *Engaging Contradiction: Theory, Politics, and Methods of Activist Scholarship*, edited by Charles Hale, 319-340. Berkeley: University of California Press.

Greenwood, Davydd, and Morten Levin. 2003. "Reconstructing the relationships between universities and society through action research." In *Landscape of Qualitative Research: Theories and Issues,* 2nd ed., edited by Norman Denzin and Yvonne Lincoln, 131-162. London: Sage.

Howe, Kenneth R. 2004. "A critique of experimentalism." *Qualitative Inquiry* 10(1):42–61.

Israel, Barbara A., Amy J. Schulz, Edith A. Parker, and Adam B. Becker. 1998. "Review of community-based research: Assessing partnership approaches to improve public health." *Annual Review of Public Health* 19: 173-202.

James, Carl, and Celia Haig-Brown. 2001. "'Returning the dues': Community and the personal in a university-school partnership." *Urban Education* 36(2):226-255.

Jordan, Steven. 2003. "Who stole my methodology? Co-opting PAR."

Globalisation, Societies and Education 1(2):185-200.

Khanlou, N., and E. Peter. 2005. "Participatory action research: Considerations for ethical review." *Social Science and Medicine* 60(10):2333-2340.

Lewin, Kurt. 1946. "Action research and minority problems." *Journal for Social Issues* 2:34-46.

Martin, Lawrence L., Wende Phillips, and Hayden Smith. 2005. "Bridging 'town and gown' through innovative university-community partnerships." *The Public Sector Innovation Journal* 10(2): article 20.

Minkler, Meredith, and Nina Wallerstein, eds. 2003. *Community-Based Participatory Research for Health.* San Francisco: Jossey-Bass Publishers.

Miraftab, Faranak. 2004. "Public-private partnerships: The Trojan horse of neoliberal development?" *Journal of Planning Education and Research* 24(1):89-101.

Nelson, Geoffrey, Joanna Ochocka, Kara Griffin, and John Lord. 1998. "Nothing about me without me: Participatory action research with self-help/ mutual aid groups for psychiatric consumers/survivors." *American Journal of Community Psychology* 26(6):881–912.

Neocleous, Mark. 2008. *Critique of Security.* Montreal: McGill-Queen's University Press.

Office of Community-Based Research (OCBR). 2009. *The Funding and Development of Community University Research Partnerships in Canada: Evidence-Based Investment in Knowledge, Engaged Scholarship, Innovation and Action for Canada's Future.* University of Victoria. Accessed September 5, 2011. http://web.uvic.ca:8080/~ocbrdev/sites/default/files/Final-CU%20SSHRC%20Report-sept%2024.pdf

Polster, Claire. 2004. "Canadian university research policy at the end of the 20th century Continuity and change in the social relations of academic research." *Studies in Political Economy* 71/72:177-199.

Purvis, Trevor, and Alan Hunt. 1993. "Discourse, ideology, discourse, ideology, discourse, ideology..." *British Journal of Sociology* 44(3):473-499.

Rappert, Brian 1999. "The uses of relevance: Thoughts on a reflexive sociology." *Sociology* 33(4):705-723.

Roche, Brenda. 2008. "New directions in community based research." Wellesley Institute. Accessed September 5, 2011. http://wellesleyinstitute.com/files/newdirectionsincbr.pdf

Rubin, Victor. 1998. "The role of universities in community-building initiatives." *Journal of Planning and Research* 17(4):302-311.

Savan, Beth, Sarah Flicker, Brain Kolenda, and Matto Mildenberger. 2009. "How to facilitate (or discourage) community-based research: Recommendations based on a Canadian survey." *Local Environment* 14(8):783–796.

Seccia, Stefania. 2010. "Protocol lacks recognition of Indigenous knowledge." *Aboriginal Multi-media Society*. Accessed September 5, 2011. http://www.ammsa.com/publications/windspeaker/protocol-lacks-recognition-indigenous-knowledge.

Slaughter, Sheila, and Larry Leslie. 1997. *Academic Capitalism: Politics, Policies, and the Entrepreneurial University*. Baltimore: John Hopkins University Press.

Smith, Bob 1996. "Addressing the delusion of relevance." *Educational Action Research* 4(1):73-91.

Smith, Linda. 1999. *Decolonizing Methodologies: Research and Indigenous Peoples*. New York: Zed Books.

Stoecker, Randy. 1999. "Are academics irrelevant? Roles for scholars in participatory research." *American Behavioral Scientist* 42(5):840–854.

Strathern, Marilyn. 2000. "The tyranny of transparency." *British Educational Research Journal* 26(3): 309-321.

Walker, Melanie, and Jon Nixon. 2004. *Reclaiming Universities from a Runaway World*. Maidenhead, UK: Open University Press.

Ward, Nadia L. 2006. "Improving equity and access for low-income and minority youth into institutions of higher education." *Urban Education* 41(1):50-70.

Washburn, Jennifer. 2005. *University, Inc.: The Corporate Corruption of American Higher Education*. New York: Basic Books.

Whyte, William, F., ed. 1991. *Participatory Action Research*. Newbury Park, CA: Sage.

Chapter 11
Lost in Translation
The Social Relations of an Institutional Ethnography of Activism

Kate M. Murray

Dorothy Smith developed her critical feminist sociology and approach to inquiry, institutional ethnography (IE), as a challenge to dominant forms of knowledge wherein information about people is constructed by and for ruling institutions (1989). Instead, Smith has suggested that research should create a kind of *map* of the myriad of social relations which organize individuals' everyday activities in the interests of ruling. Thus, her approach has been described as having both explicatory and emancipatory potential—in that it may help individuals resist domination by organizations (Campbell and Gregor 2002). In my MA thesis research, I used IE to explore the experiences of anti-poverty activists in Ottawa, Canada. During preliminary conversations with local activists, several individuals—despite generously sharing their insights—had made offhand references to the questionable value of *academic research*. New to the worlds of political work and critical scholarship, I had done very little thinking about whether or not I was doing "activist-scholarship"; I just knew I wanted to do research that local activists could *use*. Because I understood Smith's approach as able to produce an academic analysis and a specific, useable "map" for activists, it seemed that IE would fit the bill.

In my study, use of IE did produce a coherent and compelling critique of the social organization—and regulation—of the public participation activities of local activists who were members of the city's Poverty Issues Advisory Committee (the PIAC). The approach provided a systematic means of navigating a complex and large body of interview and text-based data, and focused my research in a distinct and potentially useful way. However, upon completing my research and turning my attention to its use by activist-participants, I had the distinct feeling that something *chafed* (Campbell and Gregor 2002). Through the practicalities of my project, many of IE's important assertions seemed to have been turned *upside down*. Throughout the research process I had carefully studied Smith's (e.g. 1990a, 1987, 1989, 1990b, 1999) line of thought, and especially attended to instructions about how to *do* IE (e.g. Campbell and Gregor 2002; Smith 1987). However, my insufficient consideration of how IE's conceptual premises would translate *on the ground* to some extent reproduced the very dynamic Smith endeavours to avoid—that of participant as objectified and "lost", and researcher as "position-less" expert. Within this unexpected theory-practice disjuncture, my objective to write "with and for" local anti-poverty activists had somehow gone missing.

Here, I consider my own inquiry *in practice* and *in hindsight* to unpack how this theory-practice disjuncture occurred, and to critically interrogate how IE (does and might) *work* as a basis for activist-scholarship.[138] In doing so, I critically explore my own practice, but also endeavour to illustrate how my experience relates to what Walby (2007:1008) describes as IE practitioners' insufficient attention to the approach's own "social relations of research." Among other questions, I consider whether IE's focus on the explication of *ruling* brings potential for problematic objectification and misrepresentation of participants, and does not adequately advance praxis; I connect this to lack of clarity about how accountability within IE actually *works*. In this chapter, I do not suggest that IE should be abandoned as a basis for activist inquiry; instead, I expose my own historical practice as a kind of *warning*, and also as a means to imagine how IE could be fruitfully employed—consistent with Smith's trajectory—through use by activist-scholars within co-operative, accountable relations of radical praxis.

Institutional Ethnography and Research as Problematic

Smith's (e.g. 1987, 2002) thinking is grounded in her experience during the 1970s within North American women's movements, as a mother, and as one of few women working in the abstract and male world of academia. Beginning from her sense of leading a "double life" (Smith 2002:17), Smith developed an analysis of the inadequacy of traditional methods of social research: Sociology, as society's consciousness of its own social life, has been systematically organized according to conventional knowledge; the interests and relevancies of those in power are authorized as *rational* knowledge. Those who fall outside of this ruling group learn to know themselves from the standpoint of those who have the power of *authority*—the capacity to get things done in words (Smith 1987). In particular, Smith has been interested in uncovering the extra-local, or translocal organization of activities within local and historically specific settings; she has focused on how this is accomplished through *textually-mediated social organization* wherein engagement with texts arranges and coordinates the actions of people (Smith 1984, 1987, 1990b).

Since Smith's (1987) introduction of her approach as "a sociology for women," IE has seen increasing application to contexts—varying, for instance, from mothering, to healthcare to social movements (see e.g. Smith 2006; Campbell and Manicom 1995; Frampton et al. 2006a). These varying inquiries have involved interviewing, observation, and detailed analyses of texts in order to discover and *map* the social relations through which individuals' activities are coordinated (see Dafnos, this volume, for discussion of the intersectionality of personal location and "studying-up"). In addition, there is an expanding body of work undertaken to clarify, interpret, and/or apply IE in light of various theoretical and practical projects; many authors have sought to interpret, critique, or clarify Smith's epistemological and ontological assertions—especially her conceptualization of *standpoint*.[139] Other efforts focus on elucidating IE as methodology: Campbell and Gregor's (2002) *Primer in Doing Institutional Ethnography* is frequently referenced as a guide to the practice of IE and an introduction to Smith's complex line of thought; elsewhere, DeVault and McCoy (2002) have examined processes of interviewing within IE research.

Despite its roots in the women's movement, Smith has positioned her work in relation to mainstream sociology and most accounts of IE research are articulated within academic texts and settings. Nonetheless, her approach to inquiry is commonly seen as having significant potential to inform and strengthen the community-based efforts of those who seek to challenge and dismantle ruling arrangements (Frampton et al. 2006a; Campbell and Gregor 2002; Mykhalovskiy and McCoy 2002). An early, concerted attempt to develop IE as a tool of community-based activism is marked by the work of activist-researcher George Smith (1935-1994). G. Smith's work has roots in Dorothy Smith's line of thought, but is characterized as an extension of IE and distinguished as *political activist ethnography* (Frampton et al. 2006a). More recently, Pence (2001) and Turner (n.d. in Smith 2005:221) have also endeavoured to envision how IE might inform community-based activism.

Unlike its proliferation in academic inquiry and discourse, however, Mykhalovskiy and McCoy note that IE's relation to community-based organizing and community-based research is generally not well-developed. The authors attribute this not to "poor fit," but to the "general exigencies" of writing for the community—an activity not supported by "the relevances and work organization of the academy" (2002:20). Campbell and Gregor (2002) describe difficulties related to accessing institutional data, or the potential for institutional leaders to feel threatened by IE research. Funding arrangements, organization of promotion and tenure, disciplinary orthodoxy, and ethics review requirements (not to mention the political silencing of *whistleblowers*) all constitute ways in which community-based and activist research is regulated within academic institutions (Frampton et al. 2006b; Smith 1987; see also Bourke, this volume). Other tensions relate to activists' mistrust and critiques of university-based scholars as—among other things—irrelevant, elitist, voyeuristic, vanguardist, or "parasites seeking street cred or professional advancement" (Day 2005:12; see Bourke, Dafnos, and Kip, this volume).

But while Smith (e.g. 2005, 1987) and others (e.g. Mykhalovskiy and McCoy 2002; Frampton et al. 2006b) highlight potential problems related to IE practitioners' tendency to be located within ruling institutions such as universities and research bases, Walby (2007) raises questions that are more integral to IE's own ontology and epistemology. Walby (2007:1023) asserts that "institutional ethnography is not honest about the role of theory in its practice," and suggests that those doing the practical and conceptual work of IE have avoided scrutiny of how knowledge is produced within IE itself. This chapter makes a contribution to exploring what Walby (2007) highlights as IE's own social relations of research. It also adds to recent, concerted attempts to critically explore and develop IE as a tool for activism and radical struggle (see Frampton et al. 2006a).

Institutional Ethnography in Practice

To begin my thesis research, I interviewed local anti-poverty activists, observed their public participation, and collected related documents. Campbell and Gregor (2002) suggest IE research-writers should begin by siding with informants—becoming oriented to their everyday experiences and accepting their perspectives as *true*. My informants' descriptions of their work reflected them as energetic and empowered; they described overcoming institutional obstacles, and pushing boundaries to influence policy. It was clear they worked skilfully within, and around, bureaucratic processes to accomplish their anti-poverty goals. In concert with Smith's (e.g. 1987:110, 61) characterization of informants as "expert practitioners," I thus came to understand my informants as competent and skilful *public participation experts*.

Endeavouring to work from the standpoint of my informants, I explored and documented the *actual*[140] ways in which their public participation was coordinated. Institutional ethnography does not prescribe particular research activities (Campbell and Gregor 2002). However, Smith (1987) and others outline various techniques of inquiry that can be used: I encouraged informants to speak concretely so I could identify the specific practices through which they *made real* things that otherwise existed only in the virtual form of words, ideas, directives, and policy (Campbell and Gregor 2002). I examined discursive representations of activities as a situated means of accessing the relations through which they were created (Smith 1990b).

To uncover the hidden portions of social relations, I encouraged interviewees to speak freely and paid close attention to their language. I looked for "clues" in individual accounts that indicate what informed participants' actions, where these messages came from, and how others were implicated (Campbell and Gregor 2002). To identify disjunctures between *ruling* and *experiential* versions of reality, I looked for unanswered questions and contrasts between informants' expression of their participation expertise, and their commonsense theorizing about their everyday lives (Campbell and Gregor 2002). I listened for "institutional ideologies" wherein professional training teaches people how to view the actualities of their experience in forms that are recognizable in institutional discourse (Smith 1987). Campbell and Gregor (2002) suggest that analysis should occur through the writing up of "stories" about discrete pieces of data which can later be organized. This practice is considered to maintain the standpoint of subjects and ensure the analysis is relevant to those whose experience is problematized (Campbell and Gregor 2002; Smith 1987).

Based on these guidelines, I began to write up my data. For instance, I noticed that as one informant described how city staff members were required to bring "poverty issues" forward for consideration by the PIAC, (s)he constantly used qualifying terms:

> *Theoretically*, what's supposed to happen is…
> …they're *supposed to* send…
> …we're *supposed to* be able to say…
> …we're *supposed to* have that opportunity…
> [emphasis added]

I noted that the informant's repeated use of the term "supposed to" suggested that—although (s)he was describing an official process—this was not how things *actually* happened. Further, when the informant went on to describe how the PIAC was informed about institutional rules, this narrative pattern abruptly ended; my informant no longer used qualifying terms: "*certainly* any changes to the way—the structure of PIAC or the way it works—gets sent to us … through city staff *we receive all that stuff…*" [emphasis added]. Thus, this account provided a "clue" to a disjuncture between ruling (official) and actual versions of reality; it contrasted the *theoretical* nature of the PIAC's opportunity to influence policy, with the *certainty* that the committee was made aware of institutional *rules*.

During another interview, an informant described how the PIAC receives presentations from community members. The interviewee stated that because the PIAC only has three hours per month in which to "conduct business," each community presenter is told, "you've got five minutes to make your case." I noted these statements invoked a legalistic framework, and mirrored the corporate language of *streamlining, efficiency*, and *productivity* that was common in City of Ottawa organizational documents. Drawing on Smith's (e.g. 1987) understanding of ideology, I noticed instances wherein this ideal of *efficient production of anti-poverty advice* was echoed in PIAC members' own anti-poverty participation goals and their descriptions of public participation that happened "exactly as it was supposed to" (Murray 2011).

Another interviewee described further ways in which the PIAC efficiently managed community presentations: "...so now we actually do screen our presenters; you can't just come, you have to actually submit in writing in advance why you're coming and what exactly you're hoping we'll do for you." As I wrote up the *story* of this account, I noted that PIAC's requirement for community presenters to submit a written backgrounder and to specify particular recommendations were *practices* through which institutional ideals of "efficiency" and "effectiveness" were *made real* through the work of PIAC members: documents organize work for efficiency and ease of processing Campbell and Gregor 2002; Smith 1990b).

The latter speaker's account illustrates how PIAC members expertly managed community concerns to ensure maximum institutional impact. However, Smith's (1987, 1990b) analysis of text-based social relations also highlights how requiring a backgrounder can arrange community members' efforts within institutional reporting structures and within structures of class and ethnicity (through, for example, requiring advanced formal education, computer access, and proficiency in English or French). Further, submission of a backgrounder enables the one-way transfer of community knowledge to the city government. Although undertaken to advance community concerns, requiring a backgrounder can also be understood as a practice through which PIAC members took up ruling relations and, in effect, acted as gatekeepers who managed the complex and difficult issue of poverty for city councillors (Murray 2011).

In this way, my analysis explored how the public participation work of my informants was *arranged* within ideological and actual relations of "managerial effectiveness" (Cooke and Kothari 2002), and was, in some cases, bypassed altogether. Focusing on *actual practice* in an attempt to *preserve the presence of subjects* (Campbell and Gregor 2002; Smith 1987), I began to assemble my data stories to produce a *map* of ruling relations for my informants. In this way, my research resonated with IE's objective to reverse the usual flow of inquiry through which knowledge *about people* is transferred *to institutions* that produce knowledge for ruling (Smith 1989, 2002).

Initially, this principle of a "reversal" of knowledge seemed feasible. However, bit-by-bit, the distinction between writing *for* and *about* participants began to blur. While IE's analytic focus is on *social relations*, these are often explored and illustrated via detailed description of the practices and narratives of *informants* (see e.g. Rankin and Campbell 2006; Campbell 2001; Diamond 1992; Walby 2007). My intent had been to write *for* participants and to uncover social relations, but upon re-reading my completed analysis, I realized I had written great deal *about* my informants; parts of the research read almost like critiques of activists themselves! I had (I believe) effectively used IE to uncover a myriad of social relations, but why did *participants* appear as the object of scrutiny?

IE in Hindsight: Lost in Translation

This unexpected slide—from writing for, to writing *about* my participants—produced a sense of disjuncture between my understanding of Smith's conceptual approach, and how my research occurred in practice. I had assumed my careful attention to accounts of how to *do* IE would ensure I was "collaborat[ing] with informants" (Smith 2005:140), and acknowledging them as having "experiential authority" (Smith 2005:141). Upon re-reading my research, however, I felt as though I had personally betrayed informants—first inviting them to "share their expertise", and then *translating* this into an unexpected critique. This dynamic created my own sense that a vital objective of my project had somehow *gone missing*. In the years following my research, I have endeavoured to reflect on this "line of fault" (Smith 1987) between my experience of IE "in theory" and in practice.

Knowledge Reversal? Standpoint and the Disappearance of Subjectivity

DeVault and McCoy (2002:20) describe how the "classic" approach in IE is to "'take the standpoint' of the people whose experience provides the starting point of investigation." Smith (1987:127) states that, to work from the standpoint of women "we must cede from the outset our discursive privilege to substitute our understandings for those whose stories instruct us in their experience of lived actualities." Accounts of how to do IE describe how this is accomplished through open-ended interviewing, allowing questions and research activities to emerge throughout the research process (Smith 1987; Campbell and Gregor 2002; DeVault and McCoy 2002; G. Smith 1990), and avoiding use of dominant discourses or categories within interviews and focus groups (Mykhalovskiy and McCoy 2002; Griffith and Smith 2005). G. Smith describes this in terms of his *materialist époche* device: "bracketing my own political or sociological theories and speculative accounts as part of a procedure for making sense of what people had to say on its own terms" (1990:642). Based on these practices, IE is commonly described as *maintaining* or *preserving* informants' standpoint, and their presence as active subjects (e.g. Smith 1987:105, 11, 51, 211; DeVault and McCoy 2002:44, FN 2); Smith (1987:224) states that inquiry should be undertaken such that informants "can speak to us and through us to others as subjects."

Taken together, it is my sense that these various descriptions of Smith's approach suggest a set of confusing premises. Accounts of IE highlight the embodied standpoint of both informants and researchers, but many of these seem to imply that it is possible for researchers to disown aspects of their own understanding and work instead from the perspective of informants. In fact, Smith's overall line of thinking runs contrary to this interpretation. But to some degree it appears that, in the translation of Smith's thinking to IE practice, the agency of the researcher has *gone missing*.

Smith's (1987) articulation of IE reflects her considerable awareness of relations between observer and observed, and her conceptualization of *authority* critiques sociologies wherein the invisibility of the author allows the ruling perspective to come to be equated with neutrality and objectivity (e.g. Smith 1990b:12-52). However, her discussion of this relation is generally framed as a critique of traditional sociology, and as a rationale for the open-ended practices described above (see e.g., Smith 1987:111-17). While it is common to describe IE's relations of research as reflexive and/or involving co-construction of data (e.g. DeVault and McCoy 2002; G. Smith 1990; Smith 2005), Smith's (2005:123-44) discussion of data collection and analysis as "dialogue" tends to convey this as one-way, characterizing the ethnographer as an "acute, thoughtful, and probing listener," such that the "authority of the experiencer [informs] the ethnographer's ignorance" (2005:138). Thus, Smith recognizes that participants' experience informs the perspective of the researcher, but seems to downplay the practices involved as the researcher organizes informants' narratives according to the relevancies of IE. Perhaps this relates to her efforts to go "beyond" important but insufficient feminist critiques of the relationship between researcher and "subject" (Smith 1987:111). At any rate, my sense is that IE literature as a whole does not sufficiently challenge the assumption that problematic objectification of informants only happens in *other* kinds of research.

I believe that my attempt to "take the standpoint" of my informants was integral to identifying a research problematic and to producing a meaningful analysis of social relations. However, because I understood Smith's suggestion (above) that informants "can speak to us and through us" to mean I could be a sort of impartial facilitator of participant "voice", I did not sufficiently anticipate or recognize my own subjectivity within the research process. Walby (2007:1008-1009) emphasizes how "interviewing is constitutive of the account, how transcription is an interpretive instead of straightforward process" and thus, "how research produces rather than preserves the presence of the subject." My analysis was formulated through a creative process in which I drew on my own experience, engaged with conceptual writing on IE, and actively made—and made meaning of—the activities and talk of participants both during and following my observation and interviews. Together with my research informants, I sought to better understand their work. However, I failed to recognize that as a researcher, I was engaged in my own project (distinct from that of my informants) of *producing an institutional ethnography.*

Cartographic Principles: The Discovery of Hidden Ruling

My failure to adequately scrutinize the idea of *preserving subjectivity* was linked, in part, to Smith's (e.g. 1987, 2005) assertion that IE does not aim to theorize or explain, but rather to explore and explicate; Smith (2005:52) describes IE as enabling "discovery of and learning from actualities" by proposing "cartographic principles for what might be incorporated in to the mapping of the social." However, Walby (2007:1017) suggests that the problem with this ontology of *explication* is that "it takes the world as if it was to be discovered instead of interrogating the way ontology itself constitutes the world."

Smith's overall line of thinking is not blind to the critique that Walby raises. In re-reading some of Smith's writing on this topic, I have come to understand her critique of *theorizing* and focus on "explication" of the "actual" to be a kind of shorthand articulation of her historical materialist ontology and its groundedness in her own experience. Smith and other IE practitioners acknowledge the role of theory within IE, but have attempted to distinguish IE from particular, dominant kinds of sociological theorizing that are idealist and/or positivist (see e.g., Smith 1987:106, 209-10; 2005:50; 1997:396). However, I do think many attempts to convey this distinction in its short form (i.e., "explore, not theorize") have resulted in the tendency to present and understand IE as merely descriptive. Walby cautions that the claim to *describe* rather than *interpret* can obscure the influence of the research-writer in producing research findings such that "the Archimedean point of so-called traditional sociology is actually retained in smaller parts" (2007:1013).

As an inexperienced scholar, I did not adequately scrutinize the assertion that IE "avoids imposing interpretations and collaborates with informants… in *discovery*" (Smith 2005:140). Based on the idea that I was "discovering", I did not sufficiently anticipate the specific dynamics of my collaboration with informants and thus appreciate how IE's "theorized practices of looking at the actualities of everyday life" (Campbell and Gregor 2002:17) arranged my practices of inquiry and analysis. IE's objective to explicate how the social world is organized "outside" or "beyond" what a person immediately or directly knows (Campbell and Gregor 2002:18; Campbell 1998:57; Smith 1987:89) requires elements of the research's *discovery* to surpass the everyday expertise of informants:

In the research context this means that so far as their everyday worlds are concerned, we rely entirely on what... people tell us, about what they do and what happens. But we cannot rely upon them for an understanding of the relations that shape and determine the everyday. Here then is our business as social scientists.... (Smith 1987:110)

Smith (1990b) suggests that *insider words* provide a cue to how someone, speaking about their life, misses its social organization. She draws attention to narrators' use of deictic terms (such as "now", "there", "we"), to how accounts are sequenced, and to how they are "worked up" as "fact". Smith (1987:161) demonstrates how ideological knowledge functions as textually-mediated social organization in which people "recycle the actualities of their experience into the forms in which it is recognizable within institutional discourse."

Thus, notes G. Smith (1990:644), IE requires "an acquired ability to 'see' organization in people's talk." Accounts of IE research illustrate how individuals take-up dominant discourses and ideologies—for instance, of "client-centred" (Campbell 2001), "holistic" (Rankin and Campbell 2006), or "mothering" (Griffith and Smith 2005)—even when these run counter to their lived experience. G. Smith (1990:633) describes how researchers distinguish *actual* from *ideological* ways of knowing:

> These procedures depended... on treating people who worked in the regime as knowledgeable informants. It was always important to remember that simply in order to hold their jobs they had to know their way around the regime I was interested in investigating and describing, but knew little about. These procedures, however, did not require me to believe the ideological accounts produced by a ruling apparatus.

Walby suggests that through such practices of inquiry, IE researchers listen "around and beyond words" (DeVault 1999:66) to infer "what the talk really means" (Walby 2007:1021). Thus, he asserts, the approach "relies not on the authority of the participant as an expert of their everyday life but on the authority of the institutional ethnographic frame to be able to guide the interview toward satisfaction of the ontological claims" (2007:1022). In undertaking my research, I did not adequately scrutinize how my project was organized by this ontology of *hidden ruling* wherein "inquiry is directed towards exploring and explicating what [an informant] does not know—the social relations and organization pervading her world but invisible in it" (Smith 1992:91).

Because the IE researcher's task is to explicate how ruling relations are present, yet hidden, within informants' local practices, Walby (2007) notes that IE researchers have a tendency to describe how participants "struggle in the dark" (Smith 2005:32). This tendency relates—I think—to how, as a body of discourse, accounts of IE seem to involve a second set of contradictory practices: on one hand, are claims that the researcher stands with, learns from, and preserves the presence of subjects; on the other, are procedures through which the researcher scrutinizes informants' narratives for evidence of ruling discourses. Similar to other IE accounts of ideological knowing, my research explicated how—in expertly managing community members' concerns by requiring submission of a backgrounder—PIAC members unknowingly took up institutional discourses of *efficiency* and *productivity* to act as gatekeepers. In effect, I "discovered" that what my informants took to be their own agency was in fact arranged by ruling Others. Walby (2007) states that this sociological claim to *discover something for those who are blinded by ideology* is what Sorokin (1956 in Walby 2007) called the "Columbus complex".

Preserving Subjectivity, or Producing Misrepresentation?

In this way, my own experience suggests that common practices of IE research can arrange and obscure a problematic relation between researcher and researched wherein the *insightful, technical analysis of the researcher uncovers the hidden domination of participants*. In my project, this dynamic played out in a particularly acute way. Along with my (sincere) written statement informing activists that I hoped to "draw on [their] expertise", my relative youth and inexperience—combined with formal institutional recognition of the PIAC's effectiveness—reflexively organized interviews such that many informants' narratives were accounts of how they successfully navigated political obstacles and processes to accomplish successful public participation. However, following my analytic secondary dialogue (Smith 2005) with my interview data, my written analysis introduced some of these very same accounts as "evidence" (Campbell and Gregor 2002) of informants' take-up of institutional ideologies and thus, of *hidden ruling*. Rather than defer to my "informants' experiential authority" (Smith 2005:141) I had, in effect, *translated* their stories of expertise and agency into stories of complicit domination.

I wish to emphasize that I do not consider my analysis to be problematic because it was careless, biased, or otherwise failed to capture the "truth". As far as I can tell, what I did was the credible, successful *production of an institutional ethnography*. I explicated how my informants' work was socially organized in ways that extended beyond their local practice; my analysis included extended interview quotes and document excerpts to demonstrate the *actual* practices and textually-mediated connections through which this occurred. The "map" of social relations I produced could be drawn upon to point to specific institutional practices which my informants might endeavour (and often were already endeavouring) to change. My analysis illustrated how informants sometimes worked within socially-organized boundaries and took-up institutional discourses, and other times they named these arrangements as problematic and actively worked to contest them. By and large, I think, my project did what IE is *supposed* to do.

My sense of *disjuncture* first occurred after completion and write-up of my research when, in the process of arranging to circulate my analysis, an informant read my abstract and noted that "it looks like all the other stuff that comes out of that school" (presumably referencing my university department). That brief description of my research as *looking like all the other stuff* suddenly produced for me an awareness of a possible rupture between my informant's actual experience and my account of it in text. Like Campbell's community nurse whose work with a text-based interpretive frame instructed her to "select from the client's story those pieces of information that are to go into the account" (2001:245), I had sifted through my informants' narratives, my observations of their practices, and a variety of institutional and policy documents, to select those elements that would *produce an institutional ethnography*. Thus, while my analysis to some degree conveyed informants' competence and agency, my analytic priority was the explication of *hidden ruling*. Although my work was consciously directed towards producing knowledge in the interests of my informants, this work—like that of scheduling home support (see Campbell 2006)—required integration of other priorities into my decision-making such that my informants' experiences and perspectives could become subordinated.

Smith (2005:143) states that "not all stories will be told, and of those that are, not all can be cited," but "no one story overrides; no story is suppressed." However, my experience suggests that IE's objective to explicate social organization can provide, in effect, an interpretive frame through which one story *does* override: that of individuals as *ruled*. In my analysis, although other stories (e.g., of skilful accomplishment) were certainly present, these were largely told incidentally, *on the way* to explicating the dominant storyline of *ruling*. Smith is well aware of providing a "conceptual framework for selective attention to actualities" (2005:52) and endeavours for this focus on the "mundane" to avoid "grappling with notions of truth" (1987:121). Nonetheless, my sense is that the predominant tendency to characterize IE as "preserving the subject as active and competent" (Smith 1987:142) when the objective is to *explicate how the subject comes to participate in her/his own domination* can be experienced by informants as (at the least) confusing, and (at worst) as dishonest misrepresentation (see also Walby 2007).

Accountability in IE: Is It Really So?

Smith explicitly addresses troublesome relations of power and representation in research by insisting that those who are doing the technical work of explication must be accountable and "responsible in what [they] write to those for whom [they] write" (1987:224; see also 1999:155). In particular, she describes how this accountability is made possible through IE's historical, materialist ontology:

> The social itself (as we have been specifying it) creates the conditions of its own observability. We do not therefore rely on a technical methodology for producing objectivity but on an inquiry (necessarily technical) oriented by prospective questions from others: "Is it really so?" "Does it really happen like that?" Such questions rely on the possibility that others could return to the object of our inquiry and on the basis of their own work respond, "no, she is wrong, it does not work like that but like this…. (Smith 1987:127).

Because IE endeavours to reliably *map* instead of *theorize*, and to talk about "actual people and the actual ongoing concerting of activities," Smith (1992:93) states, "there's a common ground—a real world, if you like—to which we can refer. If you're seeking to learn how things actually are put together, that dialogue with the world constrains you." Based on IE's commitment to continually address, speak of, and explicate a world known directly and practically (Smith 1987:224), Smith (2005:181) describes how "the coherence established by institutional ethnography's ontology preserves the interconnections discovered in any study for further discovery and exploration or for the making of connections with other studies." The work of G. Smith (see 1990) in particular illustrates how IE's findings can be applied, tested, and "relevant to critique" (Smith 2005:208) as individuals begin to use research analyses to confront institutional arrangements in order to understand them or to make change. However, while Smith (1987:123) states that in principle, IE's findings talk "about a world that actually happens and can be observed, spoken of, and returned to check up on the accuracy of an account or whether a given version of it is faithful to how it actually works," she concedes that "[this] practice may at times prove more complicated."

Based on Smith's (1987:170) statement that IE's analysis should "suggest how... relations might be analyzed" but is "not intended to supply a theoretical model" my project produced a detailed analysis of social organization but did not endeavour to draw conclusions or make recommendations. This approach seemed consistent with Smith's line of thinking wherein "no map tells people how to move, but only how here and there are related on the ground should they want to get from one to the other" (Smith 1993:188). In not making recommendations, I thought I was recognizing my informants as *expert practitioners* who were best able to determine the value and implications of study findings. Throughout interviewing and data collection, I did check in, and check back, with informants to ensure my accurate understanding of their work (Campbell and Gregor 2002; Smith 1987). However, I then went away to conduct what Smith refers to as the "sociologist's special business" (1987:161) wherein "the work of the ethnographer is to pass from dialogue with individuals to create a new dialogue, the dialogue between his or her records... and the making of an institutional ethnography" (Smith 2005:143).

Based on this understanding of my analytical "special business", my research subsequently laid out a myriad of social relations, but did not cultivate a space for activists to apply or respond; my project did not facilitate what was ostensibly the study's raison d'être: its use by activist-participants. I planned to circulate my completed analysis after-the-fact; the idea that I was *laying out the actual* did not contain for me, a cue to consider whether my informants should be involved in my project's analytic work. To some degree, I think this apparent gap in my project reflects my own inexperience and naïveté with respect to the role of *researcher.* However, in re-examining my project and my understanding of IE, my sense is that this inattention to the *practice* of accountability within IE research is also more widespread.

Several IE analyses, like mine, investigate institutional or social change from the standpoint of activists (e.g., Walker 1995; Rankin and Campbell 2006: Ch. 4; Turner 2001; Kinsman 1997; Turner, n.d. in Smith 2005; see also accounts of political activist ethnography in Frampton et al. 2006a). However with a few notable exceptions (e.g. G. Smith 1990; Wilson and Pence 2006; Campbell, Copeland, and Tate 1998), I have seen few accounts wherein practitioners critically describe or explore informants' engagement in IE's analytic work, or *testing* of IE findings through action. Where this is addressed, discussions often relate to questions of practicality or accessibility—for instance, the challenges of "translating" a complex and technical analysis to participants (Smith 2005:220, 21; Campbell and Gregor 2002:113), or with data analysis too tedious to keep participants engaged (Wilson and Pence 2006).[141] In general, there is not the sense that informants' involvement is integral within IE's analytic work.

In accounts of IE, it seems most common for research-writers to lay out their analyses, and then to suggest something akin to Weigt's (2006:335) statement that "[b]y recognizing the forces that shape the ways they know and experience the world, women can begin to dismantle those forces." Other accounts restrict analysis to texts and/or personal experience and thus demand less attention to relations of accountability between researcher and researched; in these cases, it is not common for authors to describe whether or how their analyses have led to change-oriented action. Even G. Smith's (e.g. 1995, 1990) descriptions of political activist ethnography, while describing how his research findings were *tested* within movement strategy, do not include detail about how these insights may have been negotiated within processes of collective praxis. Kinsman (2006:142) states:

> Even though George Smith in *Political Activist as Ethnographer* tends to write about this research as almost individual in character, it had a more collective character. It was not simply that George Smith was coming to these conclusions, many other people... were as well, and this was connected into the political development [of the group]....

Thus, while it is not altogether clear how accountability to *those for whom IE research is written* has actually played out in IE, it is reasonable to assume this may involve negotiation or even tension. Campbell, Copeland, and Tate (1998) describe challenges within their collective processes of analysis. Further, Mykhalovskiy and McCoy (2002:20) note that discord can arise due to IE's understanding of the social world that "can run counter to common-sense ways of thinking":

> [W]hile IE aims to support community organizations and social movements, its attention to ideologies and discourses of power means that

no set of practices is off limits, including the work of activists... In consequence, IE does at times produce analyses that invite community activists to reflect on their own forms of knowing. This is IE's particular contribution, although it is sometimes a hard sell.

To some extent, Mykhalovskiy and McCoy seem to portray these difficulties as associated with activist-informants' resistance to hearing a "painful truth". However, my own experience begs the familiar question: *whose* truth?

My sense is that, overall, accounts of IE downplay concern for relations between researcher and researched. Smith (2005:141, 38) emphasizes how "the controlling interest of the ethnographer... is balanced by the institutional ethnographer's deference to the informant's experiential authority and by a commitment to discovery," and thus, "asymmetries of power in the relationship seem less significant." But elsewhere, she acknowledges that:

> Whether we like it or not, that our relationships with those who are the "subjects" of our research are always ambiguous. In the contexts of our work, *we are going to take what we have learned from them and make use of it in contexts in which they do not speak*; this remains despite the care we take to return what we write to them, to check for accuracy and faithfulness with them. *We are still not doing this work for them*; we still have funding obligations to meet, reports to write that are part of them, academic papers to produce.... (Smith 1987:218, emphasis added)

Although my project produced a map which could be useful to informants, in hindsight I think it was this act of "not doing this work for them"—of *producing an institutional ethnography* in the form of a text articulated to members of the academy—that was integral to the tension I experienced.

Certainly, my informants and other activists may use, respond to, or critique my analysis on their own accord—to ask "Does it really happen like that?" (Smith 1987:127) Theoretically, my analysis did "preserv[e] the interconnections discovered... for further discovery and exploration, or for the making of connections with other studies" (Smith 2005:181). However, in the case of informants who are not members of the academy, it is unclear just when, where, or how these *prospective questions* might actually be asked.

Institutional Ethnography in Praxis: Charting Courses

Rather than a rejection of IE as a basis for activist-scholarship, what my analysis suggests are some insights and questions about how the practice of IE could be undertaken in ways that connect more integrally and reflexively with the work of struggles against capitalist, colonial, patriarchal, racist, and other forms of domination. While Smith (1992:97) views her method of inquiry as "powerfully relevant to making change," she emphasizes that "not for one moment" is this "all there is to be done or indeed all that this method of inquiry makes possible." Smith cautions that methodological strategies are insufficient and that approaches to knowledge lose their "critical force... if they are not articulated to relations creating linkages outside and beyond the ruling apparatus... enlarging [people]'s powers and capacities to organize in struggle..." (1987:225). Likewise, Kinsman (2006:135) notes that practices of activist inquiry should consider:

> how to build this type of research in the everyday organizing of social movements; how to make doing this research more participatory; and how to build dialogical, multi-voiced and non-monological discussions into movements that can link diverse research analysis and discussions.

Of course, geographic- and affinity-based networks of activists (both inside and outside of universities) are already engaged in ongoing processes of critical, cooperative analysis. These processes of organic, critical inquiry are not restricted to practical issues of strategy, but take up difficult ethical and political questions in the course of unpacking and acting within and against the contemporary complex of social relations that Day (2005) refers to as the "neoliberal project."[142] The question is not whether IE might be used to "enlighten" activists; it is whether (and how) IE might make a contribution to the radical, reflexive processes of learning and analysis in which activists are already engaged.

In envisioning how IE might be used to strengthen capacity for struggle, Smith (1987:154) has characterized IE as a form of consciousness-raising:

> ... Aiming to find the objective correlates of what had seemed a private experience of oppression. Like consciousness-raising it is also to be shared. The strategy... explicates generalized bases of the experience of oppression. Hence, it offers a mode in which women can find the lineaments of the oppression they share with others and of different oppressions rooted in the same matrix of relations.

Against understandings of consciousness-raising as something *done* to one person by another,[143] I read Smith's formulation as envisioning a means through which consciousness-raising occurs autonomously albeit within relations of mutual learning. Smith (1992:93) states that she is "increasingly formulating the enterprise of inquiry as a kind of ongoing dialogue with society, with people, in which the inquirer is always exposed to the discipline of the other." She views different locations and knowledges as different positionings from which the (ontologically present) social must be mapped (Griffith 1998), and conceptualizes knowing as "a work of cooperation" (Smith 1987:154). However, because Smith's project has been the building of a feminist sociology, her descriptions of accountability and dialogical knowing admittedly presuppose an "agentic professional" (1992:96) and seem to envision this as a text-based enterprise—the building-upon or making of connections between numerous studies (e.g. Smith 1987:177-78; 2005:181; 2002:30). In his activist extension of IE, G. Smith (1995:646) has attempted to distinguish this approach from vanguardism:

> These kinds of studies... *do not*, in themselves, *produce a political analysis* or a "political line." Doing this kind of research is not the practice of "vanguard politics." On the contrary, research studies of this sort are designed to be *written up, published, and made available to all members of a grass-roots organization for their political consideration...* they are intended to provide, on a day-to-day basis, the scientific ground for political action. (Emphasis added)

Nonetheless my own experience suggests that IE practitioners' intent to work *cooperatively* and *accountably* can be thwarted by notions (suggested in G. Smith's account, above) that one is "describing, not theorizing", and by the assumption that accountability can and will occur after-the-fact, in text. Thus, within IE, and more generally within activist-scholarship, my sense is any intellectual "division of labor" (Smith 1992:96) cannot be presupposed, but rather challenged and critically *worked-out* in practice in ways that directly oppose the potential for a slide into objectification, misrepresentation, and/or vanguardism.

This is not to advocate a liberal, power-blind, or idealized version of participation wherein all actors are assumed or required to engage equally in all aspects of inquiry. Instead, within activist applications of IE, I imagine that analytic work could somehow be worked-out through practices that embody what Day (2005:18) refers to as an ethico-political commitment to *infinite responsibility*, of "always being open to the invitation and challenge of another Other, always being ready to hear a voice that points out how one is not adequately in solidarity, despite one's best efforts." Among other things, this would entail openness to the challenge of honouring indigenous tenets, practices, protocols, and epistemology (for instance, holism, relationship to land and place, self-determination, and inclusion of elders) (see Sinclair 2003). I read a commitment to *infinite responsibility* as consistent with Smith's formulations of *accountability* and *knowing as cooperation* (above); the challenge, I think, is the working-out of such formulations within diverse configurations of praxis.

Thus, despite Smith's (e.g., 1987, 1992) and Campbell and Gregor's (2002) endeavour to distinguish IE from versions of participatory inquiry that are limited to democratization of research relations, or a focus on immediate and applied issues without attention to broader relations of ruling, I read IE as containing a systematic, co-generative approach to knowledge-making that could be drawn-upon within the praxis of radical struggle (see also Carroll 2006; Frampton et al. 2006b; Kinsman 2006; Thompson 2006). If used within worked-out relations of co-operation and accountability, Smith's formulation suggests a systematic means through which numerous individuals could work from particular experience to explore generalized and generalizing relations of ruling (Griffith 1998:370), to understand the systemic bases of human experience, and to map the way in which allegedly separate issues are interconnected (Carroll 2006:234). Within my own project, informant narratives reflected how activists were (of course) already doing the conceptual mapping work that was integral to what was allegedly "my" analysis. In hindsight, it is my sense that the working-out of processes for responsible, co-generative, analytic mapping of broader relations of struggle (Frampton et al. 2006b:248)—including processes which could expose and confront relations of academic knowledge production—would have allowed a more insightful, responsible, and useful "map" to emerge from my project.

Nonetheless, even the most complete *map* is not sufficient to determine worthwhile directions for travel. As Carroll (2006, following Marx) emphasizes, the point is not just to understand the world, but to change it. As in Smith's (1999) ideological circle, a fixation on *ruling* can produce analyses which are "trapped" within the existing terrain of negotiation and unable to imagine any alternative, thus obscuring possibility for resistance and transformation (Frampton et al. 2006b; Kinsman 2006). Citing currents in IE, Frampton et al. (2006b:259) note that "we can become much more adept at detailing shifting textual strategies of management and regulation than at identifying sites for resistance and struggle." Reflecting on my project, I am left with the sense of having produced a detailed map of only *half* of the terrain; my analytic focus on hidden ruling resulted in selective attention to *uncritical/reproductive* forms of praxis (Allman 2001) and thus did not sufficiently elucidate subjective and transformative practices which form the basis of radical change. This is not simply a matter of optimism or *cheerleading*; in my experience, grasping the complex and dialectical nature of social relations within capitalism's conditions of temporal and spatial fragmentation (see Harvey 1990) requires a rigorous analysis, as does discerning those practices which might resist, disrupt, and transform relations of domination in the most fundamental way possible. In my view, this is most effectively and meaningfully undertaken as a co-generative project wherein differently-located individuals work critically and cooperatively to fathom out, critique, and test promising avenues for radical struggle. In contrast to what Day (2004, 2005) refers to as the *hegemony of hegemony*, a form of co-operative activist "mapping" could be used non-prescriptively, to critically grasp particular moments and practices through which *ruling relations* have been (at least partially or temporarily) ruptured, resisted, or transformed, in order to identify hopeful practices and relations that might be fruitfully nurtured and/or imaginatively recreated elsewhere.

Kinsman (2006:136) notes that "it is a mistake… to see this mapping out of social relations as simply a technical matter, since it is also very much a political and social undertaking." In my mind, IE's reflexive historical materialist ontology could be drawn on within co-generative and accountable relations of learning to not only map the contours of domination, but also as a means to begin "charting courses" for change. Such an approach could both critique existing social relations and prefigure alternatives—a political commitment already evident within many of the *newest* social movements (Day 2004, 2005), and captured eloquently in Freire's (1996) assertion that individuals "learn together how to build the future—which is not something given to be received by people, but is rather something to be created by them" (in Thompson 2006:105).

References

Allman, Paula. 2001. *Critical Education Against Global Capitalism: Karl Marx and Revolutionary Critical Education*. Westport, CT: Bergin & Garvey.

Campbell, Marie L. 1998. "Institutional ethnography and experience as data." *Qualitative Sociology* 21(1):55-73.

———. 2001. "Textual accounts, ruling action: The intersection of knowledge and power in the routine conduct of community nursing work." *Studies in Cultures, Organizations & Societies* 7(2):231-50.

———. 2006. "Research for activism: Understanding social organization from inside it." In *Sociology for Changing the World: Social Movements/Social Research*, edited by Caelie Frampton, Gary Kinsman, A.K. Thompson, and Kate Tilleczek, 87-96. Halifax: Fernwood.

Campbell, Marie, Betty Copeland, and Betty Tate. 1998. "Taking the standpoint of people with disabilities in research: Experiences with participation." *Canadian Journal of Rehabilitation* 12(2):95-104.

Campbell, Marie, and Frances Gregor. 2002. *Mapping Social Relations: A Primer in Doing Institutional Ethnography*. Aurora, ON: Garamond Press.

Campbell, Marie, and Ann Manicom, eds. 1995. *Knowledge, Experience, and Ruling Relations: Studies in the Social Organization of Knowledge*. Toronto: University of Toronto Press.

Carroll, William K. 2006. "Marx's method and the contributions of institutional ethnography." In *Sociology for Changing the World: Social Movements/Social Research*, edited by Caelie Frampton, Gary Kinsman, A.K. Thompson, and Kate Tilleczek, 232-245. Halifax: Fernwood.

Cooke, B., and U. Kothari, eds. 2002. "The case for participation as tyranny." In *Participation: The New Tyranny?*, 1-15. New York: Zed Books.

Day, Richard J. F. 2004. "From hegemony to affinity." *Cultural Studies* 18(5):716-48.

———. 2005. *Gramsci is Dead: Anarchist Currents in the Newest Social Movements*. Toronto: Between the Lines.

DeVault, Marjorie L. 1999. *Liberating Method: Feminism and Social Research*. Philadelphia: Temple University Press.

DeVault, Marjorie L., and Liza McCoy. 2002. "Institutional ethnography: Using interviews to investigate ruling relations." In *Institutional Ethnography as Practice*, edited by D. E. Smith, 15-44. Toronto: Rowman & Littlefield.

Frampton, Caelie, Gary Kinsman, A.K. Thompson, and Kate Tilleczek, eds. 2006a. *Sociology for Changing the World: Social Movements/Social Research*. Halifax: Fernwood.

———. 2006b. "New directions for activist research." In *Sociology for Changing the World: Social Movements/Social Research*, 246-272. Halifax: Fernwood.

Griffith, Alison I. 1998. "Insider/outsider: Epistemological privilege and mothering work." *Human Studies* 21(4):361-76.

Griffith, Alison I., and Dorothy E. Smith. 2005. *Mothering For Schooling*. New York: Routledge Falmer.

Harding, Sandra. 1986. *The Science Question in Feminism*. Ithaca, NY: Cornell University Press.

Harvey, David. 1990. *The Condition of Postmodernity: An Enquiry into the Origins of Cultural Change*. Malden, MA: Blackwell Publishing.

Kinsman, Gary. 1997. "Managing AIDS organizing: 'Consultation,' 'partnership,' and 'responsibility' as strategies of regulation." In *Organizing Dissent: Contemporary Social Movements in Theory and Practice*, edited by W. K. Carroll, 213-239. Toronto: Garamond Press.

———. 2006. "Mapping social relations of struggle: Activism, ethnography, social organization." In *Sociology for Changing the World: Social Movements/Social Research*, edited by Caelie Frampton, Gary Kinsman, A.K. Thompson, and Kate Tilleczek, 133-156. Halifax: Fernwood.

Murray, Kate M. 2011. "Regulating activism: An institutional ethnography of public participation." *Community Development Journal* (doi: 10.1093/cdj/bsr022).

Mykhalovskiy, Eric, and Liza McCoy. 2002. "Troubling ruling discourses of health: Using institutional ethnography in community-based research." *Critical Public Health* 12(1):17-37.

Pence, Ellen. 2001. "Safety for battered women in a textually mediated legal system." *Studies in Cultures, Organizations & Societies* 7(2):199-229.

Rankin, Janet M., and Marie L. Campbell. 2006. *Managing to Nurse: Inside Canada's Health Care Reform*. Toronto: University of Toronto Press.

Sinclair, Raven. 2003. "Indigenous research in social work: The challenge of operationalizing worldview." *Native Social Work Journal* 5:117-38.

Smith, Dorothy E. 1984. "Textually mediated social organization." *International Social Science Journal* 36(1):59-75.

———. 1987. *The Everyday World as Problematic: A Feminist Sociology*. Toronto: University of Toronto Press.

———. 1989. "Feminist reflections on political economy." *Studies in Political Economy* 30:37-59.

———. 1990a. *The Conceptual Practices of Power: A Feminist Sociology of Knowledge*. Toronto: University of Toronto Press.

———. 1990b. *Texts, Facts, and Femininity: Exploring the Relations of Ruling*. New York: Routledge.

———. 1992. "Sociology from women's experience: A reaffirmation." *Sociological Theory* 10(1):88-98.

———. 1993. "High noon in textland: A critique of Clough." *Sociological Quarterly* 34:183.

———. 1997. "Comment on Hekman's 'Truth and method: Feminist standpoint theory revisited.'" *Signs: Journal of Women in Culture & Society* Winter:392.

———. 1999. *Writing the Social: Critique, Theory, and Investigations*. Toronto: University of Toronto Press.

———. 2002. "Institutional ethnography." In *Qualitative Research in Action: An International Guide to Issues in Practice*, edited by T. May, 150-161. London: Sage.

———. 2005. *Institutional Ethnography: A Sociology for People*. Oxford: AltaMira Press.

———, ed. 2006. *Institutional Ethnography as Practice*. Oxford: Rowman & Littlefield.

Smith, George. 1990. "Political activist as ethnographer." *Social Problems* 37(4):629-48.

———. 1995. "Accessing treatments: Managing the AIDS epidemic in Ontario." In *Knowledge, Experience, and Ruling Relations*, edited by M. Campbell and A. Manicom, 18-34. Toronto: University of Toronto Press.

Thompson, A.K. 2006. "Direct action, pedagogy of the oppressed." In *Sociology for Changing the World: Social Movements/Social Research*, edited by Caelie Frampton, Gary Kinsman, A.K. Thompson, and Kate Tilleczek, 99-118. Halifax: Fernwood.

Turner, Susan M. 2001. "Texts and the institutions of municipal government: The power of texts in the public process of land development." *Studies in Cultures, Organizations & Societies* 7(2):297-325.

Walby, Kevin. 2007. "On the social relations of research: A critical assessment of institutional ethnography." *Qualitative Inquiry* 13(7):1008-30.

Walker, Gillian. 1995. "Violence and the relations of ruling: Lessons from the battered women's Movement." In *Knowledge, Experience, and Ruling Relations: Studies in the Social Organization of Knowledge*, edited by M. Campbell and A. Manicom, 65-79. Toronto: University of Toronto Press.

Weigt, Jill. 2006. "Compromises to carework: The social organization of mothers' experiences in the low-wage labor market after welfare reform." *Social Problems* 53(3):332-51.

Wilson, Alex, and Ellen Pence. 2006. "US legal interventions in the lives of battered women: An indigenous assessment." In *Institutional Ethnography as Practice*, edited by D. E. Smith, 199-226. Toronto: Rowman & Littlefield.

Chapter 12

Shifting the Gaze "Upwards"

Researching the Police as an Institution of Power

Tia Dafnos

A few years ago during my MA studies I met with one of my committee members to discuss the impending ethics approval process for my thesis research. I had proposed to interview police officers and intelligence personnel about how ethnic and racial identifiers are used in the intelligence-led policing of organized crime. As I listened to the paperwork requirements and the need to ensure that research participants would not be harmed or exploited, I was puzzled. In my mind, they could protect themselves quite well against this anxious novice interviewer. I asked, or rather exclaimed, "What about me? Aren't I vulnerable?" I was feeling somewhat apprehensive about doing these interviews and felt that *I* would need some kind of protection *from them*. They have guns, investigative powers, and highly secured office spaces. I have a notebook, pen, and voice recorder. My first submission for research ethics review was not approved. The ethics review board (ERB) was concerned that while I would withhold the names of participants, my intention to identify them by their positions and organizations did not offer a secure enough guarantee of anonymity. At that time, I was surprised and frustrated to have to revise, re-submit, and wait again for approval. I did not realize it then, but that was my first taste of the politics of academic research. After going through the research process and now reflecting on that experience, questions emerge about whether the ethical framework developed to protect "marginalized" communities from academic exploitation should apply in the same way to *institutions* such as the police and intelligence organizations which form part of a police-security apparatus.

Many of the chapters in this volume take up the problematic of (re)producing marginalizing discourses through the study of and, in some cases, with "marginalized" social groups. Critiques of dominant discourses that are produced and reinforced by ruling institutions are vital to challenging them, but we also need to understand *how* they are produced—this is essential for an activist research approach that seeks to dismantle the structures of inclusion/exclusion that manifest in "marginalization". An underlying concern in this volume is with the role of academia as a dominant institution alongside government, media, and police, and the implications that this has for researchers engaged in knowledge production. One way of working through, or resisting, this dilemma of (re)producing marginalizing discourses and practices through academic research is to turn our (critical) gaze onto these institutions, including the academy. This practice of "studying up" is part of many emancipatory epistemologies and methodologies grounded in experiences of oppression.[144]

The focus of my research has been the public police institution, which plays a central role in maintaining the political, economic, and social boundaries of marginalization. Policing is a recurring character—sometimes in a lead role, sometimes in the background—through many of the chapters in this volume demonstrating how integral it is to material and discursive marginalizing and exclusionary practices. More than "studying up," my research practice is inspired by Gary Marx's (1972) call for "muckraking sociology." This is a research agenda that recognizes the power and privileges of academia and directs them towards making visible the institutional operations of the state and of corporations that are shrouded in secrecy. Like any methodology, this is not devoid of problems and self-reflexive conflicts about researcher power.

This chapter begins with a discussion of the role of academic research, particularly criminology, in marginalization and the imperative that this gives scholars to "study up". I then ground this argument in the historical relationships between the modern police institution, capitalism, and marginalization. Because of the significance of the police-security institution in the ruling relations of modern nation-states, these research practices are inescapably politicized, and confrontations with these relations have inherent potential for activist praxis. This chapter is a blend of essay and narrative, reflecting my realization that I cannot write about why and how I have engaged in my research practices without situating myself within them. Through various research encounters, it has become evident to me that the power relations of the research process are situated within the social conditions we seek to study and change. D'Souza (2009) writes that action and activism emerge from a moment or experience in which the political, social, and emotional come together in one's sense of self. In the third section, I draw on these experiences in discussing the possibilities and limitations of my research approaches in negotiating (state) institutional power, particularly in relation to the dynamics of secrecy. To end, I reflect on some of the ethical tensions associated with adopting a conflict-based research framework within the academic institution. These tensions are important catalysts for realizing the contradictions of academic work, and the potential for transforming knowledge production and other structures that sustain domination.

I: The Power of the Academic Gaze

As argued in the introduction to this volume, academic researchers have produced marginalizing discourses in studying urban marginality, often inadvertently. This is largely a result of an academic gaze focused on "marginalized" populations. The power of the selective gaze renders certain phenomena and populations problematic by *naming* them as problematic. By definition, we (sociologists/ criminologists) study *social problems*. While the intentions of some liberal and critical scholars are to sympathetically highlight the "plight" of "marginalized" communities arising from systemic power inequalities, the sources of those inequalities tend to lurk in the shadows as omnipresent, expansive concepts such as "the state", "capitalism", or "structural racism". The intangible quality of these concepts can make them seem too overwhelming to be concrete targets for intervention. Consequently, the task for potential activist scholars seeking to go beyond description to contribute to dismantling and transforming the conditions giving rise to these inequalities seems even more daunting. By turning the gaze onto these shadows, however, these institutions are more explicitly problematized and the research agenda becomes one of understanding *how* they work to produce ruling relations of power—through texts (Smith 1999), technology, decision-making processes, tactical operations, and other mechanisms. Such knowledge can illuminate the cracks and soft spots in these institutions on which to apply pressure for change.

Studying Up, Muckraking, and Conflict Methodology

In the late 1960s and early 1970s, there was a buzz in the social sciences captured by Howard Becker's (1967) statement that sociologists should "take sides" with the "underdogs" in their work. Becker was pointing out that to remain "neutral" in a world of conflict is to be biased in favour of the status quo of unequal power relations. Critiquing Becker's practice of producing sympathetic understandings of the underdogs as liberal romanticism, Alvin Gouldner (1973) argued that sociologists must do more than take sides and actually *study* the powerful. Along this line, Laura Nader (1972) coined the term "studying up" in arguing that anthropologists should focus their research on middle and upper levels of society to develop knowledge about the exercise of power "at home." This would provide a necessary complement to the tradition of "studying down"—common to both anthropology and sociology. Rather than studying colonized peoples abroad or the "culture of poverty" in the domestic context, we should make visible the cultures of the colonizers and the powerful (Nader 1972:289). The premise of studying up assumes that there is a structural hierarchy in society; however, this does not necessarily imply a radical conflict-based orientation.

The study of "powerful" groups and organizations is nothing new. There is an extensive "elite studies" and sociology of organizations literature that adopts a liberal framework. Even with critical orientations, the tendency is to invert the conventional "deviance" approach by treating "elite" groups or organizations as the exotic "others" with mysterious cultural habits, or with "deviant" or immoral behaviours to be revealed (e.g. white-collar or corporate wrongdoing, police deviance).[145] A focus on "elites" or organizations without situating them in an historical structural context remains within an individualistic, "sub-cultural" orientation. Studying up must go further than a de facto acknowledgement of a stratified society; it needs to make visible and understand how colonial, racialized, patriarchal, class structures are produced *so that we can eradicate them*. As Nader (1972:289) argues, studying up forces us to ask "'common sense' questions in reverse," thereby challenging hegemony. Accordingly, this includes rejection of the positivist ideal of a politically neutral, detached researcher, while questioning the appropriateness of conventional methodologies.

In 1972, Gary Marx called for sociologists to engage in "muckraking"—a specific form of studying up that reveals institutional practices of power that are usually hidden from outsiders. In a similar vein, others were writing about the need for a *conflict methodology* that melds critical theory with radical research practice. Proponents emphasize the "right to know" over organizational secrecy, particularly when organizations' actions govern our lives (Christie 1976). Young (1976:24) set out a rationale for conflict methodology that, like Marx, advocates for an approach using "techniques organized to obtain quality information from organizations which stand in hostile contrast to the interests of people generally for reflective self-control over their own social life." According to this perspective, dominant positivistic social science and its methods of research are directly implicated in oppression; thus, the conventional tools of the trade are unsuitable for "anti-establishment, counter-intuitive, even subversive" forms of radical and muckraking research (Marx 1972:3). New methods of inquiry are necessary, driven by a counter-hegemonic conflict framework to resist the constraints of the structures in which we work. Littrell (1993:210) argues that the independence of social science researchers depends on our being able to turn the gaze on, or against, these institutions despite their resistance—otherwise we remain "subordinated" and subservient to powerful interests.

More recent calls for studying up, such as by Harding and Norberg (2005), Hughes (2000), and Tombs and Whyte (2003a, 2003b), are indicative of its continued existence at the margins of academic research. We can attribute this in part to the symbiosis between government and corporate interests and their influence on universities and ethics review boards through a relationship of funding dependency (Tombs and Whyte 2003a; Yeager 2006). In this neoliberal climate, the increasingly precarious nature of academic employment can be a deterrent to politically critical work, never mind more radical projects. Furthermore, as Sudbury and Okazawa-Rey (2009) state, the costs and consequences of doing activist scholarship that challenges academic convention are unequally distributed along the gendered, racialized, and class-based relations of the academy. This is significant in light of Marx's (1972:14-15) observation that much of the muckraking research was being carried out by those in relatively less powerful positions in academia— younger scholars and people of colour. He suggests that these scholars have less commitment to dominant professional interests and values, and are thus "freer to innovate and offend." Further, he notes that personal experiences of oppression may drive their research practice. If Marx's observation is accurate, and if the "costs" or risks of engaging in radical research have increased, then we might expect muckraking to decline. Reflecting on the relative absence of published work on the crimes of corporate and state entities, Tombs and Whyte (2003a) argue that this has resulted in two significant self-reinforcing consequences: the underdevelopment of *research methods* for such work, and a lack of accumulated experience that can provide a *methodological resource* to other researchers.

In comparison to the marginal status of muckraking approaches, Community-Based Research and Participatory Action Research (PAR), which emerged in popularity roughly in the same period as calls for studying up and conflict methodology, have attained mainstream credibility as legitimate research methodologies. Associated with emancipatory adult education movements in Latin America, these approaches challenge dominant forms of knowledge production—and academic researcher power—by empowering the research "subject" through active participation in the research process (see Bourke, this volume, for an overview and critique). In contrast, studying up connotes a *lack* or absence of power on the part of the researcher, while the participant "has" (more) power (Schwegler 2008). This presents a reversal of the power problematic for researchers. However, following Michel Foucault (1980), we need to resist a zero-sum conception, and instead recognize power as relational and emerging, or shifting, within interactions. Academic researchers have power deriving from our privileged status as academics; vis-à-vis others in powerful structural positions/locations, the "friction" or "conflict" that can emerge during the encounter can be productive (Schwegler 2008), whether this occurs in an office or on the streets. For example, George Smith (1990), Thompson (2006), and Juris (2007) each respectively locates knowledge production as occurring in the spaces of activist confrontation with ruling regimes through participatory activist ethnography, direct action research, and militant ethnography. The privileges and power that come with being an "academic" which have been used to objectify and exploit "marginalized" groups can also facilitate access to dominant institutions; as Harding and Norberg 2005 argue, we have a responsibility to take advantage of these privileges to expose institutional workings.

The Case of Criminology

> Almost automatically, if we are studying crime, we are messing around with some of the most powerful constructs the State has at its disposal.
> (Kit Carson, in Walters 2007:221)

As someone who sometimes identifies as a (critical) criminologist,[146] questions about the role of academia in producing knowledge that is used as and for some of the most repressive forms of marginalization and social exclusion are very salient. Criminal justice institutions have a central role in social control, and criminological research is arguably more directly implicated in social control than other disciplines (Hudson 2000; Brickley 1989). Sudbury (2009) aptly describes this as the "academic-prison-industrial-complex," which situates these relations in the context of capitalism. Since the nineteenth century, criminological science and theory have engaged in the identification and sorting out of "problematic" populations that pose "threats" or danger to "us"—born criminals, vagrants, psychopaths, at-risk youth, dangerous offenders, security risks, etc.—as criminological knowledge. Whether adopting biological, psychological, or cultural forms of explanation this knowledge has (re)produced racist, ethnocentric, xenophobic, patriarchal, class-based discourses that are integral to colonization and subjugation (Kalunta-Crumpton 2004; see also Gönen and Yonucu, this volume). In addition to knowledge *of* or *about* "problem" populations, the field has been consumed with how to deal with them. Mainstream criminology is largely correctionalist—concerned with fixing the problem individual (such as through punishment, shaming, treatment, rehabilitation, or incapacitation) or improving the efficacy of the criminal justice system (CJS) (Greenberg 1993).[147] For critical and radical criminologists, the targets for change are the political-economic structures of society.

The institutional components of the CJS—law, legal system, police, courts, and prisons—are key mechanisms in producing and maintaining a social order conducive to capitalist relations. These institutions have been essential to the production and privileging of private property and to the enforcement of social relations enabling the accumulation of wealth. This social *order* of "law and order", as an idealized common good, is a powerful device that legitimizes the power of state institutions—which is increasingly extending to private entities—to deal with threats to this order. The police are a pivotal institution, empowered by law and the state's monopoly of violence; they are the front-line wielders of this power in the everyday ordering of people and spaces, and are gatekeepers to the court and prison systems.

II: Significance of the Police Institution

> There are towns because there is police [...] to police and to urbanize is the same thing. (Foucault 2007:337)

There is an historical relationship between police institutions, urbanization, and marginalization that is rooted in the emergence and persistence of capitalism and nation-states. Foucault's use of the term "police" in describing its symbiosis with urbanization refers to a broader regulatory project of which "the police" are an integral part. As Rigakos, McMullan, Johnson, and Ozcan (2009) note, the term "police" derives from the Greek root word, *polis*, which means city-state and encompasses broader notions of community and "the greater good". "Police" in its earliest sense was a prevention-oriented state project concerned with ensuring the well-being or "happiness" of the urban population through the proper management of newly emerging cities. Academic knowledge production was integral to this project in the form of "police science" (see Pasquino [1978]1991; Neocleous 2000; Foucault 2007). This police "science" was a study of the city directed by a concern with balancing and managing the relationship between state interests and the (private) accumulation of wealth by producing *order* (Rigakos et al. 2009). New urban public authorities emerged as part of this project to manage everything from health, roads, and the grain trade. The specific institution of "the police"—a quasi-militaristic "professional" bureaucratic organization—has been key to this project as front-line manager of urban disorder arising from the contradictions of capitalism and class conflict.

From their emergence in the 1800s the Anglo-American police, as Neocleous (2000) argues, have always been concerned with poverty and the production of class relations. Police have actively participated in the (re)production of capitalist class relations through the enforcement of vagrancy laws, supplemented by a moral hygiene discourse of the "idle" undeserving and threatening poor, which criminalize subsistence outside of formal (capitalist) employment. Together, this discourse and physical policing compelled participation in waged labour with the threat of violence and forced institutionalization in workhouses, hospitals, or jails. In the imperial context, police were integral to the imposition of colonial projects that are fundamental in the global relations of capitalism. Police forces have been essential to imperial state formation by protecting newly established institutions (including private corporations) and by quelling uprisings by indigenous peoples and other "problem" populations that posed threats to colonial rule (see Brogden 1987; Marquis 1997; Deflem 1994). The professional police established in Europe's industrializing cities thus shared a similar function with the colonial police forces abroad in the production, or ordering, of social relations amenable to the intersecting interests of imperial expansion and capitalist development (see also O'Connor, this volume, for a contemporary example).

While some scholars suggest that "the state" and public policing are becoming less relevant as a basis or source of power in the context of globalization and transnationalization (see e.g. Shearing and Wood 2003), the coercive and repressive capacities of the public police-security apparatus have been expanding, evident in a blurring between police and military functions and legitimized by the ideological impetus of providing security in an insecure world (Murphy 2007; Neocleous 2008). As the processes and conditions of wealth polarization, exclusion, precarious labour, and permanent unemployment proliferate on a global scale their effects are experienced materially on a local level. While a range of formal and informal entities certainly contribute to the production of social order, the public police maintain a monopoly on the most repressive forms of power.

Within cities, this is experienced in the normalization of paramilitary police units—popularly known as "SWAT" thanks to American television—which are modeled on and collaborate with military forces (Kraska and Kappeler 1997; De Lint and Hall 2009). These units are regularly deployed in urban "hot spots" populated by members of the racialized working class and those at the margins of the wage labour market, leading Chambliss (1994:193) to describe these neighbourhoods as "quasi-police states."[148] Chambliss' allusion to militaristic policing in repressive regimes evokes a colonial form of social control. Struggles for the (right to the) city must therefore literally and physically contend with the police-security apparatus on an everyday basis. Resistance by organized groups such as the Toronto-based Ontario Coalition Against Poverty (OCAP) and Montreal's Coalition to Oppose Police Brutality (COPB), as well as local community-based cop-watches, engage in everyday resistance and support work for those targeted and victimized by police (see McLennan, in this volume). One role for academic researchers in these struggles is to resist and subvert the burgeoning academic-prison-industrial-complex (Sudbury 2009) while producing knowledge that is useful to grassroots struggles.

This complex is evident in policing studies where the correctionalist impulses of criminology are resonating with neoliberal universities' thirst for community-based partnerships. Since the 1970s, there has been a tendency towards evaluative policy-oriented research of "what works" in policing (Brickley 1989; Reiner 2000; Tombs and Whyte 2003a). In large part, this is driven by the availability of state and private funding for this type of work, fuelled by academic climates favourable to partnerships—especially those that bring in research cash (Brickley 1989; Yeager 2008). A particularly glaring example is found in a recent special issue of *Policing,* a peer-reviewed journal aimed at an audience of police officers, policy makers, and academics, in which contributors advocate for more research collaborations between police and academics, including the use of action research and PAR with police. While the overall absence of counter-arguments is troubling, most disturbing is the claim by Marks and her colleagues (2010:113) that "when it comes to knowledge production the police as a community could be regarded as 'disempowered'." The authors argue that this disempowerment "is potentially very damaging" and thus rationalizes their use of PAR with this community. This is a valid statement in the sense that in the hierarchical power structure of police organizations, front-line personnel often have little if any input into organizational decision-making. They are *relatively disempowered in this context,* and certainly racialization and patriarchy would further shape these internal power dynamics. However, this is a relativistic and atomized view of power within the bureaucracy that detaches the police institution from its historically entrenched foundations in capitalism and colonialism. Wilkinson (2010:148), writing in favour of partnerships between police and academic researchers, argues that these can strengthen "the principle of policing by consent." Indeed—Gramsci (1971) argued that social control is more effective when attained through the consent of those being controlled—hegemony—rather than through repressive force.

The work of academic researchers, even when done with critical intentions, has contributed in large part to producing hegemony by legitimizing the institutions and practices that (re)produce social conditions amenable to capitalist production and accumulation. For example, while ethnographies of police organizations have been useful in describing the "back stage", these are often preoccupied with (sub)cultural explanations of police behaviour and the operations of organizations *qua* bureaucracies. In the wake of crises and scandals involving police forces, academics have often gained access to engage in evaluative research. In doing so, researchers are potentially, even if inadvertently, providing legitimacy by serving as an outlet for hegemonic voices, or by contributing to "window dressing" reforms that give the appearance that organizations are responsive to criticism without altering actual practices (Marx 1972).

III: Researching | Confronting the Security Apparatus

It is in this context of the academic-prison-industrial-complex that the methodological choices that we make as researchers are inevitably political ones. Because of its significance in producing ruling relations, the police institution is a fundamental site on which to turn the (activist) research gaze. This studying up approach can be an activist, praxis-orientated activity in two key ways: first, it aims to shed some light on the inner workings of police institutions to *demystify* their internal practices, including their production of knowledge about "problem" populations. This is a form of critique that is relatively common in critical studies of police organizations. However, in an activist praxis the question(s) underlying research inquiry emerges from the experiences and needs of those directly affected by such institutions, social movements, and grassroots activism. Research is produced for the purpose of contributing to strategies of resistance and challenge while simultaneously disrupting police power that is derived in part from their claim to authoritative expertise about "crime", "criminals", and how to achieve public order. Second, the *methodological practice* of studying up directly challenges powerful institutions' assumption of, or claim to, secrecy and "sacredness" (Manning 1977), which are both a source and a product of their power. Furthermore, the methods adopted in order to engage in radical forms of studying up are in resistance to, or subversion of, institutionalized conventions of social science that are antithetical to such research. The social interactions of this research process are inevitably grounded in broader power relations as the researcher herself is actively engaged in a political activity.

I suppose that I knew all of this in an abstract way before starting my first research project. However, although I was very conscious of the contentious nature of my research topic and questions, the implications of the research practice really did not strike me until I was actually immersed in it. My MA thesis examined how racial and ethnic identifiers are used in intelligence-led policing practices in relation to organized crime in Canada. In addition to a critical discourse analysis of official documents and statements produced over a ten-year period, I conducted face-to-face interviews with high-level police and intelligence personnel.[149] When I began PhD studies,

I did research on "diversity" training and education for police in the province of Ontario, taking up one of the threads from my thesis. Again, I interviewed police officers, but also drew on conversations with community educators who have conducted anti-racism/anti-oppression training for police recruits and officers.[150] Reflecting on my experiences with these two projects led me to think about less conventional methods—specifically, to making requests for information under access to information (ATI) laws.[151] While ATI is a legal mechanism, this can be a decidedly more conflict-based methodology depending on how we use it—Marx (1984) characterizes it as a coercive muckraking method of obtaining "data" about decision-making and operations. Underlying my decision to use ATI requests was a recognition that conventional methods are not necessarily always amenable to studying up (Lundman and McFarlane 1976). I had tentatively tested the waters of ATI during my MA research, but aware of the length of time required to process requests I decided to forgo it in the interests of completing my thesis in a reasonable timeframe. At that point, I had simply considered ATI requests to be a step towards obtaining material (organized crime threat assessments) for my discourse analysis without thinking about the requesting process itself as a key part of the research (see Larsen and Walby 2012).[152]

My current research has involved filing ATI requests for information relating to the policing of protest and dissent in Canada, with a focus on the policing of Aboriginal peoples' activism. This research stems from an observation in my MA thesis that the discourse of police and intelligence agencies framed Aboriginal peoples' protests and activism as "organized crime" and "extremism". This blurring has the effect of de-legitimizing indigenous peoples' claims to land and sovereignty while legitimizing the state's use of force against such actions. This criminalizing discourse informs operational practices of police and security forces while permeating broader popular "knowledge". Using documents obtained through ATI, I have been mapping concretely *how* the framing of indigenous peoples' protests as threats to national security underlies militaristic state responses and how this is intertwined with the negotiation of land claims (see Dafnos 2012). I have also recently been engaged in ATI-based research relating to the policing of the 2010 Toronto G20 summit. Here too, the de-legitimizing/ legitimizing dynamic of criminalization was evident. Both projects involve important collaborative relationships with academics, activists, and those directly affected by policing. ATI has been a valuable research method—obtaining records such as threat assessments, intelligence reports, emails, and incident reports can provide insights into the discursive framing of events and protestors, and the decision-making processes of those working with(in) the police-security-apparatus. Such information potentially exposes contradictions between ideological security discourse and actual practices, which challenge the legitimacy of organizations while contributing to activist strategizing and organizing, as well as to challenges in specific cases.

Although archival research is a key method in the toolbox of historians and historical sociologists, obtaining and using institutional records that are withheld from public access generally is not.[153] The antagonistic nature of using ATI legislation to *force* the release of such information is an uneasy addition to a methodological repertoire conventionally grounded in an ethics of consent, rapport, trust, and willing participation. This rupture, or disconnect, also occurs when using conventional methods like interviewing to study up with a muckraking intention. In the remainder of this chapter, I share some of my experiences in these different research projects to identify strengths, limitations, power dynamics, and ethical questions that I have encountered.

Gaining Access | Accessing Information | Information Control

As described, the police-security apparatus is intimately tied to nation-state sovereignty and is invested with the state's monopoly on violence. The legitimacy of this arrangement allows for the exercise of *secrecy* as the state is entrusted with keeping "us" safe and secure. Particularly in times of perceived crisis, the state has been able to unilaterally extend the cloak of secrecy over its operations—such as occurred after the events of September 11, 2001 (Roberts 2007; Earl 2009). At the same time, the repressive capacities of police and security forces have increased under this cloak through ongoing paramilitarization and the loosening of legal restrictions on investigative powers.[154] To challenge state secrecy by seeking information that lies beyond the public realm of access is to contest a key element of state sovereignty. This sounds like a grand claim, particularly if we are talking about one or a handful of researchers. But the measures taken by institutions to deny access to those who seek it are the materialization of ruling relations in the research process. The power of engaging in this form of resistance or challenge can be multiplied through organized, collaborative work.[155]

In my experience with procuring interviews, my requests were either flat-out denied, unanswered, or subject to organizational approval. In many instances, I had to submit my interview questions in advance. All of the people with whom I eventually did get to speak with were high-level personnel: managers, supervisors, and unit commanders. As I was told by two sympathetic officers—off the record—during my research on police diversity training, there was no way that I could hope to have police officers speak candidly about their views without the chief's formal authorization. Turning to ATI has not solved the access problem. At the most elementary level, in order to make a request for records, one must be clear about the material sought. Of course, this raises a "black box" problem of how to request specific records when we are not aware of their existence (Lee 2001, 2005). Often, one must file many requests, which can yield clues that turn up like needles in haystacks of irrelevant material (assuming that one is successful in obtaining records). Beyond this, there are significant hurdles. ATI legislation provides for mandatory exemptions of certain records, including those related to law enforcement and national defence. This can occur through redactions (removing portions of the text), the complete withholding of information, or a refusal to confirm or deny the existence of certain records (see Roberts 2006). Requests for information on politically sensitive topics or that are submitted to security organizations are automatically flagged for additional scrutiny. In Canada, as described by Rees (2003), many ATI offices have developed a screening process by which these sensitive files are forwarded to ministers' offices and their communications staff for review. This allows government to prepare media lines or responses in anticipating any damage control that might be needed once material is made public (see also Roberts 2005). More disturbingly, journalists have documented—ironically, through ATI—direct political intervention in the process as members of government are regularly reviewing requests prior to their release (see Beeby 2010; Davis 2010). In all of these examples, the politicization of information control is evident. Researchers face extensive delays, active stonewalling, and large fee estimates that can dissuade one from following through.

Like most researchers using ATI, I have run into all of these barriers (see Larsen and Walby 2012). For example, my requests, and those of colleagues, for information relating to the police and security operations of the 2010 Toronto G20 summit have been met with claims that the records we seek are non-existent or will require extensive time extensions (300 days in one case) and fees ($1342.80 in another case) to process, along with warnings from analysts to expect significant redactions. The overall effect is an attempt to discourage us, or to strip down requests significantly in our hopes of speeding things up.[156] This is directly connected to the nature of the police-security apparatus itself. Following a trend of integrated operations, security and policing for the G8 and G20 summits were coordinated through an Integrated Security Unit (ISU).[157] This policing approach blurs the lines of accountability and throws up huge roadblocks to the release of information, as all agencies involved must be consulted. Thus, for example, a request to the Ontario Provincial Police (OPP) for their incident commander notes from the summit—providing a record of operational decision-making—required extensive consultations with the Royal Canadian Mounted Police and Toronto Police Service, two of its ISU partners, among others. Initially claiming a 30-day extension, processing of the request has surpassed, at the time of writing this chapter, the one-year mark due to these two remaining consultations.

I had previously made a request for OPP incident commander notes for another project relating to the force's raid of a reclamation action by members of the Six Nations at Caledonia.[158] My first attempt was effectively deflected by the analyst who, upon telling him that I was interested in records of police practices and decision-making vis-à-vis a highly touted new guideline document for policing Aboriginal "critical incidents", defensively informed me that police practices always follow guidelines no matter the situation. I narrowed and re-submitted the request, which was assigned to a more helpful analyst. Four months later, I was told that the package of records was complete and would be sent to me as soon as it received a final sign-off of approval from the OPP. After a couple of weeks and no records in my mailbox, I inquired again. Apparently it was still waiting for the sign-off. Reflecting her own frustration, the analyst offered to describe the records to me over the phone. In the end, the OPP held up the file for five of the nine months it took for the information to be released.[159]

The frustration of the second ATI analyst points to the importance of understanding the state and institutions not as monolithic entities, but as characterized by contradictions and conflicts.[160] As Tombs and Whyte (2003b) argue, we can use these inter- and intra-institutional conflicts to expose these contradictions. In the diversity training research, the two officers who I met with off the record encouraged my research project and provided suggestions for how to pursue it in light of the police wall of silence.[161] In my MA research, institutionalized (professional) conflict between police and (largely civilian) intelligence analysts emerged during interviews, which exposed a significant contradiction to the dominant discourse about the innovativeness, importance, and effectiveness of intelligence-led policing. A methodological and activist praxis problem, or task, is to figure out how to make these contradictions useful—if we are able to negotiate access in the first place.

Research Interactions as Social Relations and Power Negotiations

Gaining access to these institutions is a social process, which becomes viscerally clear during research encounters with institutions and their representatives. Generally, my interactions with interview participants and ATI personnel have been civil and polite, if not amicable. However, they are always infused with shifting power relations. Due to the nature of their work, police and security personnel tend to view "outsiders" with suspicion—especially outsiders who come asking questions about what they do and how they do it (see Reiner 2000; Ericson 1982). Not only has professional status come into play (mine as a graduate student researcher, theirs as police commanders, intelligence supervisors, deputies, ATI coordinators), but also other aspects of our social subjectivities—in particular race and gender. Of course, this has been more apparent in the face-to-face interactions of interviews.

Research methods texts on interviewing emphasize the importance of establishing rapport with participants. With this in mind while preparing my interview guide for my thesis research, I decided that I needed to present myself as an "objective social scientist". I was most concerned that the highly politicized nature of the research topic would raise sensitivities in the people with whom I wanted to speak. I did not want to create a situation where they felt that I was being accusatory or critical and have them potentially shut down the interview. So, for example, I was conscious of not using the term "racial profiling". I saw rapport as being dependent on their acceptance of me as a social scientist rather than as a potentially trouble-making activist. Some have argued that affiliation with the academy provides an institutional "power base," the credibility and legitimacy of which is an important factor in being granted access to institutions (Marx 1972; Broadhead and Rist 1976). In the preparatory meeting with my committee member that I referred to in opening the chapter, I was also warned about the importance of appearances and needing to adopt a conservative look—but one that did not evoke a lawyerly image (because—the irony of this generalization noted—cops hate lawyers).

We're sitting in a boardroom of a large urban police force, about halfway through the interview. "Because if you're starting out looking at a criminal organization and you're looking at traditional organized crime, which is Italian organized crime, is that racial profiling." *My heart rate increases and my mind races. His question lingers in the air. More of a statement than a question—at least I hope so. He looks intently at me. Do I answer? What the hell should I say? A hot flush crept up my neck. I take a breath and suddenly he breaks his silent stare and continues speaking.* "And I think that's the big fear. That an organization or an entity is afraid that they're going to be accused of racial profiling." *I'm on edge until I leave the building.*[162]

In a moment during my first interview ever, I suddenly realized that there were some things that I could not control for—being a racialized woman and a young graduate student, asking questions about race and ethnicity in police practices. All but two of the law enforcement and intelligence participants in my thesis and diversity training research were older white men of relatively high positions within their organizations. Various layers of power dynamics must be negotiated in these interactions. As Casper (1997) and Horn (1997) discuss, women researchers, especially those who are younger, are often perceived as incompetent or at best, less qualified, researchers. At the same time, patriarchal ruling relations can be exploited to our advantage as we present a less threatening persona to participants with greater social prestige or location—especially men—and use this to facilitate access and the sharing of information. In my case however, this may have been mediated by the politicized and sensitive nature of my research and in presenting an ambiguous ethno-racial identity. In one case, a participant explicitly verbalized his assumption about my "background":

> X actually identified me as "Asian" ("with your Asian background"). I did get the sense that when they were talking about cultural differences, they were consciously aware of what they were saying to me… at least they seemed to be much more comfortable expressing themselves when we talked about intelligence, legislation and their frustrations with crown attorneys. There might have been a defensiveness—from all three—when we talked about ethnicity… Y expressed the standard line that they don't care what a person's background is, that a criminal is a criminal. (Research notes, June 2007)

In response to my question about public perceptions of the "organized crime problem," the two participants got into a discussion about how organized crime in ethnic communities is more of a problem for newcomers. First referencing his own Irish background and explaining why "Irish organized crime" is not seen as a problem anymore, one participant stated, "You know, and maybe you might know, with your Asian background, you might have some friends or people who've had a bit of contact, but as we move to being more settled here, it's not such a big issue for us." This one statement was filled with presumptions about my biography while simultaneously situating us on the bases of ethno-racial identity and immigration status. The racialized relations of this and other encounters come into play to predispose me to being perceived as inherently biased. Himani Bannerji (1995), among others, has discussed the difficulties that racialized scholars have in being taken as authoritative when speaking and teaching about racism because of this "bias". The conventional "ideal" of a "good" social scientist is one who is neutral and objective, embodied as a white (middle-class) man. The instances of subtle and not so subtle comments, and occasions when interview participants clearly controlled or steered the discussion made me feel vulnerable, embarrassed, or uncomfortable.[163] These interpersonal interactions are part of broader racialized, gendered, class-based ruling relations that underlie the processes I was researching.

At the same time, these dynamics need to be situated in the political relations of state sovereignty as our research questions challenge the invisibility of these institutions' operations. The intertwining of micro-level (inter) personal and structural relations of power emerges in these moments. As one of my interviews came to a close, one of the two participants, perhaps reflecting a degree of comfort, remarked that the ubiquitous existence of crime was a good thing because it ensured that he, and the police and intelligence community, would always have jobs. This led both participants to laugh heartily, to which I added a slightly nervous chuckle while thanking them for their time. Suddenly, the laughter broke off and the higher-ranking officer turned serious, telling me that I should not make a record of the location of their office in order to maintain its secrecy. One thing about engaging in studying up is the reality that we ourselves become objects of the gaze of those institutions and organizations that we trying to understand and make visible. On another occasion, I recounted to friends that I had to leave my cell phone at the sign-in desk at RCMP headquarters, joking that they may have bugged it while I was interviewing participants. While I though this to be mildly amusing, I was likely subject to some other kind of scrutiny. Considering the level of security at several of the workplaces in which I met with participants, it is probable that I would have been checked out before being granted an interview and thus access to these spaces. At the very least, this means being the subject of a simple internet search as a kind of background check. Larsen (forthcoming) describes how this is an automatic screening process by ATI offices of those requesting sensitive information, including any requests to police and security organizations. This raises a problem for researchers who are politically active, especially if in a visible role, because such involvement could make the denial of research access more likely. In making requests for information, we ourselves enter into the network of information databases of state institutions. This is a concession that we make, and must navigate, when doing this research—a hazard of the fieldwork is being caught up in the web of state security and surveillance.

Breaking Academic Conventions: Questions of Ethics and Legitimacy

I opened this chapter by recounting my first ethics review process. I now want to return to that initial entry into the politics of research with some reflections on the relationship between a conflict methodology and the conventions of legitimate academic research as shaped by the ethics regime. The research experiences described in the preceding sections have helped to concretize for me how the interpersonal interactions of research are embedded within broader power relations that are structured by state institutions. The nervousness, anxiety, discomfort, unease, frustration, anger, and empathy that I experienced during the research processes are embodied responses to the repressive power(s) of the state which is invested in policing and the security apparatus. This illustrates, as Lee (1993) states, that the power relations and inequalities that shape interactions between researcher and subject challenge the assumption of a consensus-based society, which underlies the dominant ethics framework for social science. At the root of the governing regime of institutional ethics review boards (ERB) is the discourse of *power*—specifically, a concern that researchers do not abuse their power by exploiting and harming subjects. Based on legal liberalism, this ethics regime revolves around the *individual*, a rational, responsible subject who can enter freely into contracts of consent—the hinge of ethical research around which revolve issues about the collection and use of data. By no means am I suggesting that this is not a crucial check against researchers' exploitation of marginalized peoples and social groups; but, what happens when the subjects of research are powerful institutions—entities whose power depends largely upon, have a vested interest in, and which enjoy hegemonic and legally prescribed means of maintaining secrecy of their practices?

One answer is simply that we do not research these institutions—if representatives do not fully consent, then we cannot do it. This is a big part of the explanation for why radical research of powerful institutions has been lacking (Punch 1986). However, this is not a satisfactory answer as the failure of researchers to turn their gazes onto the powerful maintains the status quo of ruling relations. As Punch (1986:32) writes, "to stop researching institutions…is to abdicate any pretension to change them." This underlies Nader's (1972) assertion that there should be a different ethical framework when studying up. Researchers may have power to control discussion, interpret data, and write up findings—but participants are authorities in their own right *and* are members of dominant social groups and institutions which allows them to grant or deny access, shape the interview, and, perhaps most distinctively, mobilize significant resources *against* the researcher if they are unhappy with the final analysis.[164] Marx (1984:108) is more blunt, stating that "perhaps different standards with respect to deception, privacy, informed consent and avoiding harm to research subjects ought to apply when the subjects themselves are engaged in deceitful, coercive, and illegal activities, and/or where one is dealing with an institution which is publicly accountable."

These statements by Nader and Marx raise the tension identified by Galliher (1980), who troubles the definition of the "research subject" when studying up—for example, is the police officer interviewed to be treated as an individual subject, or as (a part of) the state police-security apparatus? This was at the core of my frustration with the ERB's rejection of my initial ethics submission. The ERB was concerned that the personal identity of participants could be evident if I referred to their position, particularly if the organization they worked in was relatively small. I can understand this reasoning. The problem however, is that it contributes to a liberalistic "bad apples" approach that is unable to consider the police-security institution (and by extension, the state and capitalism) as an entity that can be the subject of inquiry. If we do not identify these individuals with their organizations and institutions—that is, to treat them as components of the state security apparatus—then we are still left with the problem of reifying "the state" or "the police" as nebulous entities that escape problematization and intervention.

The uncomfortable position for researchers is that, in pursuing a muckraking agenda to expose or illuminate the operations of institutions in structuring social relations, it is possible that the individual members of these institutions may be affected. Marx (1984) acknowledges that researchers may experience personal struggles in criticizing those who opened up to them with trust, time, and information. This indeed has been a messy aspect in my own research. I sometimes found myself alternating between empathizing with some interview participants, feeling as if I was betraying my politics by doing so, and wondering whether I had been co-opted or duped. At the same time,

I wondered whether my failure to challenge participants on problematic statements and assumptions during interviews—such as not responding "yes" to the question/statement "is that racial profiling"—was deceptive in some way. I have spent time thinking about the ethics of deception when studying up. Was I unethical in not making explicit to participants during my MA research that I was adopting a critical analytical/theoretical framework? Did I thus trick them into participating? If we call it deception, can it be justified? If I did not do what I did, would I have gained the same degree of access? With regard to ATI requests, must I clearly identify the purpose of requests when making them, or make it known that I intend to share the records with those affected by the institutions' activities? Does it make a difference whether I make requests specifically as an academic researcher, a concerned member of the public, or a movement ally?

From a conflict methodology or muckraking perspective, deception is often necessary to enable researchers to be *active* in obtaining "data" which powerful entities seek to keep hidden (see Marx 1984; Littrell 1993). This is not to say that they are the *only* suitable research tools—but that they can be important components of a research repertoire that is otherwise dependent on what is allowed by these entities through volition or slips in the control of information (Marx 1984). The argument, therefore, is that deceptive and coercive methods—such as ATI—should not necessarily be forbidden tools for a conflict research methodology.

Like all methodologies there are limitations and problems with studying up. My argument is that researchers can resist the marginalizing practices of research and adopt a radical approach in problematizing powerful groups and institutions. The flip-side of this is that we ignore the agency and ongoing forms of resistance of those who are targeted by these institutions. We thereby perpetuate the reification of "the marginalized", represented as unable to challenge hegemonic institutions without the intervention of academics. Studying the powerful should be a complement or, more accurately, a *feature of* emancipatory collaborative forms of research "from below". Activist researchers cannot rely on just one research approach, or work in isolation, if our intent is to challenge the power relations producing social, political, and economic inequalities. This means rejecting a fetishistic inclination to *possess* information ("data") for personal academic gain (e.g. theory development or publishing) and instead ensuring that it can be used for and by those engaged in ongoing resistance and organizing. If the purpose of conflict-based research is to demystify and challenge powerful groups and state institutions by exposing their contradictions, this begins with subjugated knowledge and experiences, and activist struggles.

Conclusion

By sharing my research experiences and personal conflicts in this chapter, I hope to have contributed to discussion and debate on methods of activist research aimed at dismantling oppressive structures and relations. I have argued for the importance of a radical research agenda aimed at powerful institutions, particularly the police-security institution because of its pivotal role in securing state sovereignty and capitalist relations through the production of social order. A conflict-based studying up methodology renders these structural power relations concrete by exposing *how* the production of order occurs. The contradictions between these material practices and the hegemonic discourses of "order" are important foundations for challenging the legitimacy of institutions and for collective mobilization aimed at transforming social relations.

Taking this approach brings the researcher into direct encounters with these ruling relations of power. Crucial to this is an ongoing reflexivity and realization that we are embedded in the relations of power under investigation. The consequences and discomfort we may experience in this process is evidence of our realization of the contradictions between our social-political subjectivities vis-à-vis our training within the traditional canons of theory and method. In navigating this discomfort, conflict, and friction, we cannot become immobilized in endless discussion but continue to engage in the process of developing, practicing, and discovering new methods and strategies of research. It is only through research practice that we realize what can be effective. As institutions react by finding new means of maintaining secrecy, our methods will have to respond in kind. The methods we choose, and how we use them, will depend on the specific circumstances of our research, including our relationships to our "subjects" which are shaped by broader relations of power (race, class, gender, status, etc.). Therefore, as Tombs and Whyte (2003b:266) note, there can be no strict "rules" of method in these contingencies. However, the impetus to engage in this work can be encouraged by having a cushion of experiences—our own and those of others—behind us, informing our methodological decisions.

References

Bannerji, Himani. 1995. *Thinking Through: Essays on Feminism, Marxism, and Anti-Racism.* Toronto: Women's Press.

Becker, Howard. 1967. "Whose side are we on?" *Social Problems* 14(3):239-247.

Beeby, Dan. 2010. "Tories blocked full release of sensitive Public Works report." *Globe and Mail.* February 7.

Brickley, Stephen. 1989. "Criminology as social control science: State influence on criminological research in Canada." *Journal of Human Justice* 1(1):43-62.

Broadhead Robert S., and Ray C. Rist. 1976. "Gatekeepers and the social control of social research." *Social Problems* 23:325-336.

Brogden, Mike. 1987. "An act to colonise the internal lands of the island: Empire and the origins of the professional police." *International Journal of the Sociology of Law* 15(2):179-208.

Casper, Monica J. 1997. "Feminist politics and fetal surgery: Adventures of a research cowgirl on the reproductive frontier." *Feminist Studies* 23(2):233-262.

Chambliss, William J. 1994. "Policing the ghetto underclass: The politics of law and law enforcement." *Social Problems* 41(2):177-194.

Christie, Robert M. 1976. "Comment on conflict methodology: A protagonist position." *The Sociology Quarterly* 17:513-519.

Dafnos, Tia. 2012. "Beyond the blue line: Researching the policing of aboriginal activism using ATI." In *Brokering Access: Politics, Power, and Freedom of Information in Canada,* edited by Mike Larsen and Kevin Walby. Vancouver: UBC Press. Forthcoming.

Davis, Jeff. 2010. "Cabinet ministers' offices regularly interfere in ATI requests, says Tory staffer." *The Hill Times Online.* February 22. Accessed August 3, 2010. http://hilltimes.com/page/view/ati-02-22-2010.

De Lint, William, and Alan Hall. 2009. *Intelligent Control: Policing Labour in Canada.* Toronto: University of Toronto Press.

Deflem, Mathieu. 1994. "Law enforcement in British colonial Africa: A comparative analysis of imperialist policing in Nyasaland, the Gold Coast, and Kenya." *Police Studies* 17:45-68.

Earl, Jennifer. 2009. "Information access and protest policing post-9/11: Studying the policing of the 2004 Republican National Convention." *American Behavioral Scientist* 53(1):44-60.

Ericson, Richard. 1982. *Reproducing Order: A Study of Police Patrol Work.* Toronto: University of Toronto Press.

Foucault, Michel. 1980. *Power/Knowledge: Selected Interviews and Other Writings, 1972-1977,* edited by Colin Gordon. New York: Pantheon.

———. 2007. *Security, Territory, Population: Lectures at the College de France 1977-1978,* edited by Michel Senellart. New York: Palgrave.

Friedland, Martin. 2001. "Police powers in bill C-36." In *The Security of Freedom: Essays on Canada's Anti-Terrorism Bill*, edited by R.J. Daniels, P. Macklem, and K. Roach, 269-286. Toronto: University of Toronto Press.

Galliher, John F. 1980. "Social scientists' ethical responsibilities to superordinates: Looking upward meekly." *Social Problems* 27:298-308.

Gouldner, Alvin. 1973. *For Sociology: Renewal and Critique in Sociology Today.* New York: Basic Books.

Gramsci, Antonio. 1971. *Selections from the Prison Notebooks of Antonio Gramsci.* London: Lawrence and Wishart.

Greenberg, David F. 1993. *Crime and Capitalism: Readings in Marxist Criminology.* Philadelphia: Temple University Press.

Harding, Sandra, and Kathryn Norberg. 2005. "New feminist approaches to social science methodologies: An introduction." *Signs* 30(4):2009-2015.

Horn, Rebecca. 1997. "Not 'one of the boys': Women researching the police." *Journal of Gender Studies* 6(3):297-308.

Hudson, Barbara. 2000. "Critical reflection as research methodology." In *Doing Criminological Research*, edited by Victor Jupp, Pamela Davies, and Peter Francis, 175-191. London: Sage.

Hughes, Gordon. 2000. "Understanding the politics of criminological research." In *Doing Criminological Research*, edited by Victor Jupp, Pamela Davies, and Peter Francis, 234-248. London: Sage.

Juris, Jeffery. 2007. "Practicing militant ethnography with the movement for global resistance in Barcelona." In *Constituent Imagination: Militant Investigations, Collective Theorization*, edited by Stevphen Shukaitis, David Graeber, and Erika Biddle, 164-176. Oakland: AK Press.

Kalunta-Crumpton, Anita. 2004. "Criminology and orientalism." In *Pan-African Issues in Crime and Justice*, edited by Anita Kalunta-Crumpton and Biko Agozino, 5-22. Aldershot: Ashgate.

Kraska, Peter B., and Victor E. Kappeler. 1997. "Militarizing American police: The rise and normalization of paramilitary units." *Social Problems* 44(1):1-18.

Larsen, Mike. Forthcoming. "Against opacity: The researcher as access to information applicant." In *Intense Methods: Issues and Concerns When Researching Sensitive Topics*, edited by Jennifer M. Kilty, Sheryl C. Fabian and Maritza Felices-Luna.

Larsen, Mike, and Kevin Walby, eds. 2012. *Brokering Access: Politics, Power, and Freedom of Information in Canada.* Vancouver: UBC Press. Forthcoming.

Lee, Raymond M. 1993. *Doing Research on Sensitive Topics.* London: Sage.

———. 2001. "Research uses of the U.S. Freedom of Information Act." *Field Methods* 13(4):370-391.

———. 2005. "The UK Freedom of Information Act and social research." *International Journal of Social Research Methodology* 8:1-18.

Littrell, Boyd. 1993. "Bureaucratic secrets and adversarial methods of social research." In *A Critique of Contemporary American Sociology*, edited by Ted Vaughn, Gideon Sjorberg, and Larry Reynolds, 207-231. New York: General Hall Publishers.

Lundman, Richard J., and Paul T. McFarlane. 1976. "Conflict methodology: An introduction and preliminary assessment." *The Sociological Quarterly* 17:503-512.

Manning, Peter. 1977. *Police Work: The Social Organization of Policing*. Long Grove: Waveland Press.

Marks, Monique, Jennifer Wood, Faizel Ally, Tess Walsh, and Abbey Witbooi. 2010. "Worlds apart? On the possibilities of police/academic collaborations." *Policing* 4(2):112-118.

Marquis, Greg. 1997. "The 'Irish model' and nineteenth century Canadian policing." *Journal of Imperial and Commonwealth History* 25(2):193-218.

Marx, Gary T. 1972. *Muckraking Sociology*. New Jersey: Transaction Books.

———. 1984. "Notes on the discovery, collection and assessment of hidden and dirty data." In *Studies in the Sociology of Social Problems*, edited by John I. Kitsue and Joseph W. Schneider, 78-113. Norwood, NJ: Ablex Publishing.

Murphy, Chris. 2007. "'Securitizing' Canadian policing: A new policing paradigm for the post 9/11 security state?" *The Canadian Journal of Sociology* 32(4):451- 477.

Nader, Laura. 1972. "Up the anthropologist—perspectives gained from studying up." In *Reinventing Anthropology*, edited by Dell Hymes, 284-311. New York: Random House.

Neocleous, Mark. 2000. *Fabrication of Social Order: A Critical Theory of Police Power*. London: Pluto.

———. 2008. *Critique of Security*. Montreal: McGill-Queen's University Press.

Pasquino, Pasquale. [1978] 1991. "Theatrum Politicum: The genealogy of capital—police and the state of prosperity." In *The Foucault Effect: Studies in Governmentality*, edited by Graham Burchell, Colin Gordon, and Peter Miller, 105-118. Chicago: University of Chicago Press.

Presdee, Mike, and Reece Walters. 1998. "The perils and politics of criminological research and the threat to academic freedom." *Current Issues in Criminal Justice* 10(2):156-167.

Punch, Maurice. 1986. *The Politics and Ethics of Fieldwork*. Beverly Hills: Sage.

Rees, Ann. 2003. "Red File alert: Public access at risk." *Toronto Star*. November 1.

Reiner, Robert. 2000. "Police research." In *Doing Research on Crime and Justice*, edited by Roy D. King and Emma Wincup, 205-235. New York: Oxford University Press.

Rigakos, George, John McMullan, Joshua Johnson, and Gulden Ozcan, eds. 2009. "Introduction." In *A General Police System: Political Economy and Security in the Age of Enlightenment*, 1-32. Ottawa: Red Quill Books.

Roberts, Alasdair. 2005. "Spin control and freedom of information: Lessons for the United Kingdom from Canada." *Public Administration* 83:1-23.

———. 2006. *Blacked Out: Government Secrecy in the Information Age*. Cambridge: Cambridge University Press.

———. 2007. "Transparency in the security sector." In *The Right to Know: Transparency for an Open World*, edited by Ann Florini, 309-336. New York: Columbia University Press.

Schwegler, Tara A. 2008. "Trading up: Reflections on power, collaboration, and ethnography in the anthropology of policy." *Anthropology in Action* 15(2):10-25.

Shearing, Clifford, and Jennifer Wood. 2003. "Nodal governance, democracy, and the new 'denizens'." *Journal of Law and Society* 30(3):400-419.

Smith, Dorothy E. 1999. *Writing the Social: Critique, Theory, and Investigations*. Toronto: University of Toronto Press.

Smith, George. 1990. "Political activist as ethnographer." *Social Problems* 37(4):629-648.

Sudbury, Julia. 2009. "Challenging the penal dependency: Activist scholars and the antiprison movement." In *Activist Scholarship: Anti-Racism, Feminism, and Social Change*, edited by Julia Sudbury and Margo Okazawa-Rey, 17-36. Boulder: Paradigm Publishers.

Sudbury, Julia, and Margo Okazawa-Rey, eds. 2009. "Introduction: Activist scholarship and the neoliberal university after 9/11." In *Activist Scholarship: Anti-Racism, Feminism, and Social Change*, 1-16. Boulder: Paradigm Publishers.

Thompson, A.K. 2006. "Direct action, pedagogy of the oppressed." In *Sociology for Changing the World: Social Movements/Social Research*, edited by Caelie Frampton, Gary Kinsman, A.K. Thompson, and Kate Tilleczek, 99-118. Halifax: Fernwood.

Tombs, Steve, and Dave Whyte, eds. 2003a. "Scrutinizing the powerful: Crime, contemporary political economy, and critical social research." In *Unmasking the Crimes of the Powerful: Scrutinizing States & Corporations*, 3-45. New York: Peter Lang.

———. 2003b. "Unmasking the crimes of the powerful: Establishing some rules of engagement." In *Unmasking the Crimes of the Powerful: Scrutinizing States & Corporations*, 261-272. New York: Peter Lang.

Walters, Reece. 2007. "Embedded criminology and knowledges of resistance." In *Governance and Regulation in Social Life: Essays in Honour of W.G. Carson*, edited by Augustine Brannigan and George Pavlich, 221-232. New York: Routledge-Cavendish.

Wilkinson, Sue. 2010. "Research and policing—looking to the future." *Policing* 4(2):146-148.

Yeager, Matthew G. 2006. "The Freedom of Information Act as a methodological tool: Suing the government for data." *Canadian Journal of Criminology and Criminal Justice* July:499-521.

———. 2008. "Getting the usual treatment: Research censorship and the dangerous offender." *Contemporary Justice Review* 11(4):413-425.

Young, T.R. 1976. "Some theoretical foundations for conflict methodology." *Sociological Inquiry* 46(1):23-29.

Chapter 13

Our Streets!
Practice and Theory of the Ottawa Panhandlers' Union[165]

Matthew R. McLennan

The following chapter comprises two sections. The first is an updated and edited version of a roundtable contribution I delivered to the York University graduate sociology conference "Lumpen-City: Discourses of Marginality | Marginalizing Discourses" in Toronto, Canada, in March of 2009. My aim in applying to the conference was to present in an academic setting as accurate as possible a description of the practice and theory of the Ottawa Panhandlers' Union, to which I then belonged as a voting member.

Due to my position of privilege, my claim to have belonged to the Panhandlers' Union is problematic, and requires a bit of context. My involvement grew out of already belonging to the Ottawa-Outaouais General Membership Branch (GMB) of the Industrial Workers of the World. As a wage earner without direct power to hire and fire, my membership in the GMB was uncontroversial. I developed a friendship with head Panhandlers' Union organizer and spokesperson Andrew Nellis in the context of GMB meetings and solidarity actions. At about that time, I was also supplementing my student income by busking. Earning part of my wage on the streets qualified me for membership in the Panhandlers' Union, and my offer to volunteer was met with a counter-offer to join in full participation.

I put my participation in the York conference to a vote at a Panhandlers' Union meeting, and I received unanimous support—with the amendment that I participate in the conference as a union representative. This change to the motion's wording highlighted the complex nature of my task: I had to produce a descriptive presentation while inhabiting, so to speak, that which I was describing. I had, in other words, to adhere to standards of academic integrity while approximating as far as possible, in and through my own discursive performance, the understandably partisan self-understanding of the union.

With this in mind, I presented the talk as a union representative. But because it was an academic conference, I nonetheless benefited, as a researcher and career academic, from the critical insights and methodological comments of other conference participants. Largely for reasons of time, I bracketed the question of my own experience and position in the union. In discussion with Andrew Nellis, and at the recommendation of conference participants, the editors of this volume, and other early readers of the document, I have added a second section to broadly address this question.

Because I do not think I ultimately succeed in harmonizing the conflicting claims of group solidarity, academic objectivity, and personal reflection, I have chosen to present a bifurcated rather than a unified document. If nothing else, the form reflects, to some extent, the complexity of my relation to the content. Insofar as section II is a largely methodological reflection, published after the fact of my participation in the union, the question arises as to whether or not it betrays the spirit of the union's decision to have me speak at York. My feeling is no, since section II does not contradict in any obvious respect the representation of the union given in section I; rather, it is offered in the spirit of clarifying the claim to have been able to advance that representation. Even those elements of section II which comprise generally applicable moral arguments pertaining to activists and researchers, but do not hinge directly on the Panhandlers' Union, constitute part of my methodological argument. In short, I do not cease, by reflecting on methodology and personal experience, to be a partisan of the union.

I hope in any case that besides spreading the word about a fascinating group with justice on its side, the following will be in some small measure helpful to other researchers who wish to examine their own relationships to the marginalized groups with which they are involved—especially where they are involved as outsiders.

I.

The Ottawa Panhandlers' Union is an ongoing experiment in defence and empowerment via radical street-level democracy. The union, which has roughly eighty registered members and a smaller core of a dozen to two dozen regular participants, was launched in 2003 by homeless and otherwise street-involved persons from a variety of backgrounds (see also Kip's discussion, this volume, of unemployed union mobilization in Frankfurt, Germany). At the time of its formation, it received no small amount of derision in the mainstream media and in the general public on account of its claim to actually *be* a union. A common jibe quoted in the *Ottawa Citizen*, for instance, was whether local panhandlers intended to strike for wider sidewalks.[166] Panhandlers' Union organizers have consistently responded, in and out of the press, that the popular conception of a union as a state-sanctioned bargaining service for stably employed workers, staffed by a professional bureaucracy, is in fact too narrow a definition of what a union actually is. Because many members support themselves by busking, selling artworks, helping people to park their cars, telling jokes, selling erotic services, and so on, they argue that they *are* in fact labourers and that the street *is* their workplace. Even panhandling pure and simple is viewed by some members to be a type of labour; one self-identified Buddhist member, for instance, has defined his panhandling as the selling of good karma. If we, therefore, admit that the Panhandlers' Union is made up of people providing goods and services to make or supplement their livelihoods, and, if we further admit that a union is a collection of workers banding together for mutual aid and defence, then there is no obvious reason why we cannot call the Panhandlers' Union a bona fide union—although we can, of course, admit that it is in some decisive respects an unconventional one.

It should be noted, first of all, that the union constitutes an organized workplace or "shop" of what many already consider a "real" union, the Industrial Workers of the World (IWW). The IWW is an international revolutionary union that was launched in the United States in 1905. Since its inception the IWW has striven to establish industrial democracy, which can be roughly defined as democratic worker control of the production and distribution of goods and services, organized on an industrial basis.[167] Under this watchword, the IWW has a long and continuing history of organizing and tenaciously defending what many mainstream unions, at various times, have deemed "un-organizable" sectors of the work force, such as itinerant/migrant workers, domestic workers, the unemployed, African-Americans, and recent immigrants.[168]

The IWW prefigures its notion of industrial democracy by functioning as a strongly decentralized organization. Though based in the United States, there are largely autonomous Regional Organizing Committees, or ROCs, in Germany and the British Isles. Recently, the formation of a Canadian ROC has gotten underway. The IWW is also organized around the world, by city or region, into General Membership Branches, or GMBs. GMBs are direct-democratic institutions and are relatively autonomous with respect to the ROCs. The latter are accountable to the memberships of the former, and exist primarily for purposes of coordinating the actions, communications, and so on, of GMBs in the same geographical/national region. It should be noted that many IWW members are not affiliated with a GMB (i.e. many cities do not have one); however, all members are assigned to an Industrial Union (IU) based on their current or last employment. For example, I belong to IU 620, Education Workers. In theory, the IUs would coordinate strikes and labour actions by industry and by region, by means of Industrial Union Branches (IUBs).

There is a GMB in the Ottawa-Outaouais region.[169] On the initiative of its members, it has carried out a number of small-scale solidarity actions, most notably pickets that won back-pay for service workers who had been wrongfully terminated or who had not received outstanding wages. The GMB has also provided organizational structure for the Ottawa Panhandlers' Union since the latter's inception, and it continues to assist it by means of fundraising, secretarial work, solidarity actions, and so on. It should be noted, however, that the Panhandlers' Union, though considered a shop of the Ottawa-Outaouais GMB, is a largely self-directed initiative. It adheres to the essentials of the IWW constitution, and it has voted to keep the GMB informed of its activities. But beyond that, the Panhandlers' Union is an initiative *by* street people and *for* street people. This should be stressed. Some critics have reasoned that if a union requires dues—and the IWW does, demanding sub-minimum dues of $5 per month for precariously employed or unemployed members to keep in good standing—then the Panhandlers' Union amounts in practice to an extortion racket cloaked in Leftist rhetoric. This is false. The Ottawa-Outaouais GMB pays the initiation fees of new Panhandlers' Union members, and after that it is up to individual members to stay in good standing or not. Practically speaking, all that happens to members in bad standing is that they cannot vote at the annual General Assembly of the IWW in the United States. Since few members possess the means or have expressed a desire to make the trek thus far, the issue of dues does little to get in the way of the shop's day-to-day democratic functioning. At worst, the sporadic nature of its dues payments has made it prone to fund shortages when it comes time for direct actions, legal battles, and so on. Individual members who are able have been known to pitch in more than their share when this becomes a problem.

As for what the Panhandlers' Union actually does, the question may be fairly posed what the organization of street labour along the industrial lines championed by the IWW might even look like. Furthermore, it may be asked—what concrete purpose the organization of street labour could serve. A strike situation (i.e. cessation of street labourers' provision of goods and services, many of them cultural in nature) might make the streets of Ottawa less vibrant, but it would not thereby disturb the functioning of the wage system in any obvious way. Moreover, for most street labourers there is no clear employer to struggle against. A further barrier to understanding the nature and function of the union would be the apparent recalcitrance of much of its constituency to organization. In the experience of the union, members have more often than not been affected by mental illness, or substance abuse problems, or both. This means that most of them tend to lead more or less chaotic lives. In spite of the ingenuity of its members, the union has experienced considerable organizational difficulties. It would appear to be an unlikely vanguard for establishing industrial democracy.

Nonetheless, despite the revolutionary and "workerist" rhetoric of the preamble to the IWW constitution, by the admission of Panhandlers' Union co-founder and lead organizer Andrew Nellis,[170] the purpose of the Panhandlers' Union is nothing as grandiose as the abolition of capitalism. Nellis is himself an anarcho-syndicalist with avowedly insurrectionist sympathies, but he is adamant that the union does not exist to put forward a political agenda along ideological lines.[171] The shop is "political" only to the extent that it is a vehicle for the defence and empowerment of individual street-involved people against police, reactionary politicians, landlords, and in some cases, homeless shelters. It seeks to foster such defence and empowerment by means of the direct experience of radical democracy and mutual aid—and it considers the often migratory nature of its population to be an asset, reasoning that street-involved persons will carry experiences and ideas picked up from union meetings to other cities. All of this is to say that if the Panhandlers' Union is not a revolutionary group, then neither is it an activist group of the paternalistic liberal stripe, speaking out for marginal populations who did not necessarily ask for help and who were in some cases not necessarily adequately consulted. The Panhandlers' Union aims to serve as a street-level defence organization, all the while promoting and sustaining a different type of ethic and existence for street-involved persons by means of face-to-face decision-making, action, and co-operation.

To foster this ethic is admittedly no small task. On the streets, a kind of unfettered individualism often reigns; it is usually difficult to trust other people in the same dire straits, and if a street-involved person finds a reliable way to survive, he or she generally sticks to it because his or her resource base is likely too small to provide much room for experimentation. Through the experience of direct democracy, knowledge-sharing, and skill-sharing, however, members of the Panhandlers' Union feel that their voice counts, that they matter, and that there are people who have their backs. This helps to build solidarity, facilitates defence, and ultimately gives them that trust and, to some extent, the room to experiment that was otherwise lacking.

In case this sounds like a chicken and egg scenario, where the members have to somehow trust each other enough to actually take the time to sit down at a meeting and build trust, it should be kept in mind that the increasingly draconian measures enforced by the City of Ottawa and the Ottawa Business Improvement Areas to deal with the visibility of street-involved persons has driven a large number of them to seek precisely the kind of co-operation that the Panhandlers' Union espouses. Larry O'Brien, mayor of Ottawa from 2006 to 2010,[172] effectively declared war on the poor when he compared panhandlers to pigeons and seagulls. O'Brien suggested that an appropriate response to Ottawa's homelessness problem was to stop giving money to panhandlers so that they would simply "fly away" to somewhere else. More ominously, he likened the occasional ticketing or arrest of panhandlers to shooting the odd gull at the city dump, so as to scare the rest of the flock and keep it in line.[173]

This strategy of starving street-involved persons out and intimidating them, justly criticized by Ottawa activists, is unfortunately not restricted to the public gaffs of an out-of-touch conservative politician. In fact, it is reflected in some of the city's recent legislation. For one thing, the *Vending on Highways* bylaw (By-Law No. 2005-358) makes the selling of arts, crafts, newspapers, and so on, illegal in Ottawa so long as it occurs on any "highway" —defined as "a common and public highway ... includes any bridge, trestle, viaduct, or other structure forming part of the highway and, except as otherwise provided, includes a portion of a highway."[174] The Ottawa Business Improvement Areas have been instrumental in promoting this bylaw to discourage the sale of goods on sidewalks (considered to be "part of the highway" as per the preceding definition),[175] on the grounds that such sales undercut the income of shops.[176] But the upshot of this is that police officers may apply this legislation to street labourers who are not in any way undercutting businesses, so as to "clean up the streets". Union members and other street labourers have in fact been ticketed in droves for selling crafts, artworks, and IWW newspapers.[177] The message sent by City of Ottawa meritocrats to street-labouring people is therefore deliriously contradictory: "Pull yourself up by your own bootstraps by making an honest living, but if you try to actually do so, you will be punished."

Another major problem for street-involved persons in Ottawa is the Ontario *Safe Streets Act*.[178] The Act legislates against soliciting a captive audience, which includes anyone standing in a line for a bus, or an automated teller, or a washroom, or occupying a vehicle. Of course, a "captive audience" can be, and often is, interpreted quite loosely. It is especially problematic for panhandlers in the city's centre, where literally every inch of sidewalk is near a bus stop, an automated teller, an occupied car, and so on. Presumably, panhandlers are supposed to solicit where there are no people. Notably, the wording of the Act targets squeegee kids on the grounds that they by definition solicit captive audiences. The Act thereby removes yet another potential source of income from street labourers.

The *Safe Streets Act* also legislates against "aggressive solicitation", but defines "aggressive" quite loosely as anything causing a reasonable person to fear for his or her safety—which, evidently, would include such "aggressive" behaviour as walking beside a person while soliciting, or asking again after they have refused.[179] Middle-class people, largely unaccustomed to interaction with street people, are taken here as paragons of what is "reasonable". This poses a problem for panhandlers because such "reasonable" people often over-react and fear for their safety in situations where this is not warranted. Accordingly, there are many harmless Ottawa street people being ticketed for little more than offending the aesthetic sensibilities of the financially better-off. This type of harassment and discrimination is pretty standard; it is perhaps more surprising that a paraplegic panhandler was recently ticketed under the very same *Safe Streets Act* for aggressive solicitation. This shows the overtly cynical way in which the Act is interpreted and applied by some Ottawa police officers. It is noteworthy that neither the *Vending on Highways* bylaw nor the *Safe Streets Act* have ever, to my knowledge, been applied to university undergraduates in their annual "Shinerama" drive—an often "aggressive" attempt to sell stickers and solicit money for charities from captive audiences near downtown bus stops, automated tellers, occupied parked vehicles, and so on.[180] The class bias of the legislation becomes glaringly obvious in its selective enforcement.

In such a climate, a large part of the Panhandlers' Union's efforts has gone into educating street people and the wider public about street people's legal rights, especially when speaking to police officers, and to sharing effective tactics of legally resisting police officers who overstep the legal and/or moral bounds of enforcement. There is also a regular cop-watch initiative that has been launched by the Panhandlers' Union, where volunteers from the shop as well as other local activists police the police in the city centre. In the context of such regular repression, the knowledge and support that the Panhandlers' Union provides often affects people in decisively positive ways. In the words of one new member, "I didn't know that when the cops pulled me over and went through my pockets with no cause, they were breaking the law. They won't be doing that again."

The union's meeting process contributes to this building of trust and solidarity. When a motion is put on the floor, the group tries to reach consensus. Members give a thumbs-up for "yes", a thumbs-down for "no", and a thumbs-sideways for abstention, or as it is called in the union, "standing aside". If consensus cannot be reached, there is a discussion and a second vote is taken to try again for consensus. If this fails, then the motion must be passed by majority vote. Here we have a democratic experiment in which consensus is prevented from degenerating into monarchy-by-the-veto. Rather, the consensus model is used to build good faith wherever possible. To guard against habituation to authoritarianism, the duty of chairing meetings is rotated on a meeting-by-meeting basis. Members who have been systematically disempowered, and who battle disorganizing personal problems, therefore get to experience not only democracy and co-operation, but the empowering experiences of group facilitation, direction, and organization.

Despite this overall positive picture of the union's process, there remains the question of racism, sexism, ableism, and homophobia in the meeting context. The union's most militant past and present organizers, such as Andrew Nellis, Jane Scharf, and Proshanto Smith, have all organized for a union that values and promotes respect of difference. The realities of the streets, however, often frustrate this goal. In the experience of organizers, the streets are predominantly patriarchal, racist, homophobic, and ableist (not much different, of course, than society at large …). This has presented organizers with a choice: they can either institute a "safe space" model, wherein discriminatory and threatening language is banned from meetings, or fight such discrimination via the meeting process itself. Since a safe space model would disqualify many street-involved people from participation, organizers have opted for the latter approach. This means that it is sometimes difficult for minority members to participate comfortably, and this is an ongoing battle. But it also means that participants are included in genuine debates about the validity of their language and unexamined assumptions. The union is, therefore, not perfect in this regard, but it avoids the left-liberal activist paradox of presupposing a model of values that would actually exclude a significant number of the people it claims to represent.

Another problem faced by the union is the question of drugs and drug dealers. Since substance abuse is already a problem for many of its members, and since drugs risk undermining the solidarity and organizational functioning that the union is trying to build, it is wary about seeking the support of drug dealers, though the latter are of course street-involved and are, therefore, at times invaluable allies. Moreover, drug dealers are often opposed to the kind of police heat the union has been known to bring to their stomping grounds. As with oppressive language in meeting spaces, this is a problem that has yet to be solved. Organizers have preferred to approach concrete manifestations of this problem on a case-by-case basis, in practice maintaining an uneasy truce that nonetheless sometimes spills over into conflict.

With the preceding in mind, we can move on to some of the Union's more notable practical achievements, noting as well the difficulties that have attended these. My list is by no means exhaustive, but is rather intended to provide a condensed history.

- In 2006 a member of the union was severely beaten by three security guards at the Rideau Centre, a mall near Parliament Hill, following a verbal disagreement on mall property. The Panhandlers' Union was instrumental in helping him to obtain legal counsel, after which he sued the mall for damages and was awarded a settlement out of court. The union member in question has since gotten off the streets and is steadily employed, but has come back on numerous occasions to participate and show solidarity to others in turn.
- On May Day 2006, union members and sympathizers occupied and shut down the street in front of Rideau Centre for about an hour to protest similar treatment of street people by mall security.
- The same day, members of the Panhandlers' Union and sympathetic activists and street youth occupied the lobby of the main Ottawa police station for several hours, demanding that officer Barakat, notorious for beating up street youth and stealing their property and companion dogs, be taken off the beat. The officer in question was actually promoted up from beat duty as a result. Though this result was ultimately unjust, the occupation was nonetheless deemed a success by the protestors because their immediate goal was achieved.
- May Day 2007 saw a march from City Hall to the Bank Street Business Improvement Area (BIA) in protest of O'Brien's pigeon and seagull comments and the BIA's attack on street labour. Handbills announced that "The Pigeons Peck Back." Continuing the avian theme, the building housing the Bank Street BIA was pelted with eggs by unknown protestors.
- In a display of the solidarity which the Panhandlers' Union espouses, one member volunteered to accompany another member with mental illness, anxiety,

and organizational problems to classes at the University of Ottawa. Numerous other examples of such solidarity could be cited; the important thing is to note that in many small ways the self-defeating individualism of the streets continues to be overcome by the co-operative culture espoused and built by the Panhandlers' Union.
- May Day 2009 was something of a non-event, the union's attempt to burn Larry O'Brien in effigy having been thwarted by police. Union members considered the failure of this action to stand as a lesson about tactics that is well worth examining.
- From 2008 to 2009, most of the Panhandlers' Union's funds and energies were invested in contesting a decision by the City of Ottawa to fence off a section of a pedestrian underpass where homeless people often went for shelter from the elements, and for mutual protection and company. Direct actions were carried out surrounding this issue, in addition to a human rights case against the City of Ottawa. Lead organizer Andrew Nellis was arrested in connection with a direct action concerning the fence in 2008 (protestors subsequently tried to occupy the courthouse in which Nellis was held, but were roughly shown out of the building by police). The crown dropped the charges in 2009, but Nellis is still burdened with legal fees that have to some extent hampered his organizing. The General Defence Committee of the Ottawa-Outaouais IWW has launched a campaign to raise the requisite funds. In the meantime, the City of Ottawa agreed to settle the human rights case out of court. The Panhandlers' Union was awarded seed money to open a resource centre/ commercial space. At the time of writing (summer 2011), the Union has recently hosted a May Day craft fair and is in the process of locating a financially sustainable commercial/meeting space. To this end, it is negotiating the possibility of a partnership with other Ottawa activist groups.

In sum, the Ottawa Panhandlers' Union is an embattled but tenacious organization that has managed to win some significant small-scale victories. Though it constantly re-examines its strategy and tactics, it continues to serve as an alternative to the predominant culture of individualism characterizing the streets, offering concrete support to those who need it. Above all, it has disseminated and given credence to the idea that street-involved persons are capable of a level of humanity, initiative, and organization that is seldom granted them in the popular imagination.

II.

In 1969, Vine Deloria, Jr. published *Custer Died for Your Sins: An Indian Manifesto*. He argued therein that white anthropologists who study Native American cultures are ignoramuses, charlatans, and blood-suckers. They make their academic careers on the backs of populations they do not benefit in turn; moreover, they actually harm the populations they study by obscuring the causes of social problems and contributing to clumsy, ignorant government programs and policies. They also generate or bolster objectifying, essentializing discourses. These harm in turn by fostering condescending, romanticizing, and aggressive racism in the colonizer, and fatalism and self-hatred in the colonized.

Deloria's critique of anthropologists should be read in the context of the Red Power and other decolonization movements of the 1960s and 1970s; nonetheless, its force and that of similar critiques still resonates. Critiques like Deloria's amount to a clear, decisive "Fuck off" directed by colonized peoples at colonial/settler social scientists. Above all, such critiques instantiate the colonized as a subject in face of discourses which are, consciously or not, maliciously or not, objectifying and essentializing. Importantly, for present purposes, Deloria (1969:100) also had this to say to anthropologists: if you must be anthropologists, then "get down from [your] thrones of authority and

PURE research and begin helping Indian tribes instead of preying on them." In *Indians and Anthropologists: Vine Deloria, Jr., and the Critique of Anthropology*, a retrospective volume published in 1997, Deloria tempered his argument somewhat to allow for the possibility of a more beneficent social science, closer in spirit and practice to non-paternalistic social work than to "pure" ethnology. He also speculated that anthropologists might take what they learn from subject populations in order to critique their own colonizing societies, and become concrete "problem solvers" (Deloria 1997).

Writing from a position of relative privilege in a university built on stolen land, it is impossible to take Deloria lightly. Though restricted to research on Aboriginal populations, his critique may be widened substantially to cover any discourse a researcher belonging to a colonizing/settler or hegemonic population may produce on colonized or marginalized subjects. In what follows, I will take it as axiomatic that researchers should answer Deloria's critique, producing discourse that gives back to subject-populations and, wherever possible, becoming self-reflexive, concrete problem-solvers. This axiom may be considered as moral and/or political, rather than methodological, in the sense that it posits an ultimate aim for research beyond the scope of methodological arguments. On this view, responding to Deloria's critique becomes a moral duty and/or a political decision. This is not to say that research loses its "objectivity", if we wish to retain this notion here. Rather, if we agree that research must above all serve the aims of social justice, then this will affect the kinds of questions we ask, the problems we identify and the research methods we employ.

For present purposes, all of this can be focused as follows: how can a white, able-bodied, Anglophone male with a masculine gender presentation, who has never lived on the streets, claim to belong to the Panhandlers' Union, much less represent it? How can a researcher claiming such privilege produce discourse on street-involved persons that neither replicates nor produces pernicious, essentializing representations or power imbalances? What kind of concrete "problem solving" may be produced from such research? There is perhaps no easy or straight set of answers to this line of questioning; in any case, it far exceeds the scope of the present chapter. There are, however, some rough-and-ready signposts to guide us.

Consider, for example, the issue of participation in meetings. A researcher-participant's privilege will be readily perceived in such contexts. Trust must be built, but this is difficult since social privilege manifests itself in ways that often escape the consciousness of the researcher. Many women will have noticed that even in ostensibly equal contexts of discussion, such as activist spaces or meetings, men will take up an inordinate amount of time talking or taking charge; people of colour will likely have noticed the same thing about white people. Privilege seems to generate a sense of entitlement to speak and to be taken seriously even in spaces where one is relatively inexperienced/ignorant, and where privilege is supposed to be neutralized. It is for this reason incumbent upon privileged researcher-participants to be listeners more than talkers, to abstain from voting on certain issues where they are uninformed or inexperienced, and to not make themselves fixtures or essential players at meetings.

One can never be sure, however, of having successfully navigated this problem—especially given the paradox that by hanging back and questioning one's privilege so as to check a power imbalance, the privileged researcher-participant risks treating fellow human beings with kid gloves and thereby reproduces it. There comes a point at which worrying about harming the people you are working with produces diminishing returns, and even risks becoming a type of crypto-paternalism. It might be more productive to think harder about how, and experiment with ways in which, you may concretely help your research subjects to help themselves—even if that entails certain risks. There comes a time when theory and methodological reflection must get their feet wet, so to speak; for the sake of social justice, we would do much better to test our tools of self-criticism in a field of concrete engagement.

When asking the union's permission to give the talk at York, I had to keep all of this in mind. I was encouraged when a fellow member earnestly responded: "You should spread the word. It's a good group." It most certainly is, which is precisely why, notwithstanding the important and difficult issues of power imbalance, representation, and voice, I have used my access to academia in order to publish the report you have read. Assuming then that the privileged researcher-participant's subject position presents certain seemingly insurmountable obstacles to *full* participation in groups such as the Panhandlers' Union, it does not necessarily rule out partial and even *fruitful* participation—precisely, participation conforming to what I understand as a solidarity rather than paternalistic or charity model of political activism. Assuming that research should serve the aims of social justice, the researcher-participant should care more about groups such as the Panhandlers' Union achieving practical gains than about being taken seriously by all of their members, or having a truly equal voice in decision-making processes. The union can certainly function without me; if it could not, it would be compromised to the core. It is not there to promote and protect my interests, after all (save for indirectly: I would argue that campaigns for justice, public space, cop watch, and so on, benefit everyone).

Producing reports at conferences and in scholarly texts is one thing; perhaps these avenues can be viewed as assets to such groups, to the extent that the discourse generated finds purchase in favourable policy or street-level organizational problem-solving. That said, the privilege of having attended university is perhaps best tapped for more modest "intellectual" work such as note-taking, archiving, press release writing, outreach, and so on. On a solidarity model, ultimately it is at the marginalized group's discretion how the researcher-participant may best employ his or her energies to help. What it boils down to is that the moral necessity and/or political decision to engage in activist-research or activist-scholarship do nothing to mitigate the applied-ethical minefield of such activity. This said, self-critique and reflection are indispensable—but they must not paralyze. Assuming the axial principle of social justice as a horizon for research, researchers can expect complications, frustrations, paradoxes, disappointments, but above all, the singular joys of fighting for what matters, in solidarity.

References

Bekken, John, and Fred W. Thompson. 2006. *The Industrial Workers of the World: Its First 100 Years*. Boston: Red Sun Press.

Bird, Stewart, Dan Georgakas, and Deborah Shaffer. 1985. *Solidarity Forever: An Oral History of the IWW*. Chicago: Lake View Press.

Deloria, Vine, Jr. 1969. *Custer Died for Your Sins: An Indian Manifesto*. London: Collier-Macmillan Limited.

———. 1997. "Conclusion: Anthros, Indians, and planetary reality." In *Indians and Anthropologists: Vine Deloria, Jr., and the Critique of Anthropology*, edited by Thomas Biolsi and Larry J. Zimmerman, 209-221. Tuscon: The University of Arizona Press.

Esmonde, Jackie. 2002. "Criminalizing poverty: The criminal law Power and the *Safe Streets Act*." *Journal of Law and Social Policy* 17:63-86. Accessed August 23, 2011. http://www.legalaid.on.ca/en/publications/downloads/journal_vol17/Esmonde.pdf.

Afterword
A Call to Activist Scholarship

Alan Bourke, Tia Dafnos, and Markus Kip

Each contribution in this volume engages simultaneously in a critique of dominant structures producing marginalization as well as of marginalizing discourses embedded within the academy. Since the contestation of marginalization is not bound by disciplinary affiliation or geographical location, we contend that our endeavour must also be interdisciplinary and transnational in reach. Furthermore, we caution against exhibiting any tendency towards methodological prescription or theoretical dogmatism in view of activist-scholarship. Though the issues may be particular to each context, we invite dialogical comparisons of methodological orientation and theoretical ambition which extend beyond the confines of this volume. In this, we hope that this volume will inspire readers to reflect upon their own research engagements from a new perspective, a new question. Research in one location might highlight a problem that in a different context could lead to greater sensitivity for issues previously overlooked. In particular, the contributions in parts I and II open the conceptual spaces necessary for such deliberation. To this end, can David Wilson and Matthew Anderson's critique of Obama's discourse on poverty help us formulate critiques of anti-poverty strategies in other contexts? Does Mark Willson's analysis of "homelessness" discourse in Canada offer tools to activist-scholars elsewhere? Julie Tomiak's article might lead people outside of Canada to ask: What voices and histories are silenced and what may a scholar's role be in contributing to such silencing?

Through their ethnographic research, Karen O'Connor, Silvia Pasquetti, and Markus Kip raise questions concerning the complexities of class formation and how grassroots interventions (or lack thereof) can lead to unintended consequences when confronted by the repressive sanctions of capital and state. Furthermore, although Zeynep Gönen and Deniz Yonucu, as well as Silvia Pasquetti conduct research in distinct contexts, both apply the terminology of the camp—can the transfer of this notion be useful for struggles in other contexts? In part III, there is a questioning of method and research design by contributors who seek to advance, whilst rendering problematic, emancipatory research praxis. While the contributions by Alan Bourke and Kate Murray offer critiques on the potentially conservative effects of community-based research and institutional ethnography respectively, the chapters by Matthew McLennan and Tia Dafnos advance forms of methodological engagement which have a clear applicability beyond the particularity of their given context. We ask: how can these treatments be usefully transferred to struggles in other contexts? These questions are both epistemological and methodological—the inter-relation of which reveals research to be an intrinsically political process. In other words, how are ways of knowing, or ways of acquiring knowledge of the experiential effects of oppression, integrally connected with the methods used?

We began the introduction to this volume with D'Souza's (2009) query about the different possible meanings of "activist-scholarship": Is it about activists and their relation *to* scholarship? Is it about activism *in* scholarship? Or is it scholarship *about* activism? Clearly, the diversity of approaches taken by the authors in the various contributions reveals these trajectories to be overlapping and contradictory. Yet, such approaches also exist in a necessary state of tension with each other. Granted, it is entirely possible to be an activist in one clearly defined sense of the term, and yet not in another. Such fluidity of meaning is not necessarily indicative of a problematic ideological inconsistency or lack of consensus as to what constitutes activism, but is rather illustrative of a rejection of orthodoxy as to what activist-scholarship is and can be.

First, the contributions in this volume differ in terms of the distance they exhibit between the authors and the movements that they relate to. In some cases, the author appears predominantly as an activist involved in the day-to-day activities of a particular organization or movement (see e.g. Matthew McLennan, Silvia Pasquetti, and Karen O'Connor). In other cases, the author clearly assumes the role of the scholar, less involved in the tactics and everyday life-worlds of particular struggles, although not detached from the broader strategy (see e.g. Mark Willson, Lisa Estreich, Julie Tomiak, and Markus Kip). A second line of difference between the chapters relates to the audiences that the contributors seek to address. In some cases, the contributions speak to a broader public (see e.g. David Wilson and Matthew Anderson, Zeynep Gönen and Deniz Yonucu, and Karen O'Connor). In other cases, the addressee of the writing is an academic audience in tune with contestations centred on reflexivity and voice in research (see e.g. Markus Kip, Alan Bourke, Kate Murray, Tia Dafnos, and Matthew McLennan). All these cases articulate hybrid researcher identities and thus illustrate the many ways in which we can engage the boundary between academic and activist research. In contesting the hegemonic understanding of these identities as mutually exclusive spheres, one of our aims with this volume has been to encourage such hybridity.

Although we make no claim to be representative of the many creative ways in which activist-scholars have negotiated their locations in relations of power, we also caution against adopting a *carte blanche* conceptualization of what constitutes activist scholarship, lest it become a vehicle that, with more rhetorical flourish than substantial thrust, allows one to pay lip-service to the semantics of equality, social justice, anti-racism, anti-colonialism, and so on. The potential institutionalization of critique, and the subsequent blunting of its critical force, can lead to the de-radicalization and de-politicization of social struggle. Indeed, a number of chapters have originated in this climate of disquiet—consider Markus Kip's concerns regarding the de-politicization of labour unions; Karen O'Connor's mapping of the co-optation of street sex-workers with regimes of "health promotion"; Alan Bourke's charting of the methodological conservatism of community-based research methodologies; or Tia Dafnos' critique of the use of participatory action research methods by the police themselves—all gesture toward an enveloping socio-political context which seeks to encourage compliance, if not coerce obeisance, to the status quo.

Notwithstanding such concerns, what is beyond doubt is the fact that the contributors collectively demonstrate a commitment to the power of critique as a fundamental starting point. Clearly, the contributions featured are all projects of distinctive inspiration, perspiration, and passion, and yet they are dialogically aligned in a struggle of common contestation. What the contributors collectively suggest, all working within academic spaces, is the idea that academic resources and research methods in themselves should not be dismissed simply because of the privileged social context in which they are embedded. Instead, the authors share the idea that the position of the academic, with all its power and privileges, can be used towards goals which include redefining what such power and privilege can be pressed into alliance with, and for what purposes. As a collection, these contributions suggest that the contradictions of engaging in radical praxis while situated with/in the academy can be productively exploited. Reflecting a range of approaches, experiences, and desired outcomes in navigating these contradictions, this collection is a way in which we hope to collectively learn from such negotiations. More often than not, the needs of academic institutions are at odds with those of the community. Ethics review boards, for instance, often take on the character of ethical regimes in placing disciplinary protocols and institutional fears of liability ahead of community concerns. Rather than seeking to anticipate each and every possible unintended consequence, however, the authors show us that, with sound political judgment, it is possible to engage the consequences that might arise in a productive way as the process unfolds. Clearly, there are times for reflection, but there are also times for action.

The blurring/hybridization of academic and activist identities is a troubling task, and one fraught with many problems. Indeed, the path toward an emancipatory praxis of activist-scholarship is one strewn with ill-fitting signage and bad directions. Not all the work we do as activists, for instance, will assist us in gaining access to the secure and privileged spaces of academic tenure—the security of which can, in turn, grant scholars the opportunity to further their activist goals. Conversely, not all the work we do as academics will be of immediate use for activist aims. To this end, several chapters highlight the need for conceptual spaces of reflection that are somewhat removed from the immediate exigencies of day-to-day struggles. It is in these spaces that we are offered the opportunity to rethink our goals and strategies, avoiding the traps related to particular discourses or short-term orientations. What, therefore, can be said by way of recommendation in advancing the praxis of activist scholarship? Below we draw some conclusions which have emerged from the contents of the volume. Far from a set of unifying principles to be adhered to in the praxis of activist-scholarship, we suggest they represent an ethos to be maintained against the reactionary forces which would impede their expression.

Firstly, we call for a commitment to a form of scholarly practice that acknowledges the intrinsically *partisan* character of research—that is, its affiliation and commitment to a particular cause, movement, or political agenda. Marginalization, in our understanding, implies forms of domination in which access to resources, opportunities, social recognition and political representation, are unequally distributed. Since this structural inequality is commonly legitimized in reference to deviant behaviour, laziness, a culture of poverty, the "undeserving" poor, and such, it is our conviction that activist-scholars can assist in dismantling these discourses. Indeed, we suggest this to be of greater urgency than ever before given the reappearance of "culture of poverty"-style explanations in contemporary debates on social exclusion, the concomitant hardening of a veritable socio-economic apartheid on a global scale, and considering the fact that even Saul Alinsky's *Rules for Radicals* has been utilized by the political right in grassroots mobilization. In particular, the cumulative weight of marginalizing discourses raises long-standing questions with regard to researcher neutrality and what we deem to be the misnomer of being "non-partisan".

Granted, not all partisan research is necessarily affiliated with the contestation of inequality and oppression—indeed, a recurring theme in the volume has been to demonstrate how such partisanship can be neutralized by the dominative logic of neoliberal governance. In light of this, we wish to re-emphasize the claim that all research is a deeply political act, one imbued with value-commitments and, thus, necessarily implicated in strategies of intervention/ non-intervention. Such has been a recurring tension coursing throughout the history of the social sciences—ranging from the ethos of social reformism permeating early sociological practice to all manner of moralizing discourses which have attempted to explain the vicissitudes of poverty and social exclusion in the guise of objectivity. To this end, critical scholars have endeavoured to expose the normative disguised in the descriptive, the subjective judgment veiled as impartiality, and the value judgements concealed in expressions of methodological rigour and researcher objectivity. Mobilizing data and evidence to advance a cause or movement is not solely the preserve of those who choose to make their political agendas explicit. Sociological analysis is always from *someone's* point of view, and is, therefore, inescapably partisan by virtue of its pursuit.

Second, how these different needs and aspirations can be brought into a collective movement of research *praxis* remains a question in need of individual clarification as well as collective deliberation. To be "political" is not necessarily to work towards emancipatory aims. The strategic and organizational usage of praxis that we intend here emphasizes the need for a constant cycle of re-conceptualizing the meanings of what can be learned from experience in order to reframe the strategic and operational model of activist-scholarship we propose. Debating issues of control, access, representation, reciprocity, and responsibility, in the field and beyond, requires the co-ordinated de-colonization of the methodological and gate-keeping mechanisms which are maintained by the disciplinary and institutional contours of academe. What this also calls for is a process by which participants—both "the researcher" and "the researched"—are prompted to reflexively recognize the arbitrary, discriminating, and exclusionary mindsets which find problematic replication in research practice. A critical and reflexive praxis—a blending of experiential learning through the research process with tales from the field—is a tentative step to be taken towards reconciling the bifurcated consciousness of activist-scholarly identity. In our understanding, it is also important that a critical praxis entails, and recognizes, the fact that the researcher never simply acts as an individual monad, but is rather already part of a collective movement that seeks social change. This collectivity of partisan praxis is not simply constituted by virtue of adopting a political stance, but is to be achieved, maintained, and collectively voiced through a commitment to the contestation of marginality.

Finally, nurturing bonds of *solidarity* is a pivotal link in forging connections between the abstractions of "value commitment" evident in praxis and advancing the cause of partisan research. In many of the chapters, a commitment to solidarity implies taking sides with a particular group or excluded population bedevilled by the marginalizing consequences of discursive regimes. As we have mentioned in the introduction to the volume, discourses of marginalization—as witnessed by the culture of poverty, the undeserving poor, the underclass, the lumpenproletariat, and so on—are best undermined when their contestation is collectively envisioned. If such categorizations have been strengthened by the legitimacy accrued through their association with academic discourse, as we have argued, so too should academic discourse be implicated in the possibility of their dismantling. Beyond the question of deciding the optimal form of methodological alignment in participatory, collaborative, or radical research undertakings, taking sides is recognized as an ethical and epistemological responsibility.

Accepting what solidarity entails is not merely an intellectual or epistemic choice, but rather one based upon the realization that our respective fates are inextricably intertwined. Although it may not always be a commonality of condition that is shared, solidarity arguably represents a commonality of political purpose, if not emancipatory intent, while respecting and learning from differences. While a commitment to solidarity and social equality implies analyzing marginality first and foremost in the concrete forms of its social organization, we also claim that relationships between individuals are an essential foundation in the process for social change. In this, we are compelled to jettison the binaries which demarcate, reify, and caricature the boundaries between scholarship and activism. To this end, solidarity is expressed in a collective practice that can lead to affiliations, if not relationships, friendships, or affinities and alliances. These are the relationships which often provide the sustenance for collective mobilizations and processes of experiential co-learning, and it is through such practices that we might prefigure, albeit imperfectly, forms of representational practice and human association free from domination.

(END)NOTES

Chapter 3: Legitimizing Violence and Segregation: Neoliberal Discourses on Crime and the Criminalization of Urban Poor Populations in Turkey (Zeynep Gönen and Deniz Yonucu)

1 PKK (Kurdistan Workers' Party) is a guerilla organization fighting against the Turkish State for cultural and political rights for the Kurds in Turkey.

2 While the concepts of discourse and ideology are generally perceived to be counterposed, following Hunt and Purvis's (1993:476) argument on the distinction between these two concepts, we take them as supplementary. Hunt and Purvis argue that ideology is about the external production of consciousnesses that mystifies the power relations within a class society and that discourse is inherent in all language and social relations. In turn, they suggest treating "discourse as *process* and ideology as *effect*" (Hunt and Purvis 1993:496). Accordingly, in this paper, in examining the discourses on crime and criminals, we will also question the ways in which these discourses veil and/or mystify material inequalities and conditions, and produce real effects.

3 We employ the concept "abject" *a la* Butler. Butler (1993:3) uses the "abject" for "the 'unliveable' and 'uninhabitable' zones of social life which are nevertheless densely populated by those who do not enjoy the status of the subject, but whose living under the sign of the 'unliveable' is required to circumscribe the domain of the subject."

4 In this paper, by "neoliberal" we mean the kinds of political economic practices which prioritize "the maximization of entrepreneurial freedoms within an institutional framework characterized by private property rights, individual liberty, free markets and free trade" (Harvey 2006b:145). While neoliberalism proposes "less state" in the sphere of economy, it has also depended on increasing state intervention in the regulation of the society. As Peck and Tickell (2007:33) argue: "Only rhetorically does neoliberalism means "less state"; in reality, it entails a thoroughgoing *reorganization* of governmental systems and state-economy relations. Tangentially, and more and more evidently as neoliberalism has been extended and deepened, this program involves the *roll out* of new state forms, new modes of regulation, new regime of governance, with the aim of consolidating and managing both marketisation and its consequences." By "neoliberal urbanism," we have in mind the reorganization of the space during the neoliberal era highlighting the commodity value of the city, and the processes of design and making of the cities as commodities for global investment and consumption (Mbembe 2004; Zukin 1995; Sassen 2001; Hackworth 2007; Murray 2008). Hence, cities are not just one of the spaces where neoliberal

policies are transpiring, but also constitute a central space for capitalist accumulation. During the neoliberal restructuring of the economy and society, cities undergo a process of transformation through the interventions of the state and the capital "to secure new advantages in international economic competition through the construction of territorially rooted immobile assets" (Brenner 2004:46). Further, these processes rest on the marginalization of the poor, while creating new spaces for the new middle classes of neoliberal era.

5 Scholars, such as Angela Davis, Julia Sudbury, Ruth Gilmore, Mecke Nigel and so on, who have been producing works about the contemporary criminal justice system, constitute a good example for the kind of critical research that we mention here. Their works have been indispensable for the prison abolition movement, which argues that contemporary courts, prisons, police, and other elements of criminal justice are antithetical to the production of justice. Prisons, in particular, do not solve crime, but create further problems; they exist for motives other than justice. Thus, they should be abolished and other forms of justice should be sought.

6 The headline was: "The Arena is usurped by the dogs" ("Meydan itlere kaldı"). The statement "meydan itlere kaldı" has multiple connotations in Turkish: "Meydan" can signify "arena", "space", "public space", but also existence [appearing, coming to existence], and implies "world". The word used for dog is, in fact, the slang use of dog, which when used to refer to "humans" as in the case above, it can mean evil.

7 For a detailed discussion on the pathological approach to crime see Rimke (2010), and 2011."The pathological approach to crime: Individually based theories." In *Criminology, Critical Canadian Perspectives,* edited by Kristen Kramer, 78-92. Toronto: Pearson Education Canada.

8 See coverage in: *Milliyet* September 8, 2002; *Milliyet,* January 1, 2003; *Milliyet* January 25, 2003; *Milliyet,* March 29, 2004; *Sabah*, December 15, 2005. Similarly, Gambetti's (2007) examination of the rise of lynching in contemporary Turkey suggests that the growing security and terror discourses opens up civilian violence over those seen as dangerous.

9 Among the target populations of Izmir public order police, racialized poor Kurdish youth, especially young unemployed men, occupy an important space. The zero-tolerance policies of the Izmir police strategically constitute their subjects as urban poor and ethno-racial others of the city.

10 The police chief Hüseyin Çapkın, who introduced the new policing in Izmir, has been transferred to Istanbul in 2009, as a result of his "successful" strategies against crime (Gönen 2010).

11 For example, in its fight against crime, the police forces have been undertaking quite spectacular militarized operations in particular neighbourhoods, which were known to be engaging in criminal activities. One of these operations took place in

2006, in Sarıgöl neighbourhood of Istanbul. 1500 policemen from different units including the highly militarized Special Forces were involved in the operation (*Radikal*, February 24, 2006). Similar operations took place in other neighbourhoods in Istanbul, as well as in other cities, such as Edirne and Izmir.

12 Information retrieved from *Bianet* (June 17, 2009). Accessed June 20, 2009. http://bianet.org/bianet/insan-haklari/115282-tihv-raporu-iki-yilda-polis-siddetiyle-53-kisi-oldu.

13 The first *gecekondu* neighbourhoods were constructed by the rural migrants who migrated to the big cities during the industrialization process of Turkey in the 1940s.

14 The first half of the 1950s witnessed a constant fight between the soldiers who were demolishing *gecekondu* houses, and the *gecekondu* residents who were re-building their houses after the soldiers left. The individual fights with the soldiers later turned into collective resistance, marches, and demonstrations supported by leftist students and activists. In spite of the need for a cheap industrial labour force, the government wanted to push the rural migrants/ *gecekondu* dwellers away from the city. However, *gecekondu* people were determined to stay in the city and at the end they gained their "right to city".

15 According to the *Turkey Migration and Internally Displaced Population Survey (TGYONA)*, between 1991 and 2000, 1,201,200 Kurdish were displaced from the Eastern and South Eastern regions of Turkey for security reasons (Yılmaz 2008:212). Istanbul is the city most affected by migration (Çankaya 2003). While in 1980, the permanent resident population of Istanbul was 4,133,759; in 2000 this population was 10,018,735 (State Institute of Statistics 2003, Accessed July 15, 2011. http://tuikrapor.tuik.gov.tr/reports/rwservlet?nufus2000db2=&ENVID=nufus2000db2Env&report=il_koy_sehir_cinsiyet.RDF&p_kod=2&p_il1=34&p_kod=2&p_il1=34&p_il1=34&desformat=html).

16 *Alevism* is a progressivist and a liberal sect of Islam and the *Alevi* population is a minority in Turkey. Alevi people have always supported the leftist parties in Turkey.

17 We employ the concept of "fantasy" *a la* Zizek. As Zizek (1997:125) writes, fantasy is a "scenario filling out the empty space of a fundamental impossibility, a screen masking a void"; it " constructs the scene in which the jouissance we are deprived of is concentrated in the Other who stole it from us" (1997:32).

18 In addition to the concepts of "Other Turkey" and "*varoş*", the 1990s have also witnessed the emergence of the concepts of "White Turks" and "Black Turks". While the term "White Turks" is used to refer to the middle and upper class "Westernized" "urbanites", the "Black Turks" were the ones who could not "modernize" and get "adjusted" to the modern and/or urban norms, namely the *gecekondu* populations, Kurds, etc. See Sumer (2003) for a detailed discussion on the formation of the concepts of "White Turks" and "Black Turks" in the 1990s.

19 Information available at http://www.egm.gov.tr/asayis/istatistik.asp.
20 Information available at http://www.tbmm.gov.tr/tutanak/donem22/yil2/bas/b025m.htm.
21 For instance, a newspaper article on a Kurdish neighbourhood in Istanbul depicted the residents' culture as central to the violence and crime taking place there (*Hürriyet*, September 28, 2003).
22 For the criminalization of poor and urban segregation in USA see Low (2001), Parenti (2000), Wacquant (2003, 2007); in Argentina see Auyero (1997); in France see Schneider (2007), Terrio (2003); in Brazil see Caldiera (2000), Wacquant (2003); in UK see Bauman (1997, 2004); in South Africa see Samara (2010).
23 Diken and Laustsen (2005), with reference to Agamben, argue that contemporary camps are ghettos and ghetto-like places of modern cities.
24 Fourteen thousand *gecekondu* houses have been demolished in Istanbul since 2006 (*Posta*, October 1, 2010). The municipality's aim is to demolish one million more houses in Istanbul (*Posta*, September 26, 2010).
25 For instance, in 2006 he defines the *gecekondu*s as tumours that surround Istanbul and argues that the "gecekondundu order" will be abolished (*Zaman*, April 13, 2006).
26 June 11, 2009. Meeting about forced evictions at Istanbul Bilgi University, Turkey. For detailed information about the meeting, see *Milliyet*, June 12, 2009; *Birgun*, October 29, 2010.
27 Information available at http://www.newsplink.com/2009/06/30/good-bye-gypsies/
28 Even those who have legal deeds in Ayazma had to pay the gap between the prices of their old houses and those of the houses in the projects.
29 For an insightful discussion about the relationship between political economy and crime and security see Neocleous (2008).
30 Interview, General Directorate of Security, Public Order Police Division, July 2008.

Chapter 4: Homelessness as Neoliberal Discourse: Reflections on Research and the Narrowing of Poverty Policy (Mark Willson)

31 See Victoria (City) v. Adams. 2008. BCSC. http://www.canlii.org/en/bc/bcsc/doc/2008/2008bcsc1363/2008bcsc1363.html
32 See the 2003 Woodsquat issue of *West Coast Line* 41(37).
33 *Globe & Mail*, 1977-1984.
34 As a distinct population for study, identified as those using shelter services. See Mary-Ann McLaughlin. 1987. *Homelessness in Canada: The Final Report of the National Inquiry to Canada Mortgage and Housing Corporation.* Canadian Council on Social Development.
35 "The pavement dwellers, those who must sleep in doorways, subways, and recesses of public buildings and those rendered

homeless by natural and man-made disasters, but also the hundreds of millions who lack a real home—one which provides protection from the elements; has access to safe water and sanitation; provides for secure tenure and personal safety; is within easy reach of centres for employment, education, and health care; and is at a cost which people and society can afford" (*Canadian Agenda for Action on Housing and Homelessness through the Year 2000*, 1988:117).

36 These punitive and/or space-clearing approaches have already been well-addressed by Canadian scholars, and so are not directly addressed here. See Crocker, Diane and Val Marie Johnson. 2010. *Poverty, Regulation & Social Justice*. Black Point, NS: Fernwood; Hermer, Joe and Janet Mosher. 2002. *Disorderly People: Law and the Politics of Exclusion in Ontario*. Halifax: Fernwood; Blomley, Nick. 2007. "How to turn a beggar into a bus-stop: law, traffic and the 'Function of the place." *Urban Studies* 44(9):1697-1712.

37 A British article titled "Housing or Homelessness" clearly captures this distinction and conceptual relationship, as homelessness is identified as the condition for which housing is both the cause and solution. See Connelly, Kelleher, Morton, St. George, and Paul Roderick (1991).

38 A similar though more complex move is identifiable in the strategy of the TDRC, which focused on the homeless as differentiated citizen in order to urge a collective revaluing of this specific population.

39 Cutbacks to federal investment in housing began in 1984, before the complete federal withdrawal from housing provision in 1993. According to Hulchanski (2002:12), the "supply of social housing fell from an annual level of about 25,000 new units in 1983 to zero in the 1993 budget."

40 This report offers a count of the precariously housed based on a model of the iceberg, where visible homelessness (150,000-300,000) accounts for the tip of the iceberg, with hidden homelessness (450,000-900,000) and those paying more than 30 percent of their income on housing (1.5 million), as a much larger unseen component of this problem (Wellesley 2010:4-5).

41 This perspective hearkens back to the roots of Participatory Research (PR) in the social movements and community organizing of nations of the South during the 1970s, which is notable for its challenge to the authority, objectivity and exclusivity of university-based research, and for its central emphasis on making social change. For PR practitioners, "research" was taken up as a critical and legitimizing move, challenging professionalized methods of knowledge-gathering and dissemination on one hand, and (re)valuing popular knowledges and local social justice projects on the other. See Heaney, T. W. 1993. "If you can't beat 'em, join 'em: The professionalization of participatory research." In *Voices of Change: Participatory Research in the United States and*

Canada, edited by Peter Park, Mary Brydon-Miller, Budd Hall, and Ted Jackson. Westport: Bergin & Garvey; Fals-Borda, O. and M.A. Rahman, 1991. *Action and Knowledge Breaking the Monopoly with Participatory Action Research*. New York: The Apex Press.

42 This is a matter of both an overall drop in non-precarious employment within the university alongside a rise in low-paid, limited-term or sessional positions, and a rise in professional pressures and constraints for those who are able to obtain permanent faculty positions. See, for example, Angus, Ian, 2009. *Love the Questions: University Education and Enlightenment.* Winnipeg: Arbeiter Ring; Canadian Association of University Teachers. 2010. *CAUT Almanac of Post-Secondary Education in Canada, 2010-2011*. Ottawa: Canadian Association of University Teachers.

Chapter 5: Samuel Delany's Lumpen Worlds and the Problem of Representing Marginality (Lisa Estreich)

43 On Bourdieu's conception of class as relational, and his interrogation of group-making, see Loïc Wacquant's (2008) "On symbolic power and group-making: Pierre Bourdieu's reframing of class."

44 Strikingly, the terms in which Bourdieu describes the "miracle" of the protest movement of the unemployed, in militantly confronting stigma and abject invisibility, seem inflected by the language of gay liberation: "The first conquest of this movement is the movement itself, its very existence: it pulls the unemployed, and with them all insecure workers, whose number increases daily, out of invisibility, isolation, silence, in short, out of nonexistence. Reemerging into the light of day, the unemployed give back their existence and some pride in themselves to all the men and women that nonemployment consigns, like them, to oblivion and shame" (Bourdieu 2010:155).

45 History, one scholar of African American urban history has noted in a critique of "underclass" ethnography, is no more than "personal forces writ large" (Kusmer 1996:355). In its emphasis on structural forces in the analysis of urban poverty, "underclass" ethnography glosses over the complex interplay of structural and subjective forces, perpetuating myth.

46 Samuel Delany's writing does not accord with such "neoromanticism"; his writing is closer to sociology of the 1960s and 1970s, in terms of the model suggested by Loïc Wacquant. Wacquant (2002) has provided an incisive summary of the problems afflicting US sociological representations of the poor, in particular from the 1990s onward. Such characteristic "pitfalls" include assumptions about the "underclass" as a real collective entity; insufficient theoretical framing; and a tendency toward uplift narrative which unquestioningly enshrines business ideals about the morality of work (Wacquant 2002:1473). Wacquant sees these tendencies as having a long trajectory in American sociology during the twentieth century, but also correlates these tendencies

with the unthinking adoption of tenets of neoliberal ideology. By contrast, he suggests that studies of the social and economic margins during the 1960s and 1970s, by focusing on heterogeneity and complexity within specific stigmatized subcultures, avoided such tendencies, while striving toward a critique of structures of social and economic power in the United States (Wacquant 2002:1470-1). Delany's portrayal of urban outcast cultures can be seen as aligning more closely with the latter, rather than the moralizing "parochialism" that Wacquant sees as pervading most studies of American poverty (Wacquant 2002:1522).

47 For an important formulation of this premise of black transnational studies, see Paul Gilroy's *The Black Atlantic* (1993).

48 Historian Kenneth Kusmer has noted the "curious" failure of underclass theorists and ethnographers to study the phenomenon of increased black homelessness since the late 1970s (Kusmer 1996:339). I suggest that this lacuna might have something to do with the difficulty in attributing to a highly mobile, demographically varied, and ragtag social grouping a ready-made concept of culture or reality.

49 For discussion of the relationship between colonial racial discourse and instinctual models of sexuality, see Ann Stoler's *Carnal Knowledge and Imperial Power: Race and the Intimate in Colonial Rule* (2002).

50 Delany's discernment of the limitations of the field of textual scholarship, and his will to unsettle his academic audience, can be compared with nothing so much as the extraordinary (and very funny) indictment of the humanities uttered by J.M. Coetzee's fictional character Sister Bridget, a classics scholar turned African missionary, and possible alter-ego of the Nobel-Prize-winning novelist himself. In Coetzee's novel *Elizabeth Costello* (2003), Sister Bridget—while accepting an award at a university for her humanitarian work—delivers a fifteen-minute speech before her faculty audience in which she pronounces the humanities a long-dead enterprise. Summarizing the origins of the humanistic enterprise in Biblical scholars' efforts to recover the living word of Jesus, entailing the task of translation and the study of languages, she pronounces the following:

> Textual scholarship meant, first, the recovery of the true text, then the true translation of that text; and true translation turned out to be inseparable from true interpretation, just as true interpretation turned out to be inseparable from true understanding of the cultural and historical matrix from which the text had emerged... Now, in the few minutes left to me, I am going to tell you why I do not belong among you and have no message of comfort to bring to you, despite the generosity of the gesture you have extended to me. The message I bring is that you lost your way long ago, perhaps as long as five centuries ago. (Coetzee 2003:120-122)

Pointedly, it is not the missionary who has turned her back on academe and dedicated herself to running a hospital for children with AIDS in Zululand, but her sister, the secular intellectual and "lady novelist" Elizabeth Costello, who shows herself to be narrow-minded in her understanding of African realities and cultural forms. I merely make the case here for Sister Bridget and Samuel Delany as uneasy bedfellows in their perception of the chasm between textual scholarship and "the cultural and historical matrix" from which texts emerge.

51 The name "John Marr" evokes a book of poems by Herman Melville (1922) *John Marr and Other Sailors*.

52 My use of the term "the 1960s" should be qualified as colloquial, not historical. Delany's work (including his memoir of 1988) anticipates by two decades current scholarly efforts to map social transformations of "the 1960s" within an expanded, comparative historical frame. Cf. the observations of Annette Timm and Joshua Sanborn on "the long sexual revolution" in a European context: "Historical data are demonstrating that changes in sexual behavior…were initiated by the previous generation in the 1940s and 1950s and that the popular culture of the 1960s followed rather than led social trends in the sphere" (Timm and Sanborn 2007:201). The repression of homosexuality in mid-twentieth-century America complicates this story. Samuel Delany suggests intriguing collective psychological origins for the virulence of American anti-homosexuality immediately following World War II, in *Times Square Red, Times Square Blue* (Delany 1999a:185).

53 Walter Mosley's *Life Out of Context* (2006) also addresses this predicament.

54 Delany extols Crane as a "fiercely….self-taught intellectual" whose "dense" and "energetic" poetry eluded prevailing codes of interpretation: "Twenties America had only Flaming Youth and the stodgy old professor—but no template for those between, much less one that encompassed the extremes of both. But those were the extremes Crane's life bridged" (1996b:188-189, 191).

55 Delany's portrayal of black gay self-making and self-thwarting in *Dark Reflections* might be compared with Hilton Als' brilliant portraits in *The Women* (1996).

56 This bespeaks the need for a rethinking of rights—first of all, toward an idea of sexual rights which takes on board a conception of happiness and sexual pleasure joined to wider issues of social and economic justice. For a fuller discussion in the context of late capitalism, see Hennessy (2000).

57 Hawley is no W. E. B. Du Bois, but it is implied that he may partake of some variation of the "Enlightenment ethos" (West 1999:88) on the grounds of which Cornel West has criticized Du Bois. Du Bois's intellectual values, West suggests, were premised upon a repudiation of *Lumpen* blackness, perceived as abject and ignorant. West observes that Du Bois was a New England "Victorian" intellectual, attached to ideas of formal educational striving and self-betterment which precluded recognition of black subaltern knowledge.

Chapter 6: Indigeneity and the City: Representation, Resistance, and the Right to the City (Julie Tomiak)

58 In this paper, Indigenous is used to refer to the descendants of the original inhabitants of what is now Canada. The usefulness of the term Indigenous lies in its transcendence of localized colonial contexts and state agendas (Smith 1999:7; see also Alfred and Corntassel 2005:597). At times, Aboriginal will also be used, as well as First Nations, Métis, and Inuit to refer to different groups of Indigenous peoples. Where appropriate, the names of specific Indigenous nations will be used.

59 It should be noted, however, that Census data have not accurately reflected the realities of Indigenous peoples due to chronic undercoverage, misleading categorizations, etc.

60 This European legal fiction has legitimized the large-scale expropriation of land the world over by asserting that it was uninhabited or unmodified. Together with the doctrine of discovery, it constitutes the foundation of the settler regime of legality and sovereignty in Canada (Thobani 2007).

61 Transparent space refers to the commonsensical notion that space can be seen as is, or that the representation of space is unproblematically mimetic through a gaze from nowhere (Blunt and Rose 1994:8).

62 For an overview of the Latin American modernity/ coloniality research program, see Escobar (2007).

63 For instance, the Indian Act was amended in 1911 to facilitate the removal of reserves from urban areas "in the interest of the public" (Barman 2007:5-6; see also Mawani 2005). In the debate in Parliament, Prime Minister Wilfrid Laurier stated that "where a reserve is in the vicinity of a growing town, as is the case in several places, it becomes a source of nuisance and an impediment to progress" (House of Commons Debate, 9 April 1911 cited in Barman 2007:5).

64 Said (1994:xii-xiii) explains the connection between discursive and material processes in the following way: "The main battle in imperialism is over land, of course; but when it came to who owned the land, who had the right to settle and work on it, who kept it going, who won it back, and who now plans its future—these issues were reflected, contested, and even for a time decided in narrative."

65 Cities have always been deeply implicated in the colonial project, "either as the metropolitan heartland of imperial expansion or as important nodal points in the establishment of colonies" (Anderson and Jacobs 1997:18). However, the relationship between urbanism and colonialism has been under-researched, particularly with respect to North American colonization (King 1990).

66 Texts were selected based on their description of the history of the two research sites, Winnipeg and Ottawa, or their focus on the urbanization of Indigenous peoples, more generally.

67 The pass system restricted the ability of First Nation peoples to leave reserves by requiring the permission of the Indian Agent.

68 The aim was not to work from a representative sample but to elicit a range of perspectives from the main actors involved in urban Indigenous governance and, most importantly, from Indigenous community leaders–many of whom have been working extensively with Aboriginal, First Nations, Métis, and Inuit communities in Ottawa and Winnipeg.

69 Huitema (2000) provides detailed descriptions of land policies and their impact on Algonquins in Ontario: the Crawford Purchase of 1783, the Rideau Purchase of 1829-1822, and the Williams Treaty of 1923; see also Hessel (1993:69-71).

70 See Gehl (2005), Steckley and Cummins (2007), and Lawrence (2009) for more details on the claim and issues in the negotiations.

71 As Alfred (2005:111; 1999:120) notes, modern treaty making has not challenged problematic settler assumptions and state doctrines related to Crown title; see also Asch and Zlotkin (1997) on the extinguishment controversy.

72 Its transformation into a legal right is problematic given the pitfalls inherent in rights discourse (Mayer 2009:269) as well as settler legality, more generally, as it is not only premised on the suspension of Indigenous rights, but also the suppression of Indigenous systems of law, title, and sovereignty, more broadly (Monture-Angus 1999). However, the right to the city has (at least nominally) been codified in law. Fernandes (2007) provides a discussion of its legal construction in the 2001 *City Statute* adopted in Brazil, as well as the proposed *World Chart of the Right to the City*.

Chapter 7: Palestinian Refugees and Citizens: Trajectories of Group Solidarity and Politics (Silvia Pasquetti)

73 I use the term "marginalization" instead of "poverty" because the latter evokes the static categorization of individuals according to bureaucratic definitions of who is above and below the poverty line while the former is more suitable to encompass both the symbolic and material aspects of processes of social (and often spatial) relegation at the bottom of societal hierarchies.

74 Ethnography is "a social research based on the close-up, on-the-ground observation of people and institutions in real time and space, in which the investigator embeds herself near (or within) the phenomenon so as to detect how and why agents on the scene act, think and feel the way they do" (Wacquant 2003:5).

75 The comparative approach developed in this chapter is a form of multi-sited ethnography that identifies, as its main object of research, the links between structures and experiences of marginalization as they manifest themselves at the ground level in different localities. Other objects of research, for example, the genealogy of certain institutional policies from their creation in certain centres of power to their implementation by "street-

level bureaucrats" would require other forms of "multi-sited" fieldwork. In other words, I argue that comparative ethnography is crucial for understanding how structures and experiences of social marginalization co-vary. In turn, this understanding is important for avoiding the three pitfalls I identified above: structural reductionism, voyeurism, and sanitized representations of marginalized populations.

76 The Green Line refers to the armistice line that in 1949 marked the interim border between the newly established Israeli state and the "West Bank," the territory east of the Jordan river, which during the war was annexed by Jordan (Palestinian residents of the West Bank were given Jordanian citizenship). In 1967 the Israeli state extended its rule to the West Bank. Therefore, since 1967, the Green Line has acquired a new meaning as it separates between the Israeli state and the Israeli-occupied West Bank. A similar trajectory informs "the border" between the Israeli state and the Gaza Strip, the other area that, with the West Bank, forms the Israeli-occupied Palestinian territories: the Gaza Strip was under Egyptian rule between 1949 and 1967 and was occupied by Israel in 1967.

77 In this chapter I have followed the system provided by the *International Journal of Middle Eastern Studies* (IJMES) for all transliterations from Modern Standard Arabic. For words and sentences in colloquial Palestinian Arabic I have used *Qamūs al-Quds: A Dictionary of the Spoken Arabic of Jerusalem* written by Omar Othman and Thomas Neu and adapted it to the IJMES system. The correct transliteration of *Jalazūn* and *Maḥaṭṭa* is simplified as *Jalazon* and *Mahatta*. The district in which I conducted fieldwork is called *Mahatta* in Arabic and *Rakevet* in Hebrew. In this paper I consistently use the term *Mahatta* because it reflects my experience on the ground as I conducted my fieldwork in Arabic. Finally, I use the official Israeli name for the post-war city: Lod. Before 1948, the city was called Lydda in English and *al-lidd* in Arabic. During my fieldwork, especially when I would travel between Jalazon and Lod I would often use *al-lidd* but for clarity I use Lod in this chapter.

78 It is also important to note that Gaza and West Bank Palestinian wage labourers crossing the Green Line to work in Israel have historically been denied the right to Israeli unemployment benefits, have been paid on daily basis, and have been denied access to Israeli unions.

79 See "The Inequality Report: The Palestinian Arab Minority in Israel" (2011) produced by the legal NGO, Adalah: http://www.adalah.org/upfiles/2011/Adalah_The_Inequality_Report_March_2011.pdf (Accessed July 16, 2011).

80 In 1949 the U.N. General Assembly established The United Nations Relief and Works Agency for Palestine Refugees in the Near East (UNRWA) to assist the hundreds of thousands of Palestinians who had become refugees as an outcome of the 1948 Arab-Israeli war. On UNRWA see Schiff (1995) and Al-Husseini (2000).

81 This brief account of my broader study sketches out two different logics of sociolegal control but does not address the intermediate mechanisms by which the two regimes (in their legal, spatial, and discursive components) generate different trajectories in terms of solidarity and politics.

82 The first generation of Palestinian refugees considered URNWA as a political machine used by international donors to transform the unsolved question of their political rights into a problem of poverty and unemployment. A survey of refugee attitudes, which was conducted in the 1950s, reveals the strong words that refugees used about UNRWA comparing the agency to a "narcotics castle" and its services to the "giving of a shot of morphine" (Rempel 2010:418). The episodes of collective politics that I discuss in this chapter partake to a long history of refugees' attempts to make UNRWA responsive to their material needs while at the same time explicitly recognizing that humanitarian aid is given to them because powerful actors prevent them from obtaining a just political solution to their dispossession and displacement.

83 In 1967 Israel established military rule over the West Bank and the Gaza Strip but did not grant citizenship to West Bank and Gaza Palestinians mainly for demographic reasons. By contrast, Israel annexed and claimed sovereignty over East Jerusalem and through its immigration laws created a new legal category for Palestinians living in East Jerusalem: permanent residents of the city.

84 The structure that has been under construction since 2002 in parts of the West Bank and East Jerusalem—what is often called a "separation fence"—is in reality a complex fortification system made of concrete wall, electrified fencing, deep trenches, buffer zones, patrol roads, video cameras, sniper towers, and razor wire. This structure complements the system of checkpoints, roadblocks, and by-pass roads that has fragmented the West Bank into non-contiguous areas since the beginning of the 1990s.

85 The expression of feelings of national solidarity among Palestinian citizens of Israel was mainly triggered by the killing by the Israeli army of many unarmed Palestinian demonstrators in the Occupied Territories at the beginning of the Second Intifada.

86 *Shabak* is the Hebrew acronym for Israel's General Security Service (GSS), the main Israeli security agency.

87 See UNRWA Briefing Paper (January 2010) *West Bank and Gaza Strip Population Census of 2007*. Accessed July 17, 2011. http://www.unrwa.org/userfiles/2010012035949.pdf. While the 2007 census reports that Jalazon has 7,800 inhabitants, according to UNRWA there are about 11,000 registered refugees in the camp (Accessed July 17, 2011. http://www.unrwa.org/etemplate.php?id=117).

88 See: Israeli Bureau of Statistics (*kovetz yishuvim* 2008). Accessed July 17, 2011. http://www.cbs.gov.il/ishuvim/ishuvim_main.htm.

89 There are actually four sections inside the neighbourhood: *Mahatta* is considered as state-owned land and most houses are scheduled for demolition; *warda* (Rose) and *wāḥat-al-salām* (*Neve-Shalom* in Hebrew, Oasis of Peace) are two small housing projects; *Pardes-Shanir* is an area in which the land is privately owned but it is officially intended for agricultural (and not housing) purposes; thus many houses in *Pardes-Shanir* are also in danger. I started my fieldwork in Mahatta and then extended it to *warda* and *wāḥat-al-salām*. I also visited and conducted interviews in *Pardes-Shanir*. According to the 2008 Israeli census, these four subsections of the Mahatta area include a total of about 3,500 individuals. In reality, the number is higher and today probably reaches about 6,000 people.

90 The migration of Palestinian Bedouins to Lod is part of a state policy of massive land expropriation in the Southern desert areas, which deeply affected the traditional Bedouin lifestyle based on semi-nomadic pastoralism and imposed forced urbanization over many Bedouin tribes. On Palestinian Bedouins see Abu-Saad (2008).

91 The Israeli state categorizes its Palestinian citizens into ethnoreligious categories (Muslims, Christians, Druze, and Bedouins). At the same time, Israeli public discourse often refers to Palestinian citizens of Israel as "Israeli Arabs," an ethnic category that comprises the above-mentioned ethnoreligious categories.

92 In July 2007 the members of *Hamas* (Islamic Resistance Movement) were expelled from the Jalazon camp committee in reaction to Hamas' takeover of the Gaza Strip the month before. During my fieldwork the popular committee included representatives of Fatah, PFLP (Popular Front for the Liberation of Palestine), and the Islamic Jihad. It also included some representatives of camp institutions who were close to Hamas as well as one representative of "the independents" (*al-mustaqillīn*). All members were men except for the director of the camp's women's centre. On Palestinian political factions, see Lybarger (2007).

93 International donors include the governments of Canada, Switzerland, Belgium, Sweden, Netherlands, and the United States, and the European Commission's humanitarian aid department (ECHO). See the UNRWA factsheet on JCP. Accessed July 17, 2011. http://www.unrwa.org/userfiles/2011060654643.pdf.

94 The term "mixed cities" is a folk category that refers to an urban setting that includes both Jewish and Palestinian Israelis. These bi-national urban configurations are an exception inside the Israeli state. While these cities are central to both public concerns and state policies, the term "mixed cities" does not have much analytical weight. The objective presence of members of two ethnonational categories in the same urban space does not tell much about the prevailing social and symbolic relations within and across ethnonational categories. Nor does it reveal how state and local policies manage these exceptional bi-national urban spaces in Israel. On the genealogy of this term, see Rabinowitz and Monterescu (2007, 2008).

95 After the 1948 war the Israeli state confiscated more than half of the land owned by Arabs. State land is mainly used for the development of Jewish Israeli communities. The Israeli legal regime of land also grants an official role in planning and development to the Jewish National Fund and the Jewish Agency, which exclude non-Jews. At the individual level, in 2000 the Israeli Supreme Court has recognized the right of all citizens, including Palestinian citizens, to purchase state land. This is a step that could lead to more Palestinian spatial mobility inside the state. However, there are attempts to neutralize this decision of the Supreme Court by passing new laws. On the Israeli land regime, see Kedar (2003) and Yiftachel (2006).

96 The two authors mainly refer to the first two decades of military rule over Palestinians inside Israel (1948-1966), but this is mainly due to access to archives rather than the construction of their object of analysis.

97 All names are fictitious.

Chapter 8: Sexual Violence and the Creation of a Postcolonial Ordinary: Engagements Between Street-Based Sex Workers and the Police in Machala, Ecuador (Karen O'Connor)

98 The threat of impending police sweeps altered daily life in Machala's downtown market, as the mayor, the Chief of Police, and the Provincial Health Commissioner promised that more raids would follow. The police raids against sex workers in the market began on July 1, 2006, when five sex workers were gassed, beaten, and incarcerated for four days (legally, sex workers can only be detained for twenty-four hours). The police claimed that these sex workers were arrested because they did not have their health documents in order; several did have their health documents "in order" and many people in the market noted that the police did not check these documents at the time of the raid. These raids, organized by the Provincial Health Commissioner and the Chief of Police, were accomplished with the encouragement of the Mayor as a part of the Urban Regeneration Campaign with the goal of forcibly relocating street-based sex workers to a closed, peripheral site such as *La Puente*, a "megabrothel" on the outskirts of town.

99 Health care services for Ecuadorian sex workers include mandatory gynecological exams, blood tests, and health cards which display pap smear results and negative HIV and syphilis tests. While only health officials can ask to inspect these mandatory health cards while sex workers are working, the police frequently demand to check these papers (along with sex workers' citizenship papers) during police raids or while police are harassing sex workers on the streets, in clubs, or in the megabrothel on the outskirts of town.

100 A greater focus on the shifting power dynamics, internal conflicts, and contributions of the sex workers' rights movement in Machala is warranted. The accomplishments of the sex

workers' rights movement in Machala are famous (for a brief history of the sex workers' rights movement in Machala, see La Asociación de Trabajadoras Autónomas "22 de Junio" de El Oro. *Memorias Vivas: Trabajadoras del Sexo.* Machala: IMPSSUR, 2002). However, I was asked by certain sex workers' rights activists not to publish on the current rifts in the sex workers' rights movement, and, with these ethical constraints in mind, this text has been edited and is marked by certain problematic absences.

101 I spoke with a group of sex workers who I had come to know during the previous year as a volunteer. I thought that we had developed a kind of rapport, and I was surprised by their frosty and indifferent reception of my presence in the market. One sex worker finally told me that most of the sex workers in the market were fighting with the sex workers' rights NGO (run by active and former Machalan sex workers who must answer to a paternalistic Norwegian funding company and must, to some degree, follow their guidelines) that I was volunteering with. She informed me that they wanted no involvement with anyone who worked with that NGO, looking very pointedly at me. NGO politics at this time were framed by some as extremely corrupt and self-serving in ways that resonate alongside understandings of postcolonial power dynamics, and the Ecuadorian government's normalized corruption. It was assumed that I must be corrupt and serving my own best interests to be working with this NGO. Several acquaintances who sell sex in the market spoke on my behalf and, after several weeks, my presence was eventually accepted, partially accepted, or received indifferently or ambivalently by almost all of the sex workers in the market.

102 Various forms of violence from partners, clients, friends, and family also surfaced during interviews, as well as moments where sex workers enacted forms of violence themselves, sometimes for protection and at other moments asserting their own kinds of power and extensions of abuse.

103 Many of the sex workers who I spoke with noted that whenever a new mayor, health commissioner, or chief of police came into office they often began their term by "clamping down" on street-based sex work and delinquency which included increased policing of the informal labourers and migrants in the Machalan market. The police raids in July of 2006 were preceded by the appointment of a new chief of police.

104 Carlos Falquez began his term as Machala's mayor in 2004 by announcing the beginning of an urban regeneration campaign to "clean up" and modernize the centre of Machala to prepare for development and tourism. Carlos Falquez was elected as a member of the Socialist Christian Party. Urban regeneration in Machala encompasses multiple, somewhat coordinated projects, including the upgrade of local parks, the removal of informal labourers and sex workers from downtown streets, and fixing infrastructure in Port Bolivar (a sister city connected to Machala),

in an attempt to make urban space more appealing to tourists. A sex workers' rights activist informed me that the Socialist Christian Party was in the process of implementing similar "clean up" campaigns in Guayaquil and Quito, as well as in other cities throughout Ecuador.

105 Some officers stationed at this corner took their post very seriously and carefully watched and intimidated sex workers. Other officers seemed bored and indifferent. One officer who was frequently assigned to the corner barely surveyed the street and bobbed his head to the sound of the music playing on his walkman.

106 Police raids happen periodically in the market and officers are often only able to arrest between one and six sex workers at a time. Because of this, many sex workers were able to avoid being arrested repetitively while working in the market. It is difficult to estimate how many people sell sex in the Machalan market as some people may periodically sell sex but not identify as a sex worker, and many people selling sex also perform other informal labour in the market, such as tending market stands or looking after children. It would have been inappropriate for me to attempt to do a kind of census during this period, which would have mimicked state methods of collecting information and could have been incriminating for market sex workers who were in the process of being criminalized. I would estimate that there were somewhere between 60 and 100 women who identified as sex workers and worked in the market at the time of my research.

107 Taussig defines the extra-official as the normalized state practices of corruption in Venezuela. He elaborates by saying, "[l]ike the official and the 'extra-official,' the true and the forged were flipsides of stately being; neither could exist without the other…" (1997:18). For Taussig, the state is made through the animated processes of corrupt, unofficial, and silenced state practices as well as through its official practices.

108 Some of the officers stationed in the market were young men in their early twenties from Quito, Ecuador's capital, located approximately 12 hours north by bus. Bringing in officers from outside of the province may have been a tactic to lessen the "conflicts of interest" of many Machalan officers.

109 Moser and McIlwaine (2004) differentiate between social, economic, and political violence in Latin America. The authors elaborate that social violence includes kinds of domestic and familial violence which may also occur outside of the home, economic violence includes theft or other crimes to improve the perpetrator's financial situation, and political violence includes many violent acts to further politicized causes or agendas.

110 The police have their own extra-official yet stately economy accepting bribes from informal labourers without proper licences and citizenship documents. Some people working in the market felt that these bribes were a kind of "incentive" for the police to participate in forms of violence against the urban poor.

111 On extremely rare occasions one or two queer or trans sex workers were also present on this street corner. Because "homosexuality" was illegal in Ecuador until relatively recently (November 1997), many queer sex workers may be reluctant to sell sex in public due to the pervasive homophobia that marks many dominant constructions of acceptable sexuality in Ecuador. Queer and trans sex work are not regulated by the Ministry of Public Health in Ecuador, and as a result queer and trans sex workers do not have the semi-legal status that "documented" female sex workers have. Also, some female sex workers do not identify with queer or trans sex workers, and some (although certainly not all or in the same ways) may reproduce homophobia at certain moments and bar queer and trans sex workers from the female-centered sex workers' rights movement or from the spaces where women sell sex. Due to these factors I had only a few opportunities to speak with queer and trans sex workers in Machala, as they rarely worked on the main streets of the market in the daylight.

112 Police raids against sex workers often involve degrading forms of sexually and racially loaded harassment, beatings, taunting, and rape (once in prison). Pepper spray and batons are frequently used and gun violence is sometimes threatened.

Chapter 9: Making Sense of Failure—Why German Trade Unions Did Not Mobilize Against the Hartz IV Reforms: Partisan Research in Franfurt, Germany (Markus Kip)

113 Ron Casanova (1996) presents an account of an organizer with the "National Union of the Homeless" which I found very inspiring.

114 Gouldner (1968) in fact coined the term "partisan" in the context of research.

115 For an account of this approach in the context of Italian Autonomist Marxism, see Wright (2002).

116 In 2001 Germany's Chancellor Gerhard Schröder infamously declared in view of supposed welfare abuse by unemployed workers that "[t]here is no right to laziness" (quoted in Cohen 2001).

117 For an historical account of this relationship between trade unions and the unemployed prior to the 1980s, see Rein and Scherer (1993) as well as Wolski-Prenger (1993).

118 While in post-War Germany before 1975 unemployment never reached three percent, and mostly hovered at around one percent, the numbers of the unemployed rose from 3.8 percent in 1980 to 9.1 percent in 1983 and never fell below seven percent ever since. The highest proportion of unemployment in the history of the German Federal Republic was reached in 2005 with 13 percent.

119 As in most countries in the "Western" hemisphere, trade union organization rates as well as membership figures have been falling in Germany. Since the reunification in 1990 with 11.8 million members in the DGB, numbers have been falling consistently until 2010 with 6.19 million members (DGB.de 2011).

120 The public debates leading up to these reforms were arguably kick-started by Schröder's statement in 2001 that there is "no right to laziness" in view of unemployed who live on welfare supports. Mass media played a significant role in the public framing of the problem of unemployment. This became particularly evident in 2003 when Bild-paper ran a "revelation" piece on "Florida Rolf" who managed to live in Florida on his social assistance cheque. A couple of weeks later, other cases of abuse were termed as "Mallorca-Karin" or "Viagra-Kalle". For a discussion of these, see Brühl (2004), who argues that the real number of welfare abuse cases is miniscule.

121 The demonstrations were called "Monday demonstrations," reminiscent of the weekly "Monday demonstrations" of the civil rights movement in the GDR.

122 This link between academic research on labour and trade union activity is also mediated through the trade union-led Hans-Böckler foundation, the Friedrich-Ebert foundation (close to the social democratic party SPD), as well as the Rosa-Luxemburg foundation (close to the left party—"Die Linke").

123 Of course, some trade unionists also became active in various other arenas related to welfare reform. However, my informants judged their relevance in terms of trade union mobilization against Hartz to be very slim. "The Social-Political Offensive Frankfurt" a coalition of researchers, representatives of churches, charities, and trade unionists working since the 1990s to raise public attention to local problems related to poverty, has also been voicing concerns related to the welfare reform before and after 2005. The "Rhine Main Alliance against Cuts in Social Welfare and Low Wages" was more activist oriented, but had only low involvement of trade unionists according to one organizer.

124 In the Rhine-Main region, I was able to locate only one additional unemployment initiative that was organized by ver.di (service sector trade union) in the neighbouring city of Offenbach.

125 Even after the passing of the reforms in 2005, one of the party's key demands to cancel the Hartz IV continued to attract a growing share of votes in elections. The party received 6.6 percent in Frankfurt's municipal elections in 2006 (compared to 2.3 percent in 2001). It has further reached the 5 percent threshold necessary to enter the provincial parliament of Hesse for the first time in 2008.

126 Klee's assessment fits also in the conclusion of Strümpel and his colleagues who researched the de-solidarizing effects of mass unemployment among workers (Strümpel et al. 1986:35).

Chapter 10: Participatory Practices: Contesting Accountability in Academic-Community Research Collaborations (Alan Bourke)

127 In the US context, the term community-based participatory research (CBPR) is more commonly used. Given that much of my discussion problematizes the extent to which such research can be construed *as* participatory, I have utilized the Canadian usage throughout.

128 The manifest rationale often provided for such alliances is a concern with the public service role that universities play in their surrounding communities and, to a lesser extent, their teaching (e.g. service learning) and research functions. For a comprehensive overview, see the report issued by the University of Victoria's Office of Community-Based Research (2009).

129 This is evidenced by the development of a number of community-based research networks across Canada—with some of the most notable being the Toronto Community-Based Research (CBR) Network; the Centre for CBR—a non-profit organization located in Kitchener, Ontario; the Centre for Urban Health Initiatives (CUHI) at the University of Toronto; and the Ottawa-based Community-Based Research Canada (CBRC).

130 Examples include the Office of Community-Based Research at the University of Victoria; the University of New Brunswick Community Development Institute; Trent University's Centre for Community Based Education; the MUN Harris Centre at Memorial University; and the Winnipeg Inner-City research Alliance (WIRA) at the University of Winnipeg's Urban Institute.

131 Nineteen of a total of twenty-five interviews conducted were with university-based scholars with long-standing commitments to community engagement. Located primarily within the social sciences (particularly in such areas as education, social work, sociology, and health studies), most had extensive track records of successful grant applicants at all levels of government. The rest were conducted with administrative personnel at both university and community level whose task it is to coordinate research activities between community and university partners. Questions were directed toward issues of methodological practice and the co-production of knowledge, and the effects of political culture upon research practice.

132 In effect, CBR can be classified as both an emerging and emergent paradigm—as *emerging* in regard to the sheer proliferation of CBR-style approaches to knowledge co-generation which have sought to contest traditional notions of objective impartiality and scientific pretensions to methodological neutrality; and *emergent* in regard to the context specific and localized constitution of knowledge as produced in the collaborative encounter.

133 Given that participatory research typically orients towards a collaborative and equitable social justice outcome, the absence of methodological primers for an explicitly activist praxis is perhaps of equal significance.

134 Evidence of this success can be seen in the funding allocated to these areas by the Social Science and Humanities Council of Canada (SSHRC) and the Canadian Institutes of Health Research (CIHR). Indeed, SSHRC is one of only two national research councils (the other being in New Zealand) who have an explicitly designated Aboriginal research funding stream.

135 A pertinent example could be the appropriation and augmentation of a traditional herbal remedy for commercial gain. Through the United Nation's Nagoya Protocol, the Canadian federal

government assumes sovereign jurisdiction over natural, biological, and genetic resources within its borders, without explicitly acknowledging Aboriginal rights (see Seccia 2010).

136 Several respondents suggested such capacities to be essentially twofold: a previously existing history of collaboration between communities and university programs, particularly in regard to larger and more established community agencies and organizations; and a previous history of successful grant application—a condition which greatly privileges established scholars.

137 According to Denzin, Lincoln, and Guardina (2006:772), this focuses attention on the performance *indicator* rather than the actual *performance* itself. In Canada, academics are typically ranked in their departments according to research output. An example of this from the UK context is the much criticized Research Assessment Evaluation (RAE), the last of which was conducted in 2008. Its successor—the Research Excellence Framework (REF) will be conducted in 2014. An equivalent in Australia is the Performance-Based Research Fund (PBRF)—a model that is based on an assessment of the quality and productivity of research at all participating tertiary education institutions.

Chapter 11: Lost in Translation: The Social Relations of an Institutional Ethnography of Activism (Kate M. Murray)

138 Throughout, I use the term "activist-scholarship" (or "activist-scholar") to refer to the production of radical intellectual work, whether undertaken inside or outside of institutions. Likewise, I use the term "inquiry" to refer to processes of investigation and knowledge generation, whether inside or outside of institutions. When referring to the particular kinds of scholarship and inquiry arranged by and articulated to ruling relations of the academy, I use "academic" and/or "research". In doing so, I wish to disrupt the idea that rigorous conceptual work only happens in the academy, but not to obscure the particular and often problematic social relations of academic inquiry.

139 Smith's approach is often described as falling within the category of "feminist standpoint epistemology"—a category constructed by Sandra Harding (1986), and which includes the feminist thinking of Nancy Hartsock and Hilary Rose, among others. Smith (2005:8) acknowledges that she shares with these thinkers "a common project taking up a standpoint in women's experience" however she distinguishes her own version of *standpoint* from that of others, including Harding's own use and critique of the concept. Partially due to an assumed—but false—coherence among the thinkers placed in this category, Smith's notion of *standpoint* has been critiqued as reproducing a universalized, essentialized subject, and a claim to objective truth from a vantage point "outside" the relations of ruling. However, Smith has stressed that, rather than privileging a particular knower, her notion of standpoint instead proposes a methodological "point d'appui"(1992:91), a subject position—open to anyone—from which to begin research in the "local

particularities of bodily existence" rather than in "the objectified subject of knowledge of social scientific discourse" (2005:228). This is necessarily an "insider's sociology" because it begins from "the actual social relations in which we are all participants"; there is no "outside" (Smith 1992:94). See, for instance, Smith (1992, 1993, 1997) for her engagement with several critiques and/or misreadings of this aspect of her aspect of her work.

140 Smith (e.g.1999) uses the term *actual* to direct the reader's attention towards individuals and experiences that exist outside of texts, as opposed to the *textual representation* of peoples' practices.

141 At least two accounts are exceptional in this regard; Pence (2001) has developed an interagency safety audit process through which advocates and institutional actors can collaborate in improving battered women's safety within the criminal justice system. In addition, a study by Campbell, Copeland, and Tate (1998) explored the dynamics of their participatory institutional ethnography study but found that "the project never really looked the way the literature on participatory research said it should" (in Campbell and Gregor 2002:118).

142 For Day (2005:6), this term signals the "complex web of practices and institutions that have the effect of perpetuating and multiplying various forms of interlocking oppression" in recognition that "state domination and capitalist exploitation would be impossible if it were not for the fact that neoliberal societies are divided according to multiple lines of inequality based on race, gender, sexuality, ability, age, region (both globally and within nation-states) and the domination of nature."

143 Smith has endeavoured to distinguish her approach from this view of consciousness-raising in the following comparison with the work of Patricia Hill Collins: "Collins is concerned to transform the consciousness of the oppressed. My concern is with what we confront in transforming oppressive relations" (Smith 1992:96).

Chapter 12: Shifting the Gaze "Upwards": Researching the Police as an Institution of Power (Tia Dafnos)

144 Frameworks grounded in experiences of oppression—e.g., feminist and critical race theories, black liberation sociology, indigenous methodologies—often identify the importance of studying structures and relations of domination.

145 Such frameworks often accept a hegemonic notion of "deviance" and the legitimacy of (criminal) law as a (neutral) tool of "justice".

146 I have engaged in countless conversations with colleagues about the implications of identifying as a criminologist—regardless of the "critical" modifier. My graduate training has been in sociology, and I certainly adopt a sociological perspective in my work. Yet there seems to be a political importance in identifying as a "critical criminologist", which positions one *against* conventional criminology that serves the state.

147 This is also referred to as administrative criminology.

148 See, for example, Gönen and Yonucu in this volume, on the deployment of militaristic policing in Istanbul. In the Canadian context, an example is the Toronto Police Service's Toronto Anti-Violence Intervention Strategy (TAVIS) program that targets Toronto's "priority" neighbourhoods.

149 Terms such as "Asian organized crime" and "Eastern European organized crime" have dominated the policing of organized crime. Despite official statements that these are problematic terms, they continue to be used as organizing frameworks not only discursively but also structurally by many organizations. Some police and intelligence units are organized based on these categories (e.g. Asian organized crime unit). I argue that this creates a self-perpetuating feedback loop built into the intelligence process/cycle that continually (re)produces certain groups as targets. It is based upon a racialized "othering" of organized crime as a threat to the (Canadian) nation-state, evident in dominant discourses and within threat assessment processes.

150 I spoke with three educators and four police officers directly involved in "diversity" training programs. At the core, I was interested in the same problem underlying my thesis—race-based policing practices—but approached from a different angle. It was a different experience from my thesis research—e.g., I used the term "racial profiling" freely.

151 Access to information (or freedom of information) laws have been enacted under the rhetoric of increasing transparency and accountability of government institutions to the public. The legislation allows members of the public to file requests for information with these institutions, which then, usually for a fee, provide the relevant records. See Roberts (2006) for more on the use of ATI. I use the term "access to information," reflecting the terminology of the federal Canadian legislation. Provincial and municipal levels are governed by their own laws.

152 In Canada, ATI requests are managed by designated offices and personnel in each government department or agency that is subject to the legislation.

153 It is perhaps telling that academics using ATI tend to be historians, which should give an impetus to those in other disciplines taking an historically-based approach. Journalists on the other hand, have made more use of this mechanism. This reflects Marx's (1972) concept of "muckraking", associated with investigative journalism of the early twentieth century that sought to expose activities and practices kept secret by elites—usually government and corporations.

154 See Kraska and Kappeler (1997) and De Lint and Hall (2009) on the paramilitarization of policing. Anti-terrorism legislation passed after September 11, 2001 in Canada has provided all police forces with enhanced investigative powers for "terrorism" offences, particularly by facilitating the use of surveillance (see Friedland 2001).

155 ATI is an especially useful method for this because it does not rely on the credentialism or institutional base of academic affiliation—anyone can make a request for information. Furthermore, once released, records become public record.

156 The 2010 G20 summit held in downtown Toronto resulted in the largest mass arrest in Canadian history. Of the 1,105 people arrested, 800 were released without charge soon after. About 200 of the original charges have been pursued. The state has rejected public calls for accountability in the form of a federal inquiry. Instead, a variety of disconnected, disjointed processes by various bodies have been launched, several of which have yet to conclude one year after the events. Sharing an interest in making police and government operations and decision-making visible and to support the groups and individuals targeted by police and intelligence activities, several researchers—academics, activists, journalists—have come together in a collaborative endeavour to pool and share information while making the most of ATI requests.

157 Modeled directly on the ISU structure used for the 2010 Vancouver Olympics.

158 There is a long history of struggle by the Six Nations of Grand River preceding the reclamation of the Douglas Creek Housing Estates site. The land at the root of the reclamation has been in dispute since 1784 when the land was "granted" by the Crown to the Six Nations. In 1992, part of the land was sold to Henco Industries, a land developer. The Six Nations filed a lawsuit against the federal and provincial governments in 1995 over the sale, but in July 2005, plans for Douglas Creek Estates were registered. Protestors occupied the site on February 28, 2006, setting up blockades. In the early morning of April 20, 2006, the Ontario Provincial Police conducted a paramilitaristic raid on the site and arrested 16 people. Following the raid, blockades were re-established, bolstered by a large number of supporters. On April 22, 2006, an agreement was reached between Six Nations representatives and the Canadian and Ontario governments to resume negotiations. In June of 2006, the federal government purchased the disputed land and the reclamation continues, the claim unresolved at the time of writing this chapter.

159 Was the wait worth it? I received just over 200 pages of material, heavily redacted. This included incident commander notes, which I was seeking, but most significantly, two draft versions of the operational plans for the raid on the site. Records from the day of the raid and those following were conspicuous by their absence.

160 I should note that ATI coordinators and analysts with whom we interact are often middle-persons between requesters and the organizations of interest. There are often conflicts between ATI offices and the offices of primary interest or even ministerial offices (see Beeby 2010; Davis 2010). This highlights what Tombs and Whyte (2003b) suggest is a possible conflict within institutions that can be used (exploited) to gain access and information.

161 In particular, I was advised to anticipate a slate of human rights cases alleging racial profiling and other forms of discrimination by members of certain police forces that would be adjudicated within the next year. They also suggested that I could contact the chief of police about my research with a chance that the chief would officially un-muzzle officers. I came away with mixed feelings. I sensed a genuine desire for change to the police institution from these officers, and perhaps they saw me as an outsider ally. This forced me to do some more nuanced thinking about the relationship between individual participants and the institutions they work for.

162 This narrative is a return to a moment, based on memory, transcripts, and notes I made during my research.

163 This is not to deny that the participants may also have had similar feelings about our interactions.

164 There are numerous examples of academics being censored when their findings are not favourable to state funders—see Presdee and Walters (1998), Tombs and Whyte (2003a:36-39), and Yeager (2008).

Chapter 13: Our Streets! Practice and Theory of the Ottawa Panhandlers' Union (Matthew R. McLennan)

165 I thank my brother and sister workers in the Ottawa Panhandlers' Union and the Ottawa-Outaouais Industrial Workers of the World for their input. I take full responsibility for any remaining inaccuracies or omissions that might have escaped me.

166 Proshanto Smith. 2006. "Why panhandlers need a union." *Ottawa Citizen*. March 20. Accessed September 6, 2011. http://www2.canada.com/ottawacitizen/news/opinion/story.html?id=615a7936-caaf-4613-b676-d5635bdb0790.

167 The essence of IWW industrial democracy is nicely captured in such time-honoured slogans as "Fire your boss!", "Labour is entitled to all that it creates", "Abolition of the wage system", and "An injury to one is an injury to all".

168 Readers interested in the IWW can consult the union's website at www.iww.org. For an introduction to the union's history, I recommend *Solidarity Forever: An Oral History of the IWW*, by Bird, Georgakas, and Shaffer (1985), and *The Industrial Workers of the World: Its First 100 Years: 1905 Through 2005*, by Bekken and Thompson (2006).

169 http://ottawaiww.org/

170 For a particularly good interview with Nellis, see "Interview: The IWW and the Ottawa Panhandlers Union." *Industrial Workers of the World*. Acessed September 6, 2011. http://www.iww.org/en/node/3918.

171 Similarly, though considered a revolutionary union, the larger IWW is an expressly non-political organization, in the sense that it does not advocate a particular political line. Its ranks are

made up of anarchists, communists, social democrats, Greens, "apoliticals", etc. Though clearly a rare occurrence, a fellow worker from the Minneapolis GMB has even related to me that, for a time, the branch there contained a self-identified Republican!

172 Mayor O'Brien's tenure as mayor was marked by broken election promises, a poorly handled bus strike, an elections bribery scandal, numerous questions of conflict-of-interest and the aforementioned hate speech against the street-involved poor. In 2010 he unsuccessfully campaigned for re-election, quaintly claiming that he should be mandated for a second term because he was starting to get the hang of it.

173 See CBC News. 2007. "'Pigeons' squawk over mayor's comments on homeless." *CBC News*. April 25. Accessed September 6, 2011. http://www.cbc.ca/canada/ottawa/story/2007/04/25/pigeon-070425.html. Never one to go halfway in his baffling displays of political clumsiness, O'Brien went on to publicly accuse the town of Perth of fobbing its homeless population off on Ottawa—thus reducing a critical and deep-rooted social problem to the capricious ill intent of another mayor. Likely this says more about O'Brien's own understanding of social problems and how to deal with them than it does about the mayor of Perth.

174 http://eng.anarchopedia.org/Ottawa_Panhandlers_Union

175 Union members who attended the public hearing on the bylaw note that it was mostly attended by farmers, for whom the term "highway" seemed to be of concern. It is believed in the union that the use of the term was deliberate, in order to dissuade public awareness and dissension among the urban population, who still largely believe that the bylaw does not apply to them.

176 Having cut special deals with the BIAs to stay in business, the current generation of Ottawa hot dog and chip trucks would appear to be the last.

177 For a time, a Ticket Defense Fund was in place to contest such tickets.

178 http://www.e-laws.gov.on.ca/html/statutes/english/elaws_statutes_99s08_e.htm. See also Jackie Esmonde's (2002) penetrating analysis of the Safe Streets Act in "Criminalizing poverty: The criminal law power and the *Safe Streets Act*." *Journal of Law and Social Policy* 17:63-86.

179 See Esmonde (2002).

180 Provisions are made in the *Safe Streets Act* for registered charities, but consider the following. A good friend of mine, who is an activist and certainly no stranger to the concept of mutual aid, was once followed, derided, and "shamed" by a Shinerama volunteer when she declined to donate. Presumably his moralizing insistence that she give him money after she had declined was not to be interpreted as "aggressive" because he was white, clean cut, and privileged enough to go to university?

CONTRIBUTORS

Matthew Anderson is currently a PhD candidate in the Department of Geography at the University of Illinois at Urbana-Champaign. He has a MA in Geography & Environmental Studies from Northeastern Illinois University. His research interests centre on the political economy of the neoliberal city, contemporary urban politics, and critical social and spatial theory. His current research examines the temporal dynamics of redevelopment governance in Chicago, its emergence and recent evolution, and the ways governance actors respond to evolving socio-political conditions and broader-scale processes of capitalist urban restructuring. He is also interested in the role of race and contestation in the unfolding of urban political economies and the politics of public housing reform in the United States.

Alan Bourke is Professor of Humanities and Social Sciences at Mohawk College in Hamilton, Ontario, and a PhD candidate in Sociology at York University, Toronto. His dissertation research focuses on issues of institutional accountability and disciplinary autonomy in the governance of academic research.

Tia Dafnos is a PhD candidate in the Sociology program at York University in Toronto. Her research examines the criminalization and policing of dissent, with a focus on indigenous peoples' activism in Canada. She has a forthcoming chapter, "Beyond the blue line: Researching the policing of Aboriginal activism using ATI" in Brokering Access: Politics, Power and Freedom of Information in Canada (edited by Mike Larsen and Kevin Walby, UBC Press).

Lisa Estreich is a PhD candidate at Columbia University in the Department of English and Comparative Literature. She has worked as a grantwriter for Housing Works and the HIV Law Project in New York City, as well as for the Cambodian women's rights organization Banteay Srei, about which she also produced a short documentary. Her current research interests include environmental themes in African American writing, and "green imperialism" in comparative perspective. Her dissertation focuses on urban spatial politics in several post-1960s writers, including Samuel Delany, Octavia Butler, and Doris Lessing.

Zeynep Gönen is a doctoral candidate in Sociology at Binghamton University. Her research has focused on historical and comparative questions of punishment, policing, and crime. Her recent work focuses on the neoliberal transformations in penal regulatory institutions, particularly in policing. She is currently writing her dissertation, tentatively titled: "Crime, policing and neoliberal regulation of urban poor: Izmir Public Order Police and criminalization of Kurdish youth since the 1990s."

Markus Kip is a PhD candidate in Sociology at York University in Toronto. He is an associate of the City Institute and the Canadian Centre for German and European Studies at York University. His dissertation research compares practices of trade union solidarity with illegalized migrant workers in Frankfurt and Stockholm. Prior to his graduate studies at York, he has worked as an organizer with the homeless-led organization "Picture the Homeless" in New York City. In the past, he has made a living as a day labourer on construction jobs and as a "canner" (i.e. collector of redeemable beverage containers). Having attempted organizing drives in both jobs, Markus knows what activist failure tastes like and still thinks that it is worth continuing the effort.

Matthew R. McLennan recently received his doctorate in philosophy from the University of Ottawa, where he currently teaches courses in applied ethics and critical thinking. His areas of academic specialty are twentieth century French philosophy, ethics, and political philosophy. Matt is also a member of the Ottawa-Outaouais Industrial Workers of the World. Negative experiences with police and passers-by during his stint busking on Ottawa streets as a graduate student led him to volunteer for the Ottawa Panhandlers' Union, whereupon he was generously granted full membership and voting rights by the members.

Kate Murray is currently a PhD candidate in the School of Social Work at the University of British Columbia, unceded Coast Salish Territory. She has worked in a range of community, political and academic settings, and has contributed to research on eviction and homelessness and educational texts on social welfare, social work, and social theory. Kate is currently "muddling through" thinking, research, and practice at the intersection of community organizing, activist co-learning and co-theorization, critical consciousness, and radical social change.

Karen O'Connor is a PhD candidate in the department of social anthropology at York University. Her current research explores the ways that people live with blackouts, electrocutions, and electrical theft in the Dominican Republic. Her MA work traces police violence against sex workers during an urban regeneration campaign in Machala, Ecuador. Karen lives with fellow urban anthropologist Ryan James in Toronto, Ontario, where they raise their young daughter.

Silvia Pasquetti is a Betty Behrens Junior Research Fellow at Clare Hall College at Cambridge University. She received her PhD in sociology in 2011 from the University of California at Berkeley, where she is a Research Associate at the Center for Urban Ethnography. Her article, "The Reconfiguration of the Palestinian National Question: The Indirect Rule Route and the Civil Society Route" is forthcoming in the journal Political Power and Social Theory. Her current research interests include urban marginality, humanitarianism and penality, citizenship regimes, and ethnography. In the long-term, she plans to focus her research on a comparison between regimes of sociolegal control of urban marginality in the Global South and in the Global North.

Julie Tomiak (MA, Free University of Berlin) is a PhD candidate in Canadian Studies, with a specialization in Political Economy, at Carleton University. Her research interests include decolonization, state rescaling, and the right to the city in Canada. In her dissertation, she examines how neoliberal urban governance and Indigenous struggles for self-determination intersect in Ottawa and Winnipeg, with a particular focus on the role of Indigenous organizations and service providers in transforming Indigenous-state relations.

David Wilson (PhD, Rutgers) is Professor of Geography and the Unit for Criticism and Interpretive Theory at the University of Illinois at Urbana-Champaign. He is currently investigating the racialized politics of US cities, the dynamics of neoliberal urban governances, and the contemporary restructuring of US and British cities. His most recent books are Cities and Race: America's New Black Ghetto (Routledge 2007) and Inventing Black-On-Black Violence: Discourse, Space, and Representation (Syracuse 2005).

Mark Willson lives in Victoria BC, where he is engaged in a number of community organizing projects: with Allies of Drug War Survivors, working alongside people who use drugs for quality health services, housing, income, and supports; with the Automated Project, investigating the corporatization and centralization of the university; and with the Vancouver Island Public Interest Research Group, linking students with local anti-poverty organizing projects. Mark is currently working on his dissertation through the University of Victoria's department of Political Science.

Deniz Yonucu is a PhD candidate at Cornell University in the Department of Anthropology. Her earlier works concentrated on criminalization and marginalization of working class youth in Turkey. She currently explores the emergence of "state of exception" areas at the heart of İstanbul and its effects on the working class populations.

CPSIA information can be obtained at www.ICGtesting.com
Printed in the USA
LVOW081109130112

263623LV00001B/8/P